"By virtually all standards, including his own, Emperor Maximilian II (1527-1576) was a failure. His challenges were many, his achievements few." So Paula Sutter Fichtner begins the introduction to this book, the first full biography in English of Maximilian. The Habsburg leader, though gifted, was never able to drive the Turks from Hungary, rationalize his government, or reunite Christendom or even its German components. By bringing the failures of Maximilian's reign into clear focus, Fichtner illuminates the abilities and qualities of this complex man as well as the weaknesses of the expanded Habsburg empire and the problems of ruling in an age of confessional turmoil.

Fichtner examines the dynamics of military, institutional, cultural, and family affairs in the early modern Habsburg empire and considers the reasons Maximilian was unable to shape them to his own purposes. She describes a man of tolerant disposition who allowed Protestants free exercise of their religion yet struggled both publicly and privately with the difficult religious currents of his time. From her extensive research in the primary sources, she provides a fresh portrait of Maximilian, his role in Reforma-

Emperor Maximilian II

Paula Sutter Fichtner

Emperor
Maximilian II

Yale University Press
New Haven and London

Frontispiece: Maximilian II at approximately seventeen years old. Attributed to Guillaume Scrots (Kunsthistorisches Museum, Vienna).

Designed by Nancy Ovedovitz and set in Fournier type by Binghamton Valley Composition. Printed in the United States of America by Sheridan Books, Chelsea, Michigan.

Library of Congress Cataloging-in-Publication Data
Fichtner, Paula S.
Emperor Maximilian II / Paula Sutter Fichtner.
p. cm.
Includes bibliographical references and index.
ISBN 0-300-08527-3
1. Maximilian II, Holy Roman Emperor, 1527–1576.   2. Holy Roman Empire—History—Maximilian II, 1564–1576.   3. Holy Roman Empire—Kings and rulers—Biography.   I. Title: Emperor Maximilian the Second.   II. Title.
DD186 .F53 2001
943'.033'092—dc21   00-054078
[B]

A catalogue record for this book is available from the British Library.

10 9 8 7 6 5 4 3 2 1

Helen Taft Manning
Otakar Odložilík
Ruth Kleinman—
scholars, teachers, friends

Contents

Acknowledgments

It is with utmost gratitude that I acknowledge the contributions that many have made to this book. Individual chapters profited from the alert and informed reading of the late Ruth Kleinman, Howard Louthan, and Teofilo Ruiz. Paul Rosenfeld was meticulous beyond the call of duty in his critique of the sections dealing with the revolt in the Netherlands. An anonymous reader for Yale University Press did true yeoman service. Several people helped me to negotiate the complexities of crucial archives: Adeline Rucquoi in Madrid, Andrea Schwarz and Reinhard Höppl in Munich, and Jaroslav Pánek in Prague. Some were generous enough to send me material that they thought I might need, among them L. J. Andrew Villalon, with whom I discussed the work in its earliest stages. Especially fruitful chats were held with Friedrich Edelmayer in Vienna, who also kindly provided me with offprints of his many articles, some of which were not available in the United States. Along with introducing me to the intricacies of Czech archival practice, Jaroslav Pánek also loaned me photocopies of holdings in his country's provincial repositories, thus speeding up my research considerably. The staffs of the Tyrolean Provincial Archives in Innsbruck, the State Central Archives in Prague, the Wittelsbach Privy Archive in Munich, the Court Treasury Archives and the Military Archives in Vienna were most helpful. As I have so often done in the past, I must also express my thanks to the personnel of the Austrian Haus-, Hof- and Staatsarchiv, who have done so much for so long to further my work. The late Christiane Thomas was invaluable and will be very hard to replace indeed. I was able to visit these places and work through their holdings only because of the financial support I received from the summer grants of the City University of New York and a research fellowship from the National Endowment for the Humanities in 1987–1988. I am also much indebted to the staffs of the Rare Book and Wallach Print Divisions of the New York Public Library and of the Pierpont Morgan Library for assistance in locating illustrations for the text and to the Austrian Cultural Institute in New York and its librarian, Friedericke Zeitlhofer, for indispensable help in arranging for permissions and photographic material from Austria. Finally, I owe much to Edward G. Fichtner for seeing me through the many computer-related difficulties and related emotional turmoil this project brought with it and to Margaret King for guidance through some murky Latin passages.

Abbreviations and Stylistic Notes

AN	Archivo Nacional, Madrid
AÖG	*Archiv für österreichische Geschichte*
BN	Biblioteca nacional, Madrid
CODOIN	Colección de documentos inéditos para la historia de España
FRA	Fontes Rerum Austriacarum
GHA	Geheimes Hausarchiv, Munich
HHSTA	Haus-, Hof- und Staatsarchiv, Vienna
HKA	Hofkammerarchiv, Vienna
HSA	Hauptstaatsarchiv, Munich
KA	Kriegsarchiv, Vienna
MIÖG	*Mitteilungen des Instituts für österreichische Geschichtsforschung*
OMEA	Haus-, Hof- und Staatsarchiv, Hofarchiv, Obersthofmeisteramt, Vienna
ÖNB	Österreichische Nationalbibliothek, Vienna
SOA	Státní oblastní archiv (Třebon, Litoměřice . . .)
SÚA	Státní ústřední archiv, Prague
TL	Tiroler Landesarchiv, Innsbruck

The use of [?] indicates that the spelling or date (day, month, or year) is uncertain. When [?] follows a full date, the order of the document in an archival fascicle or other external evidence strongly suggests this attribution. When [?] appears after names, the content, tone, or location of the document (or a combination of these) argues for the author or addressee given in the note. Where the uncertainty is due to damaged material, this is clearly mentioned. Contemporary dating has been left unchanged.

Introduction

By virtually all standards, including his own, Emperor Maximilian II (1527–1576) was a failure. His challenges were many, his achievements few. Historians characteristically shrink from making absolute judgments, but they have been less cautious in the case of this ruler's career. Maximilian was not always the author of the problems he faced. He may have exacerbated the wretched health that tormented him all his life, but he did not create it. Financial difficulties bedeviled the Habsburg empire long before Maximilian governed it. As German king and emperor from 1564 to 1576, he had to deal with a polity that "had no sovereign and no center" and whose members ordinarily bent to imperial will only when it suited their interest to do so.[1] But people often play masterfully the weak hands life deals them. Maximilian rarely did.

When Maximilian has found scholarly champions, they have frequently molded him to their own ideological purposes. Germany's great nineteenth-century historian Leopold von Ranke was one, making a virtue of this Habsburg's comparatively moderate religious views. Such positions, as Ranke approvingly saw it, furthered Lutheranism, the German "national" religion.[2] But Maximilian had other goals when he succeeded his father, Emperor Ferdinand I (1503–1564). The new ruler believed that the Peace of Augsburg (1555), which territorialized Catholicism and Lutheranism in the empire, had created a workable formula for confessional peace. In Maximilian's opinion, he would serve Germany's interests by reconciling the confessions spawned by the Protestant Reformation, rather than abetting the triumph of one at the expense of the other. To have religious bilateralism encourage further factionalism rather than end it was the last thing he intended.[3]

Maximilian was not the only person of influence who worked in vain to ease doctrinal tensions in the sixteenth century.[4] But his political centrality in the Reformation era made his responsibility for Christian unity heavier and his failure to advance the cause all the more salient. Especially painful to him was the hostile reception his conciliatory religious policy found with his cousin Philip II of Spain. When in 1567 the king sent an army to suppress rebellion in the Netherlands, he did much to turn the terms "Protestant" and "Catholic" from confessional labels into military and diplomatic ones.

Even when Maximilian chose his tasks more or less voluntarily and had some freedom to pursue them, his accomplishments were distressingly modest. Although he had been fiercely ambitious as a young man, he ruled tentatively, even passively, once he came to power. Aware that his dynasty's newly acquired central European empire needed thoroughgoing administrative repairs, he made few improvements. Considered by himself and others to be a promising military leader, he met ignominious defeat in battle against the Ottoman armies in Hungary. Taken together, these disappointments added up to the greatest one of all—Maximilian never outdid the achievements either of a detested uncle, Emperor Charles V (1500–1558), or of his own father.

In truth, Ferdinand I had himself fallen short of his goals. Although he had won the thrones of Bohemia and Hungary for the house of Austria, he controlled only part of the lands attached to the crown of St. Stephen. He had held Vienna against the Turks in 1529 but had never decisively beaten them. A committed though critical Catholic, he had not rolled back German Protestantism. He had done much to broker the Peace of Augsburg, but Rome had taken him to task for his efforts. His attempts to fine-tune the agreement to accommodate Protestants living in the empire's ecclesiastical principalities and Rome's property rights in newly reformed territories were only half successful. Quarrels over these arrangements raged on long after Ferdinand's death. Nevertheless, he had kept his eastern kingdoms, such as they were; the Turks never quite reached Vienna again during his lifetime; and the German princes were not altogether hostile to what passed for a modus vivendi between German Lutherans and Catholics. Maximilian believed he could do more. He never would.

Ranke and those like him, who approached the subject of Reformation history with generally antipapal views, were at least sympathetic to Maximilian. But modern historians have found fault with him for many reasons. Scholars who admire principled commitment have called Maximilian disappointing at best, and ethically bankrupt at worst. Crypto-Catholic, crypto-Lutheran, compromise Catholic, Catholic "Christian" (the last in the widest sense of that word), hypocrite, dissembler, vacillator, weakling—these are among the unflattering epithets that have been applied to him.[5] Some of the criticism they carry is unfair, even ahistorical, for it takes little account of the moral norms of his day. Early modern princes and political theorists alike endorsed dissembling; Erasmus, taking St. Jerome as his source, said that even pious men could sometimes resort to the practice. Moreover, some of the late sixteenth century's real success stories—Elizabeth of England and William of Orange, for example—were adepts in the art.[6] But most of these pejoratives hit very close in Maximilian's case, and not only in matters of creed. An earlier and careful biographer concluded that Maximilian simply lacked the willpower to accomplish much of anything.[7] The most generous construction put on his career to date is that, at least in his religious policies, he was swimming against a powerful tide of sectarianism. He was a man of peace and conciliation whose moment to rule coincided with one of the most fractious epochs in all of European history. Indeed, some of his own contemporaries said much the same thing, especially as confessional strife only worsened after his death.[8]

Played out in the luminous afterglow of Renaissance cosmopolitanism in central and east-central Europe, Maximilian's career has some appeal to modern sensibilities, as does his outlook;[9] but the temporal distance between this Habsburg and the relativism of Western liberals in more recent times argues against exaggerating any resemblance, even in spirit, between the two. At the emperor's death, central Europe had yet to endure the murderous confessional warfare of the seventeenth century that he feared and wished to prevent. In this context, the self-confessed failure of Maximilian's conciliatory approach carries more weight than the weak formal similarity of his ideas to contemporary virtues.

Nevertheless, history, in its broadest sense, is more than a record of heroic or collective achievement. Nor is its sole purpose to create links between our own lives and thoughts and those of people in earlier times, revelatory though that process can often be. As a discipline, history is first and foremost the analysis of past experience, in which defeat and inadequacy have always played a central role. Seen in this light, the response to failure should tell us as much about an individual as would a study of his or her success. At the very least, a scholar must pay careful attention to the circumstances that attended these setbacks. It will therefore also be argued here that Maximilian's inadequacies will tell us much about the institutional, political, and religious problems of his day that tried his character and frustrated his deepest hopes. He would never rationalize his government, drive the Turks from Hungary, or reunite Christendom—or, indeed, even its German components. The overall narrative is sad and sometimes complex, for the sixteenth-century Habsburgs had a hand in events throughout much of the European continent. Family policy and foreign policy were often two sides of the same coin; to follow them, we must be prepared to leap from setting to setting, each of which features its own particular conditions and cast of characters. Still, for all that it deals with major institutions and the high politics of the time, Maximilian's story is abidingly human. It is also strangely humbling.

one

A Son of Promise

Sons called for "shooting and fireworks and also an appropriate banquet," daughters something less.[1] So decided Ferdinand I of Austria on 1 August 1527. Territorial ruler of a dynastic patrimony in central Europe and newly also king of Hungary and Bohemia, he and his wife, Queen Anna, now had their first male heir, born the previous day. The elated father had already selected the infant's name: he would be called Maximilian, after his paternal great-grandfather.[2]

Ferdinand did not reveal the motives for his choice, but political calculation was almost certainly among them. Though Maximilian I had left a mob of disgruntled creditors on his death in 1519, he had been remarkably popular among his Austrian subjects, particularly in the westernmost provinces. Ferdinand, having come from Spain, by way of Burgundy, speaking no German, and reliant on Spanish and Burgundian advisers, was still cultivating the goodwill of his people. A reminder of the first son's connection to a well-liked progenitor could be helpful in such enterprises.

Ferdinand, in fact, owed a great deal to his grandfather. The lands the archduke now ruled had not come to him easily. Some of Emperor Charles V's advisers had suggested that Ferdinand remain a bachelor. If he stayed unmarried, he could not father legal offspring to challenge his older brother in the Holy Roman Empire, Spain, or both. This idea was eventually dropped, but negotiating a territorial settlement for Ferdinand took years. Only because Maximilian I ordered in his testament that his Austrian holdings be divided among his grandsons did Ferdinand receive an appropriate inheritance at all.

The birth of Maximilian I's namesake, therefore, certainly merited a cannonade. The event augured well for the house of Austria. Ferdinand believed that both he and his brother should sire heirs as quickly as possible, because the emperor's marriage to Isabel of Portugal had thus far not been especially fruitful.[3] Moreover, Maximilian appeared at a particularly happy moment in his father's career. A faction of the Hungarian estates had elected John Zápolya, the voivode, or duke, of Transylvania, king of Hungary before a second group had named Ferdinand to the same position. Ferdinand had gone to war to defend his claim, and a successful end to the campaign was in sight.

To be sure, there were also signs that dark times were ahead for central and east-central Europe and for the Habsburgs. In 1526 the Turks had pushed farther westward into Hungary than ever before, inflicting a catastrophic defeat on the kingdom's defenders at the battle of Mohács. The resources of the Austrian lands were dwindling after repeated requests by the Habsburgs for aid against their enemies, both in Constantinople and in western Europe. Nor were Ferdinand's new kingdoms equally capable of bearing the costs they imposed on the Habsburgs. Hungary and its revenues were split after 1526 among the Habsburgs, the Turks, and Transylvania, which retained a kind of autonomy as an Ottoman vassal state. The German estates had never followed the house of Austria's leadership happily; the spread of the sixteenth-century Lutheran reform rendered the princes and cities represented in the imperial diet even less docile. Indeed, the German Protestant rulers and the Habsburgs were virtually programmed for disagreement. While aware that the Church of Rome was in large degree the author of its own troubles, neither Charles V nor his brother had any intention of jettisoning his ancestral faith.

But Ferdinand was optimistic and very energetic as well. He believed that strong defenses were the solution to the Turkish menace—he only needed to create them. As for religious differences, Christians—or their official spokesmen—simply required encouragement to work them out. His finances were not hopeless. Bohemia was still rich. Though any claims Ferdinand had had in western and southern Europe had fallen almost entirely to Charles, Habsburg control now extended beyond the continent itself. The potential bounty from the holdings in the New World was only gradually becoming clear to residents of the old. Charles V had not yet voluntarily assisted his poorer brother to the east, but he had not foreclosed the possibility either.

Ferdinand thus had some reason to think that his own future was hopeful and that of his son even more so. The likelihood that Maximilian would wear at least one crown, in Bohemia, was one that his father had never enjoyed in his turbulent boyhood. The infant archduke might someday be emperor too. Charles V had agreed, at least in principle, that Ferdinand would succeed him in Germany. Though the elder brother's own first son and heir, the future Philip II, had been born a few months earlier, the boy had no automatic claim on his father's imperial title, and it was possible that the office would never interest him. The German estates, as a rule, resisted any suggestion that the emperorship was hereditary. And what if Philip died, or had no male siblings? Who was to say that the little archduke in Vienna might not come into the Spanish legacy that had been denied his father?

Maximilian, then, was a prince with an attractive future. Little about his care was left to chance. A week after the child's birth, Ferdinand sought out a wet nurse, a routine practice among the wealthy and wellborn of that day. When a woman was finally located, her brother had to swear that her husband had never suffered from "the French disease"—the highly contagious strain of syphilis then rampant throughout Europe.[4] In 1529, Ferdinand moved his entire family to Innsbruck, probably out of concern for their physical well-being. The Turks were threatening Vienna, and plague visited the city repeatedly. He himself spent the winters of 1531–1532 and 1532–1533, as well as a good part of 1536, in the Tyrol.

Most of the time, however, the king was on the road to meetings with one set of estates or another. He therefore supervised his offspring from a distance. News of their illnesses and recoveries, their daily routines at school and play came to him from their various attendants.[5] Personal physicians looked in four times a day on Maximilian and his brother Ferdinand, born in 1529—at rising and retiring and at their mealtimes, when the doctors were to make sure that the boys ate nothing harmful. If medicines were needed, the physicians were to go to the court apothecary, after checking with appropriate household officials or with Ferdinand, if he happened to be on the scene. They were to make sure that wholesome and fresh ingredients went into the preparations and that they were correctly mixed.[6]

Since princes could come into higher office at any time, it behooved their tutors to train their august charges quickly and well. Maximilian and Ferdinand's education, moral and intellectual, received close attention. To prepare the archdukes for the affairs of both this world and the one to come, their instructors were to foster temperate and generous dispositions in the two boys. A young prince had to love his elders and those close to them, as well as God. Each Saturday evening and the following Sunday, the archdukes' preceptor explained some part of the Gospel to them and instructed them in religious behavior. God, their father explained to the boys, had singled them out to rule. It was therefore imperative for Ferdinand's sons to fear and love their Maker and, as children, to obey their parents. By submitting to their elders, future monarchs learned to govern their subjects effectively. Should the archdukes resist discipline, their conduct was to be reported to the *Hofmeister*, who was then to consult with Ferdinand. With the king's consent, fitting punishment was administered, "with a rod" if necessary.

The everyday routine of the archdukes was similarly prescribed. Young Maximilian and Ferdinand could neither eat nor drink at unaccustomed hours. After arising and hearing Mass, they had a light soup; then they went off to school for ninety minutes. An hour of exercise followed. The morning meal came at ten, after which the boys returned to their studies for another hour and a half. They then had a snack of fruit and something to drink. Their next full meal came at four in the afternoon. If they wished, the archdukes could have a piece of bread or a sweet and something to drink around seven in the evening.

Ferdinand desired his sons to familiarize themselves with the tongues spoken by all their subjects, as well as to learn the languages of foreigners with whom the Habsburgs were in contact. The boys were to master Latin rhetoric and grammar as quickly as possible, taught through model phrases and sentences. The study of literature, both Latin and German, would sharpen their linguistic skills even more; the archdukes composed essays in both three times a week. To prove their command of their lessons, Maximilian and Ferdinand recited them back to their tutor. They also took part in disputations that tested their recall of their studies and their use of learning in oral argument. The only subject that Ferdinand declared off-limits in such exercises was the traditional Catholic confession. Their faith, in the king's opinion, had served his house too well in earlier times to be a topic of formal debate.[7]

Language training was also socially important for the archdukes. It enabled them to address and converse with peoples of all ranks and stations. Young nobles, or *Edelknaben,* from all the Habsburg domains were invited to the court for schooling with King Ferdinand's sons. These youngsters could not speak German with the archdukes; only Latin, Czech, or other foreign languages were allowed. Maximilian and Ferdinand's first assistant tutor (*Unterhofmeister*), Hermann von Zalesky, drilled Maximilian and his brother not only in Latin and German but in Czech and Polish. A treasury secretary, Jeronimo Jeremia, supervised them in Italian.[8]

Maximilian was an apt pupil. Even his father, who grew more critical of the archduke by the year, continued to praise his linguistic accomplishments. In 1561 Ferdinand would boast that his eldest son could hold forth in the six principal languages of Christendom, by which he probably meant German, French, Spanish, Italian, Latin, and Czech. A eulogy at Maximilian's funeral in 1576 mentioned two additional tongues—Dutch and Magyar. Questions remain, however, about how fluent he was in each of these. A Venetian ambassador, Alvise Mocenigo, thought that the archduke was not fully secure in Czech, and some described his French as rather awkward. His general proficiency in Hungarian may not have been great. Indeed, Maximilian fell back on German phonetics to render Magyar and Czech terms and phrases in a diary he kept through 1566 and 1567. On the other hand, his Italian, his Spanish, and his written French were largely free of such quirks.[9] Contemporaries generally vouched for his competency as a linguist. When the physicians who performed the autopsy on him in 1576 found his brain warm and dry (a sign of health in a time when cold fluids were regarded as the source of much illness), they considered it the result of his command of so many languages, his highly developed intellect, and his general cleverness.[10]

With Ferdinand absent for months at a time, the moral and educational program he laid out for his sons could, and did, go awry. Most alarming was the case of Maximilian's first tutor, a philologian, Wolfgang Severus, or Wolfgang August Schiefer, who joined the Innsbruck household around 1536. The scholar's background alone should have made the king wary. From 1523 to 1525, Schiefer had been at Luther's headquarters in Wittenberg. Here he had also befriended the reformer's friend and disciple Philipp Melanchthon.

Once he took up his duties in Innsbruck, troubling stories about Schiefer's confessional leanings began to circulate, finally reaching the king himself. In 1538, Ferdinand called together his children's household staff along with Maximilian, Archduke Ferdinand, their sister Elisabeth, and the chancellor, Archbishop Bernhard of Cles. Before this audience, the king threatened to execute anyone who discussed the new religious teachings with his children. Normally indulgent in almost all personal matters, and many public ones as well, he promised to beat his sons if they did not report persons who approached them with such ideas. Schiefer returned in 1539 to Wittenberg, where Melanchthon celebrated him as a living martyr to the cause of the true Gospel.

For all the furor that his presence in Innsbruck caused, Schiefer was in contact with his young charges too briefly for him to have influenced their intellectual and spiritual outlook significantly. Nor, for that matter, did his replacements. The next teacher for the princes was the noted humanist Caspar Ursinus Velius. A good Catholic and a learned man who took his duties very seriously, he apparently killed himself shortly after joining the court. The wholly orthodox Georg Tannstetter guided the rest of Maximilian's formal education, apparently without incident.[11] Certainly, the central purpose of Maximilian's religious training would be met; he would always have the utmost respect for the Almighty. But if the confessional controversies of his day in any way touched the archduke during his boyhood, the experience went unrecorded.

Sheltered though they were, Maximilian and Archduke Ferdinand, along with two sisters older than they, Archduchesses Anna and Elisabeth, soon learned to be public figures. The year 1538 was important in all their lives. It was then that the four children were called to their father's side and introduced to the role for which all of them were being schooled. Traveling down the Danube, they joined King Ferdinand in Linz at the beginning of October. Together, all went on to Vienna where they stayed until their return to Innsbruck in 1541. The ever-cautious Ferdinand ordered that at the first sign of the plague they were to leave the city for better air. But they were princes and princesses, and the time had come for them to begin the job. In Linz Maximilian had his first formal contact with foreign diplomats. And on 8 October 1539, Cardinal Jerome Aleander, enchanted at the sight of the radiantly blond youngsters, confirmed them.[12]

Maximilian and his siblings looked like a chorus of angels to Aleander on that occasion. Real relations between the two boys, however, may not have been so harmonious. Contemporaries noted that, while not as intelligent as Maximilian, Archduke Ferdinand was even better looking and more outgoing. Athletically gifted as well, he was said to be his father's favorite, "adorned with his father's name to shape him in his father's very own ways," as Caspar Ursinus Velius declared in casting his horoscope at his birth.[13] The effect that paternal preferences had on the feelings of the boys for each other is hard to evaluate. As adults the two brothers had some angry disagreements, in which Maximilian usually played the role of the injured party. Few princely houses escaped such spats, however. Generally, Maximilian and the younger Ferdinand would treat each another as cordially as the formalities of sixteenth-century dynastic establishments allowed. Certainly, they were not constantly at odds. As time went on, they readily shared the pleasures of the table and the hunt as well as more delicate pastimes such as music. Much later in his life, Maximilian saw in Ferdinand as much a friend as a brother.[14]

How King Ferdinand's preference for his second son affected the father's ties with the elder brother is another, and more significant, matter. The interpersonal dynamics of the modern nuclear family did not always drive ruling houses. Kings, queens, and their children might be separated for long periods of time, and even when they were together, their encounters were often little more than an aspect of court ritual.

Nevertheless, princely dynasties were not altogether exempt from the emotional currents affecting humanity at large. Although psychology has yet to find verifiably universal experiences, it has established categories of problems that trouble people deeply, regardless of the cultural and temporal settings in which they find themselves. Dynastic relations may very well have heightened the normal tensions between parents and children, simply because so much was at stake. Maximilian and his brothers were beholden to their father for their present and future livings. For as long as he lived, King Ferdinand chose their wives and even the teachers of their children. Should his sons forget their dependency, there were ceremonies to remind them of it. In the father's presence, the young men doffed their caps in acknowledgment of his dominance and held them until, with a wave of his hand, the king bade the archdukes cover their heads and be seated.[15]

On material grounds alone, then, all Ferdinand's male offspring—a third, Archduke Charles, would be born in 1540—had reason to feel vulnerable. But his eldest son's position was especially awkward. German princes still insisted on the right to divide their patrimonies as they saw fit among their heirs, rather than following the rule of primogeniture. Contemporaries were well aware that, even though he would probably bear the greatest responsibility for the well-being of the house, Maximilian was likely to be very poor indeed, given the irregular ways in which the imperial estates, including the Habsburgs' own lands, contributed to the support of their emperor.[16]

Would Ferdinand I prefer Archduke Ferdinand to his eldest son altogether? There is no record of Maximilian's having asked that question directly of anyone, but, from about 1544 on, he began acting like a man who was very worried about his future, which could be made considerably worse should his brother receive the lion's share of the Habsburg inheritance. The intricacies of dynastic relations and his role as an heir apparent preoccupied Maximilian more and more. His concerns intensified noticeably as he saw that both his uncle, the emperor, and his father were quick to put their interests before his. In itself, such behavior on the part of Charles and King Ferdinand was unremarkable. They too, had been schooled in the protocols of dynasticism; neither man distinguished his own welfare from that of his children. The role of the children was to accept the parental decision, to adjust their personal feelings accordingly, and to wait their turn. Maximilian would not take easily to this process.

Nevertheless, he had natural endowments that might enable him to cope with emotional challenges. Maximilian was clever, and his training had been sound. Best of all, he was the son of a king who was likely to become German emperor as well. Once his father no longer held those titles, Maximilian could certainly lay serious claim to them if he cooperated with the prescriptions of the system into which he had been born. The task would not be easy. In all probability, he would have some anxious times in the cut and thrust of family politics. He would be hard put to master the religious and military problems of his day; but he had every reason to think that he had been prepared to handle these issues and deserved the opportunity to do so.

two

An Angry Apprentice

Maximilian was sixteen when he and his father started traveling together on political missions. In 1543, the two of them, along with the younger Ferdinand, quit Innsbruck for Nuremberg and the imperial diet. From there they went on to Prague. The truly crucial trip of Maximilian's adolescence, however, took place the following year. In March 1544 the two archdukes left their parents' household for an indefinite stay in the peripatetic court of their uncle the emperor.

For Maximilian this residence lasted until June of 1548. Years later, after a series of bitter family disputes, he declared that the only lessons he had absorbed at Charles's establishment were in the art of dissembling.[1] To be sure, Maximilian could have served an apprenticeship in this delicate craft with his father, a master manipulator of men, rather than with his uncle, whom he came to despise. But the archduke learned far more than he would ever admit during his years with Charles. In the imperial court Maximilian had his real introduction to the world beyond the Austrian provinces. Traveling about Germany, he made many useful contacts and acquired a good working knowledge of most of his family's European lands and peoples. Among the places Charles and his nephew visited together were the Netherlands, where the wealth and industrious habits of the people impressed Maximilian deeply. When religious and civil war broke out in the region a few years later, he genuinely grieved over the destruction of such prosperity.

Most important of all, Charles was a respected commander; Maximilian had not been with his uncle for a year before he began campaigning with the emperor against King Francis I. Army life pleased the archduke greatly, especially because he found himself among a circle of young princes who, like himself, were in Charles's camp to study the emperor's tactics at first hand. Among them were the young dukes of Saxony: August, whom Maximilian had already met in Prague, and Maurice. The three struck up a lively friendship which would figure large in their political futures. Maximilian would soon call Maurice his closest friend.[2]

By 1546 the emperor had important work for the combat-hungry. The French seemed quiet, and the Persians had the sultan tied down temporarily on the southeastern border of the Ottoman Empire. The moment looked right for Charles to launch an offensive against the German Protestant princes. He steadfastly insisted that he was chastising disobedient vassals, and not their confessional views. Elector John Frederick of Saxony and Landgrave Philip of Hesse were charged with breaking the imperial peace in 1542 when they drove the Catholic duke Henry of Braunschweig-Wolfenbüttel from his duchy. But few believed that to be the emperor's only concern.

Charles's forces battled their way by fits and starts down the Danube, with Saxony their final target. Maximilian participated directly in the conflict, leading a cavalry division that bore the *Reichsbanner* during the siege of Ingolstadt in 1546. The honor brought him four accompanying trumpeters, rather than two.[3] But the archduke could not fully enjoy his new distinctions. His delicate constitution—the source of countless future torments—had been a subject of public comment for a year. More alarming still, his father had not waited for the war to end before summoning Archduke Ferdinand to his side in Prague. From the outset of their stay with their uncle, the two boys had kept separate households. Maximilian's had a decidedly Iberian cast. The Hofmeister, Pedro Lasso de Castilla, was Spanish, and so was Maximilian's retinue, with which the young Habsburg was often at odds. Charles claimed, not very persuasively, that the arrangement entered into his nephew's training to be King of the Romans, the title held by the elected successor to the imperial crown.[4] More likely, the emperor was conditioning Maximilian for a regency in Spain.

Indeed, Charles wanted to keep his elder nephew with him, so that King Ferdinand's call to his second son was not necessarily a sign of favoritism. But the elder archduke had real reasons for worry over his father's behavior toward him. Maximilian had already stood in for his father at difficult meetings of the Silesian and Moravian estates. He had presided at especially heated deliberations in 1546 in Bohemia, at which several noblemen voiced strong support for the Schmalkaldic Protestants. Nevertheless, crucial though those missions had been, Maximilian had yet to learn what role he would play in the Habsburgs' central European lands. Now, while Archduke Ferdinand would be at work with their father, Maximilian would still be technically under the command of the duke of Alba in Germany. He was jealous of his younger brother and did not bother to disguise his feelings.[5]

His behavior also grew increasingly irresponsible. Reports that the archduke was drinking heavily and whoring troubled King Ferdinand deeply. Upon returning to camp from an impromptu visit to his sister Archduchess Anna and brother-in-law Albrecht V of Bavaria, Maximilian sometimes ignored his uncle's orders. Once he refused guard duty.[6] His turmoil reached a startling climax on the night between 5 and 6 February 1547. Some time around midnight, he arose, left his quarters in Ulm, and clandestinely set out on the road to Prague.[7] The sad news from the Bohemian capital that his mother had succumbed to fatal complications after childbirth on 27 January may have triggered his flagrant insubordination. He may also have heard that some members of the Bohemian estates were considering him, rather than his father, to be their king.[8]

Impulsive though his escape might have looked, Maximilian had plotted it craftily, leaving behind a false itinerary to keep possible captors off his trail. Nevertheless, the ruse did not work. A chamberlain, Thomas Perrenot de Chantonnay, discovered his absence, alerted the emperor, and then set out to bring the archduke back to Ulm. He caught up with his quarry at a post station and returned Maximilian to his uncle. Maximilian never forgave the Burgundian-turned-Spaniard, even when Philip II named him an ambassador to Vienna in 1565. Chantonnay's presence still annoyed the new emperor so much that the king of Spain eventually dispatched another envoy.[9]

This bizarre escapade, along with Maximilian's other alleged excesses, caused his father grave concern. The problem could not have come at a worse time for Ferdinand. A Protestant army was poised to invade Bohemia, and Queen Anna's death had so grieved him that he shunned public appearances. But the king knew that his eldest son required serious attention. The advice he offered applied to both Maximilian and Ferdinand, a sign that Ferdinand was very concerned about future discord between them. Christian forbearance, the king said, was the remedy when they disagreed. But it was Archduke Ferdinand who was singled out to turn the other cheek now and in the years to come, and not Maximilian. The king may have been indirectly admitting that Maximilian had some cause for anger and that it was up to Archduke Ferdinand to ride this out as best he could. It is also possible that, by asking the younger son to defer to his elder brother, their father was hoping that Maximilian could be flattered into seeing how self-destructive his dissolute behavior could be. Abstemious himself, Ferdinand pointed out that excessive drinking would undermine his eldest son's mind, body, and, perhaps worst of all, his reputation. Serious men would not serve such rulers, whose governments would suffer as a result. As for Maximilian's refusal to listen to Charles, Ferdinand called to mind the Italian proverb: "He who thinks he is a stag and is really an ass, should take care before leaping over a crevasse."[10]

Despite these unhappy interludes, Maximilian's service with Charles ended on a positive note for all concerned. Philip of Hesse was defeated first. Then, before the Saxon town of Mühlberg in April of 1547, the emperor crushed Elector John Frederick and stripped him of his electorate. Duke Maurice from the Albertine line of the Wettin house, and Maximilian's comrade-in-arms, was his replacement. Perhaps because it was the only battle his nephew had ever seen, as Charles observed afterward, Maximilian enjoyed the final combat thoroughly. Whatever the cause, the experience of victory was heady stuff for the archduke, now close to twenty years old.[11]

Maximilian also corrected his moral habits very quickly. While he never lost his taste for wine and fine foods, he exercised greater control. Visits to prostitutes also became a thing of the past. His father's injunctions may have had their intended effect. A more likely cause, however, was an impending and attractive marriage. His wife-to-be was his Spanish cousin, the Infanta Maria, and his uncle and cousin Philip were actively supporting the arrangement.[12]

The emperor and King Ferdinand had opened the question of an intra-dynastic match during the Diet of Worms in 1545. Ferdinand liked the idea, though he did not specify whether Maximilian or Archduke Ferdinand would be the bridegroom. Charles was eager for his daughter to have the most prestigious and financially secure match that the house of Austria could offer. It was he, not King Ferdinand, who believed that Maximilian, as firstborn son, would be the more appropriate candidate. The emperor also demanded that Maximilian and his future wife be called king and queen of Bohemia, the wealthiest realm that the Habsburgs controlled in central Europe.[13] Charles clearly thought of Maria as a possible future sovereign. She had not renounced her rights to rule in Spain. Careful research had been done for the emperor on the Bohemian laws of succession, including their provisions for women to hold the crown.[14] Once this question was answered, the betrothal could go forward, at least from the Spanish point of view.

The relationship would do much to clarify Maximilian's future in agreeable ways. Ambassadors watching the young archduke had already noted that he liked to command. A firm claim to a royal crown was one way to guarantee himself a lifetime in that role. Were the Bohemian estates actually to accept him as his father's successor, Maximilian would be freed to a certain extent from his father's control. Ferdinand realized this in 1547 and did not like it. True, he had insisted that the Habsburgs had hereditary rights in the kingdom even before he came to rule it in 1526; assuring Maximilian of the title, as Charles wished, would be a step in that direction. But though Maximilian might have reformed morally following the Schmalkaldic War, his political behavior now worried his father. No sooner had hostilities with the German Protestants and their Bohemian allies come to an end in 1547 than Maximilian publicly declared that his father was not powerful enough to punish the rebels in the kingdom. More insulting still, he took it upon himself a year later to act as intermediary for Bohemian noblemen whom Charles and Ferdinand were determined to punish for their support of the Schmalkaldic alliance.[15]

Ferdinand, therefore, required that important conditions be met before he would allow the betrothal and marriage to go forward. Only if Maximilian swore not to interfere in the government of the realm during his father's lifetime could the archduke call himself king of Bohemia. Charles V promised that both he and Philip would see to it that Maximilian respected the compact. If the archduke broke his vow, he would lose both the title and the succession, argue though Charles did that both belonged to his elder nephew as King Ferdinand's *primogenitus*. Ferdinand, however, had some painful concessions of his own to make. The marriage capitulations, signed in 1548, obligated him to support his son's household from revenues raised in Silesia and the two Lusatias. If these fell short, the money would come out of the father's Bohemian incomes. Should all these fail, there were "the other provinces."[16]

By 1549 the Bohemian estates were ready to go along with this arrangement, though disputes over its validity could have arisen at any time. The German text of their consent was far more formal than the version in Czech.[17] But for all its shakiness, the Bohemian settlement did much to satisfy Charles, his heirs, and even Maximilian. Maria's marriage to her German-speaking and poorer cousin had been made unquestionably more prestigious.[18] Once Maximilian and Maria had wed, they referred to themselves as the king and queen of Bohemia; until Maximilian became emperor in 1564, Maria signed with that title. Their children were known to the Spanish as princes and princesses of Bohemia as well. The Bohemian ruler was also an imperial elector, another important consideration for the Spanish branch of the dynasty. That Maximilian and his offspring were archdukes and archduchesses in Austria and that they were a royal family in Hungary, were secondary distinctions, at best.[19]

The security Maximilian drew from the betrothal agreement did not last for long, however. To his great disappointment, his father immediately made Archduke Ferdinand governor of Bohemia. Nor would the king name his eldest son regent in Hungary, even though the estates there wished to see more of Maximilian in their lands. More troubling still, Charles V, for all of his eagerness to have Maximilian as a son-in-law, did not intend to further his nephew's larger career in Germany. The archduke was to go to Spain in 1548, not only to claim his bride, but to serve as his uncle's regent for two to three years.[20] The emperor's natural surrogate in the Iberian peninsula was Maximilian's cousin Philip, who had actually served in this capacity since 1542. This time, however, the Spanish prince was accompanying his father to the empire. There he was to familiarize himself with the political landscape, to meet the princes, and, at least so it seemed to his relatives in central Europe, to present himself as his father's successor.

Such notions more immediately threatened the elder Ferdinand himself. He had been King of the Romans since 1531 and, in effect, emperor-elect. But Charles's plans could change Maximilian's future as well. The archduke's pleasing physical appearance and articulate ways, his concern for things German, and his "piety" had already impressed many German princes favorably. There were even some in the empire who called him its hope and were deeply concerned that he not fall victim to Spanish deceit and "disbelief."[21] Were Ferdinand to rule Germany after Charles, he would almost certainly work to have his own son follow him as emperor. If Philip succeeded Charles, Maximilian might have a very different future. Influencing these machinations from a distance, especially when Philip would be on the scene in the empire, would be extraordinarily difficult. Very reluctantly, Maximilian left Augsburg, where he was attending a diet, on 11 June 1548.[22] He would return to Germany only three years later.

Maximilian's trip to Spain, made in the grand style, took him through Munich and the Tyrol, and then to Genoa, which he reached in the latter part of the summer. In Italy, he was to meet "persons of quality," by which the emperor probably meant local potentates and members of various knightly orders. More than seven thousand gulden in gifts were handed out to lesser folk as well along the way.[23] But a rough passage to Barcelona put an end to the pleasures that accompanied these duties and contacts. When he landed, Maximilian was seriously ill. Weak and still suffering, he arrived in the Castilian capital of Valladolid on 13 September, where he met his cousin and wife-to-be for the first time. Despite the bridegroom's condition, Cardinal Christoph Madruzzo of Trent blessed the marriage that same evening. A nuptial mass was celebrated the next day, followed by a festive banquet, which both the Castilian and Portuguese nobility attended.[24]

Maria was not beautiful. Her face had been permanently scarred by smallpox when she was a child. Though girlish and comparatively slender at her wedding, she soon became very fat and stayed that way throughout most of her life. Neither her tastes nor her temperament fitted her to be the wife of an itinerant Habsburg ruler. For all the gritty determination of which she was capable, she loathed rough roadways and paths. And she disliked rising early, even to hear Mass, though she was a staunch Catholic.[25] Unlike her polyglot husband, she spoke seven foreign languages badly. Her social contact with the imperial princes, Maximilian's preferred companions, would long be limited to her comfortably Catholic Bavarian in-laws. She remained deeply attached to her native tongue and dependent on those who spoke it, even after she acquired some fluency in German.[26] Throughout her life, she used only Spanish with at least one of her sons, Archduke Maximilian. But she was good-natured and disarmingly frank, at least about her linguistic deficits. She thanked her Aunt Maria, Charles V's regent in the Netherlands, for writing in Spanish so that she could understand the older woman's message. And she was also endowed with patience and intelligence, crucial traits for sustaining long-term ties with Maximilian. As time went by, she acquired a good grasp of state affairs. Although Maximilian certainly did not respond to her every suggestion, she would play a significant role in religious and dynastic policies at his court.[27]

The most problematic aspect of Maximilian and Maria's future relationship would be her religious convictions, much praised by Pope Pius V. However, while Maximilian took to questioning Catholic orthodoxy early in their marriage, he spared his wife from personal criticism. The archduke certainly had good cause not to offend her; Maria retained her claims to the Spanish crowns. Should her brother Philip's line die out, Maximilian and his sons would be the probable heirs to a world far beyond central and east-central Europe.[28]

Maria said that she was happy with her marriage, even at the beginning.

Given the conventions of dynastic unions, she could have hardly said otherwise. But Maximilian did visibly love and respect her. His ailments, however distressing, may ultimately have drawn them together. He sometimes refused to travel without her, saying she was his best doctor.[29] Where he was frail, she was uncommonly sturdy. Even when well along in years, she ate three or four times a day, unusual among relatively old people of the time.[30]

The marriage, however, had started inauspiciously in two major respects. Ferdinand had granted Maximilian sixty thousand gulden annually for support of his wife, and Maria twenty-five thousand crowns a year outright. Payment of the latter stipend would begin only after the union was consummated and the emperor turned over his daughter's dowry of two hundred thousand ducats. Part of that sum was to come directly from the emperor; the remainder was made up of one hundred thousand ducats from Maria's maternal inheritance and jewelry worth forty thousand Rhenish gulden. Charles relinquished these monies erratically, thereby straining the goodwill of his brother and nephew for years to come. Even after all parties to the contract settled their most serious financial differences in 1555, Maximilian and his cousin Philip continued to bicker over this matter.[31] Maximilian had also hoped that the dowry would be larger than the promised sum and that he would become the Habsburg governor in the Netherlands. Charles, to his nephew's abiding irritation, had other plans.[32] Maximilian already had a following among the German territorial rulers, whereas Philip was noticeably ill at ease in such company. The latter was an uncongenial drinking companion, try though he did to keep up with the princes in 1550 at a diet in Augsburg. Moreover, the young Spaniard tilted too genteelly in tournaments for German tastes. Unwilling to compromise his own son's future in the Low Countries, Charles dropped any thought of posting Maximilian there.[33]

But Maximilian's most immediate troubles were not fiscal. Pleased though he was with his young wife, he could not perform his conjugal duties. Just when physical vitality was something "that we very much need," his health did not mend.[34] It was a dismaying condition for any new husband, much less for one whose virility could shape the future of a dynastic line. Some observers thought that Maximilian was simply indifferent to his bride, especially when, even by November, his condition had not improved.[35] He was obviously unhappy about the situation. The fecundity of others aroused his envious fantasies. News that Dorothea, the wife of Elector Palatine Frederick III of the palatinate, was pregnant left him imagining her "weighed down with a big pregnant body" and eventually giving birth to a young prince and heir.[36]

Happily for both him and Maria, the fever had passed by December of 1548. Court gossips now told of how tenderly the newlyweds behaved toward one another. Their first child was born on 2 November 1549 to an exuberant father, who let it be known the same day that Maria had conceived soon after his illness had gone.[37] That the baby was a daughter rather than a son did not matter. He called her Anna, the name of his mother and of his favorite sister, now married to Duke Albrecht V of Bavaria; the girl had a special place in his affections and marital schemes throughout his life. In 1567, he would confess that he loved her more than all his other children put together.[38] And though Maximilian was never free of physical problems, impotence was not among them. Within the space of nineteen years, the couple produced sixteen children, ten of whom survived childhood.

Maximilian remained in Spain, more or less against his will, until December of 1550. From the nephew's point of view, the duties in his uncle's realms led nowhere. To the archduke's great displeasure, Charles closely supervised his activities in the kingdom.[39] On paper, Maximilian and Maria were jointly empowered to conclude treaties, should Charles or Philip be prevented from doing so. In practice, however, the couple could do little unless they consulted in writing with the emperor.[40] Nevertheless, they happily entertained themselves with a lively and elegant court in Valladolid, frequented by young noblemen from both Germany and Spain. Maximilian also had time to cultivate his broadening aesthetic and intellectual interests. In Spain he fell into a reckless style of patronage that would cost his treasuries dearly in the future. He acquired things because he believed that they were rare, rather than because they were intrinsically valuable or beautiful. Vague claims to learning sufficed for someone to qualify for one of his pensions.[41] Charles's earlier decision to make the Spanish royal household grander to impress his Burgundian vassals, who took ostentation very seriously, made the young couple's establishment even costlier. Debts mounted up quickly.[42]

Such surroundings seemed an improbable training ground for political or administrative responsibilities. Nevertheless, Maximilian handled the standard tasks of government well. He even learned something from them—though, once again, he would never say so. His careless private spending did not blind him to the larger realities of state finance. He quickly saw that rising prices imposed real limitations on a prince's household. Spurred on, almost certainly, by the irregularity of the income from his wife's dowry, he consolidated and enlarged his father-in-law's Spanish revenues. The emperor required detailed accounts of all activities from the king and queen of Bohemia, as they signed themselves. Generating such reports helped Maximilian to internalize procedures that he would have to follow throughout his life. Staffing problems, which the explosive growth of the Spanish court made even more pressing, questions of defense and commerce, religious affairs— all commanded his attention routinely.[43]

The archduke approached these matters with both thoughtfulness and, where necessary, some bureaucratic cunning. He knew how to deflect embarrassing questions. When Charles asked him in 1549 to explain why he had added several administrators and councillors to his government, Maximilian pleaded for time to prepare a thorough accounting. He also knew how to protect himself by shifting responsibilities to other offices. In 1550, Maximilian had to account for a substantial rise in expenditures for the fleet under the Council of the Indies, the body which administered the Spanish possessions in the Americas. As Maximilian described it, the council had only itself to blame. After postponing the organization of an armada, they undertook it at a moment when interest rates had gone up markedly. The force was therefore more expensive than it need have been. Had the body acted promptly, the vessels would have already returned with the gold and silver to pay for them, presumably at lower cost. Though critical, Maximilian was careful not to overstep his competence. The council, it was said, did not respect regents. He urged Charles to look into the matter himself.[44]

Maximilian was as fussy as his uncle about detail, at least in matters that meant something to him. When he commissioned decorative projects, he asked for reports on their progress. He specified what colors of clothing and jewelry were to be worn in family portraits.[45] Applied technology held a genuine fascination for him. Though Maximilian would never like Spain or Spaniards, he eagerly undertook publicly useful projects in the kingdom. A chronic shortage of potable water afflicted many Castilian urban centers, Valladolid included. All supplies had to be carried from a nearby river or brook, making life, in Maximilian's opinion, especially trying for the common man. In 1549 he resolved to develop a fountain and water supply system for the city. An installation found in Augsburg, which drew from a local river, the Lech, and which he had studied closely, was to be the model. Jacob Fugger, the financier-prince of Augsburg, was asked to recruit the necessary skilled workmen, unavailable in Spain, from the empire.[46]

The scheme grew in both scope and purpose as it unfolded in Maximilian's mind. It could be engineered "to greater common advantage" by making the rivers around Valladolid navigable.[47] This called for raising and lowering parts of the Pisuerga River, a procedure that would, with the aid of a waterwheel pump, force drinking water into the city. He had seen such technology in Prague and elsewhere; he asked his father to find someone in his territories who could realize it in Spain for him. Though the project never got much beyond the planning stage, it revealed yet another side of the intellectual versatility that would distinguish him in adulthood.[48]

It also showed that his personal ambition had survived his Spanish sojourn. Such undertakings were easily turned into princely statements about themselves to the world at large. "We too, want to leave something to remember us by here," Maximilian wrote, underlining the passage himself.[49] Precisely what it was about himself he wanted remembered is not clear. He could have been thinking only of his general importance, for he went out of his way to assure artisans that working for him would confer honor and fame on them.[50] But he could also have been hoping that the project would prompt Castilians to keep him and his future heirs in mind, should the Spanish line of Habsburgs die out.

Thus, the Spanish regency had a positive aspect for Maximilian. But he chafed endlessly at his subordinate role. Though forbidden to meddle in his father's Bohemian administration, he stayed in touch with his promised kingdom. The high burgrave of Prague, Wolf of Kreig, reported that the local estates feared that their future ruler would forget his Czech on the Iberian peninsula. Maximilian reassured them on that point and that he would visit Bohemia as soon as he could. Exquisitely attentive to local sensibilities in the kingdom, he suggested people who were both technically knowledgeable and fluent in Czech for offices in his future realm. Proving that he had absorbed at least one major lesson from his Spanish experiences, he urged construction of mines to augment the royal treasury.[51]

But most of all, he longed to return to Germany. "May God grant it soon," he wrote in 1550, underlining the phrase as he did so. Spain was a place from which he sought to be released.[52] He missed the hunting parties described by Maurice of Saxony, his friend and erstwhile comrade-in-arms, especially when the archduke heard that his father and brother Ferdinand were participating. He did not forget German wines, which he ordered from the Rhineland in 1549 with a connoisseur's precision. He asked that they be as "soft and sweet" as possible and that they travel in the smallest barrels to be found. This last stipulation was to ensure that the narrow road from the port of entry, Bilbao, to Valladolid could accommodate the shipment.[53] He struggled to maintain some sort of presence among the electors, if only by reporting his trip to Spain to them in 1548. Throughout his stay in his uncle's realm, he badgered German correspondents for news of the electors. Handwritten copies of official documents would do, should printed texts not be available.[54]

Indeed, by 1550, matters of great import for Maximilian were under way in the empire. His uncle and father had been tussling for several years over the Habsburg order of succession in Germany. Charles had pulled back from supporting his own son, rather than his brother, King Ferdinand, as his immediate successor. But Charles wanted Ferdinand to be succeeded by Prince Philip, and not Maximilian.[55] Upset though he was once he learned of this scheme, the archduke remained temperate in his communiqués to the electors. He cast himself as a spokesman for the peace and welfare of Germany. Phrases such as "the praiseworthy German nation" and "our beloved fatherland" were cannily scattered throughout his letters.[56] He knew his audience well. The German princes, who opposed any prospect of a Spanish succession, welcomed such language.[57]

Maximilian had long been begging to be recalled to Germany. The climate of his uncle's realm did not agree with him. He was, he argued, only learning Spanish ways which would make him unpopular in central Europe. Charles, though fearing that his nephew would return home in the same impetuous way that he had fled camp in 1547, ignored these pleas, even after the succession negotiations got under way. Indeed, the emperor implored his brother to forestall such a move. King Ferdinand assured his son that he would do nothing contrary to his interests, but he did not spell out what he planned to do for the young man. Already bitter and worried, Maximilian was now offended, as well.[58]

Ferdinand clearly felt some obligation to defend Maximilian. He denied all rumors that his son was secretly soliciting support from the electors; but he was not ready to advance the archduke's cause publicly. He ordered Pedro Lasso, his son's majordomo, to warn Maximilian that almost any kind of contact with the imperial estates was unwise. The latter received the advice frostily. He had not, he said, turned into a Spaniard because he had married one. Maximilian redoubled his efforts to cultivate the goodwill of Germany's territorial rulers, especially electors Joachim of Brandenburg and Maurice of Saxony. The young Habsburg employed every device save outright treachery to further his cause, which was far from hopeless. The princes disliked Philip on social, political, and cultural grounds, greatly resented the secrecy that enveloped Charles and Ferdinand's talks, and would never forget that the two Habsburgs had treated the empire as yet another family property.[59]

By the autumn of 1550, Ferdinand had decided that his son's presence could further the negotiations. The king was also ready to be firm with his brother. He asked Charles to summon Maximilian to Augsburg, where the family was meeting. When the emperor balked, claiming that he still needed a regent in Spain, his brother retorted that Philip could handle that job nicely. Exploiting his brother's anxiety about Maximilian's volatile moods, Ferdinand remarked that his son was no longer a child and might do something "inconvenient." Charles yielded, setting March of 1551 for his nephew's return. Maximilian did not wait. He set out for Germany on 30 October 1550, leaving his pregnant wife in her homeland until the spring of 1551, when he went back for her. The archduke arrived in Augsburg to find relations between his uncle and father so envenomed that the two could not be together in the same room. To add to Charles's displeasure, his brother had insisted on taking up the matter of aid in the struggle against the Turks, along with the succession question.[60]

Only the mediation of their sister, Mary, the regent in the Netherlands, enabled Charles and Ferdinand to communicate at all. At least publicly, Maximilian remained a model of self-control throughout the heated negotiations. In private, he canvassed actively and successfully for electoral support. As early as December 1550, he appeared to have a good number of votes in hand.[61] But Charles and Ferdinand seemed not to notice. The final agreement between his uncle and father pushed back the time for him to be German emperor, perhaps forever. The compact called for Philip to follow his uncle, and for Maximilian to succeed his cousin. Should the latter live to old age and retain the imperial crown throughout his lifetime, Maximilian might well be dead long before Philip vacated the position. King Ferdinand promised to observe the agreement to the letter. Furthermore, Philip was to be responsible for upholding the integrity of the imperial fiefs in Italy. Though the electors questioned the legality of this arrangement and Ferdinand's right to confer the so-called Italian vicariate on his nephew, Philip did indeed assume the role. Ferdinand tried to soften the blow for his son as best he could. As discussions drew to a close in February of 1551, he promised to spur Charles on in paying his daughter's dowry. Maximilian was not swayed.

He refused to assent in writing to the succession agreement. Charles, despite considerable experience with the treachery of princes, had to make do with an oral vow from his nephew to honor the compact.[62]

Nor did Maximilian keep his fury at the succession bargain to himself. His father, he said, had been far more interested in aid from the emperor against the Turks than in the welfare of his own son. He was even more critical of Charles and Philip. Seemingly forgetful of his own early excesses, Maximilian called his cousin unfit to rule and charged that he was interested only in dispensing patronage and amusing himself. His opinion of the emperor was even more scathing, and, from the standpoint of dynastic solidarity, more dangerous. At the end of 1551, Maximilian harangued Giovanni Michele, the Venetian ambassador, on the subject of his uncle's faults. Charles, to his nephew's way of thinking, was completely self-absorbed, the cause of the disorders then afflicting the entire continent. His behavior toward Ferdinand had been inexcusable, given the aid the king had rendered his brother in the past, especially during the Schmalkaldic War. Maximilian openly declared that he had no intention of abiding by the succession agreement, even if his uncle were to compensate him from his other territories. Honor, said the archduke, as his father had once declared when Charles was ready to pass King Ferdinand over in favor of Philip for the imperial office, was worth far more than possessions.[63]

The emperor ordered his nephew back to Spain in 1551 to resume his regency; the younger man flatly refused. When he left Augsburg for Valladolid that May, it was only to reclaim his wife and their two children.[64] Maximilian planned the trip to show himself in the best possible light. Bankers in Augsburg were called upon to extend credit to the Italian tailors who would outfit some of his retinue. His advance purchaser would go on to Milan to ensure the quality of the workmanship. Though the outlays were to be substantial, the archduke wanted a close accounting of them in "an orderly book."[65]

Nevertheless, the journey only added to the tension between Maximilian and his Spanish relatives. In all, he was under way six months, not three as planned. The trip to Spain went off smoothly, but mishaps plagued the return. Philip accompanied the couple, but the two men apparently did not enjoy each other's company. Until July, when they sailed together to Genoa, where the land journey would resume, they traveled separately. Once embarked on the Mediterranean, Philip witnessed at first hand a supremely embarrassing moment for his cousin. Contrary to the general policy of the house of Austria,

Maximilian had been cultivating good relations with King Henry II of France. Henry had stood as godfather to one of Maximilian's children. Nevertheless, the respect of the house of Valois for the Habsburgs was apparently none the greater. The French attacked the ship carrying the king and queen of Bohemia and the future ruler of Spain, boarded it, and carried off to their own craft several of Maximilian's horses.[66]

Things only worsened when Maximilian reached Italy. In spite of careful planning, expenditures had exceeded the archduke's estimates. By November of 1551, he could neither leave Genoa for the trip homeward nor pay his retinue. King Ferdinand forwarded an additional ten thousand crowns, a little more than half of what his son needed to get to Innsbruck. By 2 December, Maximilian reached Milan, with his creditors in hot pursuit. In Bolzano, two weeks later, he had not seen eight thousand crowns that Ferdinand had sent through Mantua. He pulled himself together enough to conduct a meeting of the Tyrolean estates in an orderly fashion, forwarding to his father their requests, marked "A," in a bundle of documents also containing his reply, marked "B," and the estates' counterreply, marked "C."[67] But his troubles were far from over.

Maximilian reached Innsbruck early in 1552. There he found his uncle as wedded to his succession plans as ever. The archduke left for a visit with Albrecht of Bavaria, who was also traveling. Shortly after he departed, however, Maximilian succumbed to a fever, followed by fainting and shortness of breath—the first of many bouts with cardiac difficulties. He believed that someone had poisoned him in Trent, where he had stopped over; his father reinforced the conviction by sending him a supply of antidotes. The archduke suspected that the culprit was Christoph Madruzzo, the cardinal bishop of the region, who was promoting Philip of Spain's succession to the imperial crown.[68] The spectacular entry of the king and queen of Bohemia into Vienna later that year may have offset some of the humiliation and discomfort of the trip. In the evening, lanterns lit the tower of St. Stephen's Cathedral from top to bottom for the occasion. More marvelous yet, the royal couple brought with them an elephant, a gift of King John II of Portugal.[69] But Maximilian's seizure in the Tyrol was associated in his mind with Philip and Catholic machinations. He would trace to it the bodily afflictions he suffered from for the rest of his life.[70]

Maximilian continued to work diligently at ingratiating himself with the electors and other key German territorial rulers. It was a policy sure to deepen bad feeling and mistrust between the two branches of his house. At least one of the princes, Maurice of Saxony, had more in mind when he dealt with Maximilian than insuring that his next emperor would be a German. The erstwhile duke, now elector of Saxony, was married to a daughter of Philip of Hesse, whom Charles had imprisoned for insubordination during the Schmalkaldic War. Maurice was under pressure from his brother-in-law, the future landgrave William IV of Hesse-Cassel, to win the release of William's ailing and defeated father. Shortly after the conflict ended, Maurice and Elector Joachim of Brandenburg persuaded Maximilian to make use of his access to his uncle to obtain Philip's freedom.

Maurice and Maximilian had become very close. It was to the ambitious elector that Maximilian exulted over the birth of his first son, Ferdinand, in 1551. He could be so open, he said, because the two understood one another so well.[71] Maximilian undertook the mission on behalf of Maurice's father-in-law willingly, though discreetly; he had already aired the possibility of a pardon in 1547 with Granvella, Charles's chancellor. It was not Maximilian himself, but the duke of Alba, one of the emperor's most trustworthy commanders, who carried the request to Charles at the Diet of Augsburg in 1548. The emperor, protesting illness, refused to consider it. He had more urgent concerns. Though Maximilian repeatedly advised against pressing Philip's case too vigorously with Charles, Maximilian continued to act as an advocate for the unfortunate landgrave. When his cause seemed to falter, the archduke was openly apologetic.[72]

On the question of Philip of Hesse, Maximilian and his father were of one mind. Ferdinand had also counseled that the emperor had far more to gain in Germany by releasing the landgrave than by prolonging his confinement.[73] Charles was deaf to this argument too, and on 15 January 1552 Maurice and Landgrave William decided to join with Henry II of France to win Philip's release. In return, the elector promised to recognize French possession of Metz, Toul, and Verdun, which Henry captured a couple of months later. Still quartered in Innsbruck, the emperor was unexpectedly attacked by the Saxon elector's forces. Charles fled ignominiously to Villach in Carinthia; he had little choice but to negotiate with the German princes the issue of Philip's release. Though he had no evidence that Maximilian had betrayed him, the emperor thoroughly distrusted his nephew's ties to Germany's territorial rulers, especially those with Maurice. Maximilian denied that there was anything suspect in these relationships, but his uncle clearly did not believe him.[74]

Maximilian made no attempt to mollify his father-in-law. The archduke's bland assurance that his only concerns were peace and restoration of German freedom, a none-too-subtle reference to Charles's high-handed efforts to steer the imperial succession, kept all tempers on edge. Nor did Maximilian question Maurice's motives.[75] If anything, his friendship with the Saxon prince seemed to grow closer. On introducing the elector to his wife, the archduke insisted that Maurice embrace Maria fully rather than simply kissing her hand, even though both visibly shrank from such a greeting.[76] Maurice would be a valuable military adviser when Maximilian went to Hungary in 1552 to oversee Habsburg military operations there. Between the two of them they kept the Turks at bay for the rest of the year.

Charles was not impressed. He remained stonily hostile to his nephew. He refused to deploy Maximilian in the Netherlands as Mary of Hungary's chief of military operations. Relations between him and the archduke he said, delicately yet pointedly, were the reason.[77]

The emperor's dynastic interests shifted westward following the death of King Edward VI of England in 1553. A marriage of Philip to his second cousin Mary Tudor, the heir apparent, was strategically and confessionally attractive; the emperor announced in 1554 that he would not press Philip on the electors as his immediate successor. Assurances of goodwill and loyalty flowed from Vienna, as both King Ferdinand and Maximilian's wife, Maria, reaffirmed their bonds to Charles.[78] Philip himself was not altogether eager to become emperor, and he made his feelings clear fairly soon. Indeed, by 1555 he declared that the imperial crown did not interest him, though he did insist on retaining his vicariate in Italy.[79]

But Maximilian had turned enduringly against almost all things Spanish. Hearing so many contrary reports of his uncle's intentions, often from members of Charles's court, the archduke did not know whom to believe. Good words, he noted, often hid quite other schemes. Maximilian's reputation for antagonism toward his uncle prompted Henry II of France to dispatch an envoy, Christoph von Roggendorf, to the archduke in 1554. His mission was to ferret out more about the discord in the house of Austria. To keep dynastic tensions as high as he could, Roggendorf was to tell Maximilian that the emperor, regardless of what he had said, still planned for his son to succeed him in Germany. Maximilian conveyed the news to his father, who received it skeptically, much to the archduke's irritation. Ferdinand was programmatically wary of anything coming from France, particularly via Roggendorf, who had once been in his service and who had provoked the king's deepest dislike. In spite of Maximilian's entreaties, his father refused to give the envoy so much as a hearing.

Throughout the 1550s, Maximilian's views of the French grew closer to those of both his father and his uncle. By 1556, war with the Valois threatened in Italy, where Pius IV, who detested the Habsburgs for their comparatively evenhanded treatment of German Protestants, was backing Henry II. Maximilian saw more clearly that the French ruler only wanted to use him against his uncle and cousin. In 1557, he refused to receive Henry's ambassador, Caius de Virail, much as his father had refused to see Roggendorf only three years before. Marriage alliances with the house of Valois were never out of the question for Maximilian. But as time went on, French support of the Turks, at least against the Habsburgs, convinced him to close ranks with his family against news issuing from Paris.[80]

Greater caution toward France did not, however, increase Maximilian's sympathy for Spain. He had left a few friends there; he was especially close to the viceroy of Valencia, the count of Benavente, who kept in touch with him about Maximilian's two eldest sons, when they went to live with Philip II in 1563. But Benavente was the exception. Even his wife vexed Maximilian with her Spanish ways and the Spanish retinue Philip had carefully selected for her. Petty quarrels between Maximilian and Maria's household were routine, leading him to remark in 1555 that he should have married a German. That same year, King Ferdinand, who was genuinely fond of his daughter-in-law, added a codicil to his will in which he urged his son to cease criticizing his wife over her Spanish servants.[81]

For a time in 1556, it appeared that Charles, hoping to win his nephew's support against France, was thinking once again of ceding the Netherlands to Maximilian, a prospect that had led the younger man to accept his marriage years before. But the price was high—the Habsburg patrimonial lands of the Tyrol, Styria, and Carinthia were to go to Philip, so that he would control the Italian border. The Spanish prince was to become emperor as well. Maximilian stiffly refused; in August of 1556 he left Brussels, where discussions with his uncle were taking place.[82] Even when Philip's accomplishments were good news for the dynasty, Maximilian took little pleasure in them. In 1557, the new king of Spain scored a major victory against the French in the Netherlands at St. Quentin. More military successes followed in 1558. Duke Albrecht V of Bavaria, a man to whom Maximilian was very close, was sure that his brother-in-law would rejoice at the news. But Maximilian saw only the sinister side of the triumph. Philip had dealt very lightly with his German prisoners in 1557, leading the archduke to suspect that his cousin was renewing his campaign for the German crown.[83]

Grievances like Maximilian's, particularly those which arose from his father's broken promises and the hostility the archduke met with at the hands of some of Ferdinand's advisers, were not uncommon among heirs apparent of any day.[84] Maximilian's case was unusual only in that he was answering to two dynastic authorities, each of whom had competing personal agendas. That the archduke was very high-strung compounded his difficulties. Moreover, the emperor and his brother had sound institutional reasons to deny Maximilian the support that he sought from them. The archduke's typical response to frustration was to rail against it. He deferred to his elders selectively, a serious challenge to the patriarchal structure of his house. His impulsiveness could be embarrassing and sometimes dangerous. Even though his father and the emperor had often disagreed bitterly over such matters as the elder Ferdinand's succession in the empire and financial aid in Hungary, they had avoided long-term ruptures. Maximilian was generally contemptuous of his Spanish relatives (except his wife) and their subjects, either openly or indirectly. His feelings about those around him swung between immoderate attachment to those he believed to be friends, such as Maurice of Saxony, and suspicion toward almost everyone else. The first attitude left Maximilian open to unscrupulous manipulation. The second reinforced a sense of isolation that presaged a troubled public career, notwithstanding the organizational talents and other skills the archduke had shown during his Spanish regency. He had yet to prove that he had the most important qualities of a successful ruler—judgment and wisdom.

three

A German Prince and the German Religion

Less volatile people than Maximilian were drawn into the confessional maelstrom that the Protestant Reformation stirred up in Europe. With his lively intellect and independent ways, the archduke could hardly have escaped some decisive brush with the new doctrines, which had taken hold throughout much of the Holy Roman Empire by his late adolescence. What was remarkable in Maximilian's religious development was neither his curiosity about evangelical ideas nor his skepticism about key aspects of Catholic orthodoxy, but his persistent cultivation of both inclinations.

The archduke had not drawn up the dynastic agendas that had so deeply offended him. In matters of faith, however, Maximilian largely created his own troubles. From the standpoint of narrow political advantage, he had little cause to antagonize Ferdinand I when it came to religion. Ferdinand's Catholicism, committed, yet reform-minded, was more or less acceptable to his family, to the German princes, and to Rome, at least until 1555 and the Peace of Augsburg. Ferdinand's careful religious politics had eased his way to several militarily crucial compromises with the Protestant territorial rulers. The imperial estates were not asking for any radical break with these views when Maximilian began courting electoral votes in the early 1550s. Either the Catholic or the Protestant camp would have welcomed the exclusive support of the emperor, but no one at that point expected to get it. For Maximilian to succeed his uncle and father, he would have needed only to assure the imperial electors, both Protestant and Catholic, that he would respect traditional German liberties and resist alleged plots in Madrid to subvert them.

Aside from the heartfelt wishes of his wife, Maximilian also had personal reasons to follow the faith of his Habsburg predecessors. Aesthetically and culturally, he was closely tied by the 1550s to his Catholic family and to Catholic Europe and would remain so all his life. His relatives supplied him with the curiosities and rarities in which he took immense delight.[1] Not only would he observe a modified version of Charles V's elaborate court ceremonial, but he acted as a patron for scholars, musicians, and painters who came from Spain, the Spanish Netherlands, and Italy.[2] Maximilian eagerly received choral compositions from cardinals in Rome. If the efforts pleased him, he forwarded the manuscripts to other Catholics. Though he truly loathed Pope Paul IV for the latter's anti-Habsburg views, Maximilian felt free to ask the pontiff for livings to support staff at the court chapel in Vienna. He was especially taken by the music of Orlando di Lasso, a Netherlander, whom he tried to bring to Vienna. When Albrecht of Bavaria snared the composer for his Munich establishment, Maximilian badgered the duke for Lasso's pieces, masses included, and tried to reciprocate with works of equal merit. If Maximilian had trouble finding vocalists, Albrecht might send him some. If, by chance, he could not use the personnel the duke supplied, Maximilian tried to place them in his father's court.[3]

Maximilian depended upon his Catholic brother-in-law for help in more mundane matters too. A variety of fish and game—live, dead, and in various stages of decomposition—traveled from Munich to Vienna or the other way around. The two men shared a lifelong taste for the red and white wines of Hungary.[4] Early in his career, Maximilian started relying on Albrecht as a general news-gatherer for information that came to Munich from throughout Europe.[5] Johann Ulrich Zasius, who often carried their communiqués, served both men and later became one of the archduke's imperial vice-chancellors.[6] Maximilian also called on his Catholic relatives to provide livings or other forms of assistance for those who had served him.[7]

Thus, Maximilian had many reasons to identify himself with the Church of Rome. Measured orthodoxy might very well have brought him the political rewards and cultural contacts that he craved. But it took several years for him to understand this, and when he did, the tactical usefulness of this position had sharply diminished. In the meantime, his spiritual development would try his entire family and bewilder outside observers.

Environment undoubtedly influenced Maximilian's eccentric confessional development. The religious climate of the king's court was as ambiguous as the mixed signals Ferdinand was giving about his eldest son's political future. In his youth, Ferdinand I had embraced the Erasmian reform that inspired his lifelong struggle for the moral and intellectual improvement of Roman Christendom. Until his death in 1564, he believed that Catholics and Luther's followers could iron out their differences; indeed, the dividing line between the two confessions in his time was quite fuzzy. These hopes, coupled with political pressures and Ferdinand's often nonchalant administrative style, brought into his government and household men of many shades of belief. During the last years of his reign as emperor, Ferdinand even ennobled Protestants at his court. Nor did he run the only Catholic establishment in his family where the confessionally suspect could gain a hearing. Albrecht of Bavaria, whose orthodoxy deepened only with age, forwarded requests to Vienna from known Protestant sympathizers, such as Hans Ungnad, a former Habsburg governor in Styria.[8]

A handful of Protestants and Protestant-inclined princes fought on the imperial side during the Schmalkaldic War—Erich of Braunschweig-Calenberg, and two Hohenzollern princes, margraves Hans of Küstrin and Albrecht Alcibiades of Kulmbach. Maximilian's regimental standard-bearer was Hans Ungnad's son, Ludwig. Maximilian appears to have been very close to both Ludwig and Duke Erich. Both men subsequently went with the archduke to Spain. Though Erich quickly ceased dabbling in evangelicalism, he remained a lukewarm Catholic, hardly an ideal companion for the restless Maximilian.[9] One of the trophies Maximilian carried away from the Schmalkaldic War was a Lutheran Bible bound in black satin, which had belonged to Elector John Frederick of Saxony. During his Spanish regency, however, the archduke gave no outward sign of religious doubt. Possibly he was on his best behavior because of the negotiations over succession then under way in Augsburg. Possibly, too, he did not want to displease his new wife, who was just then beginning her lifelong patronage of the Jesuits.[10] Maximilian attended Mass, even on early winter mornings when Maria could not rouse herself; hand in hand, they attended during the summer. He visibly enjoyed listening to sermons from clergymen he would scorn a few years later. In 1549, he wrote to the emperor that he had been very happy during a thirteen-day pilgrimage to Santiago.[11]

In dealing with problems in Spain that might have tempted him to criticize Catholic policy, Maximilian remained steadfastly correct. Not long after he became regent in 1549, he had to resolve a dispute between the royal council and the Inquisition over which office should open the streets of the Moorish quarter in Valladolid. The opportunity was there for Maximilian to criticize the Inquisition as the embodiment of Catholic repressiveness, but he did nothing of the kind. His role, he declared, was to foster temperate discussion of the matter. Should he intervene at all, it would be to cut off bickering between the two sides. In any case, he was ready to execute any decision that Charles or Prince Philip took on the issue. As late as 1555, Michele Suriano, the Venetian ambassador to King Ferdinand's court, said that Maximilian appeared ready to follow his father's lead on policies and attitudes toward the papacy.[12]

Circumspect though he may have been, Maximilian gradually became known as a evangelical sympathizer. Alvise Mocenigo, another ambassador from Venice, speculated that consideration for Protestant sensibilities had influenced Charles V to name Maximilian president of the imperial diet that met in Augsburg during 1547.[13] When the archduke arrived in Augsburg for the family negotiations in 1550, no one identified him with the new creed, but he was clearly not hostile to the movement. Its supporters found him very accessible. During Maximilian's distressing stopover in Trent a year later, Protestant spokesmen at the church council, then in its second session, asked him to arrange a long-promised hearing with the emperor. Maximilian responded cautiously though positively, recommending that the Protestants exercise patience while he tried to gain his uncle's ear. Roger Ascham, the English ambassador to the imperial court, called the archduke a pious prince in whom the German territorial rulers had placed their hopes. Exactly what the envoy meant by that was not clear.[14] But some aspect of Maximilian's religious views was obviously troubling both his family and Rome. In March of 1551, the count de Luna, Philip's caretaker in Spain, claimed to see much improvement in the archduke's religious behavior after contact with an un-named nuncio.[15]

Once Maximilian left Spain for good, he became far more active in German religious politics. He vigorously supported schemes to advance Protestant and Catholic cooperation. Throughout 1553, several evangelical territorial rulers, along with the electors of Mainz and Trier and Albrecht of Bavaria, were trying to establish the so-called Heidelberg League. Seeking to keep Germany at peace during the war that had broken out between Charles V and France in 1552, the group recommended compromise between evangelicals and Catholics until their confessional differences could be ironed out. Members also were committed to blocking any Spanish succession. In August,

Maximilian enthusiastically proposed to his father that they join the organization.[16]

Ferdinand generally endorsed the goals of the league. Nevertheless, he was loath to offend the emperor, who flatly opposed any accommodation with the new confession. Ferdinand eventually did enter the alliance, but only half-heartedly. Moreover, in September of 1553, he forbade Maximilian to meet with other signatories. The discussion between the two was stormy; the father lashed out at his son as a self-centered "hothead."[17] Maximilian could very well skip the meeting, especially after having recently begged off on attending the marriage of his sister Catherine to King Sigismund Augustus of Poland on grounds of poor health. The archduke replied that in the present instance, he really wished to attend the affair. Ferdinand reminded him that not only Charles but the entire Spanish court would be disturbed were he to go to the gathering. The Spanish would feel that way, shot back the archduke, no matter what he and his father did.

Ferdinand's admonitions left Maximilian little choice but to remain "an obedient son," as he bitterly described himself.[18] As for the Spanish, the less he saw of them, the happier he would be. He assured his Bavarian brother-in-law that he would do all he could to remain a German and to serve German interests.[19] Still fuming, he continued to press the league's cause, though he did shift the blame for Ferdinand's lukewarm support of its purposes to his father's advisers, "who listen to the grass grow."[20] The archduke also sensed that these men distrusted him deeply.[21]

They had every reason to do so. Maximilian was going through a crucial stage in his confessional development, as even his father recognized. Under the guidance of Johann Sebastian Pfauser, the king's court preacher, Maximilian began a serious program of Bible study. Born in Constance, Pfauser had entered the priesthood following the Schmalkaldic War. By the beginning of the 1550s, he had distinguished himself with pastoral work at Sterzing in the Tyrol. On the recommendation of the bishop of Trent, Christoph Madruzzo, and Kaspar von Niedruck, a man of decidedly heterodox leanings who was then in Ferdinand's establishment, the king called Pfauser to Vienna in 1554.

Describing himself as neither evangelical nor Catholic, Pfauser claimed to be seeking a middle way while preaching what he deemed to be the truth. Where matters of doctrine and practice had been called into doubt, he fell back on Scripture rather than conciliar or patristic authority. He would have nothing to do with the veneration of saints. But no one had said that Pfauser was not a sound Catholic. He had vigorously attacked both pope and Curia, but so had King Ferdinand himself from time to time.[22]

But it was not long before Pfauser stirred up heated controversy at the court in Vienna. Ferdinand tried to get rid of the priest. Maximilian argued strongly for Pfauser's transfer to his own household, and his father relented. By 1555, the cleric was known to be married, though his open conversion to evangelicalism took place only after he was forced from Maximilian's court in 1560.[23] Until that time, however, the more sharply Pfauser was attacked, the more vehemently Maximilian defended him. At the end of 1554, Ferdinand and his vice-chancellor, Jacob Jonas, confronted the archduke. Jonas charged him with trafficking in "rotten eggs" (*faulen Eiern*), that is, favoring the new German confession. Maximilian declared that his only concern was that the house of Austria have honorable servants. Jonas pressed on, accusing both Maximilian and his preacher of being evangelicals. To this the archduke retorted that Jonas was an "old papist," an epithet which he was using more and more.[24]

But Ferdinand did not issue any ultimatums to his son. His foremost concern at the end of 1554 was an upcoming diet in Augsburg. Here, once again, the king hoped to ease some of the religious discord in the empire. Raising money and troops to counter the Turks was on the agenda as well. Given the sympathy Maximilian enjoyed among evangelical princes, and even from those Catholics who were eager to reconcile confessional differences, his father could ill afford to be unduly harsh with the archduke in such matters.[25] Leaving Maximilian in charge of affairs in Vienna, Ferdinand set out for Augsburg in December.

The once circumspect regent of Spain, however, had turned into the religious enfant terrible of the house of Austria. Standing in for his father at a meeting of the Lower Austrian estates, Maximilian accepted their petition for Communion in both kinds and forwarded it to Ferdinand, regardless of the latter's order to do nothing of the sort. Ferdinand had charged the Jesuit Peter Canisius with preparing a new German catechism, to which the king himself had composed an introduction. Maximilian had no love for the new Society of Jesus; Pfauser had claimed that unnamed conspirators within the order had dissuaded Ferdinand from letting his eldest son govern Bohemia. Maximilian held up the publication of the catechism in 1555; Canisius protested to Ferdinand. The king dispatched a stern written rebuke to his son. Maximilian was infuriated; it was yet another instance of harassment from the Jesuits, whom Pfauser had called "bloodsuckers." Maximilian dispatched a messenger to Augsburg to defend the outspoken pastor.[26]

Rumors circulated at the diet that Maximilian was refusing to hear Mass and that he would soon formally join the evangelical ranks.[27] The negotiations at the gathering, which would end with the provisional territorialization of the evangelical and Catholic creeds in Germany, reached their climax in August. Nevertheless, Ferdinand found time to add an eloquent codicil to his testament. He urged all his sons to adhere to the religion of their forebears. The house of Habsburg had flourished under its auspices. Habsburg progeny and relatives, the king pointed out, were rulers or consorts in almost every European land except Scotland.[28]

Even this awesome conjunction of faith and dynastic self-interest failed to impress Maximilian—just why is not clear. He had private reasons to resent Julius III, who had long viewed the archduke as religiously suspect and had preferred Philip to his Austrian cousin during the succession crisis of 1551. Indeed, Julius had declared that Philip's election as emperor was an absolute necessity.[29] But Maximilian had no quarrel with popes inclined toward internal reform of the church. He applauded the election of Julius III's successor, Marcellus II, in March of 1555. Here was a man known to be interested in advancing the moral and intellectual standing of the clergy, and Maximilian believed that he could be won over to compromise in Germany as well. The new pontiff's sudden death two months later genuinely saddened him.[30]

More significantly, however, Maximilian kept to himself whatever theological opinions he may have formed from Scripture and Protestant tracts he studied. He had apparently come to some conclusions. He asked his wife to clasp a crucifix, rather than a representation of the Virgin, in her hands as she gave birth to their son Albrecht in November of 1559. That, however, was as far as he apparently went in asking her to accommodate his religious views, at least at that time. He was certainly not professing Pfauser's "middle way," the position with which later historians have identified the archduke.[31]

Indeed, when one discounts the bitter mood Maximilian was often in when he expressed himself, his religious utterances added up to little more than the general Erasmianism of his father and some of the king's advisers. Maximilian was much concerned about the quality of Catholic clergy and grieved when capable men among them passed from the scene. He continued many Catholic observances. Awaiting a visit from him in Stuttgart on either Friday or Saturday in 1556, Duke Christoph of Württemberg ordered fish and lobster for the welcoming meal, in the knowledge that Maximilian, at that point, did not touch meat on either of those days.[32] Though he called public sale of indulgences by the Jesuits " 'magic shows' " (*Zauberpossen*) and refused to let Jesuits educate his children, Maximilian's main difference with the order was not over fine points of doctrine. Rather, it had to do with the Jesuits' wish to bring the Inquisition into the Austrian lands and with the intrusive way the company proposed to examine every clergyman there.[33]

But the archduke was asking questions. Furthermore, a circle of people that stretched far beyond Pfauser was ready to help him find answers. Christoph of Württemberg supplied him with Luther's works, Melanchthon's *Loci Communes*, a synopsis of doctrine, and personal encouragement not to concern himself about the pope.[34] When the duke offered him Melanchthon's collected works and those of the Swabian reformer Johann Brenz, Maximilian accepted gratefully. He also asked for "other writings from theologians of the true faith."[35]

Maximilian's patronage also extended to the work of Primož Trubar, a Slovenian priest who had put together an evangelical catechism and translated the New Testament into his native tongue.[36] Through Kaspar von Niedruck, the archduke made the imperial library available to the Croatian evangelical reformer Matthias Flacius (Vlasic) Illyricus, who took a far more sternly deterministic view of original sin, salvation, and the sacraments than did the theologians around Melanchthon in Wittenberg. When Flacius began work on the *Magdeburg Centuries,* a history of the Christian Church that culminates in its restoration through the evangelical reform, Niedruck recommended sources in Vienna for the project. Maximilian allowed Niedruck to make notes from these materials and to send them on to Flacius. The Habsburg's orders opened other libraries to the scholar as well.

It is possible that the archduke's interest in the *Centuries,* at least in its early phases, may have stemmed from his general eagerness to support the arts and learning. Maximilian thought well enough of Niedruck as an historian to want to inspect his published writings.[37] But regardless of the archduke's motives for assisting the project, Niedruck declared that it would have taken far longer without such aid. When he finally finished the study, Flacius dedicated it to Maximilian, among others.[38]

More crucial to Maximilian's inner development, however, may have been Jacob Acontius, secretary to Madruzzo, the cardinal bishop of Trent. An Italian who grew into an early advocate of tolerance and some kind of provisional religious freedom, Acontius, like Pfauser and Niedruck, had begun his Austrian service in King Ferdinand's court.[39] He apparently grew quite close to Maximilian, at least according to a contemporary Dutch historian, Simon Ruytinck, a Protestant sympathizer.[40] Acontius's theology, if that is the term for it, was as much a matter of attitude as of systematic thinking, at least in the early 1550s. He did not call himself evangelical. Like Pfauser, he questioned the role of the sacraments. Salvation was possible for all who read Scripture seriously and were touched by grace.[41] The Italian's access to Maximilian may have been smoothed by his sympathy for the prince's political troubles rather than by any spiritual message. When Acontius sent Maximilian the finished version of his most important religious tract, the *Dialogo*, in 1558, he included a Latin rendering of the Psalms. Openly speaking of the Habsburg succession struggle of 1550–1551, the reformer promised that, should the archduke read the texts, he would find that he and David bore the same cross. David's career as king of the Hebrews had turned out happily, and Maximilian would have the same good fortune.[42]

Such sentiments were bound to hearten Maximilian. But he also read the *Dialogo* and seemingly took its message seriously.[43] The tenor of the tract anticipated policies that Maximilian espoused to the end of his life. Acontius took no formal position on doctrine, nor did he defend confessional pluralism as a permanent arrangement. Though he was sure that a single, incontestable Christian faith was somewhere to be found, traditional religious authority was not a reliable guide to it. Christians had to make their spiritual way for themselves. In the process, as Acontius saw it, evangelicals, and even Jews and Turks, could be helpful in correcting the mistakes of Rome. God would protect serious seekers after truth, even when they listened to heretics. In theory, a prince could silence heterodoxy in good conscience if the dissenting religious tenets were mistaken. If these were upheld as doctrine, however, their suppression by political authority would constitute a grave error. Worse yet would be for a ruler to follow such a policy at the behest of others, by which Acontius meant the pope, rather than out of personal conviction.[44]

All in all, Maximilian's behavior, the company he often kept, and the people he chose to protect reinforced hopes among a variety of religious dissidents that he would actively support them. Between 1555 and 1557, Jan Blahoslav, a leading pastor of the Bohemian Brethren, a sorely persecuted splinter group of fifteenth-century Utraquists, appeared four times in Vienna. First approaching Pfauser, who remained noncommittal, Blahoslav wanted Maximilian to intervene on behalf of the movement's leader, Jan Augusta, who had been incarcerated in semidarkness for almost nine years. Elector Palatine

Ottheinrich, who thought that the archduke was concerned about "all pious Christians and learned people," asked Maximilian to put in a word for Lelio Socini (later to be suspected of antitrinitarianism, Socini was at the time ensnared in legal problems in his native Italy). Christoph of Württemberg was also worried about Socini. Maximilian told the duke that he could do nothing to assist him. Nevertheless, he declared that he shared Christoph's anxiety.[45]

Rome was finding Maximilian ever more troublesome. When a small evangelical cell developed in Valladolid, Pope Paul IV was sure that Maximilian had inspired it.[46] Even Catholics sympathetic to the style of reforms that Maximilian and his father wished to sponsor grew increasingly uneasy. In January of 1558, the archduke asked Johann Ulrich Zasius, then advising Ferdinand I, to purchase the library of Dr. Johann Albrecht Widmannstetter, an imperial functionary and chapter member of the Regensburg Cathedral. " 'A library [of] heretical books,' " commented the councillor nervously in the margin of the order. Zasius recommended that Albrecht V of Bavaria, who was far less open to evangelical seduction, buy the books instead.[47]

Maximilian's father, emperor by 1558, could no longer tolerate such behavior in an heir apparent. He launched an aggressive campaign—Maximilian compared it to the persecution of Jesus Christ—to win his son back to orthodoxy. Rome would not be much help, because Maximilian had little respect for Pope Paul IV. Not only was the latter rigid and wholly at home with nepotism and the seamy underside of church finance, but he also wished to keep the Habsburgs as far from Italy as possible. Moreover, Paul held Charles and Ferdinand personally responsible for the success of the evangelical reform in Germany. Upon learning in 1555 of the confessional settlement reached in Augsburg, the pope had threatened to depose both the emperor and his brother, making Ferdinand's—and therefore Maximilian's—succession in the empire more problematic than ever.[48]

Ferdinand I had a sizable mission, to which he applied himself relentlessly. Those who assisted the emperor in the "assault on the sensibility" of the prince, as a nineteenth-century scholar once put it, were even more single-minded.[49] By 1560, the archduke's privacy was not a consideration, at least for the the Polish bishop Stanislaus Hosius, whom Rome delegated to work on the Habsburg prince. Upon hearing that Maximilian read Pfauser's writings while taking the thermal waters in Waltersdorf, south of Vienna, Hosius suggested visiting him there to discourage such interests. Even Ferdinand advised against that. The emperor did not scruple, however, to enlist Maria, his niece and daughter-in-law, as an intercessor with her husband in the hope that her fervent Catholicism and the couple's deep bond would return Maximilian to orthodoxy. Indeed, Ferdinand became so desperate that in 1559 he put out feelers to Rome about a possible annulment of the marriage. Maria, he said, could not remain the wife of a heretic. Distraught though she was, the queen of Bohemia rejected the idea. So did the pope, on the grounds that Maximilian had not interfered with his wife's religious observance.[50]

Maximilian responded to these pressures ambiguously, calling himself neither papist nor evangelical but simply a Christian.[51] Interviewed by Matthew Cithard, his father's court preacher, he declared that his sole concern was to rid the Church of abuses, a not wholly disingenuous claim. Though he quickly changed his mind, Maximilian welcomed the election in 1559 of Pius IV, who seemed eager to cleanse Christendom of its decay. Maximilian's attitude was all the more remarkable given that Pius, like Julius III, had supported Philip during the Habsburg succession crisis. And the archduke continued to concern himself with Catholic reform. When the last segment of the great church council of Trent would get under way in 1562, Maximilian would draw up a list of cardinals he thought were committed to genuine Catholic renewal.[52]

Ferdinand had to get Pfauser out of his son's household once and for all, though, because the archduke's attachment to the clergyman was embarrassingly public. Prompted by Peter Canisius, the king opened his campaign in 1557 and 1558. Furious confrontations ensued between father and son over Maximilian's religious views and especially over Pfauser. Ferdinand's spies attended the preacher's popular and accessible sermons and listened closely. By July of 1559, they had noted thirty-eight heresies in Pfauser's homilies. Maximilian felt more beleaguered than ever; he thought seriously of taking refuge with some German Protestant prince. Even Maria, who had complained to Charles and Philip about her husband's confessional peculiarities, begged Ferdinand to treat his eldest son more gently.[53]

But the emperor persisted. Though willing to accommodate evangelical practice temporarily for the sake of public peace, he was not ready to extend the privilege to his own family. Early in 1560, he ordered Pfauser, whose name appeared at the head of Maximilian's household list, out of Vienna. Fearing that his father would do the clergyman physical harm, Maximilian yielded to the order.[54] But his underlying attitude was unchanged. Maximilian swore in letters to Pfauser that he would remain true to his faith, though what that was went unsaid. The cleric and his family remained the archduke's pensioners long after they had left his formal service.[55]

For a moment, Maximilian was once again the emotional and headstrong youth who had defiantly fled his uncle's camp in 1547. He fired off a series of letters to the Protestant electors, asking them for support and even sanctuary. But the evangelical princes were not willing to sacrifice good relations with the emperor for the sake of his son's convictions. July of 1560 brought a cautious reminder from Elector August of Saxony that the archduke had filial duties. Maximilian was also urged to take care of his health. Elector Joachim of Brandenburg was equally vague. Most receptive was their colleague Elector Palatine Frederick III, though he warned Maximilian that he could not help him keep his titles and position once he left Vienna. The archduke's fury gradually waned. He even heard out the arguments that Bishop Hosius continued to force upon him.[56]

But it was Ferdinand I who had probably done the most to bring about the new softening of his son's attitude. As early as the summer of 1559, he had threatened to disinherit Maximilian altogether in favor of the loyally Catholic Archduke Ferdinand. The latter made it clear that he would have little sympathy for his elder brother, should their father follow through. When Maximilian asked the emperor to leave him with at least the kingdom of Bohemia, Archduke Ferdinand protested.[57] In the spring of 1560, the emperor repeated the threat, reminding his son that he could lower him to depths as great as the heights to which he had raised him. Maximilian must either submit or lose all claim to his patrimony.

Nevertheless, for all his resolve, Ferdinand clearly wished to avoid irreparable ruptures. Having shown himself ready to issue ultimatums, he also pointed to the rewards that Maximilian would enjoy were he to renounce his apparent confessional heterodoxy. Maximilian's cousin Philip, now king of Spain, was eager for his relatives in Vienna to remain Catholic. His only son, Don Carlos, was mentally and physically frail, and it was possible that one of Maximilian's sons might be heir to the Spanish crown. Negotiations to send two of Maximilian's boys to the court of their uncle in Spain had already begun. Should Carlos survive, a match with one of Maximilian's daughters might be in the offing.[58] When Ferdinand offered his eldest son an outright bribe—a handsome living of twenty-five thousand gulden a year from Pardubice in Bohemia—Maximilian retorted that such arrangements had little effect on his conscience. He did not say no, however. He was willing, he said, to obey Ferdinand in all worldly matters, but not where his soul was at stake. He insisted on communing in both kinds (*sub utraque*).[59] But he had shown that he had clear priorities, thereby opening the way for compromise with his father.

To Ferdinand's knowledge, Maximilian had not communed in orthodox fashion for about three years. The emperor feared that if the archduke were forced to do so, he would abandon Catholicism altogether. In October 1561, Ferdinand presented the case for a dispensation to Pius IV, because only the pope could permit such exceptions. After much back and forth between Vienna and Rome, and further arguments between father and son, the concession arrived in December. Pius IV was not happy about it, and he urged Ferdinand to redouble his efforts to remake Maximilian into a sound Catholic. If the archduke were granted the privilege of communing sub utraque, he must exercise it privately, and only after declaring that the ceremony *sub una* was equally valid. More stormy discussion followed, and Ferdinand himself wanted some firm commitment from his son on the question of his confessional loyalties. On 7 February 1562, Maximilian vowed before his brothers, his father, and his father's privy councillors that he would not leave the Church of Rome.[60]

That Maximilian never communed in the traditional way again is a sign that real conviction lay behind his stubborn demand for the privilege. But political calculation certainly played a large role in the archduke's declaration of 1562.[61] Ferdinand himself was also worrying about more than the future of his son's soul. The imperial election loomed, and a similar ritual was to take place in Hungary, where there was to be a native competitor. He was John Sigismund Zápolya, the son of the emperor's erstwhile rival for the Hungarian crown. The coronation ceremony called for the king-elect to commune publicly in one kind. Maximilian insisted that if he were to perform the rite at all, he would have to partake of both bread and wine. To placate all sides, at least partially, Ferdinand suggested that the archduke commune secretly, as the pope had suggested, thereby removing the stain of heresy from the act.[62] This Maximilian was willing to do, thereby bringing the immediate crisis to an end.

However painful this struggle had been for Maximilian personally, it had not weakened his good standing where it counted the most politically— among the princes of the empire. Even in the midst of his disputes with his family over religion, he continued to promote himself as a champion of German interests and an enemy of Spanish ambitions in central Europe. No one, Protestant or Catholic, would object to such policies. Whenever a prince suggested a way to advance the welfare of the empire, Maximilian was quick to act on it.[63] Indeed, Maximilian had initially been so successful in stirring up German support for his election that he had somewhat overplayed his hand. After King Ferdinand acceded to the imperial title in 1558, the archduke wanted his installation as German king to take place immediately. Citing tradition, however, the electors preferred to wait until their reigning emperor died before choosing his successor.[64]

Ferdinand I's health was not good, so they would not have to wait very long. Wishing the imperial crown to remain in his branch of the house after his death, he devoted much of his dwindling energy to securing Maximilian's election. Given the younger Habsburg's solicitous courtship of their goodwill, the electors were easily won over. In truth, Maximilian, and the house of Habsburg as a whole, had much to offer to the empire's territorial rulers, whatever they thought of the family's ambitions. Regardless of their confessional leanings, all the electors knew that the Ottomans still posed a real threat in the heart of Europe and that only the house of Austria commanded the wherewithal to defend the region effectively. The kingdom of Bohemia, it was remembered, was very wealthy. Some read the archduke's stubborn defense of his interests during the succession crisis as a testimonial to his character.[65]

Maximilian's religious opinions, like his sociable ways, were pleasing to many German territorial rulers, though for different reasons.[66] The Catholics among them, indeed even Pius IV, could live with him once they considered their alternatives. There had been talk of a Protestant candidacy for some time, and though no serious contender had stepped forward, Rome found the prospect troubling. Even the Spanish court, which could be extremely rigid in religious matters, believed that the interests of the true faith required Maximilian's election. News from Vienna about his confessional views had not been entirely bleak, even before his Communion dispensation came. Many Protestant positions apparently displeased the archduke, especially Flacianism, which had taken root at the Saxon ducal court in Weimar. Furthermore, the indisputably Catholic archduke Ferdinand had become a good deal less attractive. He had recently embarked on a morganatic marriage with Philippine Welser, a woman far inferior to him in rank, if not in wealth. Since then, he was taking the duties of state less seriously than he once had done.[67]

Protestants had, by 1562, also been reading Maximilian's career with a view to their own interests for almost fifteen years. Beginning during the

Schmalkaldic War, evangelical princes had believed that Maximilian had some sympathy for their religious views. Charles's scheme for a Spanish succession had given them a political reason to support the archduke—Maximilian's close friend Maurice of Saxony had been particularly hostile to the idea of Philip II as future emperor. For Maximilian finally to have paid lip service to Catholic orthodoxy under parental pressure was no deficit from the evangelical point of view.[68] Indeed, the quasi-inquisitorial tactics and callous disregard for conscience that had forced his hand only reconfirmed religious dissidents' antipapalism. Maximilian had indicated in 1548 to Maurice of Saxony that he would look out for the worldly interests of Luther's princely followers too. They eventually responded in kind. Promised concessions to Joachim II of Brandenburg in the bishoprics of Magdeburg and Halberstadt brought from the elector a counterpromise of support when Maximilian's election finally came up in 1562.[69]

But of utmost concern to all the evangelical territorial rulers was the preservation of the religious settlement of Augsburg reached in 1555. For this task, the Protestant electors had an ideal candidate in Maximilian, if their emperor had to be a Habsburg. The Peace of Augsburg had legitimized Luther's evangelical reform where territorial rulers followed that creed, along with the traditional faith of Rome; to continue this arrangement, Brandenburg and Saxony needed an emperor who wholeheartedly backed both the letter and the spirit of the agreement. Charles had refused to sanction the settlement; Ferdinand regarded it as a temporary political expedient. Maximilian, however, enthusiastically endorsed the peace as a way toward a lasting religious settlement.[70]

By 1562, the last round of the religious council in Trent was under way. Unlike Ferdinand I, however, Maximilian did not expect reforms by Rome to foster confessional reconciliation in the empire. Papal spokesmen, he warned the princes, were negotiating in bad faith. In his opinion, an exclusively German national council was the likeliest instrument for ironing out local religious differences.[71] And the Peace of Augsburg was, in his opinion, crucial to this process. But here too, his slant was more or less toward the evangelical corner. His sole regret about the outcome of the diet in 1555 was that his father had endorsed the so-called Ecclesiastical Reservation. Under this order, church lands remained under Catholic control in ecclesiastical principalities where a prince bishop or abbot embraced the Reformation.[72]

Thus, both Catholics and Protestants had reason to see Maximilian as the only viable successor to his father. A remarkably harmonious atmosphere prevailed at the election in Frankfurt in December of 1562. Maximilian was conspicuously attentive to the wishes of the Protestant electors when discussing the conditions under which they would vote for him. He did not, however, identify himself so closely with their program that he seemed overly beholden to them. The evangelical princes indeed grumbled at the formula that defined papal-imperial relations, that is, the relationship between the pope and the German king. Maximilian, however, persuaded them to drop the issue until after the election, when he would talk it over with each man individually.

The pervasive goodwill lasted through his coronation, which also took place in Frankfurt, to save time lost when one of the electors, the archbishop of Cologne, died during the proceedings. The only dark note was the weather, so gloomy that eyewitnesses at the public procession were hard put to make out the details. Nevertheless, crowds turned out to see the sights, especially a rare one—a Turkish ambassador. The banquets were gratifyingly extravagant. Most important, the very popular new king impressed onlookers with the lavishness of his outfit and the four thousand horses he had allegedly brought for his retinue.[73]

The elaborate ritual took careful account of all confessional sensibilities. Under papal dispensation, Maximilian communed privately sub utraque in his Frankfurt quarters. For once, his delicate health was of some use, since it served to excuse the irregular practice. His physicians, it was said, had advised him to go through the rite as early as he could. Had he waited for the coronation Mass, he would have had to fast longer than was good for him. During that service, however, he pledged his loyalty and support to the Church of Rome and the pope who spoke for it. For the actual liturgy, the three Protestant electors tactfully withdrew to the sacristy. At the crowning, however, the papal ambassadors were so far from the place where the new king took his oath that they heard very little of what was being said.[74]

Back in Vienna for a brilliant triumphal entry, Maximilian learned in March of 1563 that the pope still had serious misgivings about the emperor-elect's religious views. Pius IV had resigned himself to the archduke's succession in the empire, at least in principle, only after Ferdinand I agreed to send German bishops to Trent. Before recognizing Maximilian in his new office, the pope wanted him to pledge himself to Catholicism both publicly and in writing.[75] Maximilian had himself been anticipating trouble from Rome over his

German election for some time. As early as 1561, he had asked Philip to intercede on his behalf with the pope.[76] But once he learned what Pius wanted of him, Maximilian flatly refused.

At this moment, the house of Habsburg showed what it was prepared to do for one of its own. Believing that Maximilian might become a better Catholic out of gratitude for his help, Philip II put in a word for his cousin in Rome. Ferdinand I was concerned about the precedent that the pope's request might set; he moved speedily into the controversy too. While allowing that Pius had the right to confirm and approve the election of a king and emperor, Ferdinand argued that no pope could exact any more from Maximilian than he himself had agreed to under similar circumstances in 1560. Ferdinand's papal coronation was still pending, though Pius had invited him to Bologna for the ceremony. Protesting what he called Rome's excessive demands, the emperor resolved to put off his own crowning. His eldest son, said his father, was altogether "reasonable" about his religious behavior. By the fall of 1563, Maximilian agreed to volunteer a simple written guarantee of his Catholic loyalties and a vow to model his behavior toward the Church upon that of his uncle and father. No public profession was made. Early in the following year, Pius grudgingly accepted the compromise. At least, he remarked, the younger Habsburg was no self-confessed heretic.[77]

Maximilian finally had what he had believed from adolescence was rightfully his. Securing the German crown had taken more than ten years of dynastic infighting and aggressive politicking. On the way to his victory, strategic realities had begun to crowd out the apparent religious concerns that had made him such a problem for his family and the Church of Rome. Those areas where his alleged Protestant leanings were halfway conspicuous—his support of the Peace of Augsburg most especially—had proven to be tactically useful. The Catholic preponderance in the imperial diet derived only from the membership of ecclesiastical princes, large and small. The support of Protestant secular rulers was crucial when military aid was needed, and the Habsburgs could not take them lightly. Maximilian's criticism of the papacy and any interest he showed in evangelical ideas, however discreetly, marked him as a German and protector of German interests. The secular Catholic German princes generally endorsed that position.

But it would be a mistake to think that Maximilian's behavior was solely a product of political calculation. A man of Maximilian's considerable ambitions would not have persisted in his views to the point where he came close to losing both land and position unless he had been prompted by spiritual conviction. Maximilian would cling to positions such as communion in both kinds until he died. As a matter of general principle, he said, in the year before he became emperor, conscience came before authority.[78] And he did not give up searching. He continued to listen attentively to a wide range of Christian discourse. From 1550 to 1570, he went through eight court preachers before settling on one who was more or less acceptable, Lambert Gruter from Deventer.[79]

It was even clearer that Maximilian wanted a lasting reconciliation between the traditional faith and its evangelical offshoot in Germany and that he saw the Augsburg settlement as a way of achieving it. Even before the diet convened in 1555, he had expressed great hopes for such an arrangement. Furthermore, he adhered to the letter of its territorial provisions. He had no intention of extending similar terms anywhere to other Protestant factions, which continued to multiply. By 1562, he had distanced himself from the hapless Bohemian Brethren, the Zwinglians, and more obliquely from the Calvinists, for deviating from the 1555 agreement. The broadly constructed theology of the Heidelberg Catechism, forwarded to him from the palatinate in 1563, smacked too much of "Zwinglianism," especially in the articles on baptism and Communion. It sounded, he said, as if its authors had set out deliberately to disagree with the Lutheran Augsburg Confession of 1530 (Augustana) and make impossible the religious unity he wished to restore to the empire.[80]

All in all, though, Maximilian's election in the empire marked a sharp turn for the better in his fortunes, given the political and confessional problems he had faced for more than fifteen years. Some of his deeper spiritual concerns—the issue of his Communion, for one—may even have been answered. More happily still, he had begun to find his way back into favor with his father, who had exacerbated Maximilian's problems but had also done much to resolve them. Their growing reconciliation was an object lesson in the management of intradynastic relations, and it was timely, for the emperor did not have long to live.

four

From Father to Son

Ferdinand and Maximilian were much alike. They had the same quick intelligence and single-minded longing for office and power. Both were tenacious. They were equally excitable, though the father learned to control himself earlier than did his son. They enjoyed identical recreations—music, collecting rarities, and above all hunting—the pastime of choice among the sixteenth-century Habsburgs, both male and female. In the midst of serious communications between them, Maximilian could drift off into news of his game preserves, confident that what he had to say would interest his father.[1]

Yet, despite their similarities, the two men disagreed often and bitterly. The successful princely family was one that knew how to resolve conflicts when they erupted. Ferdinand and Maximilian had a very hard time inventing these strategies. The archduke's quixotic religious concerns and his resentment of his brother Ferdinand had made for years of strain between Maximilian and his father. Raw ambition, coupled with unfortunate circumstances, did the rest.

Emperor Ferdinand had long been accustomed to the responsibility, as well as the privileges, of rule. At eighteen, he had already been on the way to becoming a major figure in the political and military affairs of central Europe. His grandfather was dead, and his brother Charles V gave him considerable independence in managing German affairs and the Habsburg Austrian patrimony. Though similarly eager to make his mark on the world, Maximilian remained restively subordinate to his father well into adulthood.[2] With little control over his own finances, he lived in an extended adolescence. The archduke spent more or less as he pleased, but it was his father who ultimately paid most of his bills. The inevitable conflicts over money matters between the two were frequent and prolonged. Had Ferdinand been able to gratify his son's every impulse, the two might not have clashed so often. But by 1555, the king was hard put to cover the archduke's kitchen and cellar costs. Of the 140,000 gulden yearly allowance promised to Maximilian 136,000 were still outstanding. His father's pledge to make good on the balance remained unfulfilled, as Ferdinand's debts and mortgages rose to the staggering sum of 1,500,000 Rhenish gulden. Nevertheless, Maximilian pursued his claims so remorselessly that his father was reduced to begging his son to show compassion at his plight.[3]

Maximilian had little to say about the upbringing of his numerous children until after Ferdinand I's death in 1564. Indeed, Queen Maria carried more weight at first in arranging dynastic unions than did her husband. When, in 1560, Philip II proposed marrying Maximilian's second daughter, the seven-year-old Elisabeth, to the youthful King Sebastian of Portugal, the king of Spain first made contact with his sister, not her husband. But it was Maximilian's father who really managed these affairs. With fifteen legitimate offspring, as opposed to his brother's two, Ferdinand was among the most energetic dynastic marriage brokers of his day. His grandchildren gave him the capital to continue forging these schemes. By 1563, he had sketched out marriage plans for Elisabeth and her elder sister, Archduchess Anna, as well as Archduke Rudolph, in either Spain or France. Maximilian contributed little more than his consent to these arrangements.[4] Moreover, Ferdinand, not Maximilian, had Maximilian's daughter Archduchess Maria interred at Linz, the resting place of Emperor Frederick III's entrails.[5] King Ferdinand also generally oversaw the education of his older grandchildren. It was he, or sometimes Archduke Ferdinand, who found tutors and summoned them for conferences when necessary.[6] The emperor dispatched Maximilian's eldest surviving sons, Archdukes Ernst and Rudolph, off to the court of Philip II for extended schooling in 1563.[7]

More passive princes than Maximilian, knowing that they were likely to outlive their elders, might have accepted their subordinate status graciously. For the archduke, waiting to take center-stage was a near-daily exercise in frustration. His impatience only mounted as Ferdinand's managerial style grew increasingly lax during the last few years of his life. Matters both large and small suffered from neglect and lack of direction. Authorities who received Ferdinand's disposition over the body of Archduchess Maria were puzzled over who had the final word in such matters—father, mother, or grandfather.[8] Ferdinand woefully underfunded his grandsons' stay at Philip's establishment. By the time they embarked from Genoa for the crossing to Spain, their money had already run out. The boys' irate father had to rescue them, but he reminded Emperor Ferdinand that his reputation and authority were as much at stake in the matter as Maximilian's own.[9] As the emperor considered and reconsidered the order in which he, his son, and his wife were to enter Frankfurt for Maximilian's coronation in 1562, Maximilian grumbled, "It is not up to me to establish the rules."[10]

More exasperating still, Ferdinand I took his time about drawing up his final will. Maximilian, Archduke Ferdinand, and Archduke Charles were on tenterhooks for years, as their father reconsidered the division of his territories. A testament from 1543 left Bohemia and Hungary to Maximilian. He and Archduke Ferdinand would govern the rest of the Habsburg central European patrimony jointly. After 1547, the year Maximilian's behavior became especially troublesome, Ferdinand no longer talked of ceding more than Bohemia and Hungary to his eldest.[11] When, in 1554, the king settled on the idea of partitioning his lands among his three sons, he seems to have been more interested in providing them all with appropriate livings and offices than in punishing any of them.[12] Nevertheless, the settlement left Maximilian at a distinct disadvantage. He would never control the central European resources of his house completely, even though he would produce more legitimate claimants to the Habsburg patrimony than his brothers put together. Ferdinand could have changed his mind again, but he did not.

Yet another dynastic issue added to the tension between the king and his eldest son. Close relations with the Spanish branch of his house were among Ferdinand I's highest priorities. Although he occasionally challenged his brother, or even ignored his orders, he never did so conspicuously. He also repaired breaches quickly when he could. Maximilian never ceased to believe that his uncle was the key obstacle to his own ambitions and that his father was Charles's agent. The archduke's attitude had been formed during the succession quarrel of 1550–1551, when Ferdinand had not rejected Philip out of hand as his eventual successor in Germany. Even after 1555, when Charles had made it clear that he wished to resign as emperor, Maximilian believed that his uncle would revive Philip's candidacy for the office.[13]

Driven by this rich assortment of resentments, Maximilian pounced angrily on any sign that his father was neglecting the interests of his own son in order to please the increasingly moody emperor. He blamed a disappointing military campaign in Hungary from 1554 to 1556 on what he called his father's excessive desire to help Charles's armies in Italy. Such treatment, the archduke said, would make it far more difficult for him to rule the kingdom.[14] He tried to excuse himself from dynastic command performances that had anything to do with Charles. He did not want to attend the emperor's abdication in the Netherlands in 1556, complained about deferring to his uncle when he got there, and took offense at Philip's dismissive attitude toward his request for aid against the Turks.[15]

Maximilian did speculate that his father's careful treatment of Charles V was a way to ensure a future transfer of the Spanish crown to the Habsburgs in central Europe.[16] Having no direct insight into Ferdinand's purposes, however, Maximilian more often flailed wildly against his uncle's hold over his father. Sometimes the archduke overlooked his own best interests. Both Charles and Ferdinand wanted their cousin, Mary Tudor, as a daughter-in-law when she became queen of England in 1553 after the death of Edward VI. While the emperor was promoting Philip, Ferdinand was backing his second son, Archduke Ferdinand, as prospective suitor. Johann Ulrich Zasius, to whom Maximilian normally listened closely, thought that marrying Philip off in England would take the Spanish prince out of the running for the imperial crown once and for all. When King Ferdinand yielded to his brother, Maximilian exploded at what he called his father's lukewarm support for the project. Here was one more example, he fumed, of Ferdinand's assisting Spain rather than his own offspring.[17]

Maximilian's accumulated grievances brought him close at times to outright disloyalty. In 1556 he suggested to his father a league of the imperial princes and France against Spain. From the standpoint of Habsburg interests, the notion was outrageous. The archduke's defense—that anything that might benefit the public good, meaning promote German welfare, merited support—hardly justified the dynastic turmoil such an alliance would create. Ferdinand's reaction was predictably curt and negative. But Maximilian thought he had proved once again that a Spanish clique carried undue weight at the court in Vienna.[18]

Where friendships outside his family were at stake, the archduke willingly subverted the ambitions of his father. In 1534, Ferdinand had lost Württemberg, held by the Habsburgs since 1519, to the Schmalkaldic League. He did not give up hope of recovering the duchy; nevertheless, Maximilian openly and enthusiastically favored leaving the territory in the hands of his intimate

Duke Christoph. The archduke's support for Christoph cooled a bit when Ferdinand mentioned that he might make the territory part of Maximilian's inheritance, should the land come under Habsburg control once again. By 1553, it was clear that the king could expect only a financial settlement from Christoph. With no hope of actually ruling Württemberg, Maximilian sided with Christoph during the bargaining.[19]

Maximilian flagrantly breached Ferdinand's confidences to underscore his father's defects. Though the king made it expressly clear that the information was to go no further, the archduke sent materials concerning negotiations with France and Rome in 1562 and 1563 to Albrecht V of Bavaria. Aware that Ferdinand would be furious if he learned what his son had done, Maximilian begged his brother-in-law to profess ignorance of these matters. Copies of documents that the king did not even know were in his son's possession also went to Munich on Maximilian's initiative. All the archduke asked was that the materials be returned. He did not want to betray his father, he said, but his brother-in-law had to see that Ferdinand had yielded altogether too much, this time while negotiating with Giovanni Morone, a papal legate.[20]

Conflicting dynastic imperatives, then, had driven father and son very far apart. But the house of Austria was not without resources to heal itself. The interests and responsibilities of the sixteenth-century Habsburgs were so numerous and far-flung that Maximilian and Ferdinand could cooperate on some issues, if not all. Maximilian was never allowed to forget that he was his father's subordinate.[21] Nevertheless, even during the years when he feared the worst about his son's confessional inclinations, the king delegated several administrative and military functions to the archduke because no single person could effectively handle them all. In 1554, while his father was in Bohemia, Maximilian acted for him in Vienna. He did the same thing a year later when Ferdinand was at the Diet of Augsburg. The archduke's refusal during this interlude to allow the publication of the new Catholic catechism of Canisius was a shocking piece of disobedience. Yet in 1556 Ferdinand appointed Maximilian his next-in-command in a new *Hofkriegsrat*. Unable to staff the war council or to return from Prague to conduct a search, Ferdinand asked his eldest son to suggest candidates. Maximilian, who was named head of the Habsburg military administration in Hungary in 1556, was soon in charge of the kingdom's current and future military campaigns.[22] By the end of the decade, father and son were discussing policy together even as they disagreed sharply over Maximilian's religious views.[23]

Standing in for his father at meetings of local estates could be irksome. In

January of 1564, Maximilian found the representatives from Upper Silesia were "as stubborn as mules" (*wie die schtetigen esl*). But gatherings even in the most provincial of settings had their lighter moments. On this particular occasion, he derived at least one day's "comedy" from the open-mouthed astonishment with which some Silesian villagers inspected a pack animal in his train.[24] Best of all, the elector of Saxony, two margraves from Branden-burg, and three princes of Anhalt had arranged to visit. Knightly games and hunts were arranged, at least when time permitted.[25]

Duties that brought real rewards pleased Maximilian even more. In 1556, he exulted over the booty his troops in Hungary had captured from the Turks, the prisoners they had taken, and the general military prowess his men had shown. But he was also willing to put pleasure aside when affairs of state required his attention. In 1560, Bajazet, a son of Sultan Süleyman the Mag-nificent, was captured in Persia after he had led an uprising against his father. Until the military and political implications of this situation were clear, Fer-dinand wanted Maximilian with him in Vienna. Though he had been hoping to visit his brother-in-law in Munich, the archduke obeyed his father's order without protest. In 1562 plans for another trip to see Albrecht evaporated when the voivode of Transylvania, John Sigismund Zápolya, a "restless man" (*unruewigen mensch*) who Maximilian thought would be the source of future trouble, seemed to be preparing for war.[26] The lines of his strategic thinking had also begun to follow his father's model. Once a critic of Ferdinand's cautious ways with the Porte, Maximilian was becoming more guarded. He realized in 1560 that he had to put a check to the Ottoman forces' skirmishing around Szatmár, Sziget, and Székesfehérvár (Alba Jula) in Hungary. Nev-ertheless, the archduke did not want to move prematurely. Such an enemy, he now believed, required careful handling.[27]

Thus, routine dynastic responsibilities forced Ferdinand I and Maximilian to cooperate, even during their years of rancorous conflict. But without some skillful psychological orchestration on the part of the emperor, the two men would probably not have overcome as many of their differences as they did. Though clearly in training to replace his father, Maximilian remained very insecure. "I do not want to praise myself," he wrote early in 1564 to Duke Albrecht, broadly hinting that he wanted his brother-in-law to say that the archduke was conducting a set of negotiations wisely.[28] Ferdinand was very good at flattering his way into the good graces of difficult but sensitive people. Indeed, he had begun the process with Maximilian before their confrontation over religion in 1562. If Maximilian fretted over his inadequacies, his father sympathetically reminded him that it was God who had ordained certain conditions, and nothing could be done about them.[29] Ferdinand was also generous with praise and encouragement. When Maximilian was overseeing some especially difficult bargaining with the Bohemian estates during the fall of 1555, his father extolled the archduke's skill and emphasized how much the younger man was doing for his father's lands and peoples. Where Maximilian could point to genuine successes, Ferdinand congratulated him swiftly and warmly. The elder Habsburg was not too proud to admit that he could not have done better than his son.[30]

But the improved relations between father and son were not solely the result of Ferdinand's judicious praise. The emperor was too much a gentleman ever to have been wholly offensive to Maximilian. Even at the height of their religious disagreements, the king had observed routine civilities. If he accidentally saw the younger man's private correspondence, the emperor apologized sincerely.[31] More important, after exacting from Maximilian a profession of loyalty to the Catholic faith in 1562, Ferdinand actively promoted his son's political and territorial interests in Germany. He was visibly moved by the archduke's election and coronation in Frankfurt in 1562. Ferdinand did not always tell his son the details of the negotiations with Pius IV over Maximilian's declaration of orthodoxy. To find out, the archduke had to rely on his own informants.[32] Nevertheless, it was the emperor who crafted the agreement that settled the issue without compromising the prerogatives of future Habsburg emperors.

Furthermore, though Ferdinand had named Maximilian as his successor in Bohemia and Hungary only in his testament of 1555, he had long been looking out for his son's interests in those kingdoms. The Bohemian and Hungarian estates had persistently defended their right to a free election of a new ruler. Ferdinand had not refused to have Maximilian crowned king of Bohemia in 1548 only because he feared that the archduke would meddle in the royal government. He believed that, when the time came to install a new ruler in Bohemia, Maximilian would have little difficulty. If extraordinary concessions were to be asked of those estates beforehand, however, the body might demand that the archduke acknowledge their electoral powers. Ferdinand's long-term goal of making the kingdom a hereditary possession of his house would take even longer to achieve. In 1561 Ferdinand had also persuaded the Hungarian estates to accept Maximilian as his successor without any specific promises that the practice of election there would continue.[33] Last, but hardly least, the Hungarian and Bohemian coronations went forward only because

Ferdinand and his representatives won the papal concession of Communion in both kinds for Maximilian.[34]

Maximilian, therefore, had much reason to be grateful to his father in September of 1562 when the archduke was elected and crowned king of Bohemia. The ceremony and festivities in Prague had gone smoothly, despite a spreading epidemic in the capital and the cramped, airless quarters he and Maria had to occupy during the warmest months of the year.[35] His entry into the city was as grand as Ferdinand's had been many years before. Four hundred hussars rode out to meet the future ruler, as he neared the city for an official greeting. Representatives of the Jewish community stood on the bridge over the Moldau to the Hradčany, holding aloft a baldachin, which sheltered the Decalogue. The coronation took place on the twentieth of September. At the religious service associated with the rite, the bishops of Olomouc (Olmütz) and Breslau presented him to the archbishop of Prague; here was visible evidence that the church deemed him fit to be king. He was asked if he believed in, and would protect, the Catholic faith. He firmly replied "ja," then went on to take the oath in Czech. He had probably communed earlier in both kinds. The rest of the day was filled with banqueting and tournaments. On the twenty-first, his wife was crowned.[36]

The Hungarian coronation was equally joyous. Ferdinand had chosen wisely in giving Maximilian operational command of the Habsburg segment of that realm after 1552. The future king had carried out the military side of his duties well enough to arouse local hopes that he might drive back the Turks and reunify the kingdom. Maximilian threw himself into the festivities with visible gusto. The event was set for August of 1563 but was then postponed a month because several members of the estates could not reach the coronation city of Bratislava (Pozsony) on time. Nevertheless, the king-to-be started ordering fresh fish for the banqueting as early as 12 July. Here Maximilian ran into some difficulty—because the creatures could not be kept alive in the Danube water in which they were to be shipped, he was forced to settle for the salted and pickled variety. And the best of efforts could not forestall some fighting among the German, Hungarian, and Bohemian forces in the small city. But no one went hungry—provisions from Austria above and below the Enns, Bohemia, and Moravia entered Hungary duty-free for six weeks. And the ceremony went off spectacularly. The magnates and other nobility of the kingdom turned out in full regalia. Their finery and jewelry were "indescribable," according to one bedazzled observer. Maximilian was resplendent in the traditional Hungarian coronation costume of a long scarlet tunic, over which he wore a cloak draped in folds from his shoulders.[37] And he was in high, even cocky, spirits. Prior to the coronation, he had said that he would take an oath to protect justice and peace to the best of his ability and to respect both secular and spiritual authorities in the kingdom. The archbishop of Esztergom, who officiated at the rites, wanted him to swear all of this by the virgin and saints. Maximilian refused, calling instead on the Gospel as a witness to his sincerity. He could not even resist indulging in some outright teasing at the expense of the clergy surrounding him during the rites. "Don't be afraid; for the present I am not going to kill anyone," he murmured, swinging a ceremonial sword.[38]

Thus, by the end of 1563, Maximilian was assured of every position for which he had been struggling since late adolescence. He had endured deeply bitter moments, as he saw his father tend his own career more industriously than his son's. But Maximilian's primacy in his family was now secure, especially since Archduke Ferdinand had sidelined himself in a misalliance. In the end, the emperor had worked for Maximilian wholeheartedly, with gratifying results.

Ferdinand I could take some satisfaction in his firstborn as well. Maximilian was now following his father's wishes more readily, in religious as well as political matters. Even before he had foresworn outright apostasy in 1562, Maximilian had engaged Bishop Urban of Gurk as his court preacher, albeit on the condition that the employer would listen to the clergyman only when he was right! This was, however, a noteworthy reversal after the archduke's earlier rejection of the appointment. Pfauser would continue to receive a pension from the court in Vienna, tardy though it often was.[39] But by 1563 Maximilian's interest in Protestant contacts was visibly waning. He would have nothing to do with Nicholas von Warmsdorf, an evangelical councillor whom he had often entrusted with missions to Protestants. That same year, Christoph of Württemberg sent Maximilian some of the writings of Kaspar Schwenkfeld, the deeply radical spiritualist reformer who argued for removing the Last Supper altogether from the Christian liturgy. The Habsburg king ordered them destroyed, in unspoken affirmation of the Augsburg settlement, to which his father had contributed so much. Nor did Maximilian seem eager to foster any evangelical reform in the Austrian lands. In the spring of 1563, he was delighted when the Lower Austrian estates were less demanding in confessional matters than usual. He publicly sympathized with his father's strenuous efforts to bring the Council of Trent to a productive close and warned that Ferdinand was sacrificing his health to the process.[40]

Indeed, the emperor's physical condition had deteriorated alarmingly. It was a sudden and startling reversal of roles for the two men. Maximilian's ailments had given cause for concern for years. As early as 1552, hearing that their future ruler had been seized by an unspecified "weakness" (*Schwachheit*), officials in the Tyrol wrote Christoph von Eyzing, the governor of Lower Austria, and Georg von Thuen, Maximilian's *Obersthofmeister,* for further details about the malady. Assailed with episodes of illness for the next few years—in 1554, he had been plagued by heart palpitations for more than two days without relief—the archduke realized that he might be chronically debilitated.[41] By contrast, Ferdinand, who was a very hard worker, had been blessed with an unusually robust constitution throughout his life. By 1560, however, he was noticeably less vigorous. That May he complained of a recurrent fever and waning appetite. Though not otherwise uncomfortable— he slept well and suffered from neither thirst nor pain—he saw in the symptoms a reminder that he would not live forever. Maximilian was taking a cure—this time for dysentery, and his presence at his father's side did not seem necessary; Ferdinand ordered him to continue his therapy. Another episode of fever struck the emperor, though, at the height of summer in 1561; Maximilian reported that Ferdinand was dreadfully wasted.[42]

Maximilian continued to hope for his recovery.[43] He cared for his dying father solicitously, even tenderly, until the very end. It was not an easy task. "I cannot tell you in a short time every strange thing his majesty has done and how peculiarly he behaves," he told Albrecht of Bavaria in September of 1563. Ferdinand was losing not only his strength but his mind. As Charles V had done before his death, he frequently drifted off into melancholy fantasies. Regaining some grasp of where he was, he would turn angrily on others; now and then he became furious with himself. Sometimes he cried and threw things on the floor. He would pound his fists on the table, draw imaginary circles and sit in strange positions. If he came to his senses, he was cheerful but could not think consecutively.[44] Important issues were neglected, among them what to do about a Swabian knight, Wilhelm von Grumbach: his murder of the bishop of Würzburg threatened the peace of the empire. Maximilian feared that such infractions, if left unredressed, would become widespread in Germany. In those moments when the emperor could be attentive, he listened to others and not to his son.[45]

By April 1564, Ferdinand's condition had worsened to the point where Maximilian prayed that the Almighty would have mercy on him. On 21 April, apparently in full possession of his faculties, the emperor handed his various governments over to his eldest son with the injunctions to protect Catholicism and his subjects and uphold justice—and to pay his debts.[46] Maximilian continued to do what he could. At his request, his sister Anna came from Munich, and her presence pleased their father greatly. Maximilian also made sure that music continued to be played in the emperor's chambers, another source of enjoyment for the dying man.[47] For all the time and emotional energy these efforts cost him, Maximilian came to respect the tenacity with which his skeletal father held on to life. The emperor received extreme unction on 11 June, but "his majesty did not have in mind bringing things to an end quite so soon."[48] The entire process left Maximilian very critical of his father's doctors. He was particularly caustic toward anyone who "promised golden mountains" (*promittit aureos montes*) and then, when his cure did not work, claimed that the prescription had yet to take effect.[49]

Ferdinand died around seven in the evening on 25 July. The complex funeral arrangements went forward desultorily. There was nothing especially unusual in such delays, however, for the Austrian Habsburgs. Work on the tomb of Emperor Maximilian I, who had died in 1519, was still going on and would continue for some time.[50] He had asked to be buried in Prague alongside his wife, Anna; Bohemian officials had to be consulted about the dates for the ceremony and for a diet, which would have to meet at the same time. Special platforms were needed for carrying the body from the Hradčany to the nearby St. Vitus' Cathedral.[51]

When October came, the public memorial obsequies had yet to take place. Prague was not particularly safe; the deadly plague still haunted the city. The ceremonies, eventually rescheduled for 10 March, then had to be put off again, because of problems in the Austrian lands. Throughout the entire time, the new king and emperor had been too preoccupied with Hungarian and Turkish affairs as well as other affairs of state to give more than passing attention to the burial arrangements.[52] Ferdinand's resting place, therefore, became yet another ongoing project for the house of Habsburg.

Not everyone was happy to have Maximilian as emperor. There were Catholics who thought he might betray them. His laugh sounded counterfeit to some; they thought it masked something.[53] On the whole, though, his accession was welcomed. Foreign ambassadors thought him highly qualified for his new offices. Maximilian had a sharp intellect, spoke knowledgeably about matters of state, and was visibly interested in military affairs and technology. Although less talkative than his father, and a touch haughtier, Maximilian had mastered more languages than Ferdinand I. Indeed, one Venetian ambassador found the son generally more capable than his predecessor. Maximilian was also far more accomplished linguistically than his cousin Philip, who spoke neither French, German, nor Flemish and needed to have Latin documents translated into Castilian.[54] And the new emperor was good-humored, courtly, and at ease with people of all nationalities. In short, he cut a far different figure from the impetuous and irascible archduke of a few years before. He also appeared to have abandoned the religious experiments that had alarmed his father, his uncle, and even his wife. Some observers believed that, if anything, Maximilian was more Catholic than evangelical, for he now publicly followed the traditional rituals.[55] Finally, he looked the part he aspired to play. True, he was only of middling stature, and disproportionately thick lips marred his otherwise regal countenance. Nevertheless, the lively intelligence in his eyes, so similar to that which had distinguished his father as a young man, substantially offset these drawbacks.[56]

He had also encouraged lofty expectations. Even once he and his father had grown close after 1562, Maximilian had continued to criticize Ferdinand's nonchalant management of his household and government. The son was sure that he could improve on his father's record. Maximilian not only would govern his patrimony more effectively than Ferdinand I had but would rid Hungary of the Turks and bring religious harmony to Germany, all the while preserving the influence of his firmly Catholic house. It was an ambitious agenda—so ambitious that it raised serious questions in the mind of the shrewd Venetian ambassador Giovanni Michele. How, the envoy mused, would Maximilian respond if he could not accomplish all these things? Michele envisaged two possible scenarios: Maximilian might lose his self-confidence and fall into the cautious ways of his late father, or he might go to war to reaffirm his prowess.[57]

Maximilian's future might, therefore, be a test not only of his talents but of a character that was less than clear. The people who were unsettled by his laugh may indeed have been sensing something artificial about the new emperor. He had changed in unexpected ways during the last years of his father's life, in part through the late emperor's careful manipulation of his son's feelings. Whether Maximilian had been fundamentally transformed was another matter. Praise, after all, has addictive side-effects, creating a hunger for the palliative rather than for the cure. His newfound docility may also have been no more than the familiar response of a petulant child, who has finally bullied his elders into giving him what he wanted. Whatever the case, the Maximilian had yet to prove that he could withstand frustration and disappointment. He had certainly set himself up for long-term testing. Administrative reform required persistence and innovative drive; military campaigns against the Turks called for tenacity and good judgment. The challenge of uniting the Germans had already resisted the very different approaches of two talented emperors. Michele's reservations about the emperor's future behavior could not have been better founded.

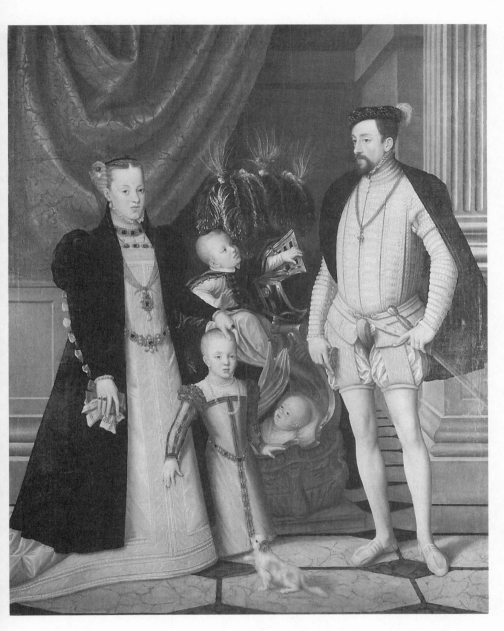

Maximilian II with Queen Maria, archdukes Rudolph and Ernst, and the infant
archduchess Anna, c. 1553. Attributed to Giuseppe Arcimboldo
(Kunsthistorisches Museum, Vienna).

Archduke Ferdinand of the Tyrol, painted by Francesco Terzio
(Kunsthistorisches Museum, Vienna).

Maximilian forwards to the tribunal of New Spain Philip II's request for information on the case of Doña Isabel, "who came of Montezuma's line," 1549, photographed by Joseph Zehavi (Pierpont Morgan Library, New York).

A stool made in 1554 from the bones of the elephant brought by Maximilian II to Vienna in 1552 (Kunstverlag Hofstetter, Ried im Innkreis, Austria).

Charles L'Ecluse, engraving by Theodor de Bry
(Archive of the University of Vienna).

Maximilian II strolling on the grounds of the Neugebäude, painting by Lucas van Valckenborch (Kunsthistorisches Museum, Vienna).

The pharmacological uses of pine nuts, from a medical tract translated into Latin by Charles L'Ecluse (Rare Books Division, New York Public Library. Astor, Lenox and Tilden Foundations).

A table to calculate the dangerous climacteric year, by Heinrich Rantzow (1580, Rare Books Division, New York Public Library, Astor, Lenox and Tilden Foundations).

Maximilian's general Lazarus von Schwendi. Attributed to an unknown south German painter (Kunsthistorisches Museum, Vienna).

guita vn altra squadra di Cortegiani, di maggior grado de i primi : delli quali intrauengono
molti di quelli , che portano li piatti, del manzar del Sienor, dimandati Chiefinir.

An Ottoman procession of court ministers and janissaries, facsimile from a
woodcut done in 1563 by Domenico de' Franceschi, in *Solyman the Magnificent
Going to Mosque* (Florence: William Stirling Maxwell, 1877), n.p. (Miriam and

Ira D. Wallach Division of Art, Prints and Photographs, New York Public Library, Astor, Lenox and Tilden Foundations).

Sultan Süleyman the Magnificent Dressed for the Hunt, facsimile of a woodcut done in 1563 by Domenico de' Franceschi, in *Solyman the Magnificent Going to Mosque* (Florence: William Stirling Maxwell, 1877), 8 (Miriam and Ira D. Wallach Division of Art, Prints and Photographs, New York Public Library, Astor, Lenox and Tilden Foundations).

Sultan Süleyman the Magnificent, facsimile from a woodcut done in 1563 by Domenico de' Franceschi, in *Solyman the Magnificent Going to Mosque* (Florence: William Stirling Maxwell, 1877), 8 (Miriam and Ira D. Wallach Division of Art, Prints and Photographs, New York Public Library, Astor, Lenox and Tilden Foundations).

The Apotheosis of Maximilian II, engraving by Jost Ammann, after Wenzel
Jamnitzer (Graphische Sammlung Albertina, Vienna).

Ringelrennen, c. 1580, with Margrave Karl of Burgau as Hercules, astride a seven-headed Hydra, pen-and-ink drawing by Sigmund Elsässer and Johannes Agricola [Hans Bauer] (Kunsthistorisches Museum, Vienna).

five

A Flawed Inheritance

Impatience and outrage, not sober analysis, had provoked Maximilian's scorn for Ferdinand I's administrative skills. Like Maximilian I before .iim, the late emperor had devoted a good deal of thought and time to improving his government. The explosive growth of the Habsburg European patrimony, the pressures of resisting Ottoman expansion, and centrality in imperial affairs spurred both men to refine existing offices as well as to develop new ones. The people affected by these changes rarely welcomed them. Local estates often voted for military aid and other forms of financial support only on the condition that structural initiatives be heavily modified. Nevertheless, Ferdinand created for Habsburg lands in central and east-central Europe an administrative machinery that endured largely unchanged until the eighteenth century. It was also widely imitated. Contemporary German princes modeled their establishments on Ferdinand's arrangements, as did leading noble houses, most notably the Harrachs of Lower Austria and the Bohemian Lobkovices.[1]

Ferdinand's government was somewhat cumbersome; it supervised the Habsburg lands, the court and household, and some imperial business. Nevertheless, it functioned more or less as intended. Its core consisted of a court council (*Hofrat*), a smaller privy council, a chancellory, a treasury (*Hofkammer*), and, after 1556, a war council (*Hofkriegsrat*). The key unit was the privy council, over which Ferdinand eventually presided himself. Advisory rather than executive, its membership was confined to a few intimates of the ruler, along with some of his highest officials. Foreign policy was discussed here, and members often carried out diplomatic missions. In Ferdinand's absence, the court majordomo (*Hofmeister*) replaced him. The much larger Hofrat dealt chiefly with legal and juridical affairs in both the empire and the Habsburg lands.

Technically subordinate to the imperial chancellory in Mainz, the Vienna chancellory handled specifically Habsburg affairs as well. It acted as a secretariat for both the privy and court councils. Nothing important went forward without the consent of the ruler, even in Bohemia, where the chancellor and one of his secretaries countersigned all royal patents. The treasury oversaw subordinate fiscal administrative bodies throughout Ferdinand's realms. One paymaster supervised civilian outlays; another official took care of military expenditures.

Ferdinand had hoped that better administrative organization would tighten his control over his lands. Until his death he was still in the process of realizing this goal. In the Austrian provinces, local captains (or, in Lower Austria, marshals) served the estates as solicitously as they did their prince, whose chief officer they supposedly were. Only the Hofkriegsrat functioned supraterritorially, and only in the face of strenuous protest from the Hungarian estates. Total integration of Bohemia and Hungary into the aulic council and chancellory never took place. Both kingdoms had retained their own chancellories, and there were no Hungarian or Bohemian members of the Hofrat.[2]

Nevertheless, without the Vienna chancellory to generate documents, the entire system would have come to a halt. It was run by two vice-chancellors, whose staffs worked interchangeably, as needed. Until 1570, Johann Ulrich Zasius and Johann Baptist Weber, both of whom had served Ferdinand I and had gathered much political and administrative experience along the way, held these jobs. Among their most sensitive responsibilities was to send instructions to ambassadors and receive their reports.[3]

Though Maximilian apparently had great confidence in both these men, he did not have to wait long for his first experience with clerical bungling. The invitations to Ferdinand I's funeral in Vienna went awry because they were misaddressed by a "small number" of people in the chancellory. Maximilian reacted to this and other lapses very decisively. No order was so well constructed that it did not bear improving; no act of negligence was to go undisciplined.[4] Stern though they sounded, however, his instructions went unheeded for the entirety of his career. Secretarial security remained a conspicuous problem. Unauthorized persons walked into the chancellory, chatted with clerks, inspected documents and registers, and often stood by as confidential materials were read aloud for copying. Supervision of off-hours access was very casual. Maximilian would try to tighten all this up again in 1571. The following year, however, a persistent ambassador, Ludwig Haberstock, from the court in Munich was allowed to duplicate papers dealing with French, Italian, and Netherlandish matters. He could even scan some of them at home.[5] Envoys on the road devised supposedly secret codes for their dispatches, then mailed them to the emperor. When missives with this information were lost, others were sent along in the same unsafeguarded way. The multiple copies of documents gave rise to secretarial errors or omissions that compromised the reliability of these materials.[6]

Vice-chancellor Weber believed that the only way to ensure confidentiality was to do business orally, rather than in writing. Such tactics, however useful, slowed everything down, decision-making included. The Viennese court was not the only one in early modern Europe to function sluggishly. " 'The original sin of our Court . . . is neither starting nor finishing anything on time,' " remarked Don Luis de Requesens, the Spanish ambassador in Milan, of Philip II's establishment. But few princes had proclaimed themselves quite as loudly as Maximilian to be administrative reformers.[7]

For all his sharp criticism of his father's government, Maximilian did not pay much attention to deficiencies of the chancellory. Quite possibly, he believed that the office had lost some of its importance. Its workload did decline, as the governments of Archdukes Ferdinand and Charles in Innsbruck and Graz increasingly took over the administration of a large part of the Habsburg Austrian patrimony during the latter third of the sixteenth century.[8] A more probable reason for the neglect was his all-consuming worry about his finances. It was here that Maximilian's criticisms of his father had some real substance. The late emperor had run territorial fiscal affairs along the lines of the contemporary "domain state," financing his government and household from the revenue he drew from his holdings. When extraordinary aid was needed, Ferdinand had also called on local estates. When he required credit, as he almost always did, he had resorted to short-term loans and other stopgap measures. These he secured in kind or through mortgages on regalian properties and incomes. Little distinction was made between the purposes for which private as opposed to public revenues were used.[9]

Some contemporary German princes, such as Landgrave William IV of Hesse-Cassel, devoted themselves single-mindedly to husbanding resources and even to changing the basis of taxation.[10] In the Austrian lands, Ferdinand did reestablish his government's control over the production and lucrative sale of salt—a program that Maximilian continued. But the late emperor had not been so successful with other fiscal reforms, including those in his eldest son's household.[11] Though he had tried to limit Maximilian's expenditures, keeping account of them was a hit-or-miss affair. Money was stored in numbered barrels, a note being made when something was withdrawn. Discoveries of unexpectedly empty containers dismayed all concerned.[12]

Maximilian had fumed, and contemporaries marveled, at the sums his father's higher officers pocketed for personal use. His own children suffered; around 1536, their household in Innsbruck was reported to have been in fiscal straits for some time.[13] Ferdinand could be maddeningly casual about debt, especially in his final years, or when favorites, such as his second son, were in need. To the Archduke Ferdinand's complaint in 1563 that he was seriously in arrears with his creditors, his father's advice was not to worry. With the help of God, such problems were easily resolved.[14]

Maximilian, whose motto was "Dominus providebit," obviously shared similar hopes. Once Ferdinand I's resources had been divided among his three sons, all the archdukes needed some assistance from the Almighty. In spite of real problems in coordinating their activities at imperial diets, where they voted as one, they worked together reasonably well, as long as money was not a central issue among them. They generally spoke with one voice in foreign affairs; for example, Maximilian negotiated peace with the Turks in 1567 in all their names.[15] All three had to approve alliances, offensive wars, and the sale or mortgaging of any patrimonial lands. They consulted on ambassadorial appointments to areas that concerned them all, such as Venice, and frequently shared envoys. In 1570, all three would agree that their representative to the maritime republic would act " 'as if the land and peoples of the exalted house of Austria were ruled through a unified, common, and collective government without differences.' " All had to consent to marriages contracted by any one member of the house; all three bore the same patrimonial titles and emblems.[16]

Providence, however, was not so merciful when it came to the fiscal side of the divided inheritance and all that touched on it. The old emperor had scarcely breathed his last in 1564 before his creditors in Bohemia began clamoring for repayment. Habsburg treasury officials in the kingdom consoled themselves that their new king was thinking about the problem, as indeed he would be for a very long time.[17] Maximilian and his brothers had to find a staggering 7,604,277 gulden to satisfy innumerable claimants, whose ranks continued to grow. A three-way division of Ferdinand I's debts took place in 1566. Maximilian, as king of Hungary, had to shoulder the unpaid costs of his father's wars there—1,066,836 gulden. Charles and Ferdinand, however, promised 150,000 gulden each to lighten that burden. The new emperor was to compensate both the younger men for renouncing their claims in Hungary and Bohemia. Of the remaining obligations, Maximilian assumed half, and each of his younger brothers a quarter. Ferdinand and Charles also promised to improve the incomes of the new emperor in Lower Austria, the poorest share in the Habsburg patrimony. Archduke Charles met his part of the bargain by not collecting the payout for his rights to Bohemia. Archduke Ferdinand continued to exact his Bohemian revenues, however, thereby setting the stage for future acrimony.[18]

The mountain of paternal indebtedness eroded slowly over time. In 1568 the brothers had yet to pay off the emperor's burial expenses.[19] Maximilian's inquiries to the Tyrolean treasury about its responsibilities for the late emperor's arrears dropped off only after 1570.[20] But Ferdinand's partition of his lands forever complicated the fiscal lives of his sons, especially that of his eldest. At the very least, poor princes had difficulty marrying off their children appropriately. With his numerous offspring, Maximilian was at a particular disadvantage.[21] Countless hours went into resolving questions about general expenses for which all three brothers were responsible. Maximilian would always have great difficulty collecting his compensation for Lower Austria from Archduke Ferdinand. Nor could the emperor count on his brothers to cooperate with him as he tried to exploit the resources of Lower Austria, Hungary, and Bohemia. Hungarian mines in Banská Bystrica (Neusohl) yielded a steady supply of copper for a lucrative trade with Italy. But Archduke Ferdinand's treasury officers in Innsbruck forbade moving copper from outside the Tyrol across the province. Hungary, they argued, was far better situated to meet the needs of Silesia, Poland, and Denmark to the north. The Hungarian ore thus traveled south, more circuitously and expensively, through Carinthia.[22]

Long-term dynastic financial obligations burdened the treasuries and patience of all three brothers. They had to fulfill monetary provisions of earlier marriage contracts, even if their liability for paying them had never been clearly fixed.[23] Though jointly responsible for maintaining their three cloistered sisters in the Tyrol, Archduke Ferdinand and Maximilian routinely tried to fob these expenses off on one another. That the archduchesses piled up their own debts in ceaseless good works did not help. Nor did Ferdinand I's slipshod record-keeping. Four years after their father's death, Maximilian had yet to receive an orderly account of the ladies' outlays. The Tyrolean treasury continued to report one figure for their debts and the treasury in Vienna another.[24]

Since the three brothers were able to make use of the same ambassadors, they might have cut down redundant expenses by sharing other employees as well. Maximilian and the younger archdukes did exchange personnel for a variety of specific assignments; they did not, however, readily part with their most capable servants, even for a short time.[25] Arguments arose over who should pay the salary of someone loaned to another archducal court.[26] During emergencies, Maximilian and his brothers ruthlessly defended their assets from one another. A grain famine that hit much of central Europe in the early 1570s would be especially trying. When some of his Lower Austrian subjects were reduced to eating acorns and tree bark, Maximilian forbade Archduke Ferdinand to provision himself from the area. Before allowing them passage through his own holdings, Maximilian charged tolls and customs duties on supplies that Archduke Ferdinand had driven up in Ottoman lands. Desperate to feed the miners of the Tyrol, Ferdinand purchased grain illicitly in both Lower Austria and Bohemia until his older brother put a stop to that as well.[27]

Most serious of all, however, was the impact of these divisions on Habsburg military effectiveness. Not only the dynasty's lands themselves, but weapons, munitions, even documents were dispersed among three governments.[28] Each of the brothers was supposed to pay a share of the imperial taxes for defense and administrative costs levied on the Austrian lands. But even under the more unitary regimes of Ferdinand I and Maximilian I, there had been little sense of commonality among the provinces and estates of the Habsburg Austrian patrimony.[29] Officials in Lower Austria saw this dark side of the partition as early as 1565. Ferdinand I, they declared, had found it hard enough to finance the defense against the Turks with united lands, let alone with the smaller portion that Maximilian now had. When military needs arose, their new territorial ruler would have to look to the empire, the king of Spain, or the pope for aid.[30] None of these, however, had been eager to help Maximilian's father, and there was no reason to think that his son would fare better.

Archduke Charles in Graz met his defense obligations more or less faithfully. But by the sixteenth century, the estates of the Tyrol were defining their military responsibilities to their territorial ruler very narrowly.[31] They rejoiced at the arrival of Archduke Ferdinand. Whereas his late father had demanded a great deal of money to meet his pan-European responsibilities, the son would be a truly resident prince, more sensitive to provincial needs.[32] The archduke lived up to their expectations. In 1566, his administration in Innsbruck declared that artillery which Ferdinand I had removed from regional armories to use in Hungary was only on loan. What had been lost, or even deployed abroad, would have to be replaced. The following year they declared that the late emperor had meant for each brother to carry out his father's testament only as best he could, not to bankrupt himself. Even under Ferdinand I, they pointed out, Lower and Inner Austria had borne heavier financial responsibilities because they were at greater risk from the Ottoman challenge. Tyrol and the other western Habsburg territories (*die Vorlande*) in Swabia had taxed themselves for Turkish defense only in times of extraordinary danger. These disputes always ended for a time when the three brothers imposed further burdens on their Austrian peasantry, which had no choice but to pay; however, the larger issue of Maximilian and Ferdinand's share of military taxes remained.[33]

Thus, Maximilian's paternal legacy was in itself problematic. It also came to him at a moment when all European regimes were struggling to keep pace with a dramatic upsurge in prices. The Habsburg lands were as vulnerable as any. From 1514 to 1566, prices on some basic foodstuffs—eggs, butter, and wine—went up by a third or more in Lower Austria and would escalate further in the remaining decades of the century. Worse yet, these increases took place in fits and starts, making it impossible for governments to anticipate their movement. The cost of iron, remarkably constant during the first half of the century, went up 100 percent in the second. Prices for staples such as grain would shoot up over twelve to twenty-four months, then fall back somewhat, only to advance again. Few Habsburg expenditures, from those crucial for the conduct of government to the pensions of lowly widows and orphans, went untouched. Mounting poverty emboldened even the humble to advise Maximilian on running the fisc. A nurse for one of Maximilian's children, who did not receive her salary from his household funds for half a year, demanded that he pay it "another way at the earliest opportunity." She suggested dipping into the army treasury.[34]

However accidental the interaction of these factors was, it created a daunting challenge for the new emperor. As he had promised, Maximilian applied himself quickly and vigorously to rectifying his finances.[35] Concern for per-

sonal prestige, never far from his mind, added to his energy. Irregular payment, even to kitchen suppliers, "brings us great harm and scorn."[36] Modest,
but positive, results came very soon. With loans and grants from all over
Europe, as well as the various Habsburg possessions, he collected 489,350
florins, 305,000 crowns, and 30,000 ducats in 1565 to cover his father's debts.
Approximately half these monies came from the lands of the house of Austria.
None of the funds, however, went toward expenses in Hungary, where troops
had yet to receive their wages.[37] Repayment of the debts Maximilian had
inherited and those he contracted as soon as he began ruling consumed more
than a third of his entire income of approximately 920,000 gulden in 1567.[38]

Stopgap tactics alone, however, were not enough for Maximilian to put
both his household and his government on a sound fiscal footing. Here too,
he seized the initiative. Unlike his cousin Philip, Maximilian never professed
ignorance of high finance. Indeed, he had taken oversight of his household
treasury out of the hands of his Hofmeister in 1561.[39] Now a ruler in his own
right, he had three strategies at his disposal—economizing, increasing his
regular incomes, and cultivating new sources of revenue.

The most straightforward of these approaches was cost reduction, and
Maximilian stuck with it, after a fashion, throughout his career. Indeed, he
thought himself schooled enough in the art to explain it to other princes. He
watched the outlays of his cloistered sisters.[40] No department or office was
too significant, or insignificant, to escape fiscal scrutiny—the military, the
armory, the court hospital.[41] Jobs were to be combined or eliminated altogether, and salaries could be cut.[42] As early as 1553, he had required his own
kitchen to cut down on expenditures by making use of heads, hooves, car-
tilage, and other bovine waste; he now turned his attention to the kitchen of
his sons. There he demanded a regular and detailed accounting of the amount
of food consumed in the household, the number of people who ate it, and
the money that the operation required. Poorly performing functionaries were
to be dismissed. Kitchen staff—those with wives and children were especially
suspect—were expressly forbidden to help themselves to the fruits of their
labors. The order also provided recipes for recycling leftovers in future meals,
though just who would consume them was left unsaid.[43] Great thought went
into the allocation and use of candles. From September to April, pages could
burn half a stick a day, from April to September, a quarter-stick. Only those
who toiled principally in the dark—in the bakery and the wine cellars—
merited half a candle all the year round.[44] People who requested paper and
ink from his chancellory were to get the worst quality available; if they asked

for cord or sealing wax, they were given as little as possible.[45] Workmen were not to be overpaid.[46]

Maximilian imposed a similar discipline on himself. A personal account book covering the years 1568–1570 shows that he managed discretionary funds conscientiously, despite impromptu gifts of small sums to local peasants who had assisted him at the hunt, a gardener's daughter, and the like.[47] In Bohemia, where he resided irregularly, he cut back on private expenditures for his kitchen, wine stock, and stables. From 1564 to 1567 he overspent the monies he received from the treasury for such purposes very modestly. In the worst year, 1566, his debits amounted only to approximately 125 florins.[48] A few years later, he would attack the monopoly of the purveyors licensed to sell everything from shoes to objets d'art at the court and would demand that the numbers of these tradespeople be cut, that their goods be of the highest caliber, and that price-gouging stop.[49]

Some of these measures had noticeable effect. Kitchen outlays at his establishment in Vienna peaked in 1566, fell back for three years, rose in 1569, and then dropped by 1572. In some categories, lighting costs, for example, he spent less as emperor than he had as an heir apparent.[50] Expenditures for his court and administration generally did rise in the 1570s, but not annually.[51] Indeed, treasury records show positive balances for five of the ten years of Maximilian's reign that are fully reported.[52] The salary base for most court officials and councillors except the paymaster remained about the same, as did their number. They did, however, receive a yearly supplement of two hundred gulden. Lowlier household members were treated proportionately. *Trabanten*, the young men who ran alongside horses in processions, who had drawn a flat fifty gulden from Ferdinand I, received an additional clothing allowance whenever Maximilian ordered them to acquire new uniforms.[53]

Cost-cutting, therefore, imposed useful fiscal restraints on Maximilian's household. It did not, however, produce the cash flow he required for his more significant official duties. For this he had to develop ways of enlarging both his regalian revenues, which included confiscations and seizures of contraband, and extraordinary income, which was normally military aid from the various estates in the Habsburg lands and the imperial diet. In Germany, where the territories always dragged out payments, he tried to speed up the flow of promised funds by working with representatives from the administrative circles into which Germany had been configured at the beginning of the sixteenth century. During a major military campaign in 1566, he also revived an earlier scheme to split the office of imperial paymaster (*Reichspfen-*

nigmeisteramt), so that one man received money from the empire and another disbursed it. Convinced, however, that this arrangement was a step on the way to the creation of a standing military force, the imperial estates would not allow it. The office therefore had to be reconstituted for every campaign, a virtual guarantee that support from Germany would always be tardy.[54]

Maximilian's chief resources clearly lay in his own lands. Lower Austria, however, had been shouldering a high percentage of the costs of defense against the Turks for a very long time and was unlikely to increase its contributions. By August of 1567, Maximilian learned that many members of the estates there were not fulfilling their financial promises to him. Significant incomes of the Lower Austrian *Kammergut* were now in the hands of local noble families as collateral from Habsburg rulers who had no other way of raising money.[55]

The newly acquired kingdoms did offer the opportunity to collect some new revenue. Only a third or so of Hungary was under Habsburg control, but this area was rich. A few great landowners built up enormous fortunes locally during the sixteenth century. The region also contained important mining towns. In 1567, ordinary royal income from Habsburg Hungary amounted to 67,277 gulden—only 19,434 gulden less than what came from Bohemia, though the latter was far wealthier.[56] But this rump kingdom was contested terrain, and its tax payments were unpredictable. Maximilian would draw no income at all from his Hungarian domains in 1570.[57] "Sauve qui peut" was the functional motto of the realm's landed aristocracy, whose loyalties, depending upon the military and political currents of the day, shifted between Vienna, Transylvania, and Constantinople. More modest officials followed the same principle. Customs collectors sold passports to transient cattle dealers, then pocketed the fees rather than sending them to the royal treasury.[58]

The kingdom of Bohemia, with its "incorporated lands"—the margravate of Moravia, the duchies of Upper and Lower Silesia, and the two Lusatias— was a somewhat different matter. It was here that Maximilian had the most reason to regret Ferdinand I's failure to centralize his financial administration. Possessed of one of medieval Europe's most versatile economies, Bohemia generated substantial income, not only from such primary sources as the famous silver deposits of Kutná Hora and Jachýmov but from manufacturing and commerce. Because the most accessible veins in the mines had begun to run out by the middle of the sixteenth century, yields were dwindling somewhat. Trade routes had also begun shifting toward the Atlantic after the opening of the Americas. Nevertheless, the kingdom, with its lucrative excise tax on beer, was still a splendid asset. Like his father, Maximilian was eager to collect these revenues.[59]

But Maximilian also noted that the highly particularistic estates of the kingdom and its associated territories had never met their obligations promptly. By the middle of the sixteenth century, their hostility to financial requests from their sovereign was all but habitual.[60] The Moravians had been the most accommodating toward their new Habsburg overlords, even recognizing them as hereditary rulers. By Ferdinand I's death in 1564, however, they too were paying taxes more grudgingly. Trying to force reconsideration of the *Biergeld* and other imposts, some in the margravate argued that such charges had lapsed with Ferdinand's passing. After Maximilian in 1565 ordered the estates to honor their commitments—indeed promised to be back for more money in the future—they complied. Nevertheless, their attitude hinted at troubles to come.[61]

Bohemia itself, which boasted a far larger economy than any of its crown lands, was central to Maximilian's efforts to enhance his revenues. It was here, however, that his father's administrative shortcomings had the most serious long-term consequences. Unable to supervise the kingdom's fiscal affairs from Vienna, Ferdinand I had occasionally conferred about these matters with his administration in Prague, but that was all. Local officers of the royal treasury remained broadly competent to supervise the incomes of their sovereign and the crown domains. These men, or at least those holding the highest offices, came from the great nobility of the kingdom and remained jealous of their prerogatives.[62]

Regalian incomes were as deeply compromised in Bohemia as they were in Lower Austria, for Ferdinand I and his predecessors habitually mortgaged them for quick cash. External claims to one sort of property could make another royal operation less productive. The electors of Saxony, for example, had rights to the forests of some royal estates that provided fuel for the smelting operations in Bohemia's mines.[63] Trade and commerce in the kingdom were additionally hamstrung at the outset of Maximilian's reign by the widespread use of debased coinage that came from electoral Saxony, Poland, and, in all likelihood, the Habsburg Austrian lands. During Ferdinand's last years, the mint in Vienna had closed down, thus opening the way for the circulation of substandard currency, not only in Lower Austria but in neighboring lands.[64]

In trying to expand his revenues in Bohemia, Maximilian did, however,

start with at least two advantages. One was to have the service of his brother
Ferdinand as his *locumtenens* in the kingdom. Ferdinand had obligated himself
to an array of underdocumented but insistent creditors while serving as his
father's governor in Prague.[65] But despite these lapses and the underlying
tension between the two men, Maximilian quickly reappointed Ferdinand to
the position. Entitled to a yearly allowance of ten thousand gulden from the
kingdom, the archduke was as alarmed as Maximilian at lagging revenue
collections.[66]

Ferdinand resorted to some masterful improvisation. Lacking the ready
cash in 1565 and 1566 to pay household servants, not to mention the interest
on his father's debts in the kingdom, he quickly set his priorities. People
dependent solely on the interest on their loans to the monarch would be the
first to receive something. But Margrave John George of Brandenburg, who
was a pensionary of the kingdom, was told to ask the treasury in Silesia for
the money due him. Other claimants had to content themselves with promises
of future payment.[67] Archduke Ferdinand also had useful ideas for permanently improving Bohemian royal revenues. He created an economic commission that would investigate ways to enlarge yields and lower expenses at
Kutná Hora. Haphazard coin stamping cost untold sums, for clipping was
easy where impresses were incomplete or off-center. In September of 1564,
the archduke revealed to the Bohemian treasury that someone working for
him in Innsbruck was perfecting a water-powered machine to standardize
minting procedures. Fiscal officers in Prague themselves quickly suggested
bringing the man to the kingdom as soon as the technique was operative.[68]

Ferdinand was a sure-handed practical negotiator as well. The bulk of
ordinary royal income came from the beer tax, but the estates transferred it
to the king's treasuries very erratically.[69] In 1566 alone, the archduke identified
more than a hundred delinquents. Some in the Lusatias had not turned over
any imposts, on beer or anything else, since 1552.[70] Maximilian peremptorily
ordered laggards to pay. Familiar with the actors from his earlier years in the
kingdom, Ferdinand granted extensions to whoever he thought simply needed
more time to comply. He scheduled gatherings of the estates for seasons when
members were likely to be settling their taxes. People who had to pay in
person could appear less often, thereby reducing their outlays for travel. The
archduke also had a realistic grasp of potential resources. When Maximilian
demanded that the archduke exact an unspecified payment from the Jews of
Prague, Ferdinand suggested 150 taler a month. Many of these people were
poor, he said, and could not give more.[71]

Thus, until he returned to the Tyrol for good in 1567, Archduke Ferdinand was a prime asset to his brother's government in Bohemia. But Maximilian also brought his own strengths to the job of improving his revenues there. Like most members of his house, he was stubborn. He resisted pressure in Bohemia to hand over significant domains to important local figures, even to men who had served him throughout his realms. Nor would he abandon crucial revenues. "Those in Prague along with the other cities are asking to be dispensed from the hereditary beer tax," he wrote in April of 1567; "this cannot be."[72] He knew the difference between form and function. The mere presence of an administrative office was no substitute for performance. Early in his career, Maximilian noted that one could have a specific department (*Kammer*) for iron, yet be short of the metal.[73] He also understood the importance of regular procedures. Individual Bohemian treasury authorities repaid creditors whom they liked, while they put others off. Such behavior, Maximilian said, weakened trust in the Habsburg court. It also made tracking expenses more difficult. He ordered that payouts be made directly from the central administration. Where his personal input seemed needed, Maximilian gave it quickly. Before eradicating the bad Saxon coinage in Bohemia, he first asked his brother to send him a sample of the inferior currency.[74]

The most impressive example of Maximilian's fiscal imagination, however, was his comprehensive *Hofkammerordnung* of 1568. Having wrestled with financial problems for four years, he echoed some themes from a similar order issued by his father in 1537. Among them were the needs for drawing up precise inventories of all fiefs and for supplementing traditional incomes with new sources of revenue.[75] But Maximilian improved on Ferdinand I's formulas in significant ways. Anticipating and tracking revenue were far more important for the new emperor than they had been for his father. Bohemian officials were supposed to issue quarterly, or at least semiannual, reports on back-payments due from the beer tax, so that their ruler would have a way of estimating income to expect from that duty. At an appropriate time before the fiscal year ended in December, the president of the *Hofkammer* in Vienna and his council were to project coming expenses and the income needed to meet them. The paymasters in his sons' households had to give weekly accountings of how much gold, coin, wax, and cloth were on hand so that a tally could be made of the money and how far it would go.[76]

Maximilian was ready to do battle with venerable court custom, if such action enlarged his resources. The incomes of official and household personnel were often enhanced through special supplements—*Provisionen, Gnaden-*

gelder, Zubuessgelder—to name only those recorded most frequently. These could be one-time, lifetime, or open-ended commitments, for widows, children, and other family members frequently asked these be continued after the original beneficiary died. Ferdinand I had been very generous in distributing such favors, which, from a budgetary standpoint, had two major drawbacks. They added up to sizable outlays; moreover, since payments were often postponed or missed altogether, recipients regularly demanded interest on them. Managing all these promises exceeded contemporary clerical skills, and Maximilian ordered that such grants cease.[77]

Another striking feature of Maximilian's Hofkammerordnung was the link it made between revenue enhancement and the economic well-being of the emperor's subjects. Though he exempted himself and his court from relying on domestic suppliers, the emperor ordered that his armies be outfitted with locally produced, rather than foreign, materials. New mines he wished to open would not only enrich Habsburg treasuries but employ poor people, who would eat better because they were working. Thirty years before, Ferdinand I had spoken merely of finding new sources of revenue. Trickle-down benefits went unmentioned, if indeed they even crossed his mind.[78]

Thus, Maximilian's schemes for enlarging his revenues ranged considerably beyond extracting more money from conventional resources. He was also prepared to work conscientiously toward his goals. But regardless of the thought and commitment he gave to these matters, the thoroughgoing improvement of finance that he promised at the outset of his career did not take place. To a certain extent, the emperor was himself at fault. Useful initiatives were inexplicably dropped. In 1570, his treasury in Vienna started to keep monthly, rather than annual, summaries of expenses and credits. Though it made tracking current revenues much easier, the practice was soon abandoned.[79] Maximilian also himself acknowledged in the Hofkammerordnung that some of his goals were little more than wishful thinking. To exploit Hungary's mineral and agrarian wealth, he admitted that he needed enduring peace with the Turks, a highly unlikely prospect.[80] Maximilian never had, even potentially, the resources that allowed his cousin Philip to think about consolidating his debts in 1556–1557.[81] And clearly he had not mastered his youthful inclination to disregard good advice. He ordered his armies to clothe themselves with fabrics from Silesia, in the face of warnings from Bohemian officials that raw materials for such purposes were not always available.[82]

External circumstance also played havoc with his schemes. War with the

Porte frustrated the best administrative intentions. In 1566, a year of heavy military outlays, Archduke Ferdinand forwarded yield from the Biergeld in Bohemia directly to the Habsburg military paymaster's office (*Kriegszahl-meisteramt*), even as Maximilian and the Bohemian treasury ordered that the money be used to pay off selected loans on which interest was very high.[83] And Ferdinand I's legacy of poor record-keeping did much to undermine his eldest son's efforts to put his government on a sounder fiscal footing. Suggestions for possible savings in running the Bohemian mines turned out to be redundant when Maximilian learned that many of the changes had already been instituted during his father's reign. Maximilian's plans to improve his revenues through technological innovation slipped through some interterritorial crack in Habsburg central Europe. Though Maximilian ordered all his subtreasuries to use the coin-stamping machines developed in the Tyrol, these devices never made it from Innsbruck to Prague in his lifetime. Indeed, they went into operation in Spain long before they did in the dynasty's lands to the east.[84]

The Hofkammerordnung of 1568 was also strikingly ambivalent when it touched on reforming traditional institutions. Even as it called for radical changes in the emperor's financial administration, it ordered that custom be respected.[85] Provincial treasury officials, especially in Prague, where they were very close to the estates, took the opening; they stubbornly resisted reform when they had a chance. At times they were simply block-headed; at times they could be quite cunning; but they almost always had their way. When a Habsburg commission to reform administrative practice at the mines in Jachýmov suggested appointing a royal captain (*Oberhauptmann*) in the town, local officers discouraged the move, saying that no such office existed.[86] With collections of the Biergeld still behind schedule in 1568, the estates did allow royal agents, rather their own personnel, to receive the money; but they balked when Maximilian proposed raising the levy. Most objectionable, however, was their king's request that the tax be delivered quarterly or semi-annually, as it was in Lower Austria. This constituted an innovation, said the Bohemians, hard to get off the ground, more difficult still to sustain.[87] When the estates themselves authorized the quarterly collection of the impost, the treasury implemented the measure unenthusiastically. Nevertheless, Maximilian pressed ahead; he asked for monthly accountings of Biergeld receipts. His administration in Prague called this pointless; the tax was due quarterly, leaving nothing to report during the intervening months. Nor, in their view, did the monthly accountings of receipts from royal holdings in Bohemia on the sale of such items as grain, fish, and wood make much sense. These items were often held off the market until the price for them was more favorable.[88]

Thus, for all the intensity with which he approached fiscal reform, Maximilian had little choice but to resume many of the practices for which he had once taken his father to task. Extraordinary revenues voted by his estates always came in irregularly. Where need outstripped resources, the latter "had to be driven up wherever we could."[89] Rather than get nothing at all from the lords of Bohemia and Moravia, Maximilian accepted partial payment, just so long as the money came quickly.[90] Systematic revenue tracking was a distant thought; the head of his treasury in Vienna, Reichart Streun von Schwarzenau, repeatedly raised vast sums on very short notice.[91] Borrowing was crucial in such operations, and Maximilian cast a very wide net. Merchants from Magdeburg to St. Pölten in Lower Austria, princes both Protestant and Catholic—all were fair game.[92] Occasionally he did not bother asking for specific sums; "substantial" ("ansehenliche") or "large" apparently said it all.[93] The wealthy Bohemian nobleman Wilhelm of Rožmberk was called upon to raise funds, with his own credit as security. Future income, both regular and extraordinary, was to serve as collateral. That some of these monies had been voted by estates for Turkish defense but not yet received was beside the point.[94] Even the bereaved offered opportunities. In 1569, Maximilian tried to track down the friends and heirs of a deceased Bohemian nobleman, Wilhelm Terzkho. They might, he thought, be in a position to extend their king the forty thousand to fifty thousand taler he needed for his troops in Hungary.[95]

Like his father, indeed like all contemporary rulers, Maximilian never thought of upending the received social and economic order in the name of fiscal integrity. Though even the Bohemian treasury delicately suggested in 1564 that noblemen as a group were not suited to certain administrative offices, Maximilian insisted on having some "distinguished" person of rank for a position in Lower Lusatia.[96] The wealth of the Netherlands impressed Maximilian deeply—he deplored the war that began there in the 1560s because it affected the trade and commerce of the region so adversely. Nonetheless, he had only a conventional understanding of how that prosperity had come about. He was sensitive to the competitive disadvantage to which his licensed court purveyors were putting merchants and artisans in the Habsburg lands.[97] But any possible relation between the public development of capital in the Low Countries and expanded rights of private property does not seem to have occurred to him.[98] Indeed, lacking the wherewithal to pay his chief officials high salaries, Maximilian rewarded the high-born who served him in time-honored fashion—with estates and other economic privileges. Large noble holdings grew vaster still, especially in Bohemia.[99] As king there, Maximilian even occasionally relied on local magnates to bargain for him with their peers.[100]

Though he had grumbled mightily about his father's abuse of the practice, Maximilian was also very generous with petty allowances and pensions, especially toward the end of his life.[101] It is true that these payments may have possibly saved him some money: covering the cost of inflation through special appropriations, rather than increased salaries, kept down his base expenditures. Such gifts also allowed Maximilian to reward those who served him well without transferring privileges in regalian holdings.[102] Grants for specified purposes were not continuing obligations, at least theoretically. Terminating these commitments, however, proved difficult; his expenses only mounted, along with the uncertainty that dogged all his fiscal operations.

Maximilian would spend a lifetime discovering that, regardless of his gifts, broad experience, and genuine concern for the business of government, the inheritance for which he had fought so hard was problematic at best. Overcoming testamentary imperatives, longstanding financial mismanagement, and deeply entrenched practice was hard and frustrating work. Nor did the list of his administrative difficulties stop there. One of the few bits of fatherly advice that Maximilian wholeheartedly accepted was that no monarch, however powerful, truly ruled alone. Good advisers were needed, for family members as talented as Archduke Ferdinand were hard to find. Maximilian was keenly aware that he needed a battery of personnel who could both guide him and carry out his plans. Lesser talents than he was had accomplished much through effective officials. Finding such people was therefore as crucial to improving his government as was having a clear notion of what to do.

six

Imperfect Men for an Imperfect World

A new monarch, particularly an energetic and ambitious one, was likely to pay a good deal of attention to personnel problems at the outset of his reign. Explicitly committed to bettering Ferdinand I's managerial record, Maximilian was no exception. During the first years of his reign, he complained repeatedly about bad service and thought often and hard about how to bring good people into his government and household.[1]

Features unique to Habsburg domains in central Europe sometimes complicated his searches—a command of Czech and German was required of supervisors at the mint in Kutná Hora—but not all of Maximilian's employees were so specialized.[2] Nevertheless, a Spanish ambassador in Vienna doubted as early as 1567 that Maximilian would ever have enough people for his enterprises.[3] Other members of the house of Austria had already encountered the problem, or were about to. In 1540, there may have been only a hundred or so men qualified and available for service with his father. In organizing a war council in 1556, Ferdinand I could not persuade leading members of the Austrian estates to serve on the body. He therefore appointed whoever would take the job.[4] Setting up his residence in the Tyrol, Archduke Ferdinand despaired of getting suitable household staff "in this abandoned wilderness." Even his sympathetic brother-in-law in comparatively urban Munich could not help. Archduke Charles had similar troubles in Graz.[5] In Spain, Philip II would never have enough trained military engineers.[6]

Maximilian had a somewhat larger pool from which to hire than did other

German princes. The emperor's cousins and in-laws throughout Europe passed along names of promising officials and other employees.[7] Maximilian was also ready to call on both Catholic and evangelical talent, unlike the bishop of Würzburg, who, in 1573, was without anyone to supervise his household because the entire region of Freiburg had no Catholic nobleman fit for the job.[8] Suitable people had strong personal reasons to join the emperor's establishment as well. Security and prestige went along with several positions. So did special benefices, pensions, and supplementary payments to offset the expenses of travel, weddings, births, baptisms, illness, or serious injuries.[9] Maximilian could be very generous to humble people generally. He willingly turned the swine kill from his estates in Pardubice over to local residents and was quick to give alms to the poor, the ailing, and the severely afflicted.[10] The wet nurses of all the archdukes received lifetime annuities of a hundred Rhenish gulden, only fifty gulden less than the salaries of responsible treasury officials.[11]

Other rewards came simply from associating with the emperor. Though convention apparently dictated the wage level at his court, gifts to Maximilian often included gifts for his staff. At a diet in Speyer in 1570, the city presented the emperor and his wife with wine, fish, grain, and a gilded silver service. Vice-Chancellor Weber, High Chamberlain Adam von Dietrichstein, Trabanten, heralds, trumpeters, and sergeants-at-arms also came away with appropriate marks of consideration.[12] Maximilian never wholly forbade even his most sensitive personnel to take small informal rewards that came to them through their jobs. Treasury officials were not supposed to accept honoraria from merchants who did business with the court. They could, however, keep fish, game, wine, and the like, for their colleagues in other administrative offices were allowed to do so.[13] A place in the emperor's service opened doors elsewhere for whole families. In 1566, Maximilian asked Pius V to confer a provostship on Joachim Zasius, Johann Ulrich's brother, "not only" because of Johann Ulrich's merits, but because of Joachim's own.[14]

Here and there, Maximilian made some first-class appointments. Many of his ambassadors served him well, submitting model reports from many of the crisis points of Europe.[15] Some were men of great experience and personal loyalty—Ogier de Busbecq and Albert de Wyss in Constantinople, Prosper d'Arco in Rome, Hans Khevenhüller and Adam von Dietrichstein in Madrid. Jacopo da Strada, his antiquary, was extraordinarily knowledgeable, so much so that he doubled in the role for Duke Albrecht in Bavaria between 1568 and 1570. And Maximilian was in a good position to discourage bad service.

Employees who performed poorly in Vienna might not find jobs at other courts if the emperor advised against hiring them.[16]

Scarce funds and lack of skilled officers may account for the more or less constant size of Maximilian's household and public staff.[17] These considerations almost certainly shaped the way the emperor thought about improving his personnel resources as well. Quality had a higher priority in his thinking than raw quantity. He stressed the need to correct faulty work habits, including his own.[18] Maximilian was also prepared to contemplate a form of meritocracy. The Hofkammerordnung of 1568 declared that social class, by itself, was no bar to employment in Maximilian's financial administration. The document directed the treasury council (*Hofkammerrat*) president and his colleagues to identify young men among the emperor's subjects whose behavior and intellect augured well for bureaucratic careers. During their studies, they would receive an allowance proportionate to their abilities. The emperor also wished to professionalize his government by putting his appointees on regular salaries drawn from ordinary income, rather than relying on special grants and allowances to cover missed payments. Maximilian suggested filling vacancies in his treasury staff on the basis of seniority. Once a position fell open, the next oldest person in the office was to get the job.[19]

Privileged though he was, Maximilian struggled ceaselessly to bring in, keep, and replace good people throughout his administrations. Indeed, these tribulations and the causes of them are the story of his government. Losing reliable personnel without replacements on hand precipitated crises. When Georg Teufl, the president of the war council in 1566, threatened to resign, the emperor faced the prospect of being left "with nothing."[20] In the absence of capable people, Maximilian made do with what he had and lived with the consequences. The treasury, the chief object of his administrative concerns, was one of the worst-run parts of his government in Vienna. Its president at the outset of Maximilian's career was Hieronymus Beck, a cosmopolitan world traveler, who had been an Edelknabe in Innsbruck. He had also worked for several years in the Lower Austrian treasury before moving to the central court office in 1563. Nevertheless, Maximilian was very unhappy with his performance. "Beck is not adequate to the job of treasury president. The treasury has never been so hard pressed as now and needs good advice and inspection," he noted in 1567. The man whom the emperor wanted for the job refused to budge from the Lower Austrian treasury. Beck therefore continued in the post until 1569, when he was named to the potentially far more remunerative post of high provisioner to the army in Hungary.[21] Further down the scale of status and responsibility, personnel shortages were also routine. Sergeants-at-arms for general audience rooms in 1562 were guarding the treasury by 1572 because no one else was available.[22] Burned-out functionaries lingered on indefinitely, even moved on to other Habsburg courts, when capable replacements did not turn up.[23]

Thus, Maximilian was only one among several sixteenth-century German princes scrambling for the best administrative talent to be found. Competition was fierce and came from beyond the empire. Rulers from all over Europe recruited experienced Tyrolean consultants for advice on mines and on engineering projects connected with them.[24] Territorial estates, which increased their administrative activities during the sixteenth century, were also on the lookout for well-trained personnel. These bodies often forbade their most highly skilled functionaries to change jobs.[25] Rulers shamelessly poached one another's officials and servants. At Ferdinand I's death, Christoph of Württemberg tried to lure Georg von Helfenstein, the Habsburg governor in the Tyrol, to serve in the Swabian circle. This was someone who really deserved his salary, as a distressed Maximilian put it, thereby implying that many did not. Maximilian himself raided his subsidiary treasuries in his outlying lands to staff his own, in effect beggaring one office to fill another.[26]

But a shallow pool of qualified candidates was only one cause of Maximilian's chronic personnel problems. Generous though the emperor could be, his administrative style sorely tested the minds and mettle of those who served him. To be sure, some discomforts often went with specific jobs. Winter in the treasury was an indoor-outdoor event for everyone; one duty of a *Hofkammerdiener* was to keep the ink from freezing.[27] Nevertheless, though Maximilian espoused the division of labor on both humane and administrative grounds—the army paymaster, he said, could "not be everywhere"—the emperor often seemed to think that increasing the workload alone would improve his government.[28]

Thus, the court comptroller, to whom the paymaster reported, was to be familiar with, and frequently reread, directions for a daunting variety of household operations. These included the kitchen, wine cellars, stables, and storerooms for lighting materials. He was to keep daily, or in some cases hourly, watch on these areas to make sure that employees were doing their jobs. He was to collect receipts for their purchases. He was also to keep track of how many horses were in Maximilian's stables, the number of foals they had produced, their breeding lines, their colors, even their names. He fined derelict employees. Only in some cases, presumably difficult ones, could he bring in the majordomo, the official ultimately responsible for the administration of the court.[29]

Maximilian expected great self-sacrifice from employees, even when he raised them to titled positions. He deeply respected Johannes Crato von Krafftheim, the surgeon and humanist from Breslau, and made him a *Pfalzgraf;* in 1568 the emperor bestowed the same rights and privileges on the physician's heirs. Ministering to the sickly emperor, however, preempted so much of his attention that Crato had little to spare for his family. He brought his wife and a frail son to Vienna only after some time in the emperor's service. No sooner did they arrive than Crato had to rush off to Bratislava, Maximilian's headquarters at the time. His wife and child were left to fend for themselves in a new home. In 1574, with the boy suffering from dysentery in the capital, Crato was prescribing to the emperor at his retreat in Kaiserebersdorf. The responsibilities took their toll: " 'I much regret to have been brought to the point . . . that I have no chance to think about my health or my life; . . . I don't know whether it would not be better to die soon and be spared mortal concerns than to find myself worn out in this splendid misery.' " Worse yet, the higher he rose in Maximilian's service, the more jealousy he believed he aroused.[30]

The peripatetic ways of both the emperor and his governments exasperated even his most dedicated servants. Pressed by a Bohemian chamberlain, Peter Vuk of Rožmberk, for 232 florins in back salary, the highly competent and conscientious court paymaster David Hag sent a polite apology in 1567 for the long delay. He reminded Rožmberk, however, that the emperor had been in Prague, then moved on to Bratislava; the authorization for such payments journeyed with him. The nobleman might have gotten his money had he been in touch with Maximilian before the latter's departure for the Bohemian capital. Funds, however, were always tight after such trips. Hag therefore suggested that Rožmberk see if anything were available in Bratislava. Hag assured him, "I am not the cause of the delay."[31]

Regardless of where he was at any time, Maximilian intended for business to continue in his capitals.[32] The many staff members who accompanied him had either to travel with their work or to remain part of an overburdened skeleton crew at home. The Diet of Augsburg in 1566 was an elaborate event, so that the retinue which attended the emperor for the occasion was perhaps much larger than for other meetings and celebrations. Nevertheless, the absence of even half the personnel that appeared with him would certainly have strained the caretakers left in Vienna. Four secretaries came from the court

chancellory, along with eighteen other support personnel, three Latin secretaries with five aides, three treasury secretaries and ten auxiliaries, three
sergeants-at-arms as well as men to handle Spanish, Bohemian, Hungarian,
Silesian, and Burgundian affairs.[33]

Maximilian's precarious finances virtually ruled out high salaries as a way
of attracting the best officials to his court or hiring anyone to assist them in
their work. Indeed, some of the imperial princes paid better wages than he
could. Among the imperial electors, Elector Palatine Frederick III was the
wealthiest. By 1576, his high court functionaries were drawing as much as a
thousand Rhenish gulden annually, considerably above what Maximilian offered, except to a very few. It was possible to come away with nothing if one
left the emperor's service before back wages were paid; much time was spent
haggling over these and other injuries that Maximilian inflicted on those who
worked for him.[34] Nevertheless, the emperor's servants, from the scarce translators to abjectly poor gardeners, were often eager to work for other rulers.
Deprived of rewards that they believed were due them, people sometimes
gave up hope of getting anything and left even for trivial reasons. Some
virtually begged to be put into the households of lesser but more generous
princes such as Maximilian's nephew, Duke William V of Bavaria.[35] Truly
prominent talents refused the emperor's offers outright. Unable to match sums
coming from the deeper pockets of the church in Rome, Maximilian eventually gave up trying to bring the composer Giovanni Palestrina to Vienna
as his chapel choirmaster.[36]

Then too, as Archduke Ferdinand untactfully reminded his elder brother,
pay not only had to be good. It also had to be regular.[37] Even though he
intended to otherwise, Maximilian fell as woefully short on the second count
as he did on the first. Even when he granted raises, gifts, and benefits to
make up for virtually stagnant salaries, he did not always release the funds
promptly. Some delay was probably unavoidable. Revenue dedicated to government and household positions sometimes came from administrative districts spread throughout the Habsburg holdings. Therefore, it was often disbursed piecemeal rather than all at once.[38] But some of the emperor's officials
received nothing at all for long stretches of time. So important a figure as
Imperial Vice-Chancellor Zasius was a typical case. His basic wage remained
an unusually high fifteen hundred gulden through his entire career. But from
1568 until his death in 1570, he apparently saw little if any of it. Rather, it
was his widow who was the beneficiary of twenty-three months worth of her
late husband's back wages. Imperial Court Councillor Georg Eder received

no salary for seven straight years. The wherewithal to live he drew on incomes from his property, most of which belonged to his children.[39] Charles V and Ferdinand I had been equally tardy in such matters, but Maximilian, of course, had promised to do better.[40]

Unpredictable compensation and burdensome work were therefore two more reasons for capable people to stay away from Maximilian's service. Even if he had been able to locate all the trustworthy employees he needed and pay them well and regularly, the emperor was neither morally nor intellectually equipped to carry administrative reform to its logical conclusions. Maximilian's eminently rational treasury and chancellory orders show only one side of his managerial thinking. The Hofkammerordnung of 1568, in which he asked for major change even as custom was respected, betrayed a certain ambivalence about structural reform that spilled over into his personnel policies too. Along with his court, Maximilian remained deeply attached to values and commitments that were wholly at odds with cost-benefit calculations and serious performance standards.

The imperial household and administrative employees were, as they had been for centuries, the emperor's personal responsibility; the longer they had served him and his house, and often the poorer they were, the more compelling his obligations to them and their families became. When toll and customs collectors died, their offices sometimes went to survivors who might otherwise fall into deep poverty.[41] One did not fire longtime servants who were too old to work. Efforts to consolidate positions went for naught when administrators argued that extensive service by some people precluded dismissing them out of hand.[42] Nor were people's skill and training the only reasons for them to continue in the emperor's government or household. Intradynastic referrals, useful though they may have been at times, often forced the emperor to take on unpromising people only because some family member of theirs had served a Habsburg relative well.[43]

Thus, as a twentieth-century scholar has put it, Maximilian was "simultaneously ahead of his time and behind it" where management of his court and government was concerned.[44] Reason may have told him where to go, but long-standing custom, along with an array of material constraints, restricted his program of improvement. He thus got no further with personnel reform than he did with bettering his revenue flow. As early as 1565, Maximilian made it clear that he would continue to use many of Ferdinand I's officials or men who had served him since boyhood, such as Georg Ilsung, the Reichspfennigmeister. Continuity of employment, not radical change, was therefore the true hallmark of both his government and his household. From 1564 until his death in 1576, Maximilian had but two presidents for his war council, two court chancellors, who were at the same time imperial vice-chancellors, two stable masters, one high chamberlain, and two majordomos.[45] The imperial office was, and would continue to be, run far more through patronage and informal channels of authority than through a precisely articulated bureaucracy.[46]

Maximilian's dependence on long-familiar employees sometimes forced him to overlook questionable opinions and behavior. Imperial Vice-Chancellor Weber would declare that he preferred to drink himself to death rather than reach the same end by working, as he claimed Zasius had in 1570.[47] Both men took sudden leave of the court to attend to personal concerns. They fled Vienna within a few days of one another in 1569 when plague struck down servants in their households.[48] But Maximilian valued Weber for the jurist's insight into confessional politics.[49] Even more important to the administration in Vienna was Zasius. In 1569 Maximilian did not think he could spare him for a time to get married, even though he thought that the excitable vice-chancellor might be calmer if he took a wife.[50] A prodigious worker, particularly with written assignments, Zasius had a wide range of contacts throughout the empire. He also shared Maximilian's stated commitment to German concerns. His religious views were closer to those of his other chief patron, Albrecht V of Bavaria. Like Maximilian, however, Zasius was a sharp critic of the papacy, especially when Rome seemed ready to thwart imperial interests.[51]

But making do with the staff he had could be very frustrating for the emperor. This was particularly true when his concern was security. As his father's commander in Hungary, he had worried about intelligence leaks and other such lapses. Some of these problems had little to do with personnel, at least directly. Sharing diplomatic correspondence from Venice, Rome, and Madrid with his brothers widened opportunities for dispersal of secret information. When Maximilian enclosed his codes with these dispatches, as he sometimes did, he was virtually inviting disclosure.[52] Most breaches of confidence, however, were attributable to the people who served him. Maximilian was a disciplined negotiator who required extensive information for his deliberations and carefully evaluated what he heard and read.[53] He thought that even the lowliest copyist in his war council should keep his business secret, not only during his period of employment, but for life. The Habsburg was especially concerned about the tidbits of information that his servants carried with them when they left his government to work elsewhere in the empire.[54]

Many sources reported to Maximilian. But his very centrality to European politics exposed him to the wiles of information-seekers. Unlike his contemporaries in the smaller German states, many of whom could not afford to maintain permanent embassies, the emperor fielded a widespread ambassadorial network. His court was a major hub for news from Europe and beyond. It was a center of transmission as well. Envoys gathered in the *Hofburg,* or even at the homes of such officials as Weber, to pick up what they could, either openly or clandestinely.[55] Spies were everywhere—Philip II had especially thick coverage in Germany—and the very people on whom Maximilian relied to manage his affairs with discretion were themselves in the business of selling information or access to their employer's ear.[56]

Informal payments were welcome to people in Maximilian's service, for their duties were heavy enough to preclude their improving their salaries by moonlighting. Accepting emoluments did not make people traitors or otherwise unfit them for Maximilian's government and household. " 'The servants of one majesty ought to be the servants of another,' " said Hans Trautson, longtime majordomo to the emperor, as he accepted a consideration of seven thousand escudos in 1572 from Spanish sources at the court in Vienna.[57] Vice-Chancellor Weber, who was also one of Philip's pensioners, was among the most venal of men. Nevertheless, though Cosimo de' Medici covered debts for some of the vice-chancellor's relatives and even gave Weber two thousand ducats, the jurist did not oblige the Florentine by pressing Maximilian to do something he clearly did not want to do—recognize Cosimo's title to be Grand Duke of Tuscany.[58] But Maximilian could never be sure of such men's loyalties, either. The emperor was furious in 1569 when he discovered that Zasius had taken money from the elector of Saxony.[59]

Nevertheless, Maximilian realized that he would not receive the variety of information he needed unless he gave something in return.[60] He therefore tolerated men who prepared and received documents in his chancellory and divulged some of their contents to other European courts, particularly those in Germany. None of their activity was clandestine. From secretaries to vice-chancellors, humanists to postmasters, several of Maximilian's most important advisers and officers compiled so-called *Zeitungen,* newsletters about the goings-on at various territorial establishments. These were then distributed to princely subscribers.[61] The court in Munich paid their Vienna correspondents—Johann Ulrich Zasius, Johann Baptist Weber, and Peter Obernburger, an imperial councillor and secretary—sums ranging from a hundred to four hundred taler a year, depending on the amount of service they had rendered. Zasius received three hundred taler, and game and horses as well, from Hesse. Christoph of Württemberg sent Neckar wine. The authors passed their news around among themselves and to others, almost always for a fee, gifts in kind, or, failing anything of that order, fresh news. When the *Zeitungsschreiber* were too busy to write themselves, they turned the job over to others, though they ordinarily signed the finished product.[62]

Zasius had a particularly dense web of informers—inquiring travelers or correspondents stationed for one reason or another in large and important countries. He was also ready to report on his own work at the imperial court. The jurist's chief German subscribers—Albrecht of Bavaria, Philip of Hesse, Christoph of Württemberg, were all well disposed toward Maximilian.[63] But the system of information-gathering in general ruled out strict control of the persons responsible for the work. Having few, if any, people at his command whose loyalty was unquestionable, Maximilian called heavily on the only person he could really trust—himself. Needing to be better informed, especially on Ottoman affairs, he took testimony from even the most casual sources. Entries in his diary often start with the tentative "there are supposed to be," indicating that, while he did not quite believe what he had heard, he could not casually dismiss it, either.[64]

The administrative constitution he inherited also encouraged him to take a hand in all aspects of his administration. Members of Maximilian's government swore allegiance directly to him, not to some abstract entity such as the state or public welfare. But if all were singly obligated to their sovereign, he stood in the same relationship to them. Maximilian was therefore charged with evaluating whatever duties and business each of them carried out, no matter how inconsequential.[65] In his case, Maximilian was temperamentally inclined toward such duties; he happily tackled minutiae such as alternate spellings of names.[66] Staffing the cultural side of his court was a kind of recreation for him. Maximilian directed the search in Rome for a kapellmeister in 1567 and 1568 both closely and knowledgeably.[67] Most important of all, his long struggle for his various titles left him acutely sensitive to his own prerogatives and reluctant to delegate any of them. On learning that Archduke Ferdinand's vice-chancellor in the Tyrol counter-signed documents with a "vidit," Maximilian warily observed that this was his brother's way of doing business. He did like to explore important matters with his privy council before reaching a decision. There were, of course, areas where only he could develop orders—measures to contain epidemics being one among many. But all in all, his sense of rule was abidingly personal, so much so that he concerned himself with the domestic lives of his officials.[68]

The range of matters, petty and substantial, that claimed his attention was staggering. His so-called *Spanische Briefbücher,* two volumes containing 655 folio pages, are largely minor letters of commendation.[69] November of 1566 found him agonizing in his aide-mémoire over finding presidents for his treasury and war office. A month later he reminded himself to keep an eye on the war council and to give it orders.[70] There were gifts to be chosen for an embassy to Persia, a decision to be made on purchasing another bison (*Auerochs*) for the menagerie in Prague, a master mason to be appointed.[71] At one point, he was formulating responses to his Hungarian councillors, arguing against papal inflexibility toward the Protestant reform, and developing Turkish policy virtually at the same time. By May of 1567, he sounded breathless on paper.[72]

Thus, from the outset of his reign, Maximilian was trying to do more things, and to be in more places, than he ever could be. There was a perverse consistency to his policy; he had, after all, criticized his father many times for leaving too much to subordinates;[73] but the results of his approach were both predictable and quick to materialize. Even before he became emperor, Maximilian was hard put to answer letters promptly; the pattern continued. In 1565, he was already excusing himself from promised meetings with the Moravian estates because of more urgent business. Two years later, he was not sure he could attend the wedding of his nephew, William of Bavaria, to Renata of Lorraine, a match he had helped arrange. Business, he explained, "multiplies from day to day, and also appears afresh."[74] Though he asked fellow princes such as Albrecht of Bavaria to send routine correspondence to the imperial secretary, Peter Obernburger, the emperor continued to be the direct recipient of many such letters.[75]

The combination of personalized authority and unqualified, often disgruntled, officials therefore left government a very loose affair throughout Maximilian's lands, tied as much to local and private interest as to the emperor's affairs.[76] Postponement and neglect, at first a tactic with Maximilian, became outright habit. Salaries went unpaid and orders unforwarded, even when officials made clear that it was imperative to take action.[77] Tolls in Bohemia were not collected, in part because many of the stations did not have copies of the appropriate orders. Only in 1575 did Maximilian get around to correcting the problem.[78] Sorting through impending tasks, the emperor sometimes forgot truly essential chores such as negotiating loans.[79]

The press of work led even Zasius to think he needed a secretary, though his extracurricular preoccupations were surely a part of his overload. The strain on Maximilian was even more apparent. Four years into his reign, he was already haggard and seemed weaker by the day. If he did not actually fall asleep over his papers at midnight, as did his cousin Philip in Spain, he probably came very close.[80] His frequent indispositions caused administrative as well as physical upheaval, for they forced him to put off everything from council meetings to diplomatic negotiations.[81] Key subordinates, such as a Bohemian comptroller or Archduke Ferdinand, had their own afflictions that slowed down business as well. But while such men often had considerable leeway in the application of policies and programs, only Maximilian could authorize these measures.[82]

It did not take long for Maximilian to see that he needed help, at least for representational affairs. By 1567, he was already asking Philip II to send Archdukes Rudolph and Ernst back from Spain. To prepare them for their coming duties, he urged their Hofmeister, Adam von Dietrichstein, to keep the boys at their studies so that they would not succumb to the Spanish malady of laziness.[83] It would be several years before his sons returned. But until then, and even after, Maximilian's administration continued the slipshod ways for which he had once scolded his father.[84] In 1571, he admitted publicly that his government resembled that of Ferdinand I, including in the way his father had treated officials.[85]

Maximilian was only one of several European rulers of his time who tried to reshape both the structure and personnel practices of their administrations.[86] None of them did an especially good job of it. The kind of loyalty and submission that a Louis XIV could eventually command from his officers and estates a century later was out of their reach.[87] What was striking about Maximilian's efforts was the close connection he made between managerial reform and personal self-image. He clearly did not realize that identifying problems and remedying them were quite different processes. Maximilian's inability to outstrip the performance of his father's government and those of other contemporary princes was a disagreeable way to learn certain of life's ineluctable realities. It was an especially trying lesson for a man who thought himself the exception rather than the rule.

seven

The Pleasures and Ironies of Splendor

"The court is a remarkable game," wrote Lazarus Schwendi, one of Maximilian's trusted advisers and military commanders, in a moment of critical reflection.[1] Contemporary princes did indeed have to be alert. Personal interests dominated the minds of those who served monarchs. Courtiers and court officers cooperated when their agendas coincided. When their aspirations differed, they were potential competitors. Officials closely watched the salaries of their peers to make sure that no one received more than his rank merited. Complex plots, devious stratagems, and boundless ambition often shaped the advice they gave. When developing policies, rulers and their surrogates had to weigh all of these factors, even as they consulted such men. At the same time, these very people belonged to the monarch's social world. The courts of Charles V and Philip II were such places; so was Maximilian II's establishment.[2]

Maximilian was psychologically armed to survive in such an environment. Years of analyzing and thwarting the schemes of his father and uncle had made him a suspicious man. Nevertheless, for all the strain that it caused him, Maximilian's court, and the central role he played in it, gave him his greatest pleasures. Though eulogized for his modest and ascetic ways when he died in 1576, Maximilian was wholly at ease with the pageantry and trappings of sovereignty.[3] The festivities, sports, entertainments, and hobbies, which were among his greatest joys, were possible only in the setting where he spent his entire life.

The spectacle of rule was part of its exercise in early modern Europe, and the princely court a kind of social gymnasium in which images were created, refined, and displayed. Though experience taught that appearances could be grossly misleading, no monarch could neglect the public ceremonial side of his office. It was the way he told the public how to think about him, and Maximilian had a sure grasp of dynastic theatrics.[4] Contemporaries thought that he put on one of the more impressive shows of his day. The emperor had "enough officials and ministers in every sort of position, to . . . populate a city, all with large stipends and provisions," noted a Venetian ambassador, blinded to the Habsburg's shaky finances by what he saw.[5] To some observers, the Viennese court was distinctively cosmopolitan as well. There were numerous Italians and Spaniards, the latter drawn eastward by the empress's household.[6]

Though the Habsburgs of central Europe sometimes invited popular participation in court festivities, the overriding purpose of these events was to persuade the wide world that a ruler was an exceptional being.[7] Developing a ruler's image began early. Like his father, eight-year-old Archduke Rudolph participated in a public tournament with his uncle Charles in 1560, and supposedly gave a good account of himself.[8] The Spanish ceremonial at Maximilian's court underscored the uniqueness of the ruling family and its relation to the transcendental order. Festivals and tableaux that typically assigned the reigning prince an exalted role and unique mission reached newly elaborate, even exotic, levels during Maximilian's reign. He and his counterparts throughout Europe participated in many such affairs personally. The Italian mannerist painter Giuseppe Arcimboldo, who worked for three emperors— Ferdinand, Maximilian, and Rudolph II—was valued as much as a designer of celebrations as he was for his canvases. His distinctive paintings of human heads as compositions of fruits, vegetables, and flowers were expressions of the harmony between the political and natural spheres that Habsburg rule was supposed to bring to contemporary Europe.[9] The garments Maximilian wore as emperor carried religious significance, possibly to reassure the Spanish court about his confessional leanings, but also to identify him with his imperial office.[10] Basic physical processes, such as eating, were arranged to underscore the singularity of the dynasty. Kitchen chamberlains of Maximilian's sons could eat some, but not all, of the dishes consumed by the archdukes.[11]

Behind almost every ceremony lay certain visual and didactic purposes. Hierarchy and deference governed Maximilian's relations even with foreign potentates. Waiting to kiss the hands of the emperor and his wife, ambassadors stood before Maximilian, as did his sons—bareheaded until he gave a sign for them to don their hats. Arriving in front of Maximilian in 1568, a Turkish orator bowed his head, took a step forward, dipped his head once again, then moved to stand directly in front of his host, where he repeated the motion a third time. He then bent especially low to kiss the Habsburg's gloved hand. Lesser members of the delegation went through an abbreviated version of the ritual.[12] When Maximilian received the Order of the Garter on 4 January 1568 from the earl of Sussex, Elizabeth I's ambassador, a diagram of the seating order of participants and their line of movement was carefully drawn up, so that no awkwardness would take away from the grandeur of the occasion.[13] Eager, as his predecessors had been, to make a lasting impression at his first imperial diet, Maximilian brought 2,280 horses to Augsburg in 1566 for himself, the empress, and several noblemen from his Austrian hereditary lands.[14]

The court itself was a separate legal entity in matters of right and wrong. When the emperor's own councillors or resident noblemen were charged with wrongdoing, the court marshal personally made the arrest, or imposed what his sovereign called the knightly imprisonment. Should the alleged offender resist, other household officials were called in to assist. The marshal, at the outset Ludwig Ungnad, attended the hearing as well.[15]

The relentless formality of these arrangements and their sometimes stressful link with active politics did not bother Maximilian in the slightest. Public duty and private amusement were, for him, virtually indistinguishable, and he carried out his assignment in this system with lifelong enthusiasm. Evaluating him as a ruler and as a man, contemporaries looked at the way Maximilian dined, the pastimes he favored, the disciplines he patronized, and the artifacts he chose to adorn himself and his surroundings. The emperor expected such scrutiny, and he was prepared to prove himself an adept in all these areas. Gastronomic excess was a feature of late sixteenth-century life in Germany, particularly among the upper classes. Therefore, princes had to work especially hard at maintaining an air of exclusivity at table.[16] Ferdinand I had eaten and drunk sparingly, but he had been a spectacular host. The number of dishes presented to him at his late-morning dinner had ranged from twenty-four to thirty, or more when guests were present.[17] At the Diet of Augsburg in 1566, Maximilian gave a banquet of five courses, each of which comprised 125 dishes.[18] Whether he followed this pattern routinely elsewhere is not clear; but no matter how ceremonial these occasions were, he enjoyed them. Although he had long ago put heavy drinking behind him, Maximilian admired good vintages, chilled on ice if possible, and the princes who served them, such as the bishop of Würzburg.[19] Over protests from the vintners of Lower Austria, he regularly imported foreign wines to Vienna, both for himself and as gifts for others. Italy, chiefly the South Tyrol, and Hungary, a separate customs unit in the sixteenth-century Habsburg empire, benefited from his patronage. To his great pleasure, territorial rulers such as Christoph of Württemberg reciprocated with samples of their local products.[20] He was equally discriminating with food. Ordering cases of fruit and nuts from the South Tyrol, even before he was emperor, he distinguished *Margranaten*, small-seeded apples, from those with large seeds. Various kinds of freshwater salmon—"Laxn, Ashen, Felchen und Reinancken"—were favorites, particularly when they were brought live.[21] His brother Ferdinand was a willing confederate, shipping him such delicacies as salmon pâtés (*Pasteten*) from Prague.[22]

Passionate horsemen and hunters, Maximilian and Archduke Ferdinand organized and participated in tournaments enthusiastically. *Ringelrennen*, a contest of Italian origin in which competitors vied to spear an elevated ring with tilting-lances, was especially popular. Though the physical challenges of the sport were not great, spectators greatly enjoyed the outfits of the riders. Costumes were often exceedingly fanciful, and their effect was heightened by makeup, all of which professional artists—Arcimboldo among them—sometimes designed.[23] Lavish anachronisms they might have been, but these games had a message as well. A good tournament performance from Maximilian bespoke prowess as a military leader, a message especially important to convey to the Turks.[24]

Sixteenth-century princes were avid collectors of rare and exotic specimens, including human ones. Dwarfs, court jesters, unusually gifted singers—all set off mankind's most singular oddity—the ruler. To possess something that no other monarch or prince had was to show proof of distinction. People who sought Maximilian's favor went to great lengths to advertise the singularity of their talents; one applicant, a composer, claimed to use the human voice in the most natural way possible and to have mastered the grand harmony of the universe.[25] But Maximilian welcomed rarities of all kinds enthusiastically, whether he discovered them himself or received them as gifts. Thrilled by the span of the antlers from three felled stags brought out of Hungary in 1563, he regretted that he could not give a pair to his Bavarian brother-in-law. Archduke Ferdinand claimed one set for himself; Ferdinand

I, who was at that time still alive, commandeered the second for the arch-bishop of Salzburg. But Maximilian was so eager for the duke to appreciate the creatures' size that he sent Albrecht a cast of one of the hooves.[26]

All Maximilian's major residences had menageries and gardens for botan-ical and zoological curiosities, which came from many parts of the world.[27] He cared for the animals with real interest in their welfare, at least by the standards of his day. The elaborate job description of the lion-keeper, for example, called for him to "purge" the beasts occasionally.[28] Maximilian oc-casionally erred in judging the response of his audience to his novelties. The elephant he brought to Vienna in 1552, "an amazing, dreadful, huge, horrible beast, is only twelve years old, grows until it is thirty, will get bigger than it already is," so dumbfounded local officials that they gave far more coverage to the creature in their welcoming speeches than to the future emperor and his consort.[29] Such miscalculations, however, were no reason to reject the general strategy. Even after the elephant died, it remained a display item. Maximilian had some of its bones turned into a three-legged stool that became a prized oddity in the Habsburg collections.

Great care went into choosing gifts as well. They were statements about the giver's means and the political significance of the recipient. In 1565, for example, Maximilian bestowed on an envoy from Florence an ornamental chain that cost 1,606 gulden; a legate from Moldavia received a necklace that year too, but it was worth only half as much.[30] Gifts brought countergifts as well, some of them very interesting. There were the "really pretty" English hounds sent him in 1566.[31] In return for some rare seeds that came from Maximilian's gardens, Landgrave William IV of Hesse-Cassel commissioned an unusual clock for the Habsburg ruler, who was known to fancy such things. After weighing the alternatives, William decided that it should be in the shape of a miniature world globe, with mechanisms that showed the motion of the planets, a calendar, and the time of day. To instruct Maximilian in operating the device, William thoughtfully sent the craftsman who had made it, along with the piece itself, to Vienna.[32]

But Maximilian was far more than a collector of curiosities. Just as genuine as his love of oddities, but even more significant for his image, was his informed passion for music. He had inherited the taste from both Maximilian I and Ferdinand I, but Maximilian II's interest was far broader. Where tal-ented artisans and musicians were concerned, he even forgot his distaste for his wife's countrymen. Spaniards predominated among his tailors, swordsmiths, gilders, and goldsmiths. The emperor was especially impressed by Spanish basses, who were prized in Bavaria as well.[33]

Performances in a wide variety of settings received Maximilian II's full support. Music was central to services in the royal chapel, an important public station for the emperor, for it was here that he demonstrated the religious associations attaching to his position as ruler. Trumpeters celebrated his appearances in secular functions as well. Chamber ensembles, in which the imperial family and its courtiers sometimes played, were another feature of his court. Such groups gave music a private importance beyond the ceremonial role it had long served in the households of rulers.[34] Maximilian not only listened to music; he read about it as well.[35] Like both his father and his uncle, he participated actively in arranging appointments to his musical establishment. He found some very good people. Though he could not entice the premier composers of his day, Palestrina and Orlando di Lasso, into his service, he engaged two of Lasso's finest students for the court chapel— Jakob Vaet and Philippus de Monte. Nor did he stop at simply engaging and listening to talented singers and instrumentalists; he supervised the storage methods for their books and scores.[36] The emperor even prescribed music as therapy for one of his sons: Archduke Wenzel was advised to listen to a kind of Spanish flute—the gaita—during an illness.[37] Maximilian himself sang alone in his chambers.[38]

Maximilian was very attentive to the pictorial and architectural side of his court as well. Rulers placed great stress on representations of themselves and their ancestors, and this emperor was no exception. Dynastic duty, however, was not the sole inspiration for his interest in art, building and rebuilding, and sculpture. Details about this side of Maximilian's life are comparatively sparse, but his steadfast commitment to these enterprises suggests the aesthetic value he found in them. A man of his time, he had little use for medieval painting, statuary, and structures. Perhaps it was for this reason that he never made the dark and decidedly old-fashioned Vienna Hofburg one of his many serious renovation projects. Maximilian prized both the works of antiquity and contemporary artists and architects who followed classical models. At least according to the testimony of his antiquary, Jacopo da Strada, the emperor much admired the latter's classicizing townhouse adjacent to the Hofburg. As with foods and wines, Maximilian ignored local sensibilities when it came to judging artistic accomplishment. The emperor charged his representatives throughout Italy with finding plants, and sketches and models of

statues, antiquities, buildings, fountains, and grottoes, to embellish his residences, inside and out.[39] Strada's particular charge was to identify worthwhile
objets d'art throughout Europe.[40] Even though Austrians resented the Italian
for both his origins and what they called intellectual arrogance, Maximilian
consulted him repeatedly.[41]

Nor did Maximilian rely exclusively on specialized advisers in making
acquisitions. He directed his collections closely and personally. Even before
he became emperor, he had supervised the purchase of decorative objects for
his household.[42] As emperor, he occasionally ordered his ambassadors to
evaluate art for him, but he himself told them what to look for. The reputation
of the painter alone was not enough to justify buying his works. When an
envoy in Venice, Veit von Dornberg, reported in 1568 that some allegorical
paintings by Titian were available, Maximilian inquired about not only the
price but the condition of the canvases. Did they show signs of age? Did the
works conform to reality? A Titian portrait of the king of Portugal had borne
no resemblance to the subject.[43] Such discrimination attracted some first-rate
artists and sculptors to Maximilian's court. The most notable among his painters, Arcimboldo, worked for Maximilian even before the archduke succeeded
Ferdinand I. Bartholomäus Spranger of Antwerp, a later addition, became
the principal artist at the court of Rudolph II. Alexander Colin, the great
Netherlander who would design Ferdinand and Maximilian's tomb in
Prague's St. Vitus' Cathedral, was also in Maximilian's service.[44]

The most immediately visible way for a ruler to establish a distinctive
public presence was through the buildings he occupied or commissioned. Just
as Maximilian rejected Ferdinand I's administrative standards, he refused to
use his father's quarters in Prague.[45] But the new emperor had compelling
practical reasons to busy himself with construction and repair projects. The
upkeep of residences was a major problem for all Habsburg princes in the
early modern period; Maximilian devoted as much attention to maintaining
buildings as he did to undertaking new ones. Careless workmanship, shoddy
materials, and flawed planning led to structural deterioration that far outpaced
routine patch-ups and remodeling. The so-called Stallburg in Vienna, conceived, though not used, as Maximilian's residence, was completed in 1565.
By 1577 it already needed a new roof.[46] Restoring the Hradčany in Prague
was a never-ending task. Most of the interior had gone up in flames in 1541,
and Ferdinand I heavily damaged the exterior by stripping defensive ordnance
from the walls for use in Hungary.[47] Ferdinand and his second son and regent
in Bohemia had intended to fix the complex. Lacking the funds to finish the

job, however, they had left it to Maximilian. Badly strapped himself, he had little choice but to do the work as cheaply as possible.[48]

Maximilian put an enormous amount of himself into his major construction and reconstruction schemes. This was especially true in the work he had done at Kaiserebersdorf and the Neugebäude on the Simmering heath, both of which were to be showcases for his collections. Competition with his cousin in Spain may have driven Maximilian as he planned these complexes; he asked to inspect plans for Philip II's Escorial palace and the king's summer establishment in Aranjuez.[49] But generally these activities were tension-free distractions from the incessant strain of political and administrative business. Here Maximilian answered to no one. Fruit trees and roses were ordered for his garden, "because we now wish it."[50] He could even forget for the moment his animosity toward Rome. Maximilian happily accepted classical sculpture for his new gardens from Cardinals Colonna and Ippolito Este, indeed, from the pope himself.[51]

As was true of his administrative schemes, however, none of his larger building and landscaping projects were fully realized. Sometimes, as in the case of the Vienna Prater, which his father had purchased, Maximilian was slow to follow through on his own orders.[52] But erratic funding and estates that balked at paying for his architectural projects, even as they sold him building materials at a profit, were the chief impediments. Even properties to which he was deeply attached, such as the so-called Katterburg, remained undeveloped. Today the site of Schönbrunn Palace, the Katterburg was a forested area to the west of Vienna that he bought in 1569 for four thousand gulden. Though he hoped to turn it into a zoological garden, he never got beyond installing an aviary, a *Fasanengarten*, and artificially stocked fish ponds.[53] Uncertain finances also made it as difficult for him to hire reliable supervisors for construction work as it did for him to find good administrators generally. Major architects, such as Andrea Palladio, avoided his service. In the absence of men with the imagination and expertise to carry out its design, an intricate complex such as the Neugebäude remained only a shell.

Yet another way for princes to enhance their reputations was to patronize letters and learning. This, too, was for Maximilian more an inclination than a duty. His pleasure in books and determination to support serious scholarship endured throughout his life. He not only read many of the volumes he received but noted mistranslations and other inaccuracies when he found them.[54] He found enough mistakes in the Spanish historian Alfonso Ulloa's history of Ferdinand I "to make correcting it as much work as writing it again."[55]

Maximilian asked Philip II's ambassador in Venice, the headquarters of Ulloa's publisher, to postpone bringing the book out until at least the most important mistakes were removed. The emperor even listed them.[56]

Maximilian respected books. In 1575, near the end of his life, the emperor would hire the first librarian for the Hofbibliothek—Hugo Blotius, a Protestant humanist from the Netherlands. The collection, gathered from Austrian, Bavarian, Rhenish, and Swiss monasteries, was rich; two-thirds of its 1,039 manuscripts were of medieval origin. It was also wildly disordered. Kaspar von Niedruck had overseen the purchase and access to the materials, but it is not clear who, if anyone, replaced him following his death in 1557. Perhaps Maximilian himself took a hand in the task. The year after Blotius began his work, he had three copyists rather than two. He had also begun to catalogue all of the holdings systematically. Financial problems took their toll on his more ambitious plans, as they did on every aspect of Habsburg administration.[57] But Blotius did suggest opening the imperial holdings for scholarly research. Maximilian approved, as long as readers were qualified and the volumes were well kept. A library that was so well endowed, yet not accessible, "was like a burning candle under a bushel whose light no one perceives."[58]

Long before he became emperor, Maximilian was cultivating the lively curiosity about the natural world and its workings that he had inherited from his father. His extended Spanish sojourn in the 1550s brought him into contact with the zoological and botanical rarities making their way back from the New World to gardens and menageries in the Iberian royal residences. All of his major retreats and residences in Lower Austria, the Hofburg included, had menageries. The emperor was also an avid horticulturist, for whom planning and keeping gardens were true recreations. In 1558, six years before Ferdinand I's death, Maximilian had already placed a major tract of plantings in the Prater. Whole families moved between his various residences to tend his flowers and shrubs. On occasion, Maximilian turned his hand to distilling oils and essences from plants. Such activities, he thought, might reveal some of nature's secrets to him.[59]

None of these activities were unusual among princes of his time, but Maximilian may have had more than an amateur's interest in pursuing them. Despite the many intellectual and aesthetic satisfactions his new position had brought Maximilian, one feature of his life had not changed—his wretched health. Some of his difficulties arose from accidents. Driving at full tilt through the streets of Vienna in August of 1563, his coach overturned, leaving

Maximilian with injuries to his left arm and right knee.[60] Some bodily strains he could not avoid. Frequent indispositions confined the emperor to Vienna, where a raw climate taxed delicate constitutions.[61] But whatever the complicating circumstances, his complaints were undeniably chronic.

Many of the scholars and scientists at Maximilian's court were there because he found their generally moderate religious views congenial to his own.[62] But the most learned among them, along with their counterparts at the court of Archduke Ferdinand in Innsbruck, had an even more useful qualification. They were often vitally interested in expanding medical knowledge to aid the suffering. Physicians from both courts consulted on medical matters.[63] They had considerable confidence in their powers, for their profession had made striking advances. Leonhart Thurneisser zum Thurn, a medical adviser who served Archduke Ferdinand for twelve years and traveled extensively in Maximilian's Bohemia and Hungary, developed charts to show how many more remedies contemporary doctors could prescribe than their counterparts in ancient times.[64] Indeed, a therapeutic strain ran through much of the cultural life at Maximilian's court. Hugo Blotius' ideal library itself, which offered prescriptions to people troubled by such problems as how to defend true religious belief, has been likened to a pharmacy.[65] According to Crato, Maximilian's most important physician, the emperor himself compiled a substantial catalogue of "experiments" to help those searching for a cure to the plague.[66]

Perhaps the most distinguished scientist to work for Maximilian was Charles L'Ecluse, a Calvinist from the Netherlands whom Crato had introduced to the emperor. Maximilian made him superintendent of the gardens in his various Austrian residences—Rossau, Kaiserebersdorf, the prospective Neugebäude, and the Hofburg itself. Clusius, as he came to be called, along with his correspondents and friends, would map and name many of the plants in the pre-Alpine region. The botanist also encouraged the cultivation of non-native species such as the tulip and the horse chestnut, which was brought back from Constantinople in 1576.[67] He was sincerely grateful for the support and stimulation he had received at Maximilian's court, and for the cooperation the emperor's agents gave him on his projects. As a young man, Maximilian himself had sent L'Ecluse a plant from Spain.[68]

But mapping the vegetation of the known world was just one element of L'Ecluse's larger program. Equally important was his commitment to understanding the pharmacological effect and uses of the botanicals which he described and catalogued. Indeed, when he could not identify some of the materials he received, L'Ecluse turned to old pharmacopoeias, as well as natural histories, for more information.[69] He had high hopes for the potential medical applications of the plants that Dutch and Frisian explorers and mercantile voyagers were bringing back from India, Africa, and America; L'Ecluse urged that pharmacists and surgeons go along on these trips. Indeed, he had already received specimens from professionals who had made such journeys. The samples were highly suggestive: a leaf from the Americas which natives smoked relieved them of head pain; parts of other plants soothed gastric upsets. The subject of possible new purgatives came up repeatedly.[70] Maximilian's was not the only Habsburg court where the ruler hoped to enlist the fauna of the New World to combat European ailments; Philip II sponsored such undertakings too.[71] But at this stage in his life, Philip's physical needs were not quite as pressing as those of his cousin.

Most closely associated with the effort to heal the emperor was Crato, the physician from Breslau, who ministered to Maximilian for the entire twelve years of the Habsburg emperor's reign. He accompanied Maximilian wherever he went; indeed, by 1575, he dined with the emperor almost daily at ten in the morning.[72] He strongly recommended moderation in all things, from diet to therapeutic and prophylactic interventions, as the key to a healthy life.[73] Where medicines were required, Crato was broadly eclectic. He was well versed in Paracelsianism, an intricate doctrine blending mysticism and chemical pharmacology, which was widely practiced at the German courts of the day, largely for its utilitarian applications.[74] The power of Christian prayer was not to be scorned, either.[75]

Crato was a crusty type, sometimes peremptory with both colleagues and students.[76] Intellectually, however, he was a careful man. Along with Clusius, he was reluctant to challenge the proposition that astrological configurations influenced the natural world.[77] He took the work of alchemists seriously when their procedures seemed to produce medically useful results.[78] In the ongoing sixteenth-century controversy over these matters, however, Crato was more inclined to look upon medical conditions as physical problems to be treated by physical means. He was very partial to the outlook of Jean Fernel, a court physician to Henry II of France, who was a vigorous advocate of observation and experimentation as a way of improving medical practice. Interested in the pharmacological uses of plants, Fernel stressed the importance of precise dosages. Like Crato, the Frenchman firmly believed that physical ailments were natural occurrences to be dealt with empirically. What the senses could not apprehend on their own terms could be left to theology. Philosophy was somewhere in between. The two physicians admired one another immensely, tossing compliments back and forth in books that they either wrote themselves or introduced for one another.[79]

Maximilian's thinking seemed to have run along these lines as well. He had a skeptical side, leading him to dismiss portents that contradicted experience, such as headless eagles that flew.[80] Though he may have harbored thoughts about the power the heavens exerted over his well-being, he did not impress his contemporaries with his interest in these matters. Heinrich von Rantzow, a North German humanist who had been in Charles V's camp at the same time as Maximilian and remained close to several Habsburgs, did not name Maximilian as a supporter of astrology in his catalogue of rulers who were adepts in the art. Charles, on the other hand, was singled out very specifically for his contributions to the discipline, as were men even closer in age to Maximilian, such as Landgrave William of Hesse.[81] Maximilian was, however, quite absorbed in the physical symptoms of his own illnesses and the various therapies prescribed to relieve them. He listened attentively to medical debates over the intense cardiac problems that afflicted him in 1571.[82]

Indeed, for Crato, as well as for the roster of other physicians at the emperor's court, Maximilian was an ongoing scientific experiment. Opinions differed rather sharply on how to cure his assorted maladies. Crato looked for ways to assist the powers of nature to heal his patient, prophylactically as well as chemically.[83] Dietary regimens, however, were an especially contentious issue. To cure a cold that afflicted the emperor in 1571, some of his doctors advised diluted wine; some recommended taking it full-strength. Only undiluted, they argued, could it whip up the animal spirits in the emperor's pituitary that would lead to his recovery.[84]

But a full-fledged cure was beyond all Maximilian's physicians. Indeed, the emperor's afflictions multiplied. In addition to the bouts of fever that seemed to befall everyone in the sixteenth century, Maximilian developed crippling gout. By 1568, he suffered badly from hemorrhoids and had experienced several more episodes of heart palpitations.[85] His preference for rich foods and heavy wines obviously did him little good. But neither did "total" purging ("per omnes partes"), even though his doctors recommended it. One such cure, reinforced by an absolute fast of fifteen days, left the emperor, by his own testimony, dreadfully feeble.[86] His belief that illness was a sign of God's anger in all likelihood reinforced the depression that often accompanied his maladies. In 1563, he had hoped that his Maker would rid him of his "weakness" once and for all.[87] By 1567, he was coming to realize that he could

never expect to be consistently healthy. Though he could jest at his pain—
he reported after one episode of gout that he had improved but was still not
prepared "to outrun" (*erlaufen*) a hare—he was at the mercy of Divine Will
in these matters.[88] If something other than illness delayed him, he stressed
the point in his apologies because it was so unusual. He had come to believe,
or so his subtext read, that all knew his body to be unreliable.[89] His very
presence, the underlying focal point of activity for everyone who served him,
was therefore more conditional than that of most men.

Maximilian's court often performed brilliantly for him. Indeed, his orchestration of it may have been his most singular accomplishment. In no
other aspect of his life were duty and preference so well integrated as in the
pursuit of his artistic and intellectual interests; indulging them was clearly
among his greatest pleasures. Both Maximilian I and Ferdinand I had made
their establishments cultural centers. In continuing the work of his predecessors, Maximilian II did much to turn sophisticated support of art and music
into a dynastic tradition. What he lacked in funds, he made up in taste and
an uncommon feel for both aesthetic and scholarly consequences. What he
requested to be done often had serious and lasting value. Blotius' work in
the Hofbibliothek was of this order. And one cannot come away from reading
L'Ecluse and his descriptions of plants and stones from all the corners of the
Habsburg *imperium* without appreciating how much his work added to understanding of the natural environment of east-central Europe.[90] But, as in
the case of the emperor's incomplete administrative reforms and building
projects, it was one thing for Maximilian's resident scientists and scholars to
describe and experiment with the world's *naturalia* but quite another to
achieve the results they hoped their research would bring. Their work, however learned, conscientious, and sincerely intentioned, would not unlock the
secret that nature had withheld from the frail Habsburg and mankind generally—new and effective remedies for mortally ill bodies.

eight

A Shaky Solidarity

No matter how troubled Maximilian's relationships with his family were, the well-being of the house of Austria and its special place in human affairs concerned him deeply. As his father's eldest male heir, he was the chief spokesman for his line in central Europe and the primary guardian of its welfare and status. Whatever its interests, grand or trivial, he attended to them carefully. Whether he was checking on the lineage of the pages in his sons' household or the layout and execution of his father's tomb at St. Vitus' Cathedral in Prague, Maximilian thought first and foremost about enhancing the good name and public standing of his family.[1] He did not suffer insults to any of its members lightly. "Treated like a whore," he commented angrily on the domestic tribulations of his sister Catherine, whose husband, King Sigismund II of Poland, had refused to consummate the union.[2]

He also enjoyed the company of other Habsburgs, even loved some of them and their attached in-laws. He was as concerned about Catherine's safety and peace of mind as he was about the dynastic implications of her problems in Poland.[3] He was very fond of his elder sister, Archduchess Anna, the wife of Albrecht of Bavaria. Infirm though he was, the emperor declared himself ready in 1568 to give her some of his blood if it could cure her of a wearisome indisposition.[4] With Albrecht, Maximilian was on genuinely affectionate terms. "[It] is a joy to me when I can do something pleasing for your grace not only in this affair but in all other possible ones," he wrote the duke in 1567, after acting as go-between in the betrothal of Albrecht's son, William, to Renate of Lorraine.[5] The emperor truly meant it. Observers at Maximilian's court noted correctly that he had a favorite among his brothers, too—Archduke Charles.[6]

Of Archduke Ferdinand, who remained sturdily self-important, the emperor was understandably wary. His tastes were even more grandiose than his elder brother's, and he could be annoyingly imperious when he indulged them. In 1565 he suggested using some of Empress Maria's Bohemian revenues to pay an organ-builder, who was to fashion an instrument without precedent in Christendom, or so the archduke claimed. The emperor grumbled when his younger brother refused to accept his corrections. Any sign that the archduke was posing a threat to Maximilian's superior authority perturbed the emperor greatly. Sometime late in 1566 or early in 1567, Ferdinand reportedly held a festive entry for himself into Innsbruck where, preceded by a herald, he appeared under a baldachin. Such ceremonies, observed his older brother, were appropriate only for reigning kings. A month or so later, Maximilian laconically noted that the "younger" cardinal of Trent had dismounted to greet the archduke while the latter remained on his horse, a sign of the Habsburg's higher status. That the emperor bothered to mention the episode at all, however, suggests that he saw something suspect in it.[7] Ferdinand, too, along with those who served him, was quick to perceive slights, both real and imagined, when Maximilian failed to communicate regarding dynastic affairs.[8]

Nevertheless, the same forces that had mended relations between Maximilian and his father prevented an irreversible falling-out between the emperor and his second brother. Both had the interests of the house of Habsburg uppermost in their minds. Maximilian welcomed—even generously acknowledged—the archduke's advice on negotiating with the Turks. Despite Maximilian's steadfast reluctance to take him fully into his confidence, Ferdinand often followed his father's advice to go the extra step in dealing with his elder brother.[9] Their exchanges even showed flashes of sympathy and understanding, particularly when illness and foreign threats were the subject. And tension between them faded completely when the two men discussed hunting and all matters connected with it.[10]

Like his father before him, Maximilian was immensely solicitous of his children's physical well-being. His acknowledged favorite was his eldest daughter, Archduchess Anna, with whom he occasionally played gambling games.[11] Close as he was to Albrecht of Bavaria, the emperor refused to lend a physician to the duke for more than three weeks when Anna required medical attention. While the archduchess was suffering from smallpox in 1567, her father postponed a meeting with the Hungarian estates until he was sure of her recovery.[12]

Maximilian's sons, especially those who remained in Austria, received the same sheltered upbringing as the emperor himself had. They developed their relations with the nobles of their lands in the *Edelknabenschule*, the pool from which the staffs of their own little households were drawn. The weather for their airings was carefully monitored, as were their companions, especially when sickness was abroad. They were not all robust. Archduke Frederick, who was especially frail, died in childhood. It was not, however, from lack of attention. The laying-on of goatskins and emeralds was prescribed for his digestive upsets. The little boys were thought to be very pretty, especially when they preceded their mother on the way to chapel for daily devotions, with the archduchesses trailing behind.[13]

Once in Madrid, Archdukes Rudolph and Ernst's relations with their father were more remote, though not impersonal. He supported them erratically; in 1567 their tutor, Adam von Dietrichstein, had yet to receive anything near the seventy-five thousand florins a year required for their expenses. The nobleman pointed out that such lapses gravely compromised Maximilian's reputation—something the emperor himself had said in other circumstances.[14] Generally, however, Maximilian was a responsible and concerned parent. He took the time to choose some very personal gifts for his sons—an illustrated calendar, for example, in 1569.[15]

After the death of Ferdinand I, Maximilian also took an active interest in the boys' education, which closely paralleled his own tastes. The archdukes read both the literature and history of antiquity and apparently absorbed some of their father's values from it. "How much discord destroys human society" was one of Archduke Rudolph's lessons for the day in 1565.[16] The future emperor and his brother were to emulate Alexander, Caesar, Charlemagne, the Henrys of Germany, Barbarossa, and Lothar the Saxon, along with their lineal forebears Rudolph I and their great-grandfather Maximilian.[17] Rudolph took his elite status seriously, describing himself and his brothers to their father as "well-born boys." They did arithmetic daily and took regular exercise. As far as Rudolph was concerned, his life added up to a great deal of work.[18] But there were many pleasures such as outings to Aranjuez, "truly a pastoral setting," as Rudolph reported to his brothers left behind in Vienna. Quantities of deer and rabbits made for splendid hunting.[19]

These and other experiences turned Rudolph into an enthusiastic Hispanophile—by 1570 he extolled his uncle's realm for its prosperity, its culture, and the purity of its faith.[20] His religious practice, however, took personal pleasure into account. After watching the public condemnation of apostates and heretics in Toledo on one occasion, Rudolph did not join the other royal children in a visit to the body of St. Eugene. He preferred, he said, to remain in a garden writing. In matters of religious politics, he was altogether flexible, at least when he was eighteen. In 1570, as Philip's forces quelled an uprising around Granada of the Moriscos, Moslems who had supposedly converted to Christianity at the turn of the sixteenth century, the archduke urged the king to forgive the rebels. Christianity was nowhere so strong as in Spain, he argued; whatever threat the Islamic community in the city posed could easily be countered by scattering these people around the country. As was so often the case when the counsel came from the German branch of his house, Philip ignored it.[21]

Maximilian's relations with the Spanish branch of his house had been tense long before he became emperor. Always somewhat uneasy at having his eldest sons at King Philip's court, notwithstanding the enticements of an Iberian inheritance, their father did not intend that they be absent from Vienna indefinitely. He worried that the archdukes would forget their German and instructed Dietrichstein to see they did not. While Archduke Rudolph sent dutiful reassurances home in 1565 on that point, Maximilian had yet other reservations about the Spanish environment.[22] It encouraged indolence, he said. By 1566, Maximilian let it be known that he might name one of the boys his governor in Bohemia, for Archduke Ferdinand was needed in the Tyrol; Archduke Ernst was the likely candidate. It was also possible that one of Maximilian's sons might follow in his uncle Ferdinand's footsteps in the Tyrol; Ferdinand's offspring by Philippine Welser would not be eligible to succeed their father. Philip did not object; if the youth was required for the position, he could go. But as in so many other affairs of state, the king put off a decision. Maximilian repeated the request in 1567, but nothing came of it.[23]

However cold-blooded dynastic policy often was, though, emotions sometimes got in the way. By 1568 Philip had become quite fond of his nephews and was reluctant to part with them.[24] The duke of Alba, a close adviser of Philip, had even more practical concerns, arguing that either of the archdukes might marry one of Philip's daughters. The young men should therefore know something about lands where they might share thrones with their wives. In Vienna, Philip's special ambassador Chantonnay and his sister Maria la-

bored to persuade the emperor that he did not need his eldest sons immediately. The Turks were not threatening; Archduke Charles could handle
Austrian affairs, Maximilian himself could take care of Bohemia.[25] Rudolph
and Ernst did not leave their uncle's household until 1571 and the birth of a
son to Philip's third wife, the emperor's favorite daughter, Anna.[26]

Maximilian himself backed away from pressing his cousin on the issue, as
a dynastic issue that had been building for several years came to a head.[27] It
had long been obvious that Philip's only living male heir, Don Carlos, was
very frail. Maximilian, among many, had seen this at first hand while serving
as his uncle's regent in Spain. Aside from the young man's health, further
shaken in 1562 by a head wound sustained in a fall, his bizarre character had
already aroused unfavorable gossip and curiosity throughout Europe. Maximilian deplored the way Philip had reared the youth—treating him with
exaggerated respect as a child, then more strictly after Carlos had been thoroughly spoiled. All this, thought the emperor, had turned the prince into his
father's enemy.[28] No one was sure how unbalanced Don Carlos really was.
Nevertheless, as Adam von Dietrichstein wrote Maximilian in 1564, what he
knew was "bad enough."[29] Carlos was pale, with one shoulder higher than
the other, the left foot longer than the right. Even worse, he stammered and
was childishly impulsive, gluttonous, and lazy. In 1567, he confessed to Dietrichstein that he was impotent, confirming what many had suspected for
years.[30] To remedy his disability, Carlos promised to drink wine, which
doubtless compounded his ailments. His spiritual life may have been equally
troublesome. In 1564, Philip wrote of his son as having been "recently converted from [a] Turk to our holy Catholic faith."[31] The prince now wished
to receive religious instruction from the prior of Guadelupe. Philip acknowledged that Carlos could be taught only "according to his capacities." Nevertheless, he hoped that the cleric would take on the task.[32]

But the emperor and Philip also wanted Carlos married, regardless of his
disabilities. Maximilian had long since decided that his Spanish second cousin
would be the husband of Archduchess Anna.[33] Himself a living witness to
the power of will over infirmity, the emperor saw Carlos's handicaps as no
bar to the match. Dietrichstein advised the emperor that marriage with Anna
might remedy Carlos's problems. The mercurial prince himself took enough
interest in the arrangement to scold his father at times for moving too slowly
on his behalf.[34]

Maximilian kept his reasons for his single-minded pursuit of the union to
himself. In all likelihood, he thought it would keep alive a possible Spanish

succession for his branch of the house of Austria.[35] Empress Maria's sons by Maximilian could legally inherit the throne, at least in Castile. Philip did have daughters, however, and such a move would all but certainly have been contested; his commitment to the match was in any case more cautious. Where marital diplomacy was concerned, the king of Spain, unlike his cousin in Vienna, was at a great disadvantage—he had few children to deploy in the service of his strategies. He was not about to be rushed into anything; his strongest trump card was Carlos, and the young man's future wife had to be chosen for maximum political usefulness. Archduchess Anna was only one of several candidates. There was also Princess Marguerite, the daughter of the late Henry II of France and Catherine de' Medici. Another was Philip's sister, Juana, once the wife of the now-dead Prince João of Portugal, who had served as regent in the kingdom for her son, Sebastian, until 1562.[36]

The French possibility put Vienna and Madrid at real odds. Maximilian, too, had nuptial interests in that kingdom. In 1565, Catherine had opened discussions about a marriage of her son, Charles IX, to Maximilian's second daughter, Archduchess Elisabeth. The emperor saw major political and military benefits in the alliance. Among them were a limit to French support of the Turks and the return of Metz, Toul, and Verdun, lost to the empire in 1552. He also wanted to thwart any future Valois candidacies for the imperial crown. Not surprisingly, the French rejected such stiff terms.[37]

Philip was much perturbed by his cousin's activities; he reminded Maximilian of his duty to keep the interests of their entire house in mind. Indeed, the Spanish monarch had his own uses for Elisabeth. Catherine de' Medici shifted her tactics with Marguerite in 1567, putting out feelers concerning a nuptial alliance with King Sebastian. Hoping to avoid near-complete French encirclement of his realm, Philip urged the emperor to offer Archduchess Elisabeth to the Portuguese ruler.[38]

Maximilian was under no illusions about the French government, which continued trying to block his discussions about establishing peace with the Turks in 1567. "Cats never give up hunting mice," as he said.[39] But he did not altogether trust either Philip's advice or the twists and turns of his marriage diplomacy, all of which the emperor read as maneuvers to keep him from a French alliance, however unlikely it was.[40] Furthermore, keeping alive the prospect of a French marriage for Elisabeth gave Maximilian leverage with his cousin regarding a decision about Don Carlos. It was not proper, the emperor argued, for the elder of his two eligible daughters to be left hanging, while the prospects for the younger advanced in Paris.[41]

Throughout these machinations, Philip was growing ever more uneasy about his son's behavior and more insistent on keeping Archdukes Ernst and Rudolph with him.[42] But no one, least of all Maximilian or his wife, who was just as eager to marry her eldest daughter off to her nephew, was prepared for the bizarre turn that events in Madrid took during February of 1568. Philip had his eccentric heir confined. The entire imperial family in Vienna fell into turmoil—Maximilian because he had no clue about Philip's motives; Maria out of sisterly sympathy for the distress that her brother's only son had brought him; and Archduchess Anna, supposedly, because she had some feeling for her cousin. As late as the third week in January, Philip had indicated that he wished the marriage of Don Carlos and his niece to go forward.[43] The king's initial accounting of the move to his relatives was so terse as to be no explanation at all; he mentioned Carlos's behavior and general life style and left it at that. He reassured his cousin that he was not angry with his son; nor did he wish to punish him. The king was certain that Maximilian would eventually see his point of view. Maximilian quickly asked for details, but since Philip remained impenetrably silent on the subject, the emperor and his wife continued to hope that the Spanish-Austrian betrothal would take place.[44]

With no evidence to the contrary, there was no real reason to doubt Philip's explanation for his decision.[45] But the more uncommunicative the king remained, the more Maximilian blamed his cousin's behavior rather than that of his son. The prince was peculiar—he might have grandiose ideas one day and forget them the next—but the emperor believed that Carlos was basically sane and certainly did not need to be confined. Maximilian may have been conflating memories of his struggles with his own father with the tribulations of his nephew.[46] Philip's silence, however, clearly offended Maximilian, and he did not like the gossip now circulating about the incident.[47] He therefore persisted. At the end of March, he offered to support the marriage of Archduchess Elisabeth in Portugal, as Philip had earlier proposed. With this concession on the table, the emperor delicately inquired what Philip intended to do for Anna, if she was not to become the bride of the Spanish prince.[48]

But still Philip delayed, both with a decision on the marriage and with his consent to his nephews' departure. He now openly said that he might not father another son; the duke of Alba thought the same.[49] Maximilian's attitude toward the king of Spain softened somewhat, particularly during the summer of 1568, when he heard that Philip believed that Don Carlos could neither govern nor sire heirs.[50] Though never completely satisfied with the king's reasons for his treatment of his son, the emperor recognized Philip's predicament. He also agreed that their opponents would be delighted to have this matter divide the house of Austria. But Maximilian still pressed for the union of Carlos and Anna, even as Philip's ambassadors worked to convince him otherwise.[51]

In the end, Maximilian got his Spanish marriage, though with different partners. On 31 August, he learned that Don Carlos was dead.[52] Whether from natural causes or violence, no one knew. Philip's report of the affair reached Vienna by the middle of September, and the emperor took it at face value. He dismissed rumors of foul play, which quickly began making the rounds; the king's only mistake, said his cousin, had been to allow his son to overindulge in food and drink immediately before his death. There was nothing to be done.[53] When, however, Philip's wife, Isabeau of Valois, died in childbirth later that year, the king looked to the German branch of his house for another bride, the same Archduchess Anna once intended for his son. Maximilian quickly accepted the proposal. The betrothal took place on 27 February 1569; the marriage by proxy, with Archduke Charles standing in for Philip, was celebrated on 4 May 1570. For his part, Maximilian yielded to the entreaties of both his wife and her brother and allowed Rudolph and Ernst to remain in Spain until 1573, when their sister gave birth to a son. Philip also gave up his opposition to a French marriage; the contract, in Spanish, between Charles IX and Archduchess Elisabeth was signed in 1570. It was not altogether impossible that the emperor would indeed gain something from the union. Though he was unable to persuade the French to begin discussions on the reincorporation of Metz, Toul, and Verdun into the empire, they did not rule out taking it up in the future.[54]

Thus, if marriage policy was a predictor of how well the two branches of the house of Austria could get along, the indications were mixed. An anonymous memorandum to Charles V had once forecast that, whether Philip or Maximilian became emperor, either would ultimately depend heavily on the other.[55] For all that the Don Carlos episode showed each man thinking primarily in terms of his own branch of their dynasty, it also suggested that Philip and Maximilian would not easily fall out. Both men came away from the question more or less content with the arrangements they had concluded. They continued to cooperate in important ways. Also a claimant to the Habsburg patrimony in central Europe, Philip realized that he had a role to play in defending it against the Turks. Appeals for help on these grounds demonstrably moved him, even though his cousin accused the king of not doing what he should.[56] Philip did send troops, good ones, to Hungary. For his part, Maximilian was ready to intercede for Philip's agents, who were scattered all over Europe, when they needed it.[57]

But the tortuous marriage negotiations over Don Carlos had also exposed the continuing mistrust between the emperor and the king of Spain. Part of the difficulty was personal. Neither man ever had enough close contact with the other for them to become each other's familiars; they therefore had little occasion to share pleasures, such as the hunt, where bonds of respect, even trust, were often formed. Maximilian remained ever vigilant for signs that Philip's interest in an imperial succession had quickened. The emperor was acutely aware that opinion of him at Philip's court was not high. Chantonnay, who made this known in Vienna, himself had little respect for Maximilian. Following the betrothal of Philip and Anna in 1569, he called the emperor a piece of paper that could be turned whatever way one wished, in this case a wholly mistaken appraisal, given the tenacity with which Maximilian had pursued the arrangement.[58] Some men might have shrugged these comments off, but Maximilian was not among them. Philip had good reasons to resent his cousin, too. The latter appeared to be intellectually and socially far more brilliant than he. Maximilian had once posed a plausible alternative to Philip in Habsburg Burgundy. In 1553, there had been rumors that the Flemish actually preferred Maximilian to himself as a territorial ruler there.[59]

But the highest bar to long-term good relations between them was religion. By the 1560s, Maximilian was ready to credit his cousin with being a pious king, a substantial concession, given his earlier slighting remarks about Philip's behavior. The emperor took great care not to send confessionally offensive ambassadors to Madrid. Adam von Dietrichstein pleased Philip so much that he made the nobleman and his son knights of Calatrava.[60] But Philip's view of Maximilian was very different. The king was no fanatic, but his Catholic faith and its place in public policy were very serious matters for him. He was as obsessive about his cousin's sacramental practices as Maximilian was about keeping Philip away from the imperial crown. Philip had never been happy with the standards of religious observance at the court in Vienna. Such advisers to the Austrian Habsburgs such as Hans Trautson, George Seld, George Gienger, and Zasius had long supported reconciliation between the religious camps in Germany, not permanent alienation, which the understanding of Christian doctrine in Madrid threatened to create. Philip had openly deplored Ferdinand I's request to permit Communion sub utraque in his lands, should it be necessary. But he did not doubt that his uncle was asking for the privilege in the sincere belief that he was furthering the welfare of the true faith. Nothing in Ferdinand's personal religious practice was suspect. While a contemporary description of his court as a monastery was exaggerated, it was a pious place indeed.[61]

Philip had no such confidence in his cousin. The earliest news of Maximilian's religious idiosyncrasies had worried the king and his advisers.[62] The emperor was not the only one of his siblings to question the traditional faith; his sister Catherine had told him that she no longer asked for the intercession of saints.[63] But Maximilian's political responsibilities were immeasurably greater; both Catholics and Protestants, therefore, scrutinized his confessional behavior minutely.

Maximilian's devotional routine had provided reassurance to his family, at least during his first years as emperor. As the empress was normally close by, he reportedly listened to Catholic preaching regularly and attended service. While traveling, he heard Mass routinely, though no sermons.[64] His public policy sometimes took an orthodox turn, as well. In 1564 he delayed, for what he called personal reasons, publication of Ferdinand I's mandate allowing general Communion in both kinds in Bohemia. When the archbishop of Salzburg announced that he would introduce the practice the same year, Maximilian demurred and tried to strike some compromise between the confessional sides instead.[65] During marriage negotiations that had been under way for some time between Archduke Charles and Elizabeth of England, Maximilian steadfastly supported his brother's request to worship privately as a Catholic so that he could live with his conscience in a Protestant country. Maximilian's tenacity on this issue, along with Elizabeth's refusal to grant religious exceptions in her realm, did much to abort the entire project.[66] Members of the emperor's establishment had to worship as traditional Catholics, and regularly. Neither Protestant nor Catholic could criticize the general moral tone of Maximilian's household, even before he succeeded his father. Blasphemy, adultery, and prostitution, he declared, all invited the wrath of God. The majordomo was to punish such lapses. He was to keep especially close watch on trabants, most likely to be young men prone to rough behavior.[67]

At times, Maximilian even had a good word to say about the Jesuits. In 1567, praising their exemplary lives, he asked Pius V to protect the order, especially a foundation they had established in Vienna.[68] As the territorial ruler of Lower Austria, Maximilian was the beneficiary of the *Bulla visitandi* granted to his great-grandfather Emperor Frederick III in 1446. This gave the Habsburgs wide control in their lands over the choice of investigators who evaluated moral practices and financial conditions in local churches and cloisters. By the sixteenth century the Church was allowing inspections to get under way even before knowing the scope of their mission. Maximilian was very active in arranging visitations to Catholic establishments, not necessarily a happy sign for the papacy, given that he was assuming more responsibility for the quality of religious and intellectual life at these institutions. But regardless of his increased powers, Maximilian suggested nothing after an inspection in 1567 to jolt sensibilities either in Madrid or among papal officials. Though he advised that rules be administered with enough flexibility to attract young people to cloistered vocations, his basic recommendation was that traditional regulations be allowed to stand. In a meeting with Austrian prelates in Vienna on 22 December that year, he made it clear that, in accordance with a policy dictated by the Council of Trent a few years earlier, he would not tolerate married clergy.[69] Nor would he ever give in easily to the demands of Protestants in the Austrian estates for religious concessions, even though he needed their financial assistance.

But some of his earlier attitudes had not changed, and his behavior fueled suspicions among those whose religious convictions ran along narrow paths. This was particularly true of Philip II. Maximilian continued to criticize the Roman Curia and its rigid response to Protestantism. He applied the decrees of the Council of Trent very selectively, calling them the product of special interests.[70] This view was not unusual among the secular rulers of the day— Philip himself enforced Tridentine pronouncements at his own discretion. But in the context of Maximilian's other aberrations, the emperor's objections to the outcome of the conclave in 1563 gave his critics one more reason to doubt his commitment to Catholicism. And given his basic outlook, one could hardly blame the king of Spain for doubting the trustworthiness of his cousin's religious principles. For all Dietrichstein's efforts to convince Philip otherwise—he reminded the king that Charles V had agreed in the Augsburg Interim of 1548 to allow the practice temporarily—the king of Spain remained steadfastly opposed to clerical marriage, tactical or otherwise. Maximilian's support of a celibate clergy in 1567 rang a bit hollow when only three years before he had written his ambassador in Rome, Prosper D'Arco, that permitting a married priesthood would improve religious observance in his own lands.[71]

Nor did Maximilian trouble himself with confessional niceties when making court, educational, and ecclesiastical appointments. By 1570, Francisco de

Córdoba, who had been so encouraged by the new emperor's behavior at the outset of his reign, said that Maximilian now surrounded himself with heretics. What Catholics were there were only lukewarm in matters of faith. And though Maximilian might praise the Jesuits for their piety, he deplored their influence on his devout sister, Archduchess Magdalena, in the Tyrol. He thought that her association with the order made her overly eager to condemn to hell even those who believed they were saved.[72] He considered a Jesuit cloister Magdalena wanted built in Hall, outside of Innsbruck, a waste of money. Two other structures were under preparation for them in the same small area, and he saw no need to support a third.[73]

No member of his house, in short, could say for sure where he stood on the Catholic-Protestant controversy, but all of them, especially in Spain, wanted to know. From 1564 to Maximilian's death in 1576, his religious behavior was reported, analyzed, criticized, and often defended in a voluminous correspondence between Vienna and Madrid. Philip, his ambassadors, the empress and her confessor, even Maximilian himself—all weighed in vehemently and often on the subject.[74] What was the content of the preaching at the imperial court? What were the religious leanings of Maximilian's advisers? How frequently, if ever, did the emperor take Communion? How often did he confess, and before whom? Dietrichstein, Spanish ambassadors, and even Zasius, set to the task by Philip, toiled mightily over the emperor's soul in the hope of getting him to commit himself formally and publicly to Catholic orthodoxy. If Maximilian could be brought to that point, thought the king of Spain, his cousin's inner conviction would take root and grow. For his part, Maximilian would stand his ground on matters of doctrine essential to him. He insisted on his personal right to commune in both kinds. Philip's fears were groundless, he said, the product of rumors spread by people who wanted to divide their house.[75]

No one suffered more from conflict between the Spanish and German branches of the house of Habsburg than the empress. Maximilian had remained very close to Maria; indeed, he trusted her as much as he could trust anyone. She dutifully accepted her subordinate status and the restrictions Maximilian placed on her, even when she wanted to do otherwise. Like her husband, she could be temperamental—in 1567 she feared giving birth, even while wishing for a child, especially a daughter.[76] But she was clearly Maximilian's confidante. She supped alone with him in the evening, and each spent a considerable amount of time in the other's chambers, the location being determined by the emperor's health.[77] Philip consulted with them both on dynastic affairs. His ambassadors sought her advice before approaching the emperor. She was frequently present when important matters were being aired; she sometimes terminated the exchanges by announcing that she was fatigued and wanted to rest, a graceful way, certainly, of sparing Maximilian prolonged contact with Chantonnay.[78]

Like her great-aunt Margaret and aunt Mary, both regents in the Netherlands, she was politically shrewd. The empress's involvement in her husband's affairs grew over time. In 1572, they held joint audiences with Hungarian bishops and other notables in the kingdom.[79] As Chantonnay and Maximilian explored the pros and cons of marrying Charles of Styria to Elizabeth I of England, it was Maria who doubted that the queen would tolerate Charles's private Catholic devotions—dissimulation, the empress called it. She also pointed out that Elizabeth had already given public proof of her Anglicanism. Agreeing to such arrangements for the archduke could lead to a dangerous revolt in her lands, which would eventually undermine the interests of the house of Austria. The French, the empress further noted, could put such developments to good use.[80] Maria was also well-informed about many of Philip's policies, if only from listening to the conversations between her brother's ambassadors and her husband.[81]

Nevertheless, Maria's Spanish connections also increased the tensions between Vienna and Madrid. Loyal to Maximilian though she was, the empress maintained a separate correspondence with Philip that kept him abreast of life at the Viennese court. Brother and sister were mutually sympathetic as personalities and intellects, especially in matters of faith. Having first made the acquaintance of the Jesuits in Spain, Maria became the special patroness of the order in Vienna. Philip trusted her enough to advise Chantonnay to consult with her on such sensitive questions as a request that came in 1568 from the Lower Austrian estates for recognition of the Augsburg Confession.[82] Philip had a considerable hold on her—she received an allowance from him of twenty thousand ducats, for which she was profoundly grateful. This, in addition to her powerful religious convictions, made her most cooperative with the regime in Madrid. Strongly hinting that were were certain matters she did not want to reach her husband's ears, she often told things secretly to Luis Vanegas de Figueroa, the second of her brother's special envoys in Vienna.[83]

Maximilian could do little about this situation; his marriage and its possible Spanish inheritance meant a great deal to him. Nor could he remove another constant irritant—his wife's Spanish household. Because Maria's German never improved much, she remained extremely dependent on servants from her home country. Even her German-born children had to communicate with her in Spanish.[84] In his search for information, Philip II consulted sources far beyond his immediate court and ambassadors, and Maximilian, with some justification, believed that many on his wife's staff were spies. The emperor, of course, had his contacts in Madrid. Philip's governor in Valencia, the count of Benavente, whom Maximilian regarded as one of his supporters in the imperial succession, acted as a useful informant.[85] But where religion was concerned, Philip had little to hide. Maximilian's vulnerability on religious matters, however, encouraged his cousin to spy on him relentlessly. In the interests of maintaining cordial relations with his wife, Maximilian had no alternative to living in close proximity with Spaniards whom he disliked intensely.

Thus, while Habsburg dynastic machinery could function effectively, it also contained serious stress points. In addition to the financial complications that division of the family patrimony in central and east central Europe had created, lines of separation on matters of religion had begun to deepen. Maximilian refused to commit himself to the Church of Rome; yet his Spanish relatives, even his wife, would have no great confidence in him unless he did. It was hardly an environment conducive to smooth family relations, even without other major disagreements between its branches. When these arose, as they did, the unity of the house of Austria could create as many difficulties for its members as it did advantages.

nine

Defeated at Arms, Broken in Spirit

In no area did Maximilian II's administrative problems do more damage than in the ongoing Habsburg confrontation with the Turks. The enemy from the east had acquired a timeless familiarity for him—the "hereditary foe" (*Erbfeind*), he called them.[1] Though driven away from Vienna itself in 1529, Sultan Süleyman the Magnificent had spread his rule as far west as Buda and Pest by 1542. He was also the tributary overlord of the easternmost third of Hungary, Transylvania, ruled by a nominally elected duke, or voivode. The incumbent by 1564 was John Sigismund Zápolya, a truculent and impetuous man whose father had been Ferdinand I's rival for the crown of St. Stephen.

Ferdinand had begun erecting a defensive border against the Turks, which would eventually slow their expansive drive. Maximilian's contemporaries had no way of knowing this, especially when they and subsequent generations exaggerated the sultan's control over his empire as a way of underscoring the superiority of Christian freedom. But Süleyman was indeed a daunting challenger for the Habsburgs. Where Maximilian was conspicuously weak, his counterpart in Constantinople was strong. At a time when the Habsburgs and many of their counterparts in the West were struggling to bring system and greater central authority to their governments, the sultan had gone a long way toward doing so. The military implications of these accomplishments were widely recognized by Habsburg ambassadors to Constantinople as well as others. They often remarked on the sharp contrast between the relatively brisk way in which Süleyman made and delivered policy and the protracted bargaining required to move the imperial German diet into action. The Ottoman ruler's officials received systematic training for their jobs. An orderly method of taxing peasants and populations grouped as millets, that is, by religious affiliation, supported local government and legal institutions. Süleyman had something close to a standing army.[2]

Turkish expansion followed a predictable pattern. Local societies and economies were first weakened by small-scale skirmishing campaigns. As time went by, fortresses went up in key locations, though large stretches of terrain remained unoccupied for some time. Gradually, however, Ottoman government spread to these areas; the sultan resumed large-scale campaigning and finished off his work of conquest. Hungary had not conformed to this model exactly. But observers saw that Turkish military organization had played a major role in subduing the kingdom and that it threatened to bring further success. Worse yet, from the Habsburg perspective, some Protestants, along with abjectly poor Catholic peasants and serfs, had concluded that Ottoman rule was preferable to what the house of Austria and traditional local landlords had to offer.[3]

Whatever clashes took place between Maximilian and the Turks thus came at a moment when the latter's administrative and military effectiveness had peaked.[4] Encounters with German troops up to the middle of the sixteenth century had only improved Ottoman combat readiness. The musketeers and arquebusiers who defended Vienna in 1529 had inflicted heavy casualties on the sultan's army. Since then, Süleyman had enlarged his forces, trained them for greater mobility, and equipped them with the newest ordnance. For his part, Maximilian was working with essentially the same war-making machinery that his father had used during his long and frustrating quest for a decisive victory over Süleyman's forces. Ferdinand I had always been able to cobble together sizable armies. But to do it, he had to call upon the German territories for aid, a very cumbersome procedure. Each direct vassal of the emperor was bound to give his sovereign a contingent of troops, the number to be determined by the size of the land a given prince ruled. Mobilization took place in stages, with very small increments at each step. The so-called Austrian circle was responsible for 120 cavalry and 600 foot soldiers the first time around. Should more men be required, second and third mobilization quotas were then filled. Their pay came from special taxes, "Roman Months," with the amount determined by the actual number of men under arms and the length of their service. The real challenge was to supply these forces and discipline them, especially when they were in the field. Mutinies were routine, even among the well-trained Spanish troops prized by both Ferdinand and Maximilian. Between 1572 and 1607 during the war in the Netherlands, they turned on their commanders forty-five times.[5]

In Hungary and the Austrian lands, to which the Habsburgs, as territorial rulers, could turn for additional help, the estates organized provincial levies and set the time of service. Depending on the gravity of the situation, they were expected to fund every thirtieth, tenth, or fifth soldier, who served usually from three to six months. Practically speaking, this meant a summer and then some, a short tour of duty, to be sure, but one that made a certain kind of sense. The estates could not always raise the taxes they voted in, which were based on income rather than property value. Maximilian turned to his lands for mercenaries, most of whom had little experience. Their foreign counterparts, especially those from Spain and Italy, rarely showed up in the numbers promised.[6]

At his death, Ferdinand had left a standing army of about nine thousand scattered around the Hungarian borders. Maximilian had thoughts of continuing the practice; the imperial estates, however, concerned about maintaining some control over the military plans of their sovereign, did not support him. Therefore, German monies were usually slow in coming. Campaigns often started before the imperial paymaster (*Reichspfennigmeister*) had collected the sums authorized for previous wars, leaving the officer no alternative but to borrow, often on his personal credit. It was George Ilsung's private resources, not exceptional administrative gifts, that led Maximilian to choose him for this position. Nor did the court war council (*Hofkriegsrat*) control these funds; all financial matters went through the court treasury, which was careful to see that enough resources were on hand to cover expenses.[7]

The war council presented a special, and unfortunately sensitive, case of the pervasive disorder Maximilian had diagnosed in his father's government. His first large-scale order for his officialdom in 1564 attacked the casual work habits and security arrangements in the body. Behavior problems abounded— "lewdness, screaming, scolding, annoying, or frivolity" were explicitly forbidden.[8] Interpersonal relations were no better—officials were neither to plot, presumably against one another, nor to circulate rumors. Little seems to have come of these prescriptions, however. By 1566, Maximilian concluded that the council required his personal supervision. He did not trust its advice.[9]

Vienna's standards of military administration also bothered the emperor's chief commander in Hungary, Lazarus von Schwendi. He had won a few skirmishes against Ottoman forces in the east of the kingdom during 1565 and 1566. Though it irritated the Turks mightily, his success had attracted much attention in Europe. Schwendi, who was of Swabian origin, was a man to whom Maximilian listened closely. Seasoned in the armies both of Charles V and Ferdinand, he was in some ways Maximilian's *Doppelgänger*. Both men prized political stability. They shared generally irenic religious views, which made them suspect in Catholic circles. They had the same broad cultural interests and innovative turn of mind. Schwendi had acquired a solid grounding in humanistic studies in Basel and Strasbourg; Maximilian's librarian Hugo Blotius was the tutor of the general's children. Though Schwendi's respect for the rules of confidentiality was as casual as that of anyone else in Habsburg service, he was a sounding board for many of Maximilian's political and religious ideas, even after he had left the emperor's service.[10]

Schwendi was often torn between contradictory military imperatives. Like generals before and since, he always needed more of everything—men, money, or matériel. When his quantitative standards were met, qualitative matters bothered him.[11] He believed that great masses of undisciplined and poorly organized men were little better than no army at all. His recipe for successful warfare followed Maximilian's general prescriptions for administrative improvement—a trained staff for the Hofkriegsrat and a standing army that was reliably provisioned, financed, and supported with experienced technical personnel. Schwendi urged that military financing be separated from the Hofkammer and that the Hofkriegsrat project its expenditures for at least a year. Like Maximilian, though, he often had no choice but to improvise; and like other commanders of his time, Schwendi often borrowed to keep his forces together.[12]

Maximilian had one great advantage in dealing with the Turks at the outset of his career. He had already played an active and successful role in Hungarian-Ottoman affairs even before his father died.[13] The sultan's court had not thought much of Ferdinand I. Only when Charles V in Spain gave his brother his full support, which was a rare occurrence, did the Turks take the younger man seriously. Their reaction to Maximilian was very different. The news that he was now emperor hit them "like hailstones on their throats," in the words of a communiqué to the new emperor in October of 1564.[14] His well-publicized interest in military affairs worried them, as did the good opinion both the Hungarians and Germans already had of their new ruler as a leader and strategist. An inept mock siege celebrating Maximilian's arrival in Vienna following his coronations in 1563 had not altered these views.[15]

Süleyman, now quite feeble, Ferdinand, and Maximilian had concluded a truce in 1562. Its provisions, however, made future conflict all but inevitable. Each of the belligerents had the right to improve his fortifications behind the treaty lines. The agreement also stressed the need for timely execution of its financial provisions, which obligated the Habsburgs to deliver thirty thousand ducats annually to the sultan. But the peace for which the house of Austria was paying in 1562 was broken locally many times during the following two years. Maximilian responded by delaying payment indefinitely. One could not, he explained, send money along routes that Ottoman-backed marauding had made unsafe.[16]

Nevertheless, for all these flash points, neither side was eager for combat in 1564. Maximilian's Hungarian council, in the past eager to have the Habsburgs pursue the reunification of the kingdom aggressively, were pleased when Maximilian wrote Süleyman that he wanted an enduring, not an eight-year, peace between them. The sultan seemed well disposed toward receiving an embassy from Vienna and vowed to uphold the 1562 agreement.[17] Even before Ferdinand died, Maximilian had assured the Turks of his pacific intentions, and Germany was his first concern once he succeeded his father. In 1565 the sultan was preoccupied with taking Malta.[18]

But this superficial lull did not mean that the causes for open war had disappeared. The most likely among them was the position of Transylvania. While Süleyman had personally renounced the territory in the 1562 accord, no one was sure how far John Sigismund's claims extended to other areas of Hungary. His general truculence made the situation even more explosive. Both the Habsburg and Ottoman sides knew this and had worked at forging some kind of alliance with Zápolya. Within the month after Ferdinand had died, Hungarian councillors urged the new emperor to incorporate the voivode formally into any peace with the Turks. Not too many years before, Süleyman's son and eventual heir, Selim, had proposed a confederation to John Sigismund. Süleyman had rejected the idea, but his views were not binding on his successors.[19]

Maximilian had also interceded several times on John Sigismund's behalf with Emperor Ferdinand and expected some gesture of goodwill from the Transylvanian leader. Such hopes faded in 1564 when Zápolya, on his own initiative, attacked Habsburg castles in Hungary. Local defenders beat him off, thereby reinforcing the general impression that the new emperor was not to be trifled with. Generally comfortable with military issues, Maximilian was much encouraged. He threw himself into gathering an army to counter the voivode's challenge more decisively. Confidence surged among others in the Habsburg camp, most notably Archduke Ferdinand.[20]

The next round of skirmishing was equally heartening. Despite poor supplies of men, equipment, and horses, Maximilian's troops, led by Schwendi and Erasmus Mager von Fuchstaat, commander of the fortress of Szatmár, not only held the Habsburg positions but captured the strongholds of Tokaj and Szerencs from Zápolya. John Sigismund was pushed not only well east of the Tisza River, but to the peace table. An armistice was reached in March 1565. Complaints did come from Constantinople about the seizures, and Süleyman began to mobilize. But he did not seem to have ruled out a negotiated settlement of differences. Both Zápolya and Maximilian were his tributaries, and what truly angered him was that both men were cavalierly trafficking in his lands without consulting him. Indeed, Süleyman believed Maximilian had the greater grievance and promised to force the voivode to cede formally what the Habsburgs had taken.[21]

Once-timid advisers now urged Maximilian to entrench himself further in Hungary. Although they balked at the expense of continuing the campaign, his Lower Austrian provincial council did not want him to fall back from the Tisza. Schwendi regretted that the outermost Habsburg defense line lay so deep inside the kingdom, but he did not wish to withdraw. As he saw it, there could be no peace as long as John Sigismund was alive. Whatever fighting the commander had to do was better carried on from positions he now held. Schwendi did not advise extended pursuits.[22] Indeed, he was full of warnings about Maximilian's limited military options and still hoped for some negotiated stay of hostilities. One should, as he put it, avoid scaling great heights because of the steep fall one could take. Archduke Ferdinand recommended using the talks to buy time for building up the imperial army and refining its tactics.[23]

Maximilian did indeed open discussions, which an astrologer had predicted would be successful.[24] The seer could not have been further from the mark. When the talks went badly, both sides signaled their displeasure by limiting the movement of each other's ambassadors or actually imprisoning them. Such maneuvers only provoked further discord and delay.[25] Bad communications reinforced the suspicion each party had of the other. Certainly, the Turks had good cause to question Maximilian's good faith. The emperor sent two special missions to Constantinople in 1565 and 1566. Neither carried the tribute that Süleyman expected. At one point Maximilian commented that he kept up these contacts only to clear himself from blame for resumption of hostilities.[26] Süleyman and his grand vizier, Mohammed Sokolli, began to aid John Sigismund more actively.[27]

Maximilian's inconsistent responses, now provocative, now temperate, reflected the wide range of counsel he was hearing and continued to receive. His general position was not wholly unfavorable, as his brother Charles pointed out. Unlike any of their immediate predecessors, the current generation of Austrian Habsburgs was at war with the Turks alone. All of Italy, save Venice, was armed against the infidel; the king of Spain was harassing Süleyman in the Mediterranean. Archduke Ferdinand had a grand strategy that called for striking some kind of alliance with the Persians, a long-standing nuisance on the sultan's borders, and using Spain to neutralize the Turkish fleet at sea.[28] No one pursued the idea for very long—indeed two thousand Persians appeared in the army Süleyman eventually brought with him.[29] But such schemes betokened active military planning in Vienna. More oblique encouragement was forthcoming from the estates of Lower Austria, which doubted that the calm of Ferdinand I's last years would endure for long, given the behavior of both John Sigismund and the Turks.[30]

Schwendi himself saw both sides of the issue. He questioned the wisdom of major offensives, yet he argued for policies that made full-scale war a likely outcome. He counseled Maximilian to keep the new outposts he had won at the Tisza, even as the Turks complained about the loss of them. While recommending that the emperor hurry peace negotiations along, Schwendi urged him to begin military preparations. His theory was that a strong military posture would force more favorable terms from the Porte. The buildup required to make this policy credible, however, easily translated into a sign of insincerity, especially when Maximilian would not yield his newly won spoils. Such behavior certainly made John Sigismund's claims that the Habsburgs would campaign further in eastern Hungary all the more plausible.[31]

By November of 1565, Süleyman had decided to launch a major strike into Hungary, though it took him some time to organize it.[32] Maximilian spent the winter of 1566 trying to raise the aid from abroad that his estates and his commanders claimed he needed. Ordinarily, first campaigns were the most important ones a sixteenth-century ruler would lead and were drawn up with utmost care. Their outcome forecast future successes or failures and did much to establish a leader's general reputation. Maximilian's renown was even more on the line, because Schwendi had persuaded him to lead his armies as well as to organize them. Acutely aware of what was at stake, the emperor threw himself wholeheartedly into preparing for a not unwelcome challenge.[33]

Medieval castles were still the key defensive units in the Habsburg portions of Hungary. These were neither outfitted nor designed, however, to withstand sieges of more than a few days, especially when heavy artillery joined the assaults. The empire had contributed to the upkeep of the units but done little else, even though Germany was, after the Austrian lands themselves, directly in the line of Turkish attack.[34] Maximilian had long identified himself as a protector of German interests and carefully cultivated the Protestant princes with the future of military aid against Süleyman in mind. None of these blandishments speeded the deliberations of the Diet of Augsburg in 1566, which bogged down in a dispute over the place of Calvinism in the empire's confessional makeup. Though Maximilian eventually got most of the help he wanted—the elector of Saxony promised a thousand cavalry for three months, and other members of the estates were equally generous—it was a discouraging experience. Given its men and material resources, he commented bitterly, Germany could be very powerful were it united.[35]

More ominously, the imperial estates made plain in 1566 that they would not support Habsburg military ventures much longer. Maximilian's relations with the princes in these matters, therefore, seemed destined to be as conditional as those of his forefathers.[36] The rest of Christendom was no more responsive. Philip II, though well disposed toward Maximilian on the issue, was carrying a load of prohibitive debt, swollen by the expenses of his armada in the Mediterranean. At first there were hints that anywhere between a hundred thousand and two hundred thousand ducats would be forthcoming.[37] But none appeared, a decision shaped substantially by the opinion at the Spanish court that Süleyman was too old and weak to break the peace.[38]

Those who did contribute named their price. In Florence, Cosimo de' Medici agreed to extend a loan of two hundred thousand ducats, but only if Maximilian sanctioned his elevation to the rank of grand duke, a step Pius IV was supporting for his own political purposes. Maximilian had to give that matter some thought; the gesture had ramifications for both the Spanish and the Austrian branches of his house in Italy. Cosimo wanted to be an archduke, but this would have offended both of Maximilian's brothers. Johann Ulrich Zasius came up with the substitute title of grand duke, and Maximilian went along with the proposal, though he left open a number of ways he could extract himself from the arrangement. The pope and Genoa did, however, promise fifty thousand ducats. Lucca would give something too, but no sum was mentioned. Maximilian did his part, allowing goods from these areas to pass toll-free through Austrian customs.[39]

Inclined to immerse himself in detail of any kind, Maximilian had been micromanaging his campaign for some time. Indeed, he probably had little choice in the matter, for even in the final stages of preparation, he could not find capable people, especially any who were familiar with the Turks. He worked tirelessly to hold logistical and other support at optimum levels. Defeat, should it befall him, would not be due to slovenly planning and unnecessary expense. He tried not to take on any more people than he could use at any time.[40] To keep his forces from being stripped of cavalry and dray animals, he forbade the export of horses from Bohemia.[41] An adequate and wholesome food supply was essential; Christoph Teufel, the chief provisioner (*Proviantmeister*) was to determine the best times for purchasing these goods in Austria above and below the Enns. Overruns in the baking of bread were to be avoided. Subordinate buyers were to be supervised to forestall private profiteering. All transactions, even the most minor, had to have a counter-signatory.[42]

Through March and April of 1566, with news coming from Schwendi that he had neither the money nor the equipment to keep his forces from plundering an already depleted countryside, Maximilian labored to correct these and other problems. But for all his efforts, an air of improvisation hung over the entire undertaking. Tactical issues were rarely addressed, for the emperor was not sure of how big his own army would be; nor did he know the size of the Turkish force or, most important of all, whether Süleyman would lead it himself.[43]

Maximilian did have access to some reliable external sources of information about the Turks: the German princes and his own ambassadors. Among the latter, Franz von Thurn in Venice was especially sharp when it came to evaluating intelligence that came his way.[44] Generally speaking, however, much of Maximilian's knowledge of his enemy was the product of an erratic and disorganized flow of data gathered by people of varied, if any, training.[45] Few of his sources were fluent in Turkish; when he did find people minimally qualified to serve as translators on missions to Constantinople, he had trouble paying them.[46] Zealous subordinates could hold up dispatches from Constantinople to find out whether the emperor preferred to have the documents translated before they were forwarded to Vienna.[47] The Turks suffered from similar problems, making relations between the belligerents even more uncertain. Letters to Süleyman's officials could lie unanswered if no one was about who could read Latin.[48] Like every one of his princely counterparts, Maximilian had spies; however, they complained bitterly at the nonchalant way he directed them to send their findings, which were often worked into appendices of letters ostensibly dealing with commercial affairs and sent as mercantile correspondence.[49]

The emperor, therefore, was working with cloudy and inconsistent reports about Ottoman operations throughout the first half of 1566. As early as January, a massive offensive from Constantinople seemed imminent. But what was Süleyman's precise target?[50] And would the Ottoman ruler lead his troops personally? The sultan's health had been a topic of morbid speculation for several years. On so-called good authority, he was dead as early as October of 1564. But by 1565 and 1566 Maximilian's ambassador in Constantinople and others were saying that Süleyman himself would campaign. Yet the envoy, Albert De Wyss, was not absolutely sure; nor did he know when the Turkish armies would begin to move westward—perhaps, he said in 1566, by the end of March. By spring, however, Süleyman's physical condition had worsened, forcing him to remain in his capital at the end of April.[51] Nevertheless, the very possibility that the Ottoman ruler would be on hand influenced Schwendi in persuading Maximilian to command the imperial force personally. Indeed, the general wanted all three Habsburg brothers on the scene to maintain order in the ranks.[52]

By the end of July, with troop contingents drifting into Vienna, Maximilian was aware that a powerful Turkish army was on the march. This he had anticipated. He was clearly taken off guard at the beginning of August, however, by the news that not only was Süleyman leading his troops, but that the Ottoman ruler had laid siege to the fortress of Sziget as well. Someone claimed to have heard the sultan vow that he would either conquer the fortress or die before it.[53] Maximilian lamely hoped that the stronghold would not fall too quickly; he would do what he could to aid the "upright folk" who were its defenders.[54] His personal stake in the conflict was high. He would do all he could, he assured his brother-in-law, to support the effort so that "many should see, that nothing will be neglected; reputation can be endangered and damaged in such a way."[55]

The behavior of many troops in and around Vienna did not bode well for the campaign to come. The rowdy men stole horses and wagons and probably much more as well; people were sometimes routed from their homes. Doors to wine cellars went up in flames as well. Maximilian noted somewhat cryptically to himself that the shooting within camps should be stopped once guard duty began. And he was still not altogether certain of the size of the force at his command. He still did not have a quartermaster. Come what might, however, they would be fed; his chief provisioner talked of surpluses.[56] He therefore resolved to move into Hungary, along with his brother Ferdinand as his chief lieutenant. The latter arrived in Vienna on 9 August with his units. Three days later, "with brilliant numbers in the name of God," they left the Hofburg and went down the Kohlmarkt to the heart of the city—St. Stephen's square and the Wollzeile—and thence eastward. An array of other princes and noblemen accompanied them; more joined along the way—Bohemians and Moravians and a force led by Günther von Schwarzburg. All in all, they numbered somewhere around 86,300 men—an enormous assemblage.[57]

But on arriving in Hungary, they did little more than sit there for almost two months—first in Magyarovár, then in Győr. September came, but Maximilian still had no firm insight into Turkish movements. Until the end of the month, the emperor was wholly unaware that the sultan had died in the field on 4 September, four days before the capture of Sziget. Indeed, Maximilian did not learn this until the middle of October.[58] The prolonged waiting sapped camp discipline, which in any case had worsened when supplies grew short. Angry soldiers turned on one another.

To keep national animosities at bay, Maximilian placed the Germans as far as he could from the Hungarians and Italians. Archduke Ferdinand was supposed to police these arrangements, but it was Maximilian himself who rode back and forth daily from one unit to another to preserve order. All this was a clear signal that without his initiative, nothing would get done. Even when he was clearly in evidence, though, Italian and German troops got into fights.[59] Nor were Maximilian's best commanders on the scene—Schwendi was in Transylvania; Miklos Zrinyi, a veteran Hungarian captain, was leading the force defending Sziget.[60] Their talents were needed in those positions, too, but the emperor did not trust all of the officers in the field with him. "He is a dangerous and false man," noted Maximilian in his diary of Philip von Reiffenberg—a man who said one thing away from Maximilian, another when he was close by.[61]

Maximilian's immediate challenge was to help lift the siege under way in Sziget. Both he and Zrinyi thought that they had some time. The captain believed that his fortress was well supplied. The emperor had calculated that Sziget, surrounded as it was by swampland, would be hard to take. Encamped in Raab, he weighed contradictory advice from his various military advisers. Some urged him to push on; others counseled caution. Clearly perplexed, Maximilian deferred a decision. He still gave some thought to making peace. Maximilian was not altogether kindly disposed toward Zrinyi, who had excused himself from the Habsburg's Bohemian coronation in 1562 because the invitation came on too short notice. But he was a brave and tenacious man, as he would soon prove. Maximilian finally did send aid to him. It arrived too late, however, owing to some negligence in the emperor's chain of command. Prolonged drought enabled the Turks to move across the land far faster than the emperor had estimated, and the fortress fell on 8 September.[62] Even as the defense of Sziget was still holding its own, Maximilian and those counseling him considered other plans of action. Someone suggested attacking Székesfehérvár in Transylvania itself, even though John Sigismund had not formally come to the sultan's aid. The chief officers, however, deemed this plan too risky, for the days were already getting short, the nights long and dark; moreover, the trails through the forests were narrow, and water was scarce along the way.[63]

Maximilian himself decided to lay siege to Esztergom, then in the hands of the Turks. He alone was fully committed to the operation. The catastrophe that unfolded was therefore largely his responsibility. As the army moved into position, Maximilian's personal troops were positioned behind the units of two leaders most opposed to the maneuver—Count Günther von Schwarzburg and Philip von Reiffenberg. Their men were in a sullen mood; they had mutinied over lack of pay, even though Maximilian claimed that there was money for them. But they refused to move. The whole plan collapsed; by October, the troops disbanded with the maximum possible disorder. Pleading illness, Archduke Ferdinand precipitately left the field on the fifteenth of October, despite his brother's entreaties and appeals to his honor. Ferdinand was prone to the deep moodiness that afflicted many members of his house, so that he may have been acting on no more than a wild impulse. But Maximilian sourly attributed such bizarre behavior to rumors that the archduke's wife, Philippine Welser, had been unfaithful. "Would that the bitch were stuffed in a sack and nowhere to be found."[64] He blamed a rampage among Bohemian and Moravian contingents on the archduke's irresponsible departure, a charge that was probably unfair. Nevertheless, Ferdinand's exit "hatt nix geholfen" (didn't help at all), as the despairing emperor put it. Indeed, for one very bitter moment, Maximilian suspected that Ferdinand, who was von Schwarzburg's immediate superior, might himself have provoked the rebellion among those troops to get to his wife all the sooner.[65]

A final, and equally chaotic, attempt to rescue the expedition by driving the Turks from Székesfehérvár ended ignominiously, as well. Corporal punishment, Maximilian thought, might bring his forces back into line, but it was impossible to administer. He ordered them to his borders and other key defensive outposts. His own camp he broke late in October. Near Komorn, the emperor was assailed by heart palpitations, but he returned to Vienna on the twenty-ninth of the month. On the thirty-first, the city had the first snow of the winter season yet to come.[66]

Maximilian did not give up immediately. Schwendi advised him to do so as early as December of 1566—"it is all treachery," the emperor commented bitterly in his diary.[67] He considered approaching the German princes again for aid; many of them had yet to pay their share for the recent campaign. But Maximilian was not quite certain of how to go about it—in writing, by calling a meeting of the imperial circles or some other subsidiary authority short of a formal imperial diet. And the search for good personnel went on—a chief weapons master and a shipmaster, the last one having turned out to be nasty, careless, and selfish. Could his current commanders be used more effectively elsewhere? But even as he pushed himself to think these matters over quickly, the emperor admitted that he lacked many things needed for a future campaign.[68] Schwendi had been suffering since the middle of October with pain and colic; his recovery was in doubt. Even if he improved, he was demanding very substantial changes in Maximilian's military administration before he would agree to stay on. Among other things, he wanted the appointment of a general war commissar, a *Kriegsobrist*, who would direct the staffing of all military offices.[69] Nothing was done; the Swabian commander retired in 1568, dismayed about conditions at Maximilian's court and the people in it.[70] Most important of all, the emperor's resources for such undertakings were growing ever tighter. By 1568, he would ask the estates of Lower Austria to take over his debt of two million gulden, along with service that amounted to five hundred thousand gulden more.[71]

Maximilian did turn occasionally to improving his intelligence gathering operations. In 1567, Archduke Ferdinand recommended that a mission going to Constantinople to discuss yet another peace initiative take along both someone knowledgeable about warfare and fortifications and a skilled artist. They were to view and sketch Turkish military installations along the Danube, then analyze what they saw when they could work undetected at night. Further inside the Ottoman lands, they were to note and draw topographical features, such as mountains, valleys, waterfalls, and forests.[72] Maximilian agreed, but this was no signal of systematic reform. To the end, his information-gathering was more improvised than purposeful, and material came from unscreened and insecure sources. The embassy to Constantinople in 1567 hired a local translator. In 1570, the imperial ambassador in Rome was begging that information about the Turks not be sent to him until safer routes were available.[73] The emperor's domestic front was equally porous; indeed, Turkish merchants were buying military equipment in Vienna and shipping it from there.[74]

The defeat he suffered in Hungary in 1566 had wrought a visible change in Maximilian. When he returned to Vienna, disappointment was written all over his face, according to those who were with him. Where once he took his meals genially in company, he now brooded for days on end over his humiliation. Something came over him like the black depression into which Charles V had fallen after Maurice of Saxony had attacked him in 1552.[75] He recovered enough public self-control to discuss the affair coolly, if he had to. Any lingering anger with Archduke Ferdinand did not show.[76] But privately, he made very clear how crushing the experience had been. His careful preparation for the campaign made the reversal even more hurtful. Sometimes he tried to shift some of the blame for his humiliation to his advisers and to nature itself. His army, he said, had retreated because of death and desertion. How could he have known of Süleyman's demise when even the Ottoman high command was ignorant of it? The people Maximilian had tried so hard to find had proven themselves mediocre at best and downright unfit at worst. His commanders had not even been able to agree on Süleyman's intentions. Although the emperor did not say so, Zrinyi, his father's appointment, was a conspicuous exception. No one had thought that Sziget would fall so quickly. Particularly venomous were Maximilian's feelings toward Günther von Schwarzburg, who, according to the Habsburg, was more a hindrance than a help. Dealing with such men was enough to drive one "mad and senseless." The emperor alluded to conspiracies and betrayals, all unspecified; he also complained about how few reinforcements were available to him.[77] How he would have controlled even more troops when he could not discipline the ones he had was an open question. Perhaps he was too frustrated and embarrassed to think straight.

Worse yet, such feeble excuses impressed no one. Albrecht of Bavaria suggested renewing peace negotiations with the Turks; the duke had heard rumors that the emperor's reputation was now so low in Constantinople and among his own men that no one would fight for him. The Bohemian administration also thought that a truce was in order, and for equally unflattering reasons. They pointed out that Maximilian's personal leadership of the campaign, along with good domestic and foreign support, had not sufficed to defeat the Ottoman armies. It was highly unlikely that their king would enlist that kind of assistance again any time soon. The Habsburg's Austrian and Hungarian councils were more tactful—the Austrians spoke of his concluding a peace that would preserve his esteem, and the Hungarians regarded the move simply as the lesser of two evils. Neither body was ready to raise a major force for the emperor in the near term. His brothers finally joined the chorus.[78]

Foreign sources of aid that Maximilian had called upon in 1565 and 1566 did not look promising either. The new pope, Pius V, was an ascetic Dominican who had until his election served as general inquisitor. He was far more bent on cleansing Europe of Protestantism than on ridding it of the Turks, at least as the emperor saw it. Approached for help in 1568, Pius gave something only for the support of standing fortresses. In 1570, citing the needs of other parts of Christendom, he refused to contribute anything. Hungary was not the place to wage another battle. If that should happen, the pope said, the country would be fit for no prince.[79] Indeed, the Habsburg troops who remained in the blighted kingdom could not be paid regularly. This, as Schwendi reminded the emperor and his brothers, was yet another blot on Maximilian's reputation.[80]

A peace concluded in February of 1568 endured precariously until 1593, longer than anyone expected. The new sultan, Selim, was more given to women and drink than to military adventures. He died in 1574, and his successor, Murad III, appeared far more aggressive, but Maximilian himself had little time left to live.[81] A relative calm descended on the Austrian eastern front, a relief of sorts for Maximilian, but hardly in the way it had come about. He was keenly aware of how far he had fallen in the eyes of others as a result of the 1566 campaign. Even if no one had told him about it, he would have had painful images of tongues wagging behind his back on the subject. He was, after all, the man who had once criticized his father for passivity in the face of Turks who broke truces and brutalized local Christian populations. The conflict had produced its share of Ottoman atrocities once again, yet all Maximilian had been able to do was follow a decades-old policy.[82]

> Possessions lost—nothing is lost.
> Courage lost—much is lost.
> Honor lost—all is lost.[83]

Lazarus Schwendi's motto fit his emperor more than it did the general himself.

ten

Christians Divided

Like most of his contemporaries, Maximilian was uncomfortable with religious plurality. Unity betokened strength; multiplicity suggested weakness. "Sects, errors, discord, and disunity," as one of the emperor's Bohemian mandates put it, were dangerous for any realm.[1] Outright unbelievers were the worst. Bohemian Jews practiced "unchristian usury and other evil, treacherous Jewish customs," harmful to not only his own treasury but the common man.[2] Maximilian's thinking about his fellow Christians was more nuanced, but he did not like the divisions that were multiplying among them.

Restoring Germany to a single faith was, therefore, high on Maximilian's list of priorities. To do this, he needed the goodwill of both evangelicals and Catholics, and he began his reign by showing both sides that he had some understanding of their interests. Catholics were reassured when he neither banned the Jesuits nor rejected the Church of Rome. Disappointed Protestants breathed easier when, in the early autumn of 1564, he decreed that students at the university of Vienna needed only swear that they were Catholic Christians to receive a degree.[3] Later that year, however, Maximilian informed the archbishop of Salzburg that he intended to follow in his father's religious footsteps. He hoped that "the old, true Catholic faith" and its sacraments would be the key to salvation. He would do his part, he declared, to eradicate sectarianism and "excessive enthusiasm" (*Schwärmerei*).[4]

Maximilian did unequivocally endorse the Peace of Augsburg of 1555, which appeared to advance both his political and his confessional goals. The arrangement effectively turned the emperor into a "guardian of religious peace rather than a defender of the Christian Church," a role that highlighted Maximilian's centrality in German affairs and minimized his obligations to Rome.[5] The accord also called for the new emperor to recommit himself to general civil tranquillity in Germany, as laid out in the great imperial peace of 1495. Few princes dared oppose on principle any sovereign who espoused these ideals.[6] Most important, although the peace had not explicitly required parity between Lutherans and Catholics, it had established a territorial modus vivendi for the two churches in the empire. The next step was to be the lasting and comprehensive resolution of their differences that Maximilian believed he could promote.[7]

But Germany abounded in opportunities for religious conflict. Efforts to reconcile the Swiss reform movement with Lutheranism had already failed. Other groups, collectively, if imprecisely, called Anabaptist by contemporaries, added to the turbulence of the religious life of the age, to the dismay of monarchs for whom multiple confessions were an unwelcome novelty. With the spread of Flacianism, which rejected Philipp Melanchthon's relatively flexible approach to such questions as the adiaphora and the place of free will in Luther's theology, evangelicals themselves were regrouping into separate camps.[8] "In so short a time, three different confessions have been created," Maximilian noted in his diary. It did not take him long to conclude that Flacius' followers would be very troublesome, especially in Habsburg lands.[9]

Most threatening to confessional good order was the Genevan reform of the transplanted French humanist and theologian John Calvin. The movement had no standing in the Augsburg agreement, but it was making inroads in the Rhineland. Elector Palatine Frederick III's Heidelberg Catechism of 1563, though not wholly based on any single Protestant confession, was, as Maximilian read it, a clear departure from the evangelical Augsburg Confession of 1530. Worse yet, Maximilian had heard as early as 1560 that, wherever it went, Calvinism stirred up sedition—in France, for example. While serving under Philip II in the Netherlands, Schwendi reported to his future emperor that the French nobles were adopting the new faith eagerly, and not only out of concern for their souls. While the French king, Francis II, was still in his minority, they had the chance to seize spiritual leadership of the realm. Not only were they persecuting Luther's followers, but a secret group among them was plotting to overthrow their ruler.[10] Other communiqués to Maximilian forecast religious war in the kingdom and an irreversible decline from France's former eminence.[11]

Some German princes were content to see France so afflicted, because its kings had refused to return Metz, Toul, and Verdun, lost under Charles V, to the empire. Maximilian was not among those who rejoiced. Even before Ferdinand I died, Francis asked Maximilian to help persuade the Germans to withhold aid from the Huguenots. At stake were not only confessional principles, but the entire monarchical order.[12] By 1565 Maximilian agreed wholeheartedly:

> The condemned, evil Zwinglian and Calvinist sect, apart, and excluded from the common religious and secular peace in the Empire, contrary in the highest degree to the confession of many [members of the] estates and the Christians subject to them, introduces its confession through [an] altogether objectionable and unseemly deception and establish it by compulsion and force. . . . [It] for the most part directly contradicts the clear content and literal meaning not only of our and the empire's religious and secular peace but also of the Augsburg Confession.[13]

In the palatinate, however, Elector Frederick III thought otherwise. In 1566 he formally adopted Calvinism. A convert to Lutheranism before that, he had genuinely agonized over the decision. Nevertheless, all his fellow electors deplored the move. The ecclesiastical princes among them opposed Protestantism in any form. Joachim of Brandenburg and Augustus of Saxony, Lutherans both, were a bit more temperate. While not comfortable with the political implications of the innovation, they were loath to offend Protestant sentiment of any sort. Though Frederick continued to look for a way to unite the various strands of Protestantism among his subjects, he would not go back on his decision.[14]

Eager to resolve the problem of Calvinism quickly and decisively, Maximilian put it on his agenda for the diet in Augsburg in 1566, the same gathering at which he was hoping to raise funding for his war against the Turks. He had a great deal at stake and wanted the meeting to be impressive. To underscore the august nature of the affair, the emperor asked the highly respected Archbishop Daniel of Mainz to serve as its president.[15] Tournaments, banquets, and *exotica,* such as visiting foreign delegations, enriched the social life of the whole city temporarily.[16] Religious partisanship was not allowed to trouble the spectacle. Protestants objected to having the local clergy carry the baldachin under which the emperor walked when he opened the diet. Maximilian suggested restoration of an older custom, by which the city council designated men to bear the canopy. And this was not the only procedure Maximilian rearranged into order to ingratiate himself with the estates. He abandoned the customary use of a spokesman to defend his agenda before the delegates, in favor of arguing his case in person. Indeed, he continued the practice at future diets.[17]

The emperor staged a remarkable state occasion, judged at least from a visual standpoint. As a new emperor, he had to distribute the *Reichslehen* to the imperial officers, who had decked themselves out as lavishly as he did. The most modest among them, the elector of Trier, had 166 horses in his party. The Habsburg's character and public speaking skills also left a highly positive impression on his audience. His linguistic proficiency, in particular, distinguished him from the other princes, who spoke only their homely vernaculars.[18] He also had some reason to think that the secular Protestant electors would ultimately line up with him in his defense of the Augsburg settlement. Maximilian was friendly with key members of the imperial estates, among them Augustus of Saxony. One of the emperor's favorite hunting companions, Augustus also owed a great deal to the 1555 accord. It reaffirmed his electoral title, which Charles V had placed in Augustus' line, the house of Wettin, following the Schmalkaldic War. The elector had even contributed a contingent of troops for Hungary at his own expense in 1565. Other significant princes also had their particular reasons to support the Augsburg settlement wholeheartedly. It had strengthened the hold that Christoph of Württemberg had on his lands. Both he and Elector Augustus had found that their principalities were functioning quite smoothly as Lutheran polities and saw no reason to change things. On the Catholic side, Albrecht of Bavaria had used the territorial religious prerogative the 1555 peace had given him to eliminate evangelical leanings among his subjects.[19]

Still, there were just as many reasons to expect that such considerations, however significant, would not bring Christendom " 'to its senses' " in 1566 as Maximilian hoped.[20] Lutherans, by 1566, had serious questions about Calvinism's apparent denial of the real presence in the sacrament. As for Elector Palatine Frederick III, he was very unlikely to accept an imperially dictated compromise with Catholicism. To him the Mass had become a "popish abomination."[21] The behavior of his coreligionists was even more alarming. One pamphleteer had called for free exercise of religion in lands where the territorial ruler and his subjects did not share the same confession. Two Huguenots, supposedly intent on murdering Pius V, had been captured in Rome. Maximilian himself, for all his public magnanimity, had brought with him a squad of theologians prepared to do battle. A few days after the emperor's arrival in Augsburg, his court preacher, Matthias Cithardus, delivered a stinging homily against the doctrines coming from Geneva. Most menacing of all in the eyes of Protestants was the very energetic presence in Augsburg of the papal legate, Giovanni Francesco Commendone, for whom any negotiation on religious matters subverted the Catholic cause.[22]

The elector palatine was stubborn, but he had not spent a lifetime in imperial politics without having learned how to deal with his fellow princes. Imperial resolutions, especially in confessional matters, had often been ineffective in the past. At the Diet of Speyer in 1529, a protesting minority had successfully resisted a decision withdrawing territorial religious privileges first extended to the evangelical and Catholic princes three years earlier. But even if the imperial diet had respected majority rule, neither the emperor nor the estates had the power to execute policies decided this way.[23] Consensus, therefore, was almost always what the German princes and electors sought, and Frederick III seemed willing to work toward it. His soothing answer to the worries of his colleagues about confessional innovation was to say that the differences over Communion might not be great at all.[24]

Such openness contrasted sharply with the surprisingly inflexible policy that the emperor put forth at the outset of the gathering. The Peace of Augsburg was to continue unchanged; a truly comprehensive German religious settlement was, for Maximilian, apparently a dead issue. Calvinism and other confessional movements that the Augsburg formula did not cover were to be eradicated. Even Lutherans, who were explicitly privileged by the 1555 arrangement, detected a pattern of collusion between the emperor and Rome.[25] Their suspicions were not wholly unjustified. Soon after Maximilian arrived in Augsburg, Pius V asked him to remove from consideration any items preempted by decisions taken at the Council of Trent. Rather than focus on religious questions, the imperial estates should discuss a common alliance against the Turks. This the pope promised to support—just what Maximilian wanted to hear at the moment. Though he would not jettison past agreements with the estates, he replied to Pius very cordially.[26]

Unsettled by Maximilian's imperiousness and Commendone's endless maneuvers, Lutherans refused to ban Calvinism as their emperor had asked. Nevertheless, the emperor was bent on ridding Germany of this new confessional development, and, with Commendone's encouragement, he pressed on. Since his conversion, Elector Frederick III had aggressively secularized several monasteries in his lands. A committee of the diet had worked out a formal complaint, which Maximilian supported with orders to sequester those establishments. Beyond that, he asked once again for a vigorous denunciation of Calvinism.

The harsh tone of these measures alienated the delegates to the gathering even further. Nevertheless, the imperial marshal, who was the elector of Saxony, commanded Frederick to appear before his sovereign to defend both himself and what Maximilian termed "the Calvinist seduction." This the elector did with remarkable eloquence. The emperor and the princes heard him out in respectful silence. Indeed, it did not take much effort to convince Lutherans that they and the Calvinists had some common interests. Aside from Frederick's forceful presentation, partisans of the Augsburg Confession were growing worried about the official repression of Calvinism that had begun in France and the Netherlands. Should such policies succeed, might not Lutheranism be next in line?

Frederick fell ill following his appearance before his inquisitors. Maximilian was sufficiently moved by the elector's courage and sincerity to dispatch one of his chamberlains to inquire after the prince's health. But such graciousness did nothing to move business in the direction the Habsburg wished. On 26 May the estates refused to condemn Calvinism. Though they did not sanction it either, they asked that the issue be part of the agenda at some future diet. Two days later, the emperor declared that he was still determined to eradicate the movement. But if Maximilian had been hoping to court goodwill in Rome with his attack on Calvinism, as German Protestants suspected he was, he had not succeeded. Papal spokesmen in Augsburg reported that Maximilian had taken significant steps toward religious orthodoxy, but Pius still found the emperor too close to Protestantism for Catholic tastes.[27] Nor was the pope as forthcoming with aid against the Turks as Maximilian had hoped. Though Pius did contribute something to the Hungarian campaign in 1566, he shortly began turning down Maximilian's further requests. Pius, too, was defending lands against the Ottoman forces, and the North African Moors. Fortifying Malta and shoring up Mary Stuart in England, he said, were also costing him dearly.[28]

The Augsburg diet of 1566, therefore, had only encouraged confessional pluralism in Germany, thereby leaving the emperor further from his chief goal than ever. Toward the elector palatine, the Habsburg was very bitter. Upon hearing that Frederick had toasted Commendone during a courtesy call to the papal envoy before leaving Augsburg in 1566, Maximilian simply laughed. Frederick III was, he said, establishing some "strange things" in matters of religion. A year later, the emperor learned that the Calvinist elector was actively aiding the French Huguenots. Such behavior, Maximilian said, was not to be forgotten.[29] Indeed, he began to sense by 1567 that even two protected confessions were more than he could handle.[30]

The emperor's inflexible attitude toward Calvinism was clearly a tactical blunder. Yet his fears that the movement posed a serious political threat to the empire were not ill-founded. Even during his stay in Augsburg, Maximilian was confronting truly seditious activity in Germany. During the early 1540s, a Franconian nobleman named Wilhelm von Grumbach locked horns with the bishop of Würzburg, Melchior Zobel, in a territorial dispute. For the cleric, the disagreement ended in 1558, when one of Grumbach's servants murdered Zobel while trying to capture him. The bishop had, by almost all standards, behaved dreadfully toward Grumbach and his family. Nevertheless, the successor to the see, Friedrich von Wirsbach, was equally unsympathetic to the disgruntled nobleman. Grumbach turned to the emperor. Receiving no satisfaction, he and a group of confederates attacked Würzburg in 1563.

Ferdinand I, still emperor at the time, first declared that the knight had broken the public peace and then placed the imperial ban on his head but did not follow up on this initiative. Grumbach, who was far more energetic, evoked considerable sympathy among his peers. Some of them turned to Duke John Frederick of Saxony for support. The duke responded, publicly claiming that he hoped to pacify the dissident knight. But the Saxon prince's real motives were very different. Ousted as elector in favor of the Albertine branch of his house by Charles V after the Schmalkaldic War, John Frederick hoped to have Grumbach's help in regaining his title.

Maximilian's initial response to what promised to be a crisis was relatively measured, especially by comparison with that of some German princes who thought they were in for a major uprising. Elector Augustus of Saxony was particularly alarmed. Only recently installed in office, he was bent on preventing the restoration of his uncle's line to its erstwhile dignity. The elector's chancellory in Dresden mounted a major propaganda campaign against Grumbach, often put together from exceedingly casual intelligence. The knight was said to aspire to make himself a duke of Franconia, to unseat Albrecht of Bavaria and replace him with Duke Wilhelm of Zweibrücken, and to attack Cologne, Trier, and Mainz. In short, the expected offensive against electoral Saxony was made to seem part of a vast deposition conspiracy.[31]

Maximilian held back from military measures, hoping to persuade John

Frederick to drop his schemes. Overly precipitous punishment, the emperor thought, could turn the duke into a martyr in the eyes of his German peers. He also believed that Grumbach might be useful against the Turks. The emperor's attitude changed sharply, however, when he heard that the knight was plotting to kidnap Elector Augustus. Shocked, Maximilian renewed the imperial ban on Grumbach, which he extended in December 1566 to John Frederick as well.[32]

But it was possible Calvinist involvement in the confused affair that turned the Habsburg's deep concern into open fear. A certain Peter Clar, a French Huguenot "practicant," as the emperor described him, had transmitted to John Frederick sixty thousand crowns raised by sympathizers of the Genevan reform. The duke and Grumbach were clients of Charles IX; it was the emperor's understanding that the king of France, too, would support the rebels. John Frederick was already signing himself as John Frederick II, born elector, and minting coins depicting himself with the title.[33] As more information and half-information about the murky relationship linking Grumbach, Calvinists, and the king of France came his way, Maximilian recalled Charles V's experience with princely sedition in 1552. John Frederick and those helping him now became "sworn enemies of the imperial crown." Sure that an uprising against him in Germany was imminent, he swiftly undertook military action.[34]

On 18 April 1567, Elector August captured John Frederick and his residence in Gotha. Twenty years before that to the month, Charles V had beaten him at Mühlhausen. "God be praised," noted Maximilian in his diary.[35] Grumbach and several of his followers were executed five days later, and the luckless knight himself was drawn and quartered. Maximilian had some qualms about the dispatch with which all this took place, but he did not disavow the procedure either. Delaying punishment for a month, he said, let alone a year, as some of the more cautious spokespersons in the imperial estates had requested, would have made the situation impossible to remedy. Though Maximilian saw little hard evidence of a grand conspiracy, Grumbach's papers, which Augustus of Saxony had captured and forwarded to the emperor, contained truly slanderous material. According to Maximilian, the documents suggested that he wanted to root out all princely government in the empire. The ultimate goal of the conspirators, moreover, was to divide Germany among themselves, then create a republic. Such regimes were Maximilian's idea of chaos, an invitation to further Turkish conquest.[36] He condemned John Frederick to lifelong imprisonment, despite the tearful entreat-

ies of the duke's wife and pleas for clemency from sixteen members of the
imperial estates. Though frail, the Saxon prince lived on in Habsburg-funded
confinement until his death in 1595.[37]

Maximilian had several reasons to give thanks for Augustus' victory. It
upheld "holy justice" and his honor and authority in the empire.[38] It helped
him to recover some of the military reputation he had lost in Hungary over
the previous year. Archduke Ferdinand tactfully commented that the Turks
might think twice before risking another invasion.[39] But even as one set of
troubles associated with the Grumbach affair seemed to ease, another took
its place. The brutal end of the knight and some of his confederates stirred
up a wave of hostile responses in print. Particularly alarming was an anonymous doggerel pamphlet called *The Nightingale* (*Die Nachtigal*), published
at Frankfurt in the spring of 1567. A copy of it had been found in booty
captured at the fall of John Frederick's fortress of Gotha-Grimmenstein. The
authorship of the tract has yet to be determined; Maximilian thought it was
written by a Swiss theologian William Cleobitius, or Klebitz. The contents,
however, were unambiguous. It was a ringing indictment of the Saxon elector's reprisals in Gotha. Justice, it thundered, was ill served by such actions;
the emperor, as guilty as was Augustus himself, did not have long to wait
for his punishment:

> As you received the golden crown,
> You assented to the gospel too.
> Think what it is to God you do,
> When now, with that very crown,
> You aid the whore of Babylon.
> The Almighty seated on his throne,
> Has, for years, exactly known,
> The day your rule will disappear.
> That very time is drawing near.[40]

The text defended Grumbach and argued that John Frederick had merely
confused the knight's grievances with his own. It urged the princes to rescue
the duke from Habsburg captivity; it also extolled the Flacian Magdeburg
Confession, a slap aimed at Elector Augustus, for ducal Saxony was a center
of this recent strand of Lutheran thought. Some passages openly insulted the
emperor by advising Maximilian that if he really wanted to be bold militarily,
he should retake Sziget. According to the rector of the university of Heidelberg, Sigmund Melanthon, students were especially enthusiastic readers of

Die Nachtigal. Protestant though its contents were, the leaflet was too incendiary for even the elector palatine Frederick III, who ordered it out of circulation.[41]

Maximilian studied the piece and was appalled to find that it libeled himself, his father, and the imperial office. He set Duke Christoph to combing Württemberg for all the copies he could find and either send to Vienna or destroy himself. Not knowing who the author was, the emperor had the printer thrown into chains and brought before him.[42] In Frankfurt, where booksellers from every corner of Europe did business with people of many religious leanings, the city council was charged with finding out who had written the noxious pamphlet. Cleobitius himself hastily fled to Paris. Maximilian continued to ask for his return, particularly when he learned in 1569 that the man had turned out an even more offensive broadside with the same general thrust.[43]

By 1570, after a number of these polemics had been confiscated throughout Germany, Maximilian would grow somewhat calmer. He had released the printer earlier on the condition that the latter keep him abreast of Cleobitius' whereabouts if he knew them. When he eventually reported to Maximilian that the writer had died, the emperor fully absolved the unfortunate craftsman of any responsibility for the work.[44] But the episode hardened Maximilian's convictions about the danger that Protestant factionalism posed to his authority. From 1568 on, his chancellory periodically forbade the sale of incendiary political writing. Though the policy had little effect beyond that of now and again requiring publishers to draw up detailed lists of their offerings, the very existence of such directives betrayed the emperor's increasing concern.[45]

The Grumbach episode made Maximilian generally more circumspect in imperial religious affairs. He began to pay far more attention to balancing the concerns of the two German confessions, as opposed to seeking permanent resolution of their differences. He certainly did not want to be unduly identified with Catholic interests. When Chantonnay urged him to be watchful in dealing with Augustus of Saxony, the emperor simply declined to commit himself.[46] He urged the papacy to intrude in German affairs as cautiously as possible, even if Rome had good reason to do so. After Archbishop Frederick von Wied in Cologne refused to introduce the Tridentine catechism, even though his cathedral chapter had sanctioned it, Pius V demanded a profession of faith from him. Maximilian counseled patience; Frederick was in poor health and might resign very soon. Were Wied to stay on, the emperor promised to concoct some face-saving formula that would encourage the archbishop to leave. A more decisive move by Pius risked stirring up German resentment.[47] But Maximilian did not ignore papal sensibilities either. Looking for someone to guard Duke John Frederick, the emperor twice asked Archduke Ferdinand to find an impeccable Catholic. Only on the subject of Calvin's followers was the emperor plain-spoken. He did not trust them.[48]

Maximilian's problems with confessional differences were not confined to the empire. His patrimonial inheritance in Lower Austria was among the most doctrinally corrupt and fractured regions in central Europe, a continued source of embarrassment for its Habsburg ruler before Catholics and Protestants alike. He was aware of moral and intellectual failings among the local Catholic clergy well before he became emperor. A report given to him in 1562 concerning conditions in Enns was typical. One priest had several wives and children. He was also exceedingly indolent, as a result, said the inspectors, of chronic gout. Another pastor was pious and learned, but his congregation could not follow his train of thought. Indeed Maximilian had heard of at least one such figure who allegedly did not even understand himself.[49] Another investigation during the same year brought to light 135 women and 223 children kept by resident clergy in thirty-six monasteries in Austria above and below the Enns. Such conditions reinforced the strength of the Protestant appeal in the Austrian lands, as one town and region after another succumbed to some version of the Protestant reform.[50]

The Peace of Augsburg opened the way for the Habsburg emperor to dictate the faith of subjects within his own lands. This could be Lutheran, Catholic, or some confession that both sides could agree upon. As he had done in Germany, Maximilian initially addressed the issue with at least a superficial evenhandedness. At the outset of his rule in Lower Austria he ordered that neither Catholic nor Protestant pastors be molested.[51] In truth, such a policy amounted to a tilt in the Catholic direction. Protestantism had yet to be formally established in his lands, and its weight at any bargaining table depended on its continued displacement of Catholic institutions. In practice, Maximilian certainly seemed to think that any resolution of Lower Austria's confessional controversies should retain a recognizably traditional character, however improved. He criticized the "evil people" who pamphleteered against Catholics.[52] But impatient with the pace of Catholic renewal, he created a *Klosterrat* in 1568. To be sure, this office was to estimate how much churches and monasteries could contribute toward defense against the Turks and to make sure they paid their fair share. Nevertheless, he also hoped that such scrutiny would requicken intellectual and spiritual life in those institutions.[53] Maximilian took a keen, though critical, interest in Catholic preaching. "So-so," was his judgment on a presentation from the suffragan bishop of Cosnitz in 1567.[54] On a personal level, he continued to observe certain sacraments and the veneration of relics. That confessional disorder had caused some people to die unbaptized or without the last rites dismayed him.[55] Even though he said that marriage might help restore credibility to some clergymen for whom celibacy was too great a test, the emperor thought that wives were not for the truly devout among them.[56]

Nevertheless, minimal Catholicism, if that is how Maximilian conceived it, impressed few. His pious sister in Munich, Archduchess Anna, judged Maximilian to be sufficiently orthodox that she asked to have her son, Duke Ferdinand, stay for a time at her brother's court.[57] Unlike the emperor, however, the pope wanted to bring Protestants back to the true faith as quickly, and with as few concessions, as possible. Five months after his election in January, he tried to limit Communion in both kinds in the Austrian lands, including Styria, where it had never been introduced at all. Such measures would clearly antagonize Protestants even more, something Maximilian clearly wanted to avoid. He urged Pius to think again; people throughout the area were eager for the privilege, and orders from Pius might only accelerate lapses from Catholicism.[58]

The pontiff was not pleased, and he was hardly happier with Maximilian's attempts to reform monastic life in the Habsburg lands. No matter how the emperor might argue that he hoped to conserve both the moral and material standing of Catholicism and that Ferdinand I himself had sponsored visitations, the pope remained very wary of Maximilian. Pius did approve the inspection of clerical institutions that Maximilian ordered in 1568. At the same time, however, the pope dispatched Commendone once again to negotiate the territorial scope of the investigation, along with other matters. Two more visitations took place in 1569 and 1575, both of which concluded that little reform had taken place in religious establishments.[59]

For their part, large numbers of Maximilian's Lower Austrian subjects had long since rejected confessional tokenism as a response to their concerns. Protestant functionaries sat on the imperial court council (*Reichshofrat*), but so did Catholics, some of whom, such as Dr. Timotheus Jung, were converts from Lutheranism and thus doubly obnoxious to evangelicals.[60] Their faith continued to spread. By the late 1560s, most of the regional nobility of Lower Austria, and probably a majority of the lower classes, paid at least lip service to some sort of reformed creed.[61] Noting that no territorial prince had approved these changes, Maximilian sourly resigned himself to them and to the increasing numbers of dissidents who found their way to his lands from abroad.[62] There were Philippist Lutherans from Württemberg and Flacians from ducal Saxony, the latter especially welcome. Ordained Lutheran pastors were in short supply in the Austrian lands, and a number of Flacians brought such credentials.[63] There were also the so-called *Winkelprädicanten*—pastors and congregations of indeterminate confession who worshipped in strict privacy. None of them gave much thought to the divisiveness they were creating, but none were ready to accept others' differences either. The intransigent, as well as the unusually tolerant Schwendi, thought that altogether too much religious freedom reigned in Maximilian's holdings.[64]

Having already asked Ferdinand to allow free exercise of their confession, the evangelicals petitioned for the privilege once again when they swore fealty to Maximilian in 1564. A year later they demanded that Catholicism be abolished altogether. Neither proposition appealed to the new emperor. Behind all of these demands was the provincial nobility, over whom, taken individually, Maximilian had some control. They held their titles thanks to their territorial prince.[65] Inflation, currency devaluations, and higher taxes had severely affected the landed class in Maximilian's Austrian holdings, try though the landholders did to pass added costs on to the peasantry. The financial favors accruing to court position exerted a powerful attraction on many landed nobles. "Were it not for the service of his majesty, they couldn't afford soup," sneered imperial court counselor Dr. Georg Eder, a fervent Catholic partisan who in this case knew whereof he spoke.[66]

Nevertheless, Maximilian depended on these men as a group for funds. He was therefore almost always under pressure to grant religious concessions to them in the estates in return for financial aid. He weighed tactics in dealing with spokesmen for Lower Austria very carefully. "Should I confront the estates with a show of absolute power or consult with the local inhabitants or meet with them either before, during, or after a future meeting?" he ruminated in 1566.[67] But from 1564 to 1568, he staved off demands for Communion sub utraque in Austria above and below the Enns and free preaching of the Gospel.[68]

Nevertheless, Maximilian could not avoid showing some signs of goodwill toward his Protestant subjects; his ignominious retreat from Hungary in 1566 seriously undermined whatever sway he exercised over them. By the end of that year, he had agreed to create a commission in Austria below the Enns made up of six members delegated by the estates and six chosen by the government. The body was to work out a general confessional settlement for his Austrian lands. In December, Maximilian repeated the concession in Linz to nobles and knights of Austria above the Enns in return for 120,000 gulden.[69]

This turn of events was not altogether unwelcome to the emperor. Haphazard popular religious usage in his lands, where Communion both in one and in two kinds could take place at the same altar, was not to his liking. But by 1568 the Protestants were in a position to extort from him what they really wanted. With his state debt standing at 2.5 million gulden, he asked the Lower Austrian estates to assume it. Quick to jump at such an opening, evangelicals demanded official permission to exercise the Augsburg Confession in his lands freely, in return for assuming Maximilian's financial liabilities.[70] The emperor yielded, but very guardedly, pointing out that his father and uncle had entered into similar bargains. He was "not unwilling . . . in appropriate measure" to allow the knights and lords of Lower Austria to worship according to the Augsburg rite, though only in their country castles and residences. He would not give the privilege in perpetuity; it was valid only pending the completion of a unitary confession for Lower Austria. Towns and markets, which the Habsburgs were beginning to treat as regalian properties, were not affected.[71]

The work of Maximilian's commission, which had been discussing these matters for almost two years, became more urgent than ever. The only outcome acceptable to the emperor was one that left Catholic institutions more or less intact and that committed Protestants to a single order of ceremony and dogma. This was possible only where the "Agenda," as the program would be called, incorporated points of agreement, or virtual agreement, between traditional practice and the Augsburg Confession. It was an enterprise for theological moderates, among whom Maximilian was certainly one. "Above all advance the honor of God, banish sin, debauchery, and blasphemy, and be one and reconciled with God without which things are nothing," he had noted to himself a year or so earlier.[72] People of such temper and persuasion were not springing from the woodwork; Flacians in the Protestant estates pushed hard to have their views represented on the commission. Nevertheless, Maximilian invited Joachim Camerarius and David Chyträus to oversee the task. The former, an elderly Lutheran humanist, was a professor of theology at Leipzig. He taught religion as a kind of moral system, thereby sidestepping questions of ritual altogether. Renowned for his broadmindedness, Chyträus lectured at the University of Rostock. Seeing some divine purpose behind the charge, he accepted it enthusiastically.[73]

Catholics were up in arms against the project before either man set foot in Vienna; they bombarded the emperor with their complaints at every opportunity. The court preacher, Martin Eisengrein, was particularly relentless. Born to prosperous evangelical parents in Stuttgart, he had converted to Catholicism around 1558 while a student in Vienna. After stints of preaching at St. Stephen's Cathedral in the Habsburg capital and in Duke Albrecht's Munich household, he entered Maximilian's service in 1567. There he was supposed to stay for a year.

Eisengrein exemplified the rigid Catholicism that Maximilian would never be able to satisfy. As long as the two men saw eye to eye on such practices as veneration of saints and opposition to iconoclasm, they got along. Eisengrein despised the Habsburg's measured approach to his Protestant estates, however; "the fish has been stinking at the head," was the way he put it in August of 1568.[74] In September 1568, the emperor took Eisengrein aside and tried hard to clarify his reasons for promoting confessional reconciliation. In response, Eisengrein declared that the project could very well destroy Catholicism. For a moment, Maximilian lost his temper—he was, he asserted, doing nothing he could not justify before God and the world. He ordered Eisengrein from the room, then stopped him at the door to ask the stubborn cleric to continue reporting any matters he thought noteworthy.[75]

If the emperor meant to silence Eisengrein with such conciliatory gestures, he failed. The clergyman vigilantly noted how often the Habsburg heard Mass—infrequently—and how often he attended vespers—not at all.[76] Eisengrein never tired of commenting that anyone named Chyträus— "cooking-pot" in the German vernacular—could hardly be entrusted with reforming religion in Austria. As for Camerarius, he was a learned man but a poor theologian.[77]

Eisengrein's welcome in Vienna cooled quickly. Even the empress, who treated her husband with utmost tact despite his religious ideas, saw that the pastor's tirades were only hardening Maximilian's resolve to push the work of his commission through to completion.[78] Maximilian let his displeasure be known, at first through surrogates. Zasius was delegated to inform Eisengrein that his sermons were too long-winded. His Swabian accent was an added drawback.[79] After the cleric delivered a vehement discourse on sin, Hans Trautson, Maximilian's majordomo, urged him "not to knock people on the head."[80] Not long after that interview, Eisengrein left Vienna for Ingolstadt.

There he continued his polemics—though, thankfully for Maximilian, at a distance.[81]

Maximilian could always dismiss obstreperous subordinates, such as Eisengrein. But other Catholic opponents of the commission's work were permanent fixtures in the emperor's network of relationships. There was King Philip in Spain, who had decided that permitting the Augustana was "unworthy of his [Maximilian's] imperial dignity." More specifically, he feared that all the estates of the Habsburg Austrian patrimony would ask for the privileges Maximilian had tentatively extended to Lower Austria. Philip was concerned for his sister's religious feelings as well.[82]

Answering his cousin, Maximilian repeated, or embellished, a ringing defense of his policy that he had offered to Archduke Ferdinand. The emperor's military needs were different. The disordered confessional makeup of his holdings made them unlike the Tyrol and the Iberian kingdoms, which were all solidly Catholic. He had yielded very little to the Protestant side, and he made it clear to the estates of Lower Austria that they did not have full religious freedom, even though many among them believed otherwise. When Vanegas, the resident Spanish ambassador in Vienna, consulted with the emperor on the letters Philip had sent, Maximilian gave him the comforting reply that he had recently met with the estates of Lower Austria and told them that he could not yet sanction free exercise of the Augustana. He further assured Chantonnay that he had not set a time when conditional use of the confession could begin. Overcome by joy, both envoys had kissed Maximilian's hands in gratitude for the good news. Even Philip was happy to learn that nothing precipitate was in the offing.[83] But none of these men endorsed the emperor's larger project.

Chantonnay and Vanegas also pressed Maximilian to solicit the wisdom of Pius V on religious affairs in Lower Austria, a duty the Habsburg ruler found altogether distasteful. Pope and emperor had already differed on a number of matters, and Maximilian was uncomfortable with Pius' rigid ways. Up to 1568, no open break had occurred between them.[84] But the religious concessions of 1568 ended whatever pretense of cordiality there had been in their relationship. Pius first made known his unhappiness by refusing to see Maximilian's spokesman in Rome. He then announced his intention to recall his nuncio from Vienna. Maximilian took all of this very bitterly. "The pope would be well suited as an inquisitor or to direct a monastery," he remarked to Michele, the Venetian ambassador, "but ruling the world is quite another calling."[85] Maximilian repeated what, for him, was becoming a routine line of argument—compromise with the Augsburg Confession was by far the least of several evils.[86] It was familiar to Pius too, but he did not believe a word of it. He asked Philip II to bring whatever pressure the king could upon his cousin in Vienna.[87]

Upon hearing of the emperor's invitation to Chyträus, Pius V also dispatched Commendone to the Austrian lands. Remembering how the envoy had antagonized Protestants at Augsburg in 1566, Maximilian tried mightily to keep him away. A messenger went off to Innsbruck, charged with convincing the papal representative that he should go back to Rome. Commendone would not hear of it. Maximilian resigned himself to hoping that the legate would find things to his satisfaction.[88] But Commendone immediately set about trying to get Maximilian to withdraw his concessions, using rhetorical ploys that looked counterproductive even to the sympathetic Chantonnay. Maximilian, noted the Spanish ambassador with considerable insight, was "perceptive and wants to be taken as such." He did not listen happily to lectures on matters he thought he understood perhaps better than anyone else; he also liked to reach conclusions without being tricked or forced into doing so.[89] Even the devout Eisengrein remarked that people on both sides of the confessional divide at the court in Vienna wished that the ambassador had drowned somewhere along the way on his journey.[90]

Maximilian had at least one quite practical reason for encouraging Catholic observance in his lands. He had six sons, he told Commendone, and only his patrimonial holdings as a legacy. If these split over religious differences, he would be hard put to cobble together livings for his heirs. He met at least one papal request by promising not to grant further concessions to the Lutherans.[91] But that was all. To the distress of both factions in this tense atmosphere, Maximilian gave no clear signal that he favored either of them as negotiations on the Agenda proceeded.

Camerarius and Johannes Crato, who, as an evangelical sympathizer, took a considerable interest in the work of the commission, had hoped to begin serious writing in the fall of 1568. Chyträus, however, did not arrive in Lower Austria until close to the end of the year. Camerarius left shortly thereafter because of poor health, so the finished draft of the Agenda, ready by 26 February 1569, was largely Chyträus' handiwork. The theologian turned the document over to Zasius, who, in turn, passed it on to the emperor. Maximilian ordered that it not be published until he and Zasius had read it through. He also wanted his Lutheran treasury minister, Reichart Streun von Schwarzenau, his chief mediator with the evangelical side, to inspect it.[92]

Insofar as the proposal generally strove to reach a consensus on religious practice in Lower Austria, it met the emperor's goals; but although the historical traditions of the Church had inspired much of the work, the Augsburg Confession and other territorial codifications of Lutheran doctrine dominated the proposed liturgy. The Lutheran catechisms, both great and small, were to be followed in perpetuity in Maximilian's Austrian lands. Long-familiar elements of Catholic ritual that the emperor himself wished to retain, such as the elevation of the host at the Mass, the donning of surplices during the office, and the use of altar candles, were stricken from the new service. Episcopal authority over the clergy was also in doubt. Practically speaking, therefore, the draft all but recommended what Maximilian had wanted to avoid—a separate and equal Protestant church.[93]

At the end of March 1569, Protestants and Catholics began discussing the adoption of the Agenda. Though he tried to avoid open partisanship, Maximilian was under heavy pressure from Commendone to protect Catholic interests. Spurred on by Vice-Chancellor Weber, no confessional extremist but a man who almost always preferred long-standing arrangements, the traditionalist faction at court also urged the emperor to restore the familiar ceremonial. Maximilian yielded and asked Chyträus to amend his draft accordingly. The scholar refused; he saw little point in such rituals, however venerable they were. Nor would he recognize the authority of Rome's bishops, unless they permitted Lutherans to worship freely in areas still supervised by the Catholic hierarchy.[94]

As the emperor hung back from any final decision, the estates of Lower Austria amended the document further, then made it public. Maximilian said that he was favorably disposed toward the program, but he still would not approve it formally. No one was happy with this state of affairs. May gave way to June; Chyträus was eager to leave for Rostock. His university called, and his health was bad, as was that of his wife, who had recently given birth. The estates were unwilling to let him go; they still hoped he could privately persuade the emperor to accept the Agenda, though they were growing ever more doubtful that he would. It seemed to them that the Catholic side now had the Habsburg's ear.

Under pressure, the Lower Austrians went on the offensive. Expanding their list of demands, they called for, among other innovations, a public house of worship in Vienna, their own superintendent and consistory, and a school of theology.[95] Chyträus was authorized to ask the theologian Martin Chemnitz, who was openly committed to repairing the growing factionalism among

Lutherans, to come to Vienna and replace him at the head of the commission. Once again, the emperor hesitated to go through with the change. By 30 July, Chyträus would wait no longer.[96] Maximilian had already said at the end of May that neither he nor his father could keep the barons and nobles of his land from having their own preachers. He continued to reassure the Spanish ambassador that he would do nothing to prejudice Catholic belief and interests. He even joined, though he did not lead, the Corpus Christi procession in Vienna that year. But Catholics around him were not celebrating.[97]

They were even more distressed when, on 13 August, Maximilian granted the high nobility and knights of Lower Austria free exercise of the evangelical faith, though he did not confirm the Agenda as a whole or permit a public house of worship in Vienna. It was the way "the Austrians pretend to establish their religion," said the disapproving king of Spain.[98] Philip grew even more openly critical of the emperor as his spies informed him that Maximilian had not been seen taking the sacraments. Such behavior, said the Spanish ruler, scandalized the Catholic world and set a dangerous example for heretics. That Maximilian had Catholics in his imperial court council made no impression on Philip. Maximilian had to rid his administration and household of all Protestants to meet the standards of Madrid. Maximilian's policies were putting Catholics, his reputation, and the emperor's very soul at risk.[99]

Maximilian's confidence that religious compromise was possible was clearly fading. Advising Archduke Charles in the fall of 1569 on granting religious concessions in Styria, he spent as much time analyzing the political hazards of these measures and the colloquies that accompanied them as he did assessing their value. Protecting one's authority was the truly important task a ruler had in all these situations—and temporizing, the safest tactic. He admitted that his efforts to promote such talks had merely goaded Catholics into demanding that Protestantism be eradicated and had rendered him suspect in the eyes of both the pope and Philip in Spain. Misgivings about the house of Austria, which he did not specify, were circulating throughout the empire as well. Although Maximilian did not rule out the possibility that future deliberations could be useful, he was, he said, reporting his experience as he saw it.[100]

Though he did not say so, Maximilian had virtually revived his father's confessional strategy of maintaining public peace and loyalty to the house of Habsburg, while conceding as little as possible to the particular demands of any one confession. When Maximilian had to give answers, he did, but he phrased them as opaquely as possible.[101] Since becoming emperor, he had generally chosen his words with care to promote a serious end—the resolution of religious difference through compromise; but his goals were becoming far less visionary and a good deal more self-interested.

Pragmatism, however, got him no further with the confessional parties in his lands than had the ideal of religious reconciliation. By 1570, the Lower Austrian estates had paid nothing on the emperor's debts, for Maximilian had not yet confirmed and formally established the Agenda. On 30 May of that year, the financially needy Habsburg committed himself and his heirs to protecting the Augsburg Confession and its exercise. This was still not enough for the Protestant nobility of the land.[102] The emperor, therefore, asked that the Agenda be rewritten. The task went to Christoph Reuter, a clergyman who had worked with Chyträus and whose understanding of Lutheran doctrine ranged broadly over the confessional map of the day. Made public in 1571, his text differed considerably from Chyträus' original draft. It was still, however, a very Lutheran document. Catholics tried to suppress it; the bishop of Passau complained that Maximilian had overstepped his ecclesiastical authority in allowing it to appear.[103]

Not all Austrian Protestants endorsed it either. Their Lutheran clergy as a group had not participated in the recasting of the text, and they bitterly resented their exclusion. Flacians were even more critical. Anything done with the emperor's encouragement was suspect, as far as they were concerned, for Maximilian was still nominally Catholic. Nor did they like the prominent role which the Lutheran nobility had arrogated to themselves in determining the confessional fate of their land.[104] Theologians in Wittenberg, miffed because their colleagues to the south had not consulted with them, also received the Agenda coolly. The Austrians did not take to this pronouncement kindly. Their reply would be a pamphlet entitled *Specimen of All Frogs Against the Austrian Agenda.*[105]

But the estates' continued refusal to pay forced Maximilian to yield still further. In 1571, he issued the so-called religious *Assekuration*, which restated, in writing, the religious freedom of the Lutheran high nobility and knights when they were in their castles and on their lands. Members of the immediate household, including servants, could worship in these places as well. Though intended to limit the spread of the new confessions, the restriction had little effect. Private services in knightly castles and on noble estates were open to local townspeople. A note of impermanence still ran through these arrangements—they were in force only until the empire as a whole could agree upon a uniform style of worship and confession. Nevertheless, Lower Austria's great and small nobility accepted the scheme at the beginning of 1572.[106]

In the long run, Catholics probably gained more from this state of affairs than Protestants, who, split between the Flacians and those closer to Wittenberg, still had no institutionalized church in Lower Austria to protect them.[107] Religious freedom was but a personal privilege of the nobility, and therefore subject to fluctuations in the preferences and interests of this class. That Lutheranism's hold on Austria was precarious was not obvious to contemporary observers, Maximilian included. Indeed, every effort the emperor had made to contain religious factionalism both in his own lands and in the empire had shown just how much staying power the Protestant reform in central Europe really had, and how powerful were the strategies at its disposal. If there was any place where Maximilian should have been able to solve confessional issues, it was in his Austrian patrimonial lands. He was on familiar terrain, and his personal relations with his subjects were relatively good. He enjoyed the same advantages in dealing with the German princes, as well. But neither of his tactics, short-lived displays of power or evenhanded mediation, had brought him any closer to the confessional uniformity he so desired. Worse yet, his maneuvers were alienating him from his own house.

eleven

Two Habsburgs and the Netherlands

"Religious matters in the Netherlands get only worse," wrote Maximilian apprehensively around 1566. He was watching a situation that had very serious implications for his political position both within the empire and in his own family.[1] Profits were sagging by 1560, but the wealth of the Low Countries was still the envy of many princes. Now governed by Philip of Spain, the region had a diverse and developed economy. Textile manufacture and maritime trade were the engines of this prosperity, and, by the sixteenth century, the city of Antwerp, with around ninety thousand inhabitants, housed a lucrative market in financial services. The Habsburg title to these provinces came through Maximilian I. In 1477 he had married Duchess Mary of Burgundy, who would be the last direct heir of her line, a cadet branch of the French royal house of Valois. The kings of France and their successors therefore had claims to the area that had already set the groundwork for one of Europe's more durable dynastic rivalries. While the duchy of Burgundy had fallen back to France, the house of Austria had generally survived challenges to their titles in the Low Countries.[2]

Maximilian's connections with the Netherlands were exquisitely complex. As German emperor, he had theoretical sovereignty over much of the area, but his predecessors had exercised such power only with difficulty. The constitutional status of the Low Countries in the Holy Roman Empire was very unclear. An imperial reform at the beginning of the sixteenth century had drawn up twelve circles, or districts, responsible for keeping the peace in

Germany and aiding their sovereign when the security of the entire polity was at stake. A Burgundian unit was one of them. But Charles V, who had been born in Ghent and had grown up at the court of his Aunt Margaret in Mechelen, had never recognized German rights to revenues from the various Burgundian holdings. A compact agreed to in 1548 left the Netherlands virtually independent of the empire. Imperial levies for military purposes were assessed on the Burgundian circle after that time, but the district paid them no more promptly than did other regions throughout Germany. The estates of the Low Countries did, however, accept the suzerainty of the emperor and acknowledge him as their protector.

For all these ambiguities, German territorial rulers continued to assert that the Netherlands had a formal link to the empire. None of these men happily wrote off any potential revenues. In the Low Countries themselves, some members of the estates held lands elsewhere in Germany and had married into German families. Among them were Philip de Montmorency Count Hoorn, and Prince William of Orange. The prince shared with his brother the castle of Dillenburg in Hesse. Hoorn was inscribed in the register of the empire; his eponymous county overlapped both the Westphalian and the Burgundian circles.[3] Such people had a real stake in the emperor's charge to enforce the imperial peace wherever his suzerainty was recognized. Prominent Netherlanders had married into German families as well. Hoorn was husband to Walburgis von Neunahr, the offspring of a prominent Rhenish family. The wife of Lamoral Count Egmont, another important figure, was from the palatinate line of the Bavarian Wittelsbachs.[4]

Maximilian's great-aunt Margaret of Mechelen and aunt Mary of Hungary had, as regents for their male relatives, governed the Netherlands with distinction. Nevertheless, both women wore themselves out in the job. Local nobilities viewed the Habsburgs with great suspicion and feared that the slightest change in the constitutional relationship between ruler and ruled might give the dynasty wider access to the wealth of the provinces. They were also eager to retain control over religious life in the region. Local courts often tried and punished heresy. Abbeys and bishoprics, furthermore, provided sinecures for aristocratic families with more offspring than means to support them.[5]

A crisis was brewing by the time Philip's natural step-sister, Margaret of Parma, became regent in 1559. That she was inexperienced and that she was given to hysterical verbosity, at least on paper, were only two of her problems. Added to the routine fiscal tensions between the estates and their rulers was now religious divisiveness. Lutherans, Anabaptists, and Calvinists had all put down roots in the Netherlands, despite harsh, though erratic, persecution. Had Maximilian been regent, had he been given the provinces outright, as was suggested during the negotiations over his marriage, he might have treated the local confessional problem in quite another way. At least this is what some of his contemporaries thought.[6] But it was Philip who ruled here, and he had a quite different view of the situation than did his cousin in Vienna.

Philip hoped to govern the Netherlands more or less directly from Spain. Among his greatest concerns was ecclesiastical administration. The Catholic establishment throughout the provinces was profoundly corrupt, and the success of the Protestant reform, as Philip saw it, lay in its withering attacks on such abuses. In 1559, he persuaded the pope, Paul IV, to reorganize church governance in the Low Countries. Philip and his successors were unequivocally vested with the right to nominate candidates for the newly drawn episcopal sees, except for Cambrai and Liège, which were independent ecclesiastical principalities. He also decided to attach a chapter of the Inquisition to each of the proposed dioceses.

Experience should have made the king of Spain think twice before taking that step. In 1522, Charles V and the pope had established a special apostolic Inquisition in the Netherlands. Even though the office was both inefficient and independent of the established bishoprics, its penalties, when applied, were severe. The local population resented them deeply. Philip seemed ready to administer these measures far better, especially when he added Maximilian's old Spanish nemesis, Antoine Perrenot, Cardinal Granvella, to Margaret's council of advisers, to see that the royal will was carried out. Catholics and non-Catholics alike were outraged.[7]

Such policies, along with the garrisoning of Spanish troops in the region, jeopardized the influence of important members of the estates. Vigorous opposition from such noblemen as Prince William of Orange and Counts Egmont and Hoorn, as well as from a faction of moderates at the Spanish court centered around Ruy Gómez de Silva, the prince of Eboli, led Philip to recall Granvella in 1564. But the papal Inquisition stayed, and turmoil mounted. Philip was taken aback. He had not visited the region since 1559, but he agreed in 1566 to return in an attempt to calm the situation. As a show of good faith, he lifted the papal Inquisition and indicated that he would be generous in issuing pardons.[8]

Philip had vigorously opposed Pope Paul IV's excommunication of Elizabeth I of England in 1559 on the grounds that it would exacerbate tensions between Catholics and Protestants. The situation in the Netherlands, however, affected him directly.[9] In 1565, he had privately commented that moderation in religious affairs was all but useless politically. On 9 August 1566, he swore before a notary and witnesses that his promise of clemency for the Netherlands had been made under duress. Although he did not rescind his offer outright, he declared that he was still empowered to punish heresy and offenses against his sovereignty. The king's attitude stiffened further after the beginning of September, when news of iconoclasm and looting of churches in the Netherlands reached him. This havoc was allegedly the handiwork of Calvinists, who had first appeared in the Low Countries during the 1550s. French Huguenots, who were fleeing the persecution of their own king, were now reinforcing their ranks. Catholics, both clerical and lay, had been harassed on Assumption Day, and a Calvinist-inspired mob had seized Valenciennes. Such reports weighed on Philip's delicate religious conscience. He decided to name Fernando Alvarez de Toledo, duke of Alba, who had been among the witnesses to Philip's notarized oath, captain-general of an army to bring order to the Netherlands. The Spanish monarch also ordered the arrest and trial of leading opponents of his measures, among them William of Orange and Counts Egmont and Hoorn. The Inquisition was to be restored, and the reconstituted bishoprics installed.[10] Persuaded, as was Margaret, that only military force could end the upheaval in the provinces, Philip asked his Austrian cousin for permission to recruit in the empire.[11] Should the German princes object to Spanish policy in the Netherlands, the emperor could smooth things over.

On one matter, Maximilian and Philip agreed. Effective rule was personal rule. As Maximilian later put it, matters that affected the king's authority, his heirs, and his possessions should be dealt with by him alone. No one else enjoyed the same respect—not his governors, not his captains-general, not his other officials. Therefore, the emperor applauded Philip's resolve to visit the provinces, the sooner the better.[12] Neither man, moreover, was a friend of sedition or of Calvinism. Maximilian was as sensitive to questions of his authority as Philip was.[13] Civil disobedience of any kind was bad, much less truly destructive behavior.[14] Vandalizing of churches and idiosyncratic notions about the sacraments troubled the emperor deeply too. In principle, therefore, Maximilian endorsed Philip's stand and would continue to do so.[15]

Maximilian, however, had a source of worry that Philip was spared— Germany. The emperor had several reasons for not wanting his cousin nearby with a Spanish army. Since the Schmalkaldic War, mistrust in the empire of the Spanish had grown so much that any nearby show of force by Philip might have nasty repercussions. That these troops might enter lands that were indisputably part of Germany made the situation even more dangerous. German participation on any side of a conflict in the Netherlands might undermine the fragile religious peace created in 1555. Not everyone, it is true, was sure that the Augsburg settlement applied in the Low Countries. But by attending the conclusion of the recess in 1555, representatives from the region had led the German princes to think that the formula did indeed extend to Luther's followers in those territories.[16] And any sign from Philip that he intended to impose his will militarily would unleash a wave of sympathy for the rebels among Calvinists wherever they were, including in the Rhineland.

Compared with William of Orange and Egmont, who were tentatively soliciting help in Westphalia, the Upper Rhineland, and Lower Saxony for their rebellious enterprise, Philip was behaving like a model imperial citizen. He had actually sought his cousin's permission to recruit.[17] Several emperors, Ferdinand I most recently, had tried to control German mercenary traffic abroad, but none had really succeeded. Loopholes abounded in the constitutional regulations covering this question, as Maximilian soon found out. Imperial troops could serve in foreign armies against rebels, so long as they neither waged war on the emperor or a member of the imperial estates nor assembled within the confines of the empire. Because no one had ever enforced these stipulations rigorously, Philip had good reason to think that his request would not be denied. The emperor and his father, moreover, had already allowed troops from Germany and from their own domains to fight for the king of Spain when he needed them.[18]

But Germans drawn into combat in the religiously fractured Netherlands might end up taking sides against one another. All of Maximilian's arguments against his cousin's policies, therefore, were designed to prevent the militarization of the turmoil in the Low Countries. He quickly advised his cousin to treat his turbulent subjects as magnanimously as possible. Encamped in Győr in 1566, Maximilian even offered to mediate the dispute. With links to both sides, he was well positioned to do so. At the Diet of Augsburg in 1566, on the one hand, Maximilian had already upheld Philip's interests by refusing to allow William of Orange to recruit in the empire. On the other hand, Schwendi had earlier told Orange in confidence that the emperor would work to satisfy German, as well as Spanish, concerns in the Netherlands if he ever had to.[19]

Philip was as jealous of his prerogatives as was Maximilian, though. The king did not want his cousin as a mediator; in September 1566 he quietly ordered Margaret of Parma to withhold Maximilian's conciliatory offer from William of Orange and Egmont. A few months later, he explained himself. As a matter of principle, he did not like having Maximilian solve his problems. The troubles in the Netherlands were his alone and subject to his authority, not his cousin's.[20]

A sense of crisis prevailed at both courts. In Vienna, L'Ecluse found himself worrying so much about events in the Netherlands that he could not concentrate on his research. But decisions in Madrid were implemented as sluggishly as they were in Vienna. Alba's appointment was not firm until December 1566 or January 1567; he did not make it to the Netherlands until the following August.[21] In the meantime, the two cousins wrangled at a distance over how to handle the issue. Debate turned angry when dynastic imperatives clashed with personal prerogatives and constitutional mandates with strategic necessities. It revealed much about the character of both men and their understanding of their offices, practical and theoretical. It also set the tone for the relationship of the two rulers until Maximilian's death in 1576. Advisers and family members participated actively. Even the youthful Archdukes Ernst and Rudolph in Spain were set to writing an essay "Pro pacificatione belgica" by their tutor.[22]

Philip did not relish going to war in the Netherlands, nor did he want any serious ruptures with the central European branch of his house. But should the king of Spain move an army into the Low Countries, he would not be risking the loyalty of his other principalities, whose interest in the region was marginal at best. For Maximilian, cordial relations with Spain and with the imperial estates were of nearly equal importance. Alienating either of them would have serious financial, military, and diplomatic consequences.

Maximilian, therefore, had no alternative but to work at persuading Philip to take the lightest hand possible in disciplining his troublesome subjects, especially their alleged leaders among the nobility. It was not altogether out of the question that at least some of the antagonists could be reconciled. Many prominent Netherlanders were worried by the role of prostitutes, habitual drunkards, and outright criminals in the Antwerp riots; William of Orange himself had put to death some of the ringleaders before things quieted down.[23] Furthermore, the emperor was receiving intelligence from Madrid that it was the king's advisers, not Philip himself, who were urging that Alba restore order in the Netherlands by force if necessary. Behind them, Maximilian told himself, was certainly Cardinal Granvella. This was something of a misperception—Granvella was also telling Philip to go to the Netherlands to see the problems for himself.[24] But as long as Granvella could be blamed for Philip's attitude, the king was not a lost cause.

Philip, however, was no more open to Maximilian's pleas for moderation than he was to acceptance of his cousin as a mediator. In November of 1566, the emperor's ambassador, Dietrichstein, reported that the king intended to crush the rebellion and restore Catholicism *in pristinum statum,* as he put it, no matter how much force was required. Philip now regretted his brief experiment with magnanimity, since it had not changed the dissidents' minds. Indeed, the situation might have turned out better if he had been more severe at the outset.[25] By the beginning of 1567, he had also rethought his plan of going to the Netherlands. He was unable to gather a large enough force to protect himself against foreign attack—a thinly veiled reminder to Maximilian that there were Germans who were supporting Philip's seditious subjects. What the king really wanted was not Maximilian's advice, but permission to recruit in the empire, along with an order that no one should aid the rebels. About the only comfort Maximilian could take from Philip's position, at least as stated, was that the king viewed the uprising in the Netherlands as a challenge to his general political authority. No mention was made of religion.[26]

But the king would soon be hearing from important people that confession was indeed a central Catholic concern in the Netherlands. His confessor, other clergymen, and Pius V himself were busily whetting his Catholic sensibilities. In March 1567, Philip received a letter from Rome over Pius' name. It urged the ruler to abandon all illusions about being able to subdue his opponents in the Low Countries while at the same time tolerating confessional heterodoxy, "perversity and license," as the superheated rhetoric of the time had it.[27] By the end of the year, these exhortations were working their desired effect. "Most zealous," is the way Adam von Dietrichstein described the monarch in matters of faith.[28]

None of these developments would go down well in Germany. But with Margaret of Parma reminding him that his charge to keep the imperial peace extended to the Netherlands, Maximilian had already relented a bit on the recruiting issue. In the fall of 1566, he allowed Philip to raise troops in the empire on the condition that the entire Habsburg patrimony in central Europe be exempted from the king of Spain's reach. By the end of December, the emperor had modified that stipulation as well. It was only Bohemia, which he protected as jealously as Philip and Margaret did the Netherlands, that was to be left untouched.[29] In late winter of 1567, the emperor even suggested an alternate line of march for Philip's army—from Savoy to Lorraine, north over Metz through Philip's holdings in Luxembourg, then on to Namur and Brussels. In this way, the king could move as he wished, yet avoid coming under fire from both the Swabian and the Rhenish circles.[30]

German interests also had to be considered, however. Though he had clearly met Philip's central request, Maximilian put off disclosing his decision to the empire until 16 February 1567. Furthermore, though Margaret and Philip implored him to do so, Maximilian did not forbid the imperial estates to help the dissidents. Most problematic of all, the emperor had also agreed with Germany's evangelical German princes that the Peace of Augsburg applied to the Netherlands.[31]

Ambassador Chantonnay thought that political calculation rather than conviction prompted Maximilian to take this step, but the two motives were, in this case, not mutually exclusive.[32] The civil strife roiling the Netherlands and France genuinely frightened many in the empire. By way of contrast, ten years or so had gone by since the Germans had territorialized two confessions, and the religious climate of central Europe had remained relatively calm. A sense of common Christian identity lingered among most elements of the German population, certainly in the imperial estates.[33] From Maximilian's standpoint, the settlement more or less worked. Just how sound an understanding he himself had where the Peace of Augsburg applied in the Netherlands is unclear. Making the case before the king of Spain almost two years later, Archduke Charles specified Guelders and Frisia, both of whose relations with imperial authority were quite ambiguous, along with what he nonchalantly called "some other principalities."[34] At the same time, any extension of the accord could do much to improve Maximilian's own image in the empire. If harmony prevailed, he could win the gratitude of a nervous population. The place of Calvinism had yet to be resolved, but Maximilian bore no constitutional responsibility for its welfare. No Catholic would ever reproach him for wanting to rid Germany of the movement, and followers of Luther's reform were eager to see their increasing numbers in the Netherlands protected. He could also play one side off against the other if he found the policy advantageous. Should he fail, of course, the emperor might be open to the wrath of Catholic and evangelical alike, but this prospect did not keep him from trying.

Neither Philip nor Margaret, however, was open to this argument, though for different reasons. The regent denied that the confessional arrangement of

1555 or any recess of the imperial diet had any force in the Low Countries. Echoing Charles V, she declared that the provinces had no obligation to the empire beyond that of occasional special contributions, voted freely by the estates. She questioned the wisdom of allowing the exercise of the Augsburg Confession; such ploys only encouraged Calvinists to claim equal treatment.[35] Philip readily called himself an imperial prince; the title allowed him to recruit in Germany for the purposes of suppressing rebellion. He was willing to enforce the imperial peace in his Burgundian patrimony. But he heartily disapproved of the German religious settlement. His answer to Maximilian's brief for Lutheran exceptionalism in the Low Countries was to insist that religion was not at issue in the disturbances; the Augsburg formula, therefore, was irrelevant to this situation.[36] Philip's operatives in Vienna argued the question with Maximilian even more pointedly. Chantonnay contended that if a duke of Saxony, indisputably bound by the Augsburg agreement, could forbid Catholicism in his territories, Philip could proscribe the Augustana in his. Clearly on the defensive, the emperor slipped back to his arguments for general moderation. Even if Luther's ideas had no standing in the Netherlands, Philip did not have to take military action.[37] Not only the emperor had difficulty in working his way through these contradictions; during early winter of 1568, the normally judicious Augustus of Saxony publicly demanded that Philip recognize the Peace of Augsburg in the Netherlands, yet forgo exercising the *jus reformandi* there.[38] At least Augustus' religious sympathies were clear, even though his thinking left something to be desired. Maximilian was providing no one with that satisfaction.

However off the mark his reasoning about the Peace of Augsburg may have been, the emperor's predictions about the reaction of the imperial estates to Philip's apparent intentions in the Low Countries were wholly correct. The king's assertion that the rebellion in the Netherlands was solely a political affair persuaded no one; his apparent plan to crush the seditious Netherlanders with force stiffened the resolve of the German princes to thwart him wherever possible. Christoph of Württemberg, Maximilian's erstwhile intimate, forbade his subjects to serve in campaigns to suppress the Augsburg Confession in the Netherlands.[39] The emperor's integrity was also in question. Talk was circulating throughout the empire of a planned confederation of the pope, the emperor, and other rulers to fight the Turks, and Protestants thought that such an alliance could be turned against the Netherlands as well. To avoid undue identification with his cousin's causes, Maximilian tried to discourage the visit of a Spanish emissary at a meeting in Erfurt of the delegates from the imperial circles during the summer of 1567, where military aid against the Turks was on the agenda. Worst of all, from the emperor's standpoint, a very few German territorial rulers were also ready to support actively the cause of their co-religionists to the west.[40]

Thus, the question of the Netherlands rather quickly showed that serving the empire while furthering the interests of the house of Austria was a delicate task. Even before the duke of Alba set foot in the Low Countries, political alarms went off somewhere in Germany any time the emperor so much as hinted that there was some merit to Philip's cause. For his part, Philip much resented having his concerns subordinated to German needs, regardless of what he heard about Maximilian's true feelings. The king was particularly displeased, of course, when Maximilian discouraged Spanish recruiting in the empire or in his own lands in central Europe.[41] But he disliked just as much being assaulted with arguments, practical, flattering, or specious, for treating the rebels leniently.[42] The Spanish ruler never denied that his presence in the Netherlands—Maximilian's way of insuring relatively mild treatment of the dissidents—was desirable. In 1567 Margaret of Parma solicited funds for the entourage required for such an expedition, thus giving Maximilian some reason to keep hammering away at his cousin on the matter.[43] But Philip also continued to mobilize.

Alba finally arrived in the Netherlands in August 1567 and soon made it clear that mercy had little place in Spanish policy. He asked Maximilian to have Orange declared an outlaw. The prince was then to appear before the commander, presumably to beg for clemency. Maximilian refused. Orange had already ignored prior mandates, and the emperor, once more mindful of his role in central Europe, feared that such a strategy would encourage the Germans to believe that Maximilian favored the Spanish cause.[44] But the duke was not inclined to wait. At the beginning of September, he arrested and imprisoned Egmont and Hoorn. A Spanish-directed purge of heretics and political dissidents began. Later generations of historians and polemicists have undoubtedly inflated the number of executions that took place. In all probability there were around a thousand—a modest figure by the grotesque standards of the twentieth century. Nevertheless, the duke's actions shocked contemporaries, probably because the bulk of it took place at the outset of the conflict and over a short span of time in 1568 and 1569.[45]

Maximilian too was horrified. The effect on Germany, he was convinced, would be pernicious; both counts were "German" as far as he was concerned. He still refused to believe that Philip could be so harsh, or even Alba, for that matter. Rather, he persisted in seeing the hand of Granvella in the decision, thus making life in Vienna even more uncomfortable for Ambassador Chantonnay, the cardinal's brother.[46] Regardless of who was making decisions in Spain, the German evangelical princes stepped up pressure on their emperor to intercede with Philip on behalf of Lutherans in the Low Countries. Even if not all the territorial rulers were wholly convinced that the peace of 1555 applied in the Netherlands, they had no firm reason to jettison their belief that the provinces were "related" to the empire. Maximilian, as emperor, therefore bore some responsibility for asking Philip to exercise care in handling his subjects in those provinces. Once again, some members of the imperial estates asked themselves if they could trust their emperor. Yet again it was being said that Maximilian was in league with the Spanish and the pope, all of whom were supposedly plotting to suppress the Augsburg Confession in Germany. In other words, a rerun of the Schmalkaldic War was in the offing.[47]

These were precisely the sentiments that Maximilian had wished to keep far from the empire, along with Alba's army. At the end of September 1567, he once more begged Philip to distinguish Lutherans and their privileges under the Augsburg settlement from other Protestant movements, chiefly the Calvinists, whom Philip could chastise as he pleased. Maximilian assured his cousin that he did not intend to have Lutherans worshipping wherever they liked—they could be exiled, after all.[48] At the emperor's court, the Spanish ambassador labored just as tirelessly to convince Maximilian that Philip had imprisoned Egmont and Hoorn not for religious reasons—both men were Catholics—but because they were disobedient vassals. The German princes, however, thought the procedure was altogether high-handed, and they came to Vienna with their arguments too. Hoorn's wife appeared before the emperor, begging him to intercede with Philip on behalf of her husband, a member of the imperial estates in good standing, and his family. In relaying her request to Philip, Maximilian added that Hoorn had done estimable service for the house of Habsburg, had a lot of friends in the empire, and even belonged to the august Order of the Golden Fleece. Countess Egmont sent an envoy, too, to request lenient treatment for her spouse. As in Hoorn's case, Maximilian promised to do what he could.[49] But German Protestant mistrust of anything Catholic and Spanish only grew. As Maximilian and Albrecht V of Bavaria planned the wedding of Albrecht's son to Renate of Lorraine in October of 1567, they hesitated to invite the pope and the king of Spain. They finally decided to ask both but to have surrogates appear for them at the ceremony. Otto Cardinal Truchsess of Augsburg stood in for Pius V, and Alba, of all people, for Philip.[50] By November, even Christoph of Württemberg, Maximilian's onetime confidant, had begun to doubt the emperor's support for the Peace of Augsburg. He was wrong, Maximilian noted bitterly in his diary, but the emperor did not record how he could change the duke's mind.[51]

Moderation, therefore, had fallen on deaf ears in Madrid and was becoming increasingly suspect in Germany. Philip, through Alba, had ruled out displays of clemency in the Netherlands, and the princes were becoming wary of an emperor who avoided making a wholehearted commitment to them. The chances that the empire could distance itself from the violence in the Netherlands grew ever dimmer during autumn and early winter of 1567. William of Orange had fled to Germany and was openly recruiting for his cause. The duke of Alba was doing the same.[52] Armed clashes between Huguenots and Catholics had broken out again in France by September 1567—certainly, Maximilian thought, a clear example of disobedient subjects' taking up arms against their king. The court in Vienna concluded that Philip's policies in the Netherlands had encouraged the outburst. Such an interpretation was, of course, a matter of debate; but one thing was clear—all sides in the unfolding struggle looked to Germany for military reinforcements and financial aid.[53]

To France, Maximilian spoke both as an emperor and as a Habsburg politician and without some of the ambivalence that plagued him in the Netherlands. He was hoping to have Charles IX as a son-in-law and could reassure the French ruler in good conscience that he had given no help to the Huguenots. He could constitutionally proscribe aiding the rebels and remind German Protestant princes, who were gathering help for the dissidents, of how dangerous such activities were. In 1567 and 1568, he issued mandates against William of Orange's recruiting in the empire. An order forbidding his subjects in the Habsburg lands to enter foreign service circulated as far east as the kingdom of Bohemia.[54]

But how would Maximilian enforce such decrees? His performance in Hungary had tarnished his credentials as a military leader.[55] Contemporaries also knew that the Habsburg was too poor to fight sedition, heresy, and the Turks all at once, should that be necessary. Even if Maximilian had been willing to force obedience from his vassals, there were no operative legal guidelines for such a policy. Neither the emperor nor the estates and the imperial circles, whose memberships overlapped, had a monopoly on arms.[56] Maximilian sometimes used redundant jurisdictions to his advantage—in

1568, without going to the imperial diet, he persuaded a gathering of the circles to lend him aid against the Turks.[57] On the whole, this distribution of power was ill suited to handling the complex problems that the conflict had raised in the Netherlands. Consensus, therefore, remained the modus operandi by default, but it was extraordinarily hard to come by in questions such as limiting recruiting and solving religious problems in the Netherlands and France. However useful biconfessionalism had been in maintaining German public peace, it did not help much in the conduct of religious politics abroad. The electors were almost always divided in their opinions, usually along confessional lines, on how to handle these issues.[58]

In such a setting, Maximilian was not likely to force his policies on anyone, at least by himself. Therefore, Germans who supported Protestants in France and the Netherlands, or who simply did not like the Spanish close to their borders, did as they saw fit, straining constitutional niceties and the patience of their emperor along the way. Even the emperor's brother-in-law, Duke William of Jülich, was already sending cavalry to the Netherlands, and, from there, to France.[59] Among the electors, only Frederick III, in the palatinate, talked about actively helping his Calvinist co-religionists in France. While he held back from sending troops personally, he looked the other way as one of his sons, Count Palatine John Casimir, assembled a force for the purpose.

Maximilian had known from the beginning of 1567 about William and John Casimir's activities. Under pressure from Chantonnay in November, the emperor ordered the former to stop. The princes of the palatinate, however, truly challenged their sovereign's authority. Maximilian dispatched a mission to both Frederick III and his son instructing the two Wittelsbachs on their constitutional duty to withhold aid from France. He also appealed to John Casimir's concern for his personal reputation and the interests of his house.[60] But the count stood firm, especially when the electors of Saxony and Brandenburg opined that what he was doing was within the law. His French expedition, he argued, had been undertaken in defense of Christendom. He was also rescuing a sovereign, not France's Charles IX, to be sure, but Jeanne d'Albret, the queen of Navarre who supported the Huguenot cause.[61] In December of 1567, John Casimir, with eight thousand cavalry and a regiment of infantry in tow, joined the Huguenot leader, Louis I de Bourbon, the prince of Condé and Jeanne's brother-in-law, in Pont-à-Mousson, about twenty miles south of Metz. They contributed materially to the successful Huguenot siege of Chartres a few months later. The following October, the count's cousin, Wolfgang of Pfalz-Zweibrücken, arrived in the kingdom with twenty thousand men and the astounding offer to serve free for a month.[62] And despite his early interest in Maximilian's advice to negotiate with seditious subjects, King Charles also resolved to go to war. "French diseases," Maximilian called both moves, his sense of humor still intact. His responsibilities still weighed heavily on him, as well. It was his duty to protect Christendom from harm, and he turned down the Valois ruler's request to recruit in the empire. The French, like everyone else, however, were not deterred.[63]

Whatever hopes Maximilian harbored for pacifying the Netherlands without dragging Germany into the fray evaporated when both Egmont and Hoorn were publicly beheaded in Brussels in June of 1568.[64] The execution did not arouse widespread religious indignation in the empire, for neither of the victims were Protestants. It did, however, heighten fears that the duke would move deeper into Germany for strategic reasons, as indeed he did. Already under orders to provision his armies locally, Alba began plundering East Frisia, which he would eventually use as a granary for his unruly forces. Important Calvinist partisans lived in the region, among them Ludwig of Nassau, who was William of Orange's younger brother. The reigning Count Etzard and his city of Emden sympathized with Orange as well.[65]

Alba's moves in northwestern Germany forced Maximilian to weigh starkly conflicting imperatives. Nassau had met his imperial obligations conscientiously and felt his emperor owed him protection. Maximilian himself did not want the Spanish to proceed on to Trier, as they threatened to do. Philip's forces in the Netherlands were behaving abominably. Nor was the emperor comfortable with Alba's high-handed style of generalship, which entailed communicating with Maximilian only when he needed him. At the same time, Maximilian was certainly not sorry to see Calvinists and their supporters punished, and it was this imperative, among the many to which he answered, that prevailed. As long as the duke stayed out of things that were none of his business, the emperor took it upon himself to keep the empire from aiding the rebels. This he would do, even if his defenses against the Turks suffered, a very strong statement from him.[66]

Themselves spokesmen for the empire's constitutional integrity, the German princes had more reason to suspect that Maximilian was "lying with the Spanish under the covers," as the emperor bitterly put it.[67] They reopened the cases of Hoorn and Egmont, complaining that the emperor had not intervened vigorously enough on the noblemen's behalf. All he had done was remind Philip that Egmont had served the Habsburgs well and that fellow members in the Order of the Golden Fleece deserved gentle treatment. The emperor had overlooked constitutional considerations that might have saved the two counts. Though Hoorn and William of Orange were members of the imperial estates, they had been stripped of their lands. Such punishment was disproportionate to their offenses, and they had every right to the protection of German law.[68]

By May 1568, Maximilian was even ready to justify Alba's entrance into Frisia. To the emperor's hearty displeasure, the counts continued to support the dissidents in the Netherlands. Not only were they forgetting their responsibilities toward the imperial peace, but they were aiding rebels who were destroying their own "nation." Maximilian promised to send the Spanish general what intelligence he could. The delighted Alba agreed with the Habsburg's constitutional reasoning entirely. He recalled once more Maximilian's argument that Philip's possessions in the Low Countries made the king of Spain a full-fledged member of the Holy Roman Empire and entitled him to its protection.[69]

Following Alba's successful strike in Groningen against supporters of the uprising in the Netherlands during the summer of 1568, the emperor congratulated him lavishly. The victory, Maximilian said, was a boon not only to the king of Spain but to the house of Austria in which he and Philip were "the closest of blood relations."[70] He defended Alba when Duke William of Jülich protested the rough conduct of the Spaniard's forces. He called William of Orange a conspirator against Philip, Philip's administration, and against the imperial peace. Once more, the duke concurred.[71] And Maximilian remained attentive to Alba in smaller ways. If a subject of Philip's from the Netherlands approached Maximilian about entering his service, the emperor touched base with the commander to make sure that there were no objections from that quarter. Maximilian cultivated connections with the duke's family as well, in one case promoting the career of a Habsburg servant with the general's son.[72]

By the fall of 1568, one of Philip's ambassadors in Vienna believed that the emperor's authority had deteriorated so badly throughout Germany that should he need serious aid, he would have only Philip to call upon.[73] But this state of affairs did not change Spanish opinion of him. Like the German princes, Philip and his commander still had many grounds for doubt about his commitment to, and understanding of, their position. Maximilian had shown in the Grumbach affair that he was willing to use force when his own authority was at stake, even in the face of hostile public opinion. His tiresome arguments for princely magnanimity in the Netherlands therefore reflected his interests in Germany, and not some higher principle. With Alba, he indulged in open self-pity. Though he applauded Alba's success at Groningen, where the general had been quite generous toward the defeated counts of Emden, the emperor believed that the imperial diet would spell only trouble for himself. The general was asked to imagine what it was like to face accusations from the embittered princes.[74] Indeed, Maximilian's self-serving ways with his cousin in his dealings with the Netherlands bordered on insult. Philip was not the German emperor precisely because Ferdinand I and Maximilian had done everything they could to exclude him from the office. Moreover, the duke of Alba's orders were to put down sedition, not to ask questions about constitutional niceties. All these considerations Maximilian shamelessly ignored when pleading his case for moderation.

And he certainly could not divorce himself from German concerns. He continued to relay German complaints to Alba about his treatment of Lutherans, the damage his campaigns were doing to trade, and the duke's abuse of "German freedom" generally. He also saddled the duke with responsibility for handling such problems.[75] In December of 1568, Alba took exception to criticisms of his troops from an assembly of the Rhenish, Westphalian, Upper Rhenish, and Swabian circles. Maximilian granted that the German princes, especially the Rhenish ones, had been most unfriendly to the Spanish forces and their leader. But he also told Alba that these districts generally were a force for political stabilization in the empire. Only if the territorial rulers overstepped their legal limits would he intervene to help the Spanish commander.[76]

Finally, even though he issued mandates against William of Orange, Maximilian seemed ready to pacify the prince rather than to repress him. In September 1568, an unidentified imperial councillor prepared a memorandum which promised Orange that Maximilian would do everything to get Alba out of the Netherlands. The emperor's government would do what it could to put together a regime in the Netherlands that its people would find more acceptable and that would function more harmoniously with its "neighbors," meaning the empire. In return the seditious prince was to abandon military activities. He was also to keep Maximilian, or others who had the interests of the "fatherland" at heart, abreast of his movements. A code was thoughtfully enclosed for his use.[77]

Maximilian's efforts to be an imperial peacemaker in the king of Spain's Burgundian lands were proving as futile as his attempts to reconcile Christians elsewhere in the empire and within his own patrimony. It was hard enough dealing with the confessional divisions affecting Germany's princes. The addition of an unpopular foreign king, who was also the emperor's cousin, and an even more unpopular army to the struggle under way in the Netherlands complicated Maximilian's tasks there immeasurably. The emperor's only success so far was to have analyzed the implications of the situation well. Going to war, as Philip had done, set off a chain of sympathetic responses that were only sharpening confessional differences throughout western Europe and in the empire. The hopes for religious conciliation that had inspired the Peace of Augsburg, and Maximilian's reliance on that agreement, were growing ever more remote. Trying to balance his generic support of monarchy, his need for cordial relations with his richer Spanish cousin, and his responsibilities vis-à-vis a constitution that gave no clear guidance on dealing with the Netherlands and other important issues, the emperor could only respond to these pressures rather than master them. "Dreary and care-ridden times," he called the year 1568.[78] From his perspective, he had a point.

twelve

Confronting Inadequacy

Maximilian's reputation domestically and abroad was measured largely by his ability to defend and further German interests.[1] His contorted and fruitless maneuvering in the Netherlands raised serious questions in all confessional camps about his fitness as an emperor. Nor, by 1570, had he resolved two embarrassing disputes in Italy, which, like his predicament in the Netherlands, stretched the Habsburg between obligations to his office and to his dynasty. Insufficient material resources made his position even worse.

Generations of emperors had claimed suzerainty over an array of northern Italian fiefdoms—Milan, Florence, and Ferrara among them.[2] Practical control of these lands, however, had shifted many times over the centuries. Each change had inspired learned juridical argument on both sides of the Alps over the relation between regional and imperial institutions, but nothing had been settled.[3] While local rulers in the Italian city-states normally distanced themselves from German affairs, they were eager to have the emperor recognize their titles officially and to retain his favor when they needed it. In Florence, Cosimo de' Medici had for some time been badgering Maximilian to confer the title of grand duke on him. When the emperor refused to cooperate, Pius V granted Cosimo's wish in 1569—a reward, he said, for aid the Florentine ruler had sent to the king of France against the Huguenots. Both Maximilian and Philip were furious at a concession that, as they saw it, challenged their influence on the Italian peninsula.[4] Aided by his loyal ambassador in Rome,

Prosper d'Arco, the emperor authorized archival and historical searches to turn up justification for his objections.[5]

Disregarding the advice of the empress and a new Spanish ambassador in Vienna, Francisco Hurtado de Mendoza, count of Monteagudo, Maximilian viewed the dispute as a matter of conscience and thought he could mobilize Protestants in the empire to come to his aid. At a diet in Speyer in 1570, he discussed a possible military strike against Florence with the secular electors. Though they readily acknowledged that the emperor ought to protect imperial prerogatives and urged him to do so, neither Saxony, Brandenburg, nor the elector palatine would assist him actively. Unable to launch the undertaking by himself, Maximilian had to let the dispute drag on. Only in 1575 did the affair come to an end, and it was money, not sovereign power, that settled it. In need of papal support in his quest for the Polish crown, Maximilian grudgingly recognized the Medici title in Florence. To sweeten the otherwise distasteful bargain, a new prince, Grand Duke Francesco, shipped along a hundred thousand badly needed scudi to Vienna.[6]

More humiliating still was the other conflict in Italy, which was as much a test of Maximilian's dynastic prestige as it was of his abilities as emperor. At stake was the tiny margravate of Finale, an imperial fief on the Ligurian seacoast. Here a local insurgency started in the 1560s had driven the tyrannical Margrave Alfonso del Carretto to Vienna for refuge and protection. The emperor felt that he and Philip of Spain owed something to Carretto; the margrave's father had been killed serving Charles V. Maximilian and Philip also agreed by 1569 that the emperor's authority was at issue.[7] Imperial commissioners went to the area to restore order and the legitimate ruler, but in vain. As early as 1567, Maximilian had considered returning Carretto to power through military intervention; as an imperial prince, Philip was asked to participate. At first unenthusiastic, the king then endorsed the idea so warmly that the emperor suspected his cousin's motives. Nevertheless, Maximilian charged the Spanish ruler in September of 1569 with carrying out the *Reichsexekution* in the margravate. He also reminded his cousin that the latter was undertaking the mission as a member of the empire and "brother" of its emperor, not as the ruler of Spain.

Two weeks later, Philip informed his ambassador in Vienna, Chantonnay, that he might incorporate Finale into his Italian holdings to make his own borders more secure. Two years went by, however, and neither he nor Maximilian moved decisively in the region. But in 1571, Philip seized Finale for himself. He had moved, he declared quite frankly, not out of duty to the empire, but simply to protect the principality from a French invasion he thought was imminent.

Maximilian was caught completely off guard.[8] He was enormously upset and remained so; Philip's strike was a blow to the emperor's reputation and sovereignty, as well as to the standing of Germany as a whole.[9] Even Monteagudo, the Spanish ambassador, saw Maximilian's authority as so shaky that the emperor had to take such incidents seriously. This he certainly did; Maximilian would eventually say that he woke up thinking about Finale in the morning and went to bed with the question at night.[10] Nevertheless, to the distress of Germany's territorial rulers, the emperor was unable to resolve the problem. Monteagudo's attitude did nothing to improve German-Spanish relations, either. Upon hearing from Vice-Chancellor Weber and Court Marshal Hans Trautson that attacks on imperial interests in Finale were unacceptable to the princes, the ambassador replied that Philip respected only threats from God.[11] The Spanish ruler did return the territory to theoretical imperial control in 1573. He also correctly predicted that Maximilian lacked the money to make good his commitments to Carretto. Maximilian never could fully pay the troops that would carry out the margrave's restoration. A partial imperial occupation of Finale, erratically funded, always dispirited, and carried out while the margrave was still absent, was in place when Maximilian died in 1576. The territory eventually fell under Spanish control in 1617.[12]

Such episodes further reduced Maximilian's stature among German princes whose reservations about the emperor's policy toward the conflicts in France and the Netherlands were mounting. Philip's forces did not go away; indeed they had become a major irritant to Germany's territorial rulers. They wanted Maximilian to do something about it, and quickly. They did, of course, have different goals. In the eyes of the Protestants, the greatest service Maximilian could perform would be to restrain his own cousin, who continued to recruit in imperial territory. Catholics, whose attitudes toward Spain relaxed a bit during the 1570s, were more eager to keep the Germans from aiding the cause of Protestant rebellion, wherever it occurred.

Maximilian's chief concern had become retaining the support of all the princes in the midst of these cross-currents. If doing so required him to confess to weakness, he did. Acknowledging Catholic concerns in 1568, Maximilian refused to order German troops to leave Philip's army. Protestant complaints brought a feeble reply from him that the soldiers would probably not obey his orders to withdraw. But the German evangelicals could not be ignored either, and Maximilian offered to confront Philip more directly than he had in the past. The emperor's youngest brother, Archduke Charles, would go to Madrid for face-to-face negotiations with their royal cousin. The two Habsburg lines had some purely dynastic issues to air: the imperial succession and the marriages of Maximilian's daughters. But the Netherlands and the problems of Spanish recruiting in Germany were the central items on the agenda.[13]

Maximilian was gambling dangerously with his reputation. Philip had been consistently unsympathetic to his cousin's private arguments; Charles's mission was an invitation for the king to take the same position more publicly. Philip had made it known that he had little regard for German politics and the emperor's role in them. "A prince of his station," said the Spanish ruler of his cousin in October 1568, should not have to listen to the German rulers.[14] Even before Charles presented his case, Philip expected that he was coming simply to intercede for Orange and "the rest of the heretics" who had violated the true faith.[15] Flawed protocol did not make Philip any more receptive. The Spanish ambassadors in Vienna, not Maximilian himself, first told the Spanish ruler that the archduke was coming. The king had also heard rumors that he would be asked to relinquish the Netherlands to the empire outright, or hand over its government to Charles or one of Maximilian's sons.[16]

Charles arrived in Madrid on 10 December 1568. Philip was indeed supremely chilly, at least when discussing the Netherlands. Through the winter of 1569, the Spanish monarch, the archduke, and sometimes the emperor, fired their views back and forth with no change on either side. Even the young Archduke Rudolph was called upon to perform and delivered a plea for negotiations with William of Orange and the return of his confiscated lands. The king remained unmoved. Maximilian's problems in Germany, he said, were his alone; Philip would not adjust Spanish policy to ease the emperor's burdens. The archduke tried again, reminding Philip that Maximilian had a duty to end dissension in the empire and to restore public peace. Philip was not impressed.[17]

Toward the end of January 1569, the king handed over two statements of his policy in the Low Countries. One was for Maximilian; a second was in Latin for the German princes who did not read Spanish. Philip's ambassadors in Vienna knew about the harsh contents of both messages by March. The king of Spain had dropped all pretense that his quarrel with the rebels in the Low Countries was purely secular; he now talked openly about defending the "true" faith of Rome. Anticipating a very hostile reaction in Germany to

the communiqués, Chantonnay and Vanegas said nothing about them. Maximilian had yet to read either document by the time a meeting of the princes'
representatives took place in Frankfurt on 14 April 1569. Both versions finally
found their way to the emperor some time between the end of the month
and the second week of May, but, seriously indisposed, he did not deal with
them immediately. Philip permitted his cousin to edit out some of the most
incendiary passages; Maximilian and Vice-Chancellor Zasius, who wanted
desperately to soothe the imperial estates, took him up on the offer.[18]

There was, however, no way to prettify the Spanish ruler's firm denial
that the Netherlands were part of the German empire. Imperial laws and
recesses had nothing to do with his lands. He had listened to Maximilian,
through Archduke Charles, only because of dynastic ties. Indeed, Philip went
to some length to point out that Maximilian was ill suited to advise him or
to ask for his consideration. The emperor's persistent refusal to embrace
Catholic orthodoxy and remove the confessionally suspect from his court left
Philip with the impression that he alone was expected to change his policies.
Countering the general argument that leniency in the Netherlands would
redound to his honor, Philip took the highest of roads. While such worldly
concerns were real, he said, they were trivial compared with those touching
upon the honor of God, His Holy Church, and its general promise of salvation.[19]

Philip had obviously dug into the Netherlands for the long haul, and
Archduke Charles's mission had failed. Indeed, William of Orange and the
more committed of the Protestant princes in Germany had seemingly been
unwilling to await its outcome. During the winter of 1569, Orange began
maneuvering around Hagenau in southwestern Germany. The area was crucial for the prince; it lay directly on the line of march for mercenaries going
to join Philip's armies. Administered by Archduke Ferdinand of the Tyrol,
it was also part of the Habsburg patrimony. Worse yet, Count Wolfgang of
Zweibrücken had taken an armed force into France, thereby raising the likelihood that Charles IX might go to war against the empire. French royal
troops did indeed begin moving toward Zweibrücken.[20]

By comparison with Count Wolfgang, said ambassador Vanegas to the
emperor, Alba was the soul of moderation. Orange's incursions into Ferdinand's territories disturbed Maximilian, too. It was time for the emperor to
tilt toward Spain and Catholic France. A detailed mandate went out against
Wolfgang and Orange. Though the indictment of Count Wolfgang read like
a lecture on constitutional law, its thrust was clear enough. Under threat of

the imperial ban, Wolfgang was to dismantle his forces in Alsace out of consideration for both Archduke Ferdinand and the estates and principalities of the empire. Orange was banned outright. The circles were put on military alert. In Cologne a *Deputationstag*—a meeting of delegates from the circles— was to consider aiding both Ferdinand and the neighboring bishop of Strasbourg.[21] But other dynastic considerations persuaded the emperor to modify his orders almost as soon as he gave them. The imperial princes were always on guard against Habsburg use of the empire for narrow dynastic ends. Maximilian had tried to avoid open partiality toward the house of Austria, and the ban on William visibly advanced Habsburg interests most of all. The emperor therefore did nothing to curb the prince and moreover turned down Archduke Ferdinand's request to activate the dormant Austrian imperial circle in defense of the Habsburg holdings. Nevertheless, even apparent restraint in dealing with the interests of his own brother, along with Maximilian's consistent criticism of Philip, did not impress the poorer German princes, who hoped to see the wealthier circles mustered quickly to counter any French invasion.[22]

At a diet held in Speyer during the spring of 1570, Maximilian made a last comprehensive effort to gain some control over this complex situation. Protestant electors were now worried about a current rumor that their emperor and Pius V were conspiring to depose them. Preposterous though the tale was, the elector palatine was urging his secular colleagues to join forces in the face of the alleged threat. For their part, Catholic ecclesiastical princes wanted to reopen the issue of Ferdinand I's Ecclesiastical Reservation. Maximilian, however, refused to discuss religious matters at all; he put off until a future meeting reconsideration of the Ecclesiastical Reservation. Instead, the emperor tried to modify the venomous environment that often surrounded these deliberations. He asked the estates to forbid the publication of broadsides in which the confessions attacked one another.[23]

Maximilian's main proposals, however, centered around an elaborate scheme for imperial reform, which Lazarus Schwendi had drawn up. Part of the plan called once more for regulating recruitment of mercenaries in the empire. This commerce was as lively as ever, and the king of France was complaining bitterly about the help reaching the Huguenots, chiefly from the palatinate. Maximilian and Schwendi proposed to give the emperor the last word regarding the practice. It was the only way, they argued, to spare the empire divisive military engagements in France and the Netherlands. Wolfgang of Zweibrücken, who had ignored his emperor's warning the year before, was again forbidden to recruit. Maximilian volunteered to assume the responsibility, held by the captains of the imperial circles, for mustering all districts in case one among them should be attacked. He also asked once more for the establishment of a standing imperial force.

Aside from the last suggestion, which the princes opposed almost reflexively, the emperor's program was not wholly improbable. A gathering of the imperial deputies in Frankfurt in the spring of 1569 had authorized Maximilian to command the circles that had been ready to aid regions threatened by Wolfgang and Alba.[24] But none of Maximilian's ideas received a serious hearing at Speyer. Though the princes had quickly protested when Wolfgang of Zweibrücken bivouacked in their holdings on the way to France, their worries ebbed once the count was safely in another realm. Possible French retaliation was a distant evil. Sensing no pressures to alter the status quo, German territorial rulers, Protestant and Catholic alike, were reluctant to enlarge the powers of their emperor. Though Maximilian pointed out that large-scale foreign recruiting might cut into the number of men available to meet imperial emergencies, the argument went nowhere. The princes remained free to allow troops from their lands to serve in the armies of other princes, provided that the appropriate circle captain approved. Maximilian was utterly defeated. "Tiresome" (*langweilig*), he called the diet, his last effort to strengthen his executive authority in the empire.[25]

All the qualities that distinguished Maximilian from his father and once recommended him to the princes—his articulate mastery of their language, his openly German orientation, his genuinely cordial relations with key figures, and his open lines of communication with all the electors—were of little help now.[26] Maximilian continued forbidding Germans to recruit in aid of foreign powers, but to no avail.[27] If anything, all sides in the struggles in France and the Netherlands intensified their quests for German troops. William of Orange felt sufficiently certain of himself to argue his case as sloppily as did other belligerents of the day. An imperial mandate in 1572, he said, overstated the closeness of the legal connection between the Netherlands and the empire. In practically the same breath, however, he declared that had the Netherlands been included in the Peace of Augsburg, many of the current difficulties would not have arisen.[28]

Here and there, opportunities appeared for the emperor to pursue the only policies that remained to him—finding grounds for compromise among people who acted out of "impassioned, heated feelings" and maintaining the goodwill of all sides.[29] He could be exquisitely sensitive. In 1570, Maximilian supported the candidacy of Prince Ernst of Bavaria as archbishop of Cologne, a step that delighted both Philip and Alba. Local evangelicals, however, wanted the incumbent, Salentin von Isenburg, to continue in the position. Though a man of proven administrative skills, Isenburg had never taken holy orders or enforced the Tridentine catechism in his see. So unorthodox a figure reassured supporters of the new confessions, and Maximilian deferred to their concerns. The emperor decreed that Ernst would reside in Cologne long enough to be plausibly eligible for the position but that Isenburg could remain in office until that moment came.[30] Maximilian was consistently thoughtful in promoting good relations with Protestant princes, particularly those who were reliable champions of the Habsburgs in Germany. One such was Duke Julius of Braunschweig-Wolfenbüttel, who, on the christening of his off-spring, received warm congratulations, along with tactfully ecumenical as-surances that participation in such ceremonies was a good work in the "King-dom of Christ."[31] Sometimes belligerents did have the same interests. Orange's marauding "Sea Beggars," for example, plagued Alba and the rulers of Frisia alike. Maximilian went to the rescue of both the duke and the counts in the spring of 1572, using troops he himself had raised in the empire. But such moments were rare. More often he listened to partisans on all sides of the religious conflicts in France and the Netherlands and their imperial epi-centers and responded mechanically to demands as they appeared, rather than harmonizing them. Should Alba complain, as he often did, about help that the counts of Emden sent to Orange's forces, Maximilian would dutifully order them to cease and desist. If the counts turned out to have been more contrite than Alba had let on, Maximilian would just as dutifully revise and soften his directive.[32] Neither side paid much attention to him. The Frisian princes continued to do more or less as they pleased. And Alba remained uncooperative, even when the issues between him and the empire did not bear immediately on confessional politics and warfare. In 1570, the Diet of Speyer had reconfirmed an earlier imperial resolution to regularize the erratic systems of coinage in the empire. The Burgundian circle was specifically charged to reduce the silver and gold content of their money to a level that approximated other German coinage—specifically, the one circulating in the neighboring Westphalian circle. Despite repeated reminders from Maximilian, Alba never complied.[33]

Maximilian's view of the confessional situation in Germany darkened con-siderably. He was unhappily beginning to think that the imperial constitution and, more specifically, the religious settlement of 1555 was a flawed and ineffective instrument. Neither Protestants nor Catholics were open to reason. Moreover, the biconfessional structure of the arrangement was becoming obsolete. The Augsburg Confession of 1532, he declared in a fit of bitter exaggeration during the summer of 1570, had no more than six partisans left in a land where there now were as many opinions as there were heads. The papal camp was no better off; Pius V, while not without his Christian virtues, lacked prudence and good sense. Faithful Catholics, he lamented at the end of the year, were also shrinking in number.[34]

Calvinism, by way of contrast, seemed to be winning the day. Early in 1572, as Count Palatine John Casimir opened contacts with many German princes and electors as well as the admiral of France, Maximilian saw the empire falling to the Heidelberg Catechism. When Ambassador Monteagudo pointed out the affinity between those who had left the faith a long time ago—meaning Luther's followers—and those who had abandoned it more recently, the emperor remained silent.[35]

Maximilian resisted heavy pressure in the early 1570s to join the Catholic League, a proposed reconstitution of the Landsberg League that Ferdinand I and Albrecht of Bavaria had cobbled together in 1558 to halt Wilhelm Grumbach's marauders. They could count on his backing for anything that encouraged general tranquillity, he said, but this idea was clearly not of that sort.[36] Though the original organization included a few Protestant territories, as well as Catholic principalities, the general tendency of its policies was to serve the interests of Rome. The revised version, an alliance of the orthodox, with Philip II at its head, would stretch from Bavaria across the Rheintal and into the Spanish Netherlands and rescue the region from heresy.[37] Leagues, however, bred counterleagues, said the emperor; it would be best if the organization included Protestants. In effect, he was blunting the confessional thrust intended by the alliance's organizers. The league never got off the ground.[38]

Meanwhile, institutionally and even emotionally, Maximilian was growing closer to Philip. The implications of the uprising in the Netherlands for established order troubled him to the core. He never did wholeheartedly embrace the Church of Rome as the king of Spain wished, but in other ways the emperor became more consistently responsive to his cousin's interests. Though he urged the king of Spain to take local suspicions into account, Maximilian allowed Philip to raise two German regiments in the empire for the Netherlands in 1571. Indeed, the emperor was glad to cooperate. The following year found him comparing William of Orange to Grumbach, thereby at least implying that the prince should be executed.[39] As Philip gathered 12,600 men for the Netherlands in 1572, Maximilian forbade the princes to disrupt their movement; his cousin's campaign, he now said, was constitutionally just, a defense of the king's own lands that were part of the empire. The rebels' behavior was an intolerable breach of the imperial peace, creating such "barbarischen confusion" in the Netherlands that no remedy could be found for the dispute there. On 15 July he met one of Philip's key demands by stripping Orange and his supporters of whatever rights, privileges, and immunities they had enjoyed in the German territories.[40]

Thus, Maximilian was drifting toward a position that seriously weakened whatever confidence Germany's Protestant princes had had in him. However artfully he could balance confessional interests when he had to, the emperor's ultimate loyalty was to his house, which was fast becoming Europe's premier Catholic dynasty. Worse yet, to the thinking of Lutherans and Calvinists alike, he seemed eager to reinforce that status through marriage alliances, not only in Spain but in France. Indeed, these schemes were one of his chief motives for keeping Germany tranquil and free of military entanglements abroad. For a marriage between Charles IX and Maximilian's second daughter, Archduchess Elisabeth, to take place, imperial mercenaries who were serving in the Huguenot cause had to quit French soil, and Maximilian urged German troops to leave the kingdom. The emperor did not altogether ignore Protestant interests as he pursued his dynastic ambitions. Between 1569 and 1570, he advised the young French monarch to remain as neutral as he could in the ongoing French conflict. If his prospective son-in-law appeared open to some freedom of conscience—a notion that found its way into the royal Declaration of St. Germaine of 1570—the need for German forces in France generally would end and Charles's subjects would obey him once again.[41]

As a strategy, moderation was as unlikely to work for the king of France as it had been for the emperor. The French queen mother, Catherine de' Medici, who had overseen her son's regency, had been relatively flexible in confessional matters. Nevertheless, many French Catholics chafed against this regime; the most resolute among them hoped to eradicate Protestantism not only in their own kingdom but in Europe as a whole. Strongly orthodox elements among the population of Paris had reacted vehemently to a limited declaration of tolerance issued by the crown at as early as 1562. But Maximilian had no other ideas to offer; he was pleased when the Valois monarch said, in 1568, that he would follow his counsel.[42]

By 1572, Maximilian had realized his most important objective—Elisabeth was now the consort of Charles IX. But confessional relations in the kingdom were deteriorating. Especially in Paris, Catholics protested measures promoting further religious harmony; Huguenots continued to aid their co-religionists in the Netherlands.[43] Maximilian himself had lost patience with all Calvinists, especially when he saw them as linked with sedition. In 1569, the emperor had cheered Charles's victory at Jarnac over Huguenot rebels and congratulated the king that the leader of the dissidents, Louis Prince of Condé, was dead.[44]

In this unstable atmosphere Charles gave the signals that set off the savage massacre of French Protestants on 23–24 August 1572 during the feast of St. Bartholomew. The slaughter went on both in Paris and in the provinces. The first grisly news to reach Vienna sobered Protestant sympathizers at the emperor's court considerably. Living and dead had been hurled into the water or piled into graves; ears, genitals, and finally heads had been cut off—all in all, a picture "the likes of which could be found in no histories."[45] The leadership at Charles's court was disorganized. Maximilian tried to establish the facts of the matter with the French ambassador in Vienna, Jean Vulcob, as best he could. A special envoy from France, Montmorin, who arrived at Maximilian's court a month later, reconfirmed the analysis. The crown had resolved that France was to be Catholic only, at least as far as public worship was concerned, for the good of the realm.[46]

Both versions depicted the massacre as a king's defense of his throne against conspirators, thus tidily confirming Maximilian's low opinion of Calvinists. He and his Spanish cousin even found some advantage in this situation. Philip II welcomed the general confusion into which France had fallen, for it was likely to limit whatever aid the Huguenots might give to abet the sedition in the Netherlands. Maximilian's reasons were more purely dynastic. He was now pursuing the Polish crown, either for himself or for a member of his house, and one of his rivals was the duke of Anjou, later to become Henry III of France. The duke had played a role in the French bloodbath, as the emperor was eager to make public, for despite his abhorrence of Calvinist rebellion, Maximilian was badly shaken by the dreadful violence in his son-in-law's kingdom.[47]

By October 1572 the massacre was causing Maximilian serious political trouble in Germany. The election of his successor in the empire was looming, and Maximilian needed the support of the Protestant secular electors more than ever. He had tactfully discouraged Philip's thoughts about making one of his Austrian nephews governor in the Netherlands. Germans, said the emperor, did not like to see Habsburgs passing imperial lands back and forth among themselves.[48] But the St. Bartholomew massacre was calling the emperor's carefully nurtured reputation for religious moderation into question. Going through a bundle of correspondence, in itself suspect because it had come to him with a broken seal, Maximilian read that his marriage policies in Spain and France had convinced many German princes that he, along with Pius V and Philip II, had assented to the killing.[49]

Charles IX had, in fact, taken full responsibility for the episode, but rumor believed carried the force of truth, at least for a time. Maximilian had to labor mightily to defend his innocence. He chastised himself for the French marriage he had once thought so desirable. He regretted deeply, or so he said, that his daughter had wed in a realm where such an unchristian bloodbath could take place. All that the emperor could say in Charles's defense was that the king was not in full control of his government.[50]

Fear that any connection drawn between him and the violence in France might cripple his quest for the Polish crown gave the emperor all the more reason to be evenhanded in confessional matters. As long as Alba remained in the Netherlands, Maximilian begged him to show mercy to individuals, including such bothersome ones as the counts of Frisia, and to stop threatening the empire.[51] The Habsburg welcomed the son of the executed Count Egmont to his court in Vienna.[52] At some level, he may have been reasonably sincere, for he continued to criticize violence as a way of resolving religious differences even after Henry of Valois was elected king of Poland in April of 1573.[53] At the same time, however, Maximilian continued to support Philip's cause in the Netherlands; in the name of dynastic solidarity, the emperor urged Archduke Ferdinand to do the same.[54] When, in December 1573, Philip replaced Alba in the Low Countries with Don Luis de Requesens, who had orders to follow a more conciliatory path, Maximilian did not entirely applaud the move. He deplored the economic hardships that the war had inflicted on the Low Countries, and he urged the new governor-general to be merciful. But, he was quick to add, the stubborn disobedience of the rebels fully justified the stern measures that authorities were taking against them.[55]

Still, Maximilian was clearly becoming so weary of this unproductive balancing act in the Netherlands and in Germany as a whole and with confessional problems generally, that he was losing interest in thinking about either condition. In May of 1573, Monteagudo had lectured him on both the empire's weaknesses and Maximilian's own. The emperor was neither resentful nor angry. He merely made light of such matters, publicly and in private.[56] Certainly his credibility in Germany was much diminished, even among personal friends. Speaking with a Venetian envoy in 1574, Albrecht of Bavaria said that Ferdinand I, hostile to Protestants though he was, was at least sincere and therefore highly regarded in the empire.[57] Maximilian, or so he implied, was another case altogether.

The emperor's judgment was now considered questionable as well. For all his apparent fumbling in the Netherlands, Maximilian could plausibly maintain that up to 1570 or so, his advocacy of accommodation and moderation in German religious affairs had fostered public peace. Now he was among the few people who still believed that war did no one good. Aid was flowing to the rebels in the Low Countries from several quarters. By 1573, the elector palatine together with France had sent Orange a hundred thousand crowns and forty thousand gulden for arms. Another count palatine, Christoph, was fighting openly for the rebel prince, as were counts Ludwig and Henry of Nassau. At the same time, Count John Casimir continued to support the French Huguenots.[58] In spite of the emperor's tilt in their direction, his religious policies found no more favor with Philip's advisers than they ever had. In 1573 some anonymous councillors in Madrid recommended that the Netherlands be returned to Catholicism on the model of the Tyrol, Bavaria, and the Catholic cantons of Switzerland. The religious practice at Maximilian's court was not even mentioned.[59]

Still stunned in 1574 at having been linked in people's minds with the St. Bartholomew's massacre, Maximilian once again voiced his regret to Schwendi over his son-in-law's role in the affair. Had Charles IX actually sought his advice, he would, "as a father," have counseled him very differently. As for what had gone on in France, and what was still laying waste the Netherlands:

> Things are no different than I have correctly (*vernünftiglich*) written you, that affairs of religion cannot be adjudicated and dealt with by the sword. . . . Furthermore, Christ and his apostles taught this over and over. For their sword is the tongue, their message God's word and Christian behavior: for their lives should inspire us, the way and how far they came to follow Christ, to follow them. . . . To summarize, Spain and France do things as they wish, and they will have to answer to God, the righteous judge. For myself, God willing, my behavior will be honorable, Christian,

loyal, and just. It is [my] entire hope that God will grant his blessing to me in this endeavor, so that I can be responsible for my thought and action before God and this world. And if I can do this, I shall not trouble myself with this wicked and godless world.[60]

Though the fiery eloquence with which he wrote was striking, Maximilian had more or less thought these things for many years.[61] Now, however, he was stating a private position, not proposing a widely applicable solution to Europe's religious divisions. To a proposal from Schwendi that same year that religious toleration be instituted in the empire, the emperor shrugged politely—this, even though Schwendi promised that Maximilian might be known as the "father of the fatherland" if tranquillity were guaranteed in Germany thanks to such a step.[62] As Maximilian now saw it, the Germans had brought their troubles on themselves. Personal pleasure and personal interests, not concern for the public good, dictated their behavior. If there was a cure for this, it lay in God's hands.[63] The Spanish ambassador found the emperor equally unresponsive. Following a warning from Monteagudo about rumors of a large-scale German invasion of the Netherlands, Maximilian nonchalantly commented that Monteagudo's informants could not have given him reliable information. The very same people had sent the emperor reports and not mentioned such threats. As for the Netherlands, he had told Philip many times how to handle the problem. It was up to the king of Spain to find his own remedies. Maximilian heard out the remainder of the ambassador's pleas in courteous silence.[64] When the Rhenish electors asked their emperor in May of 1574 to mediate once more in the Netherlands, he granted that it was in his power, but only if Philip was willing. Earlier efforts, such as Archduke Charles's mission to Madrid in 1568–1569, had been fruitless. He had brought the parties together for a time, but nothing had come of their deliberations.[65]

If Maximilian saw any alternative to confessional reconciliation through compromise and accommodation, he never disclosed it. His consistency of purpose may argue for his unwavering belief in his policy, or it may be evidence of weak imagination, overall exhaustion, or both. In any case, his commitment to religious tolerance was at odds with the political realities. The ambiguities and limitations of the German constitution, which he professed to respect, frustrated important initiatives at crucial moments. Philip's dual status as imperial prince and dynastic representative was particularly trying for the man who was both his suzerain and his cousin. A reform of the entire system was out of the question; many before Maximilian had attempted it and fallen short, even in less turbulent times. Frustrated in all his efforts to lead Germany out of its religious difficulties, in the end the emperor simply allowed the problems to wash over him. Sometimes he leaned toward the Catholic side, sometimes toward the Protestant, especially in dealing with questions about the Netherlands. It was a way of surviving, however, not of leading.

thirteen

Staying Afloat

In 1564 the Venetian envoy Giovanni Michele had predicted that thwarted ambition might turn Maximilian into a passive man. Little more than six years later, the ambassador seemed to have been proved right. The military adventures Michele had envisaged the Hapsburg ruler undertaking in self-justification lay beyond the emperor's energies. After 1566 and his humiliating defeat in Hungary, Maximilian treated warfare as cautiously as he did German religious affairs.[1] His reluctance to renew the offensive against the Turks disappointed many, his military leaders among them. So much money, sighed one commander, Johann Rueber, and so little to show for it. Maximilian must hardly have enjoyed reading the comment, which was forwarded to him.[2] For the Diet of Speyer in 1570, Schwendi had revived the timeworn idea of founding a crusading order to push back the forces of Islam.[3] No one, including Maximilian, endorsed it.

Fear of renewed hostilities on the part of Constantinople, not active plans to recapture Hungary, shaped the emperor's diplomacy in eastern Europe. In Graz, his brother Charles worried about the aimless drift of negotiations in 1570 with John Sigismund Zápolya in Transylvania. So did Archbishop Salentin of Cologne. When the voivode died on 14 March 1571 (whether by poison or naturally no one in Vienna knew), Maximilian let slip an opportunity he and his father had awaited for years, in hopes of tightening their hold on Transylvania.[4] Maximilian promised to retaliate if the sultan intervened militarily in the region, as some men there were urging, but that was all.[5] Another local candidate, Steven Báthory, no friend of the Habsburgs, became the new voivode. Once named, he refused to have anything to do with Maximilian's representatives; he preferred to listen to Turkish emissaries instead. At that point the emperor considered invading Transylvania and bringing it under his direct control; however, his own commanders, who were closer to the scene, thought that temporizing with the new voivode was a more prudent course. War, they said, was too dangerous, both for Hungary and for Christendom. Indeed, they did not even want Maximilian to correspond with them: any letters from the emperor that fell into Báthory's hands were likely to be forwarded to Constantinople. Maximilian appeared to agree. By 1575, some Habsburg supporters in Transylvania still believed that Maximilian could have captured the territory, had he moved expeditiously. Now all that they could look forward to was retribution from the incoming territorial ruler.[6]

Where the emperor did not act, others stepped in. Though Maximilian bore final responsibility for defending Inner Austria against the Turks, Archduke Charles in Graz assumed the greater part of that task. The resentful Styrian estates believed that Vienna should be doing far more, and they haggled bitterly over every florin they had to add to their defense costs. By 1575, they were still waiting for further help from the emperor, and the Ottoman forces were apparently skirmishing at will on their borders.[7] Leadership of Christendom's struggle against the Infidel shifted from the timid in central Europe to the more daring in the Mediterranean. Here Spain, the papacy, and the Venetian Republic, acting together, met with stunning, if short-lived, success. The three governments had for some time discussed combining their forces against the Turks, though so experienced a Spanish hand as Khevenhüller had doubted that they could ever agree. Pius V was enthusiastic about the undertaking. Philip, tied down by conflict in the Netherlands and by unrest at home, was not. The fall of Cyprus to the Turks in 1570, however, made the Spanish ruler think twice.[8]

The so-called Holy League came into being on 21 May 1571. Maximilian was a conspicuous nonmember. While at the diet in Speyer the previous year, he had been asked to join but had refused, believing, like Khevenhüller, that the talks would go nowhere.[9] The victory of the Christian forces over the Ottoman navy at Lepanto, however, on 7 October 1571, made the defeatists at Maximilian's court look somewhat foolish. Lured by such success and the promise of more to come, some left the emperor's entourage to join the Christian force.[10] Though Maximilian had once longed for such a triumph, he was quick to acknowledge the success of others. His personal courier carried warm congratulations to Pius. Equally hearty commendations went to the naval commander, Don Juan of Austria, Maximilian's natural cousin.[11]

The emperor believed that one victory had made others likely; it had solidified the alliance as well. Nevertheless, he declined to participate, even when he was reinvited.[12] Though magnanimous in his formal approbation, Maximilian still resented Pius V's installation of Cosimo de' Medici as grand duke of Florence. The league, grumbled the emperor, was only a way of distracting him from this controversy. He had strategic worries, as well. Should the alliance fall apart over particular interests, a result that Maximilian by no means thought out of the question, he might be facing a hostile Ottoman army by himself. Turkish forces had amassed on the borders of his depleted lands. His peace with Constantinople, struck in consultation with the electors and the estates of the empire, had not been easy to come by. Only serious reasons would persuade him to break it. Were the Turks to turn on him again, he would be defenseless. Moreover, he said, his general reputation as a Christian prince did not allow him to break his current truce with the sultan.[13]

Indeed, the league soon collapsed in squabbling over who should receive credit for the victory at Lepanto. Claiming that only Spaniards had manned the ships in the campaign, Don Juan reproached the Venetians for not pulling their weight. Spanish irresolution further undermined morale.[14] Those trying to reconstitute the alliance once again entreated Maximilian to join them. He admitted that the organization was important and strategically valuable, and even that opinion in the empire was swinging toward support for the league; but the cost of violating his arrangement with the Turks was too high.[15]

On balance, the emperor was probably wise not to join the Mediterranean offensive against the Turks. The Holy League was indeed fractious, and Maximilian could have jeopardized himself and his lands by actively supporting it. If the Turks had attacked central Europe, the league's members would not have been likely to rush the emperor's aid. But his habitual avoidance of risk was a clear sign that Maximilian's day as a Christian leader had passed. In renewing his treaty with the Turks in 1574, he turned the other cheek to provocations from Constantinople that had once fired his indignation and concern. Some among his subjects, he said, welcomed the enemy, thereby undermining his own position. Piously, but apathetically, he asked God to forgive and bless them.[16]

In his own lands and at his court, damage control was also the rule of the day, particularly in religious matters. Such a policy pleased no one who had anything to gain from Maximilian's support in the Austrian territories and Bohemia. All the confessional camps of the Habsburg lands wanted Maximilian's exclusive commitment to their particular cause, regardless of his diminished reputation. Fury over his recognition in 1568 of the Augsburg Confession in Lower Austria did not subside in Rome and Madrid. To retain Protestant loyalty, Maximilian always had to be ready to defend this step and others that buttressed it. He had to be equally responsive to indignant Catholics, his Spanish cousin and the pope chief among them.

Pius V and Philip continued urging the emperor to disavow whatever compromises he had made in Lower Austria with evangelical concerns.[17] Maximilian did not budge much. Indeed, he produced an especially strong statement of his policies in 1569, absolving himself of any responsibility for the Reformation and defending his own Catholic practice. He recommitted himself to protecting his patrimony from confessional bloodbaths.[18] The Spanish ambassador, Monteagudo, reported his exchanges on these matters with the emperor to Philip exhaustively but with some sympathy, and the king seemed more understanding of Maximilian's public plight. Philip admitted that his cousin's confessional tactics in his patrimonial lands had to take into account opinion in his estates, especially when financial support was contingent on religious concessions. And when the emperor told Monteagudo that his immediate goal was to preserve things more or less as they were and to avoid new exceptions in matters of faith for his nobility, the ambassador advised Philip that all the pressure that had been put on the emperor might have been counterproductive. Better, Monteagudo said, to foster an atmosphere in which Maximilian could think that he had initiated a course of action rather than having been led to it by others. The utterly reliable empress could also play a key role in this strategy.[19]

The ambassador's recommendation may have had some effect. Maximilian's tilt toward Catholics in the empire after 1570 extended to his own lands. Some of these moves were easy for him. The Council of Trent had called for monastic institutions to be cleansed of corruption and moral abuses; in such undertakings, the emperor, or those who spoke for him, could be models of diligence. When his inspectors visited the cloisters of the Friars Minor, Augustinians, and "Preachers" (Dominicans) in Vienna during 1574, doors and windows were to be guarded so that no miscreant escaped.[20] Discovery of corruption in cloistered places was embarrassing for Catholics, but Maximilian could be discreet. Upon hearing that an abbot in Garsten, in Upper

Austria, had married—a hypocrisy evangelicals thundered against gladly—he ordered the local governor to remove the wayward cleric from the establishment immediately, but at night, so that no one knew.[21]

He also seemed more kindly disposed to the Jesuits, at least publicly. In 1569 Maximilian paid for the repairs toward the tiling of their college in Vienna; a year later he helped its residents survive both famine and inflation with donations of grain and wine.[22] Despite an order forbidding interconfessional debate at the University of Vienna, Jesuits had occasionally appeared there for public argumentation. By 1573, Monteagudo had persuaded the emperor that the Church of Rome was best served by having regularly appointed Catholic faculty members, including Jesuits, participate in professorial disputations. Impressed by the intellectual quality of the members of the order, Maximilian established two university lectureships for it in Vienna on the condition that the incumbents speak German comfortably. The vernacular was used in faculty meetings and in many learned discussions of theological tracts. Maximilian also wanted his Lower Austrian subjects to understand what they heard when Catholics preached. The emperor further allowed Jesuit professors to hold administrative offices at the university.[23]

Catholics also had reason to hope that Maximilian was drawing closer to them as he turned his attention to Bohemia in the early 1570s. Here, too, there was a growing clamor for religious concessions similar to those he had made in Lower Austria. Absorbed through much of his career with German problems, Maximilian had spent relatively little time in Prague or in any of the lands associated with the crown of St. Václav. The embarrassment of his 1566 campaign in Hungary had considerably lessened his stature among Bohemia's magnates and nobles. This episode, combined with his long absences, had weakened his authority and encouraged officers of the estates and other local administrators to take an even more active role in the affairs of the kingdom. The Bohemian estates traditionally exercised considerable influence in spiritual affairs as well. They hoped to increase such powers, particularly those connected with the oversight of local clergy.[24]

Bohemian Catholics and Protestants alike were quick to leap to the defense of their political and confessional privileges. In matters of religion, Maximilian had followed Ferdinand I's temperate approach in the kingdom. More vigorous measures caused no end of trouble. In 1568 Maximilian had been so unpolitic as to call for a *Generalreformation* of the Bohemian Catholic clergy that followed the outlines of a program he had introduced in Lower Austria. Even his administrative officers in Prague questioned the orders. Although they did not openly refuse to carry them out, they thought that the matter required discussion with the high officials of the kingdom. Bohemia, they argued, could not be treated like the Austrian provinces. Local lords and knights had a territorial and juridical stake in clerical affairs; the Moravian prelates were a separate estate with the same privileges as knights and lords. One land was not like another; proceeding as if such differences did not exist might violate the privileges and freedoms of the nobility in the kingdom.[25]

Future diets could retaliate by refusing to support more taxes or by withholding the lucrative impost on beer. Maximilian backed off, contenting himself with orders to close all the Czech Brethren's places of worship. Catholics at his court, especially the papal legate Commendone, who was in Vienna at the time, had every reason to take heart.[26] The Brethren were the enemy of every other confession in the kingdom, and the emperor would not be seen as meddling in Catholic affairs. He continued to follow a seemingly pro-Catholic line in Bohemia for the next few years, even though by 1571 he was in a truly difficult situation. Maximilian desperately needed money from the Bohemian diet where opposition to his financial requests had been growing. The body was well positioned to thwart his requests; only the officers of the estates could collect the property tax, which had risen modestly in 1567; moreover, the nobility as a group was chronically delinquent in paying its assessment. The towns were almost as unreliable.[27]

Maximilian had some suggestions for easing his fiscal plight, but the Bohemian nobles would hear none of them. If new taxes were imposed, the bourgeoisie and the lower classes would have to shoulder them. Furthermore, the diet, or at least many Protestants in it, wanted their king's permission to follow the Augsburg Confession and to have a church free from the control of the territorial ruler. Called neo-Utraquists by modern historians, these people now were the majority in the estates. Lutherans in all but name, they had substantial differences with the long-established Utraquists, who theoretically recognized papal authority and the royal right to appoint their consistory.

In Prague with the imperial party, Monteagudo implored Maximilian to turn down the neo-Utraquist demands. The emperor's reply again reassured the steadfastly orthodox, particularly the Spanish envoy and the empress. Experience was beginning to show, Maximilian said, how dangerous it was for a kingdom to exchange Catholicism for another faith. That the new confession was the Augustana made no difference, now that there were so many readings of it.[28] Before a Lutheran spokesman in Bohemia, the emperor professed himself to be a Catholic "as were his ancestors," and furiously denounced those who had taken him for a Lutheran sympathizer. Monteagudo had never seen Maximilian so angry. When he indeed refused to sanction the Augsburg Confession, claiming that his Christian obligation and coronation oath to uphold the Bohemian *Compactata* compelled him to do so, the Spanish camp rejoiced again.[29]

Even in less formal exchanges with the Bohemians, Maximilian scored points against evangelical deputies who were pressing him to grant the Augsburg Confession. He asked these men if they were acquainted with the document, meaning the text. When, somewhat naively, they said no, he sarcastically rebuked them for requesting something about which they knew nothing.[30] Returning to Vienna, Maximilian also ordered copies of the Austrian Agenda, which he had not cleared for publication, to be removed from the streets. Those who sold it, or even had it in their homes, faced punishment. All these measures were taken "to the satisfaction of all," or so the Spanish ambassador said.[31]

But such gestures, as always, fell far short of the total commitment that supporters of the Church of Rome wanted from the emperor. While Maximilian remained a promising work in progress for Monteagudo and Maria, Lower Austria was a bleak confessional environment for Catholic sympathizers. Religious practice was fast moving from the corrupt to the anarchic. There were places where something close to a genuine Protestant ritual was followed, places where there was an evangelical majority but no organized worship, and a few areas where no serious split from the old church had occurred, even though orthodox practice was in great disarray.[32]

Moreover, for every moment that Catholics and the Spanish contingent at his court saw the emperor leaning their way, there were times when he appeared very far from them indeed. Though he took the Austrian Agenda out of public circulation, Maximilian did nothing to keep it from being printed in the castle of a local nobleman. In 1572 he forbade Archduke Rudolph to commune publicly during his coronation in Hungary, an event that the emperor was otherwise bent on making as imposing as possible. His rather lame explanation was that the ceremony was inconvenient for the archbishop of Poszony.

Rudolph was deeply angered; he wanted the ritual to take place in full view of all, in a sanctuary. Without consulting his father, he vowed to open the doors of his quarters so that everyone could see him at his devotions. Maximilian also asked him to skip passages in the rites where he swore allegiance to God and to his church. At that, the young man threatened to swear his fidelity to the Trinity, the Almighty, the Virgin, and the saints. Happily for the Spanish, Rudolph prevailed. But Philip was deeply disappointed to hear about Maximilian's maneuvers.[33] Crypto-Protestants remained at his court. Maximilian tolerated them in the hope that they would keep the general peace if he did not harass them.[34] It was hard to be a serious Catholic and loyal to such a ruler at the same time. In 1572, Hans Khevenhüller declared that being in a "steadfast land of old-fashioned, praiseworthy, good Christian practice" had been the greatest pleasure of a Christmas visit to Count Ernfried of Ortenburg in Carinthia.[35]

In 1573 a controversy over a tract by Georg Eder, a court councillor and a good friend of Martin Eisengrein, dismayed Catholics even further. The title of the work began darkly with the words "Evangelische Inquisition."[36] A kind of guide for the confessionally perplexed of the day, it was somewhat less intimidating than the incipit suggested. Nevertheless, the contents were inflammatory enough to put Protestants on full alert. Eder's targets were so-called Court Christians (*Hofchristen*), half Catholic and half evangelical, as he described them, as well as any persons who trimmed their confessional behavior according to the company they kept. Maximilian and many at his court, especially Vice-Chancellor Weber, who may have advised the emperor to denounce the pamphlet, were clearly those whom Eder had most in mind.[37] Others involved were chamberlain Johann Freiherr von Heissenstein, Crato, Christoph Zott, another court councillor, and secretaries Johann Hegenmüller and Wolf Unverzagt. Hegenmüller had strongly protested the *Inquisition*'s description of Protestants as worse than Jews, Turks, and heathens.[38]

Maximilian's name had been on the imperial privilege to Sebald Mayer, the Dillingen printer who had published the pamphlet four years earlier. Just how this happened, no one seemed to know, but such an oversight, if it was that, added to the awkwardness of the emperor's position.[39] Nevertheless, he ordered Eder to take copies of the leaflet out of circulation on 2 October 1573. The argument of Adam von Dietrichstein, his high chamberlain, that one could not deny to Catholics what was permitted to Protestants, was to no avail. Upon hearing that Archdukes Rudolph and Ernst had two books that the now-dismissed Eder wanted to take with him, the emperor seized those, infuriating his sons in the process. He forbade Eder to write on religious matters again. No one in the imperial chancellory could remember such a sharply worded mandate—they seemed to have forgotten Maximilian's vehement reaction to the *Nachtigal* a few years earlier.[40] The emperor meant it all; he had the order read back to him before issuing it. Similar materials were appearing elsewhere, and he was all the more anxious to suppress Eder's text.[41]

Wild rumors sprang up about Eder's fate—that he had been beheaded, that he had been burned with a white-hot crown, that he was in chains at his home.[42] Though nothing so drastic happened, Eder was publicly reprimanded. The mandate against him was read at a sitting of the privy council in which he functioned; it was posted in Vienna at the Lügeck, where foreign merchants congregated; it was passed around wine houses. It appeared both in bookshops throughout Germany and in private homes.[43] Maximilian refused to retract his order, and Catholics at his court believed that he was attacking their faith directly.[44]

Though Monteagudo thought that Eder was not an ideal champion for the Catholic cause—the ambassador would have chosen a theologian rather than a jurist—he and Maria took up cudgels for the victim. Maximilian stood his ground. He had inherited an empire full of heretics from his father and uncle, he said, and could do little against them.[45] Monteagudo speculated that Maximilian was trying to convince Germany's Protestant princes that his sons had survived their Spanish education none the worse for wear. Such a strategy may indeed have occurred to their father, because Rudolph's election in the empire was under discussion; but regardless of the politics involved, Monteagudo found it hard to believe that Maximilian was simply dissembling. And the empress was genuinely wounded by her husband's stubborn refusal to back down, even when she discussed the Eder affair with him privately.[46]

The Eder episode was only one of several to dim hopes among Christian traditionalists at Maximilian's court that the emperor would become one of them. Up until his death in 1576, Maximilian was generally willing to tolerate Lutherans in his Austrian lands so long as they fought neither with Catholics nor among themselves.[47] As in the rest of the empire, such a policy did not go far enough for Protestants, either. Nor did the kingdom of Bohemia, in which Maximilian would make his final attempt to iron out deep religious differences among his subjects, take much interest in his approach in Bohemia. There, too, balancing the interests of all sides was something only he thought useful.

Despite the emperor's rejection in 1571 of neo-Utraquist demands for free exercise of the Augsburg Confession in the kingdom, agitation for the privilege had continued.[48] Catholics had a modest but distinct agenda too; the archbishop of Prague had also asked for direct control of certain parishes, a proposal that the estates read as a violation of their traditional freedoms. Compounding these issues were the now open hostility throughout the kingdom to Maximilian's financial policies, and a thoroughgoing generational change in his local administrative officers. Most of the high officials who had served both his father and him, and who functioned as representatives of their ruler, were now dead. The new high burgrave after 1570, Wilhelm of Rožmberk, behaved more as a spokesman for the estates than for his king. Compounding these problems was an issue that now concerned Maximilian mightily—gathering votes in the Bohemian estates for the election of Archduke Rudolph as his father's successor.[49]

Maximilian convened a diet in 1574 to address all these issues, but illness kept both him and Archduke Rudolph from attending. In their place, the inexperienced Archduke Ernst went. The young man could not control the deliberations, as delegates grew very impatient with the incessant to and fro of couriers between Prague and Vienna relaying Maximilian's wishes to the estates. Speaking for the Bohemian lords on 9 January, Wilhelm of Rožmberk, whom Maximilian had begged for support, spoke only of the harm that the Habsburg had done the kingdom. Its resources were exhausted, its borders insecure, its religious life still in turmoil. Ignoring Maximilian's worries about funding the defense of his Hungarian borders, all the estates dug in their heels against higher taxes. When Maximilian refused to negotiate, the gathering broke up.[50] Rudolph's fate, however, still hung in the balance. The emperor called another diet for 1575.

Religious concessions had been pried from the Habsburgs when they were negotiating from very weak positions, and Maximilian's tactics would be carefully monitored by deeply interested parties. Both Monteagudo and a papal representative, Cardinal Delfino, went to Prague with the emperor to make sure that he did not cave in to pressure from the evangelical side. In Heidelberg, Elector Palatine Frederick was watching the emperor's response to the Bohemian Protestant demands as he tailored his own position for an upcoming imperial diet.[51] Maximilian and his spokesman before the estates, Reichart Streun von Schwarzenau, therefore had to thread their way very carefully between the various constituencies represented at the meeting. The emperor did not want either to strengthen the hold of the estates on the kingdom or to add to the religious factionalism already there. But his finances were worsening by the day. The second state bankruptcy of Philip II's reign was making the king's cousin more dependent on domestic financial resources than ever.[52]

Thus Maximilian was ill positioned to reject outright demands that he accept what was called the Bohemian Confession. Inspired by both the earlier Austrian Agenda and an agreement struck in 1570 between Lutherans, Calvinists, and the Czech Brethren at Sandomierz in Poland, the evangelical camps in Bohemia had come together for discussions during the spring of 1575. They hoped to formulate a modus vivendi among themselves, then present it to their sovereign for his approval. What they produced would have allowed Lutherans, Calvinists, and the Brethren to worship in ways acceptable to each creed in Bohemia without fear of repression. The most disputed issue among Protestants generally, the question of the Eucharist, was carefully laid out in such a way that the majority of Lutherans and Calvinists could live with it.[53]

Though the overwhelming majority in the diet supported the proposal, there were just enough divisions among members to leave Maximilian some room for maneuver. He exploited all the possibilities to his own advantage in the small conferences or one-on-one sessions that he almost always preferred when he was negotiating seriously.[54] He put as little as possible in writing and asked again and again that all who talked to him on the religious question accept his oral assurances. In the end, however, the emperor was handed a completed document that required him to respond. At this, he balked; on 2 September 1575, he announced that he was neither approving nor rejecting the Bohemian Confession.[55]

His lack of commitment implied an absence of support; some thought Maximilian was actually making fun of the arrangement. Monteagudo and the envoys from Rome, who had worked very hard to advance Catholic positions, rejoiced that the Habsburg had not publicly sanctioned the Bohemian proposal. They were happier still when Maximilian would not even allow it to be printed. Nevertheless, he moved quickly to repair relations with the evangelicals in the estates. On the same day that he effectively tabled the confession, Maximilian called a meeting with the Bohemian nobility. Once they had come together, he read them a declaration, at least part of which was in Czech, in which he vowed that he would follow a policy of religious tolerance and moderation in the kingdom. To underscore his trustworthiness, Maximilian struck himself on the breast in front of his audience. But again, he had satisfied no one, and he was clearly growing weary of such conflicts. While strolling during the diet with one of the Moravian magnates, Johann Žerotín, Maximilian asked whether the Czech Brethren had their own confession. Upon hearing that he had received it, the ordinarily well-informed emperor admitted that he had not read the material.[56]

Maximilian did not go away from the Bohemian diet altogether empty-handed. Though the estates had been grumbling for some time about the dynastic preoccupations of their ruler, they did agree to accept Archduke Rudolph as his father's successor. The coronation ceremony took place in October 1575, with Rudolph communing publicly in one kind, to the distress of Protestants and the acclaim of Catholics.[57] Maximilian did not exploit the occasion to ingratiate himself or his eldest son with his increasingly disaffected Bohemian subjects. So eager was the emperor to put the matter behind him that he cut the festive entry of the new king into Prague insultingly short.[58]

What he all too obviously wanted was to get to Regensburg, where he would conclude the negotiations to make Rudolph the future German king and emperor. Maximilian's physical frailties were now compromising his work routinely; his death was clearly not far off. The imperial Golden Bull of 1356 allowed the election of one emperor in the lifetime of another under certain circumstances, but whether these applied to the case of Maximilian and Archduke Rudolph was in question.[59] Confession was another problem, for Germany's religious camps had somewhat different takes on the candidate. Rudolph's mother and Philip II fretted a great deal about the spiritual perils that awaited the archduke in an evangelically contaminated land. In 1574, the empress still wanted it clearly understood that if either Rudolph or Ernst showed signs of succumbing to the Protestant virus, they could return to Spain. But weighty considerations offset such fears, and Catholics generally were very eager to have Rudolph back in Germany. As early as 1569, Vice-Chancellor Zasius had pointed out that if the emperor died without an heir having been determined, a heretic might rule Germany. Some evangelical princes, most notably Elector August of Saxony, were allegedly interested in the title.[60]

Protestants were simply worried by Rudolph's Catholic upbringing at Philip's court. A singular remoteness characterized the young prince. Contemporaries took it as arrogance, but it was more likely a sign of the eccentric reclusiveness that he would display in later years. His Catholicism, however, once he arrived in Vienna, appeared to be impeccable. Both he and Archduke Ernst followed Spanish practice as if they were in the Alcázar of Madrid, to the delight of their mother, Maria, but the bewilderment of others.[61] Such behavior disturbed many German princes, especially when they could link it to a Spanish upbringing. Maximilian was already too close to Spain for the comfort of some; Rudolph would seem no improvement.[62]

This was a challenge that Maximilian met decisively. Almost as soon as the archduke returned in 1571, his father had begun advocating Rudolph's succession with the imperial electors. The young man's first contacts with the princes went badly. He was far too serious and Spanish, the same deficits the Germans had seen in Philip years before. His father, however, defended him artfully. When Elector August of Saxony made known the reservations he and his colleagues had about the young archduke, the emperor pointed out that no one could accuse his son of dissembling. August responded positively, and Maximilian was sure of his support. The empress was campaigning on this front, as well, and urging her son's merits on August's wife, Electress Anna. The elector of Brandenburg had heard that Rudolph did not think much of the German princes and did not hesitate to show it, especially where Protestantism was concerned. The young prince had allegedly told his chamberlain that, without any further knowledge about a person, he could smell a heretic when one entered the room. Maximilian, declaring his son to be too unassuming and judicious to have said such a thing, professed not to believe this story. Lazarus Schwendi also praised the young man's virtues.[63]

By the end of 1573, Maximilian had apparently lined up the support Rudolph needed. The young Habsburg was virtually guaranteed positive votes from the clergy among the electors; Augustus of Saxony was willing to go along, as was John George of Brandenburg. This left as the only holdout the aged elector palatine, Frederick III, who hoped for an interregnum in which he would play the role of imperial vicar. At this point, Maximilian's illnesses, negotiations with the Turks, and the Bohemian election interrupted the campaign.[64] Protestants took the added time to demand further religious concessions in return for their support. Other movements were to enjoy the same privileges as followers of the Augsburg Confession, and the application of the Declaratio Ferdinandea, which protected Lutherans who lived in ecclesiastical principalities, was to be discussed anew. An emperor from the house of Austria, however, might be useful for Protestants. Habsburg preoccupation with the Turks promised a secure future for "German liberty." Even Delfino, the papal nuncio in Germany, thought that regardless of Rudolph's private beliefs, his respect for his father would keep him from taking openly pro-Catholic positions. Such considerations persuaded the Protestant princes ultimately to postpone consideration of religious issues until 1576, when a diet was projected to take place in Regensburg.[65] The election could go forward.

Rudolph's coronation and the attendant festivities took place on 9 October 1575. A banquet following the ritual, which featured two fountains of wine, one red, one white, with four spigots each, relaxed tensions for the moment. To the delight of Spanish observers, Rudolph left little doubt that a Catholic was coming to the German throne. A report went to Madrid that the night before the ritual, the archduke privately confessed "as a good and Catholic Christian son of the Roman Church." Maximilian's performance some years earlier, also recounted in the letter, went uncommended. Both the German king-elect and Ernst assisted at the Mass that accompanied the ceremony. But the general tone of the gathering was surprisingly harmonious. The empress received her very Catholic Bavarian sister-in-law in her quarters, along with a duchess from Saxony. Indisposed once more, Maximilian himself had been absent from the ceremonies. He joined the three women, however, for what was described as a very pleasant encounter. Altogether remarkably, given their unshakable orthodoxy, Maria and Monteagudo also visited Duke John William of Saxony-Weimar, the protector of the Flacian Lutherans, the following day.[66]

Maximilian had thus done significant service for his dynasty; he had deftly piloted Rudolph through channels that brought his heir crowns in Bohemia, Hungary, and Germany. All these offices were crucial to sustaining Habsburg preeminence in central and east-central Europe. Should Rudolph die—or abdicate, as Charles V had once done—a string of brothers stood ready to replace him. With regard to his male offspring, the emperor had otherwise been a neglectful father. He had done little to assure the continuity of his house beyond the one generation he himself had sired. Maximilian's sons were on the whole an intelligent-looking lot; Archduke Matthias, the third of them, was clearly possessed by the will to rule that had once driven his father.[67] By 1575 none of them, including the twenty-three-year-old Rudolph, had a wife. His father had once considered marrying him to Philip's daughter Isabel. The king of Spain had been interested, but the matter was not pursued. Years later, a Venetian ambassador, Jerome Soranzo, would trace Rudolph's neurotic eccentricities to his angry renunciation of marriage after his Spanish prospects fell through. In truth, the archduke himself had never been wholeheartedly committed to the arrangement. The empress, who had been overjoyed at the idea, had become highly distressed by 1573, by which time this and other nuptial schemes had failed.[68] Speculation about possible matches for Rudolph continued for a while. During a stopover in Dresden on his way to the imperial ceremony, the emperor-to-be four times asked the twelve-

year-old daughter of the elector to dance in the course of one evening. Some
observers thought that an engagement was in the offing.[69] But there the matter
ended, along with Rudolph's marriage prospects generally.

From the standpoint of politics, Maximilian's neglect, not only of Rudolph
but of all his sons' marital needs, is inexplicable. Normally very sensitive to
dynastic issues, he had worked zealously to create Spanish and French unions
for his eldest daughters. With five male heirs living as his life came to a close,
he may have felt no pressure to marry them promptly. Habsburg successions
often worked their way laterally through one generation rather than from
father to son. Maximilian's shallow resources did make it hard to subsidize
the households of his unmarried offspring, let alone the more elaborate establishments attached to wedded sons; but neither did he set them up with
clerical livings, even though he had given those some thought. Moral scruples
could not have been troubling him. Maximilian happily rewarded people with
ecclesiastical benefices whenever it seemed useful. He did not hesitate to place
superannuated court personnel in cloisters, even if they were Protestants
unwanted by reform-minded local abbots. It was Rudolph, as emperor, and
not his father, who worked to find German bishoprics for Archdukes Matthias
and Maximilian.[70]

One can never discount the possibility that some specific calculation lay
behind Maximilian's apparent indifference to his sons' dynastic futures. It was
clear, however, that his vitality was ebbing, to the point where he was losing
his grip on dynastic affairs generally. His comparatively vigorous pursuit of
Rudolph's crowns was a striking exception to otherwise slipshod performance. Nowhere was this more visible than in his clumsy pursuit of yet
another throne for his line, this time in the kingdom of Poland.

The Jagellonian rulers of the sprawling realm to the northeast of the
Habsburg lands had been a source of concern to Ferdinand I throughout his
career; in 1526 he feared that Sigismund I might join the Turks to drive the
house of Austria out of Bohemia and Hungary. He even toyed with the idea
of pushing Maximilian's candidacy for the Polish crown but eventually
thought better of that. Ferdinand did arrange marriages for two of Maximilian's sisters in succession with Sigismund II Augustus, the last of the
Polish-Lithuanian royal line. At the very least, the archduchesses could keep
him abreast of activities at their husband's court. Both of these unions had
been emotionally disastrous and childless, but Sigismund Augustus was technically still the husband of his estranged consort Catherine when she died in

1572. A few months later, he too went to his grave, leaving no legitimate male heirs.

Maximilian had followed his father's Polish policy faithfully. As early as 1565, he had begun exploring the idea of a Habsburg succession in the kingdom with some of its influential grandees, most importantly Michael "the Black" Radziwiłł, a Lithuanian magnate whose house had long resisted central control from Kraków. At that point, and for some time after, Maximilian feared that John Sigismund Zápolya, a nephew of Sigismund Augustus, would claim the crown.[71] That would have represented the worst possible outcome in the emperor's eyes. The voivode was quite willing to cooperate with the Turks, and "no crow," noted the Habsburg, "pecks out the eyes of another."[72] John Sigismund's successor in Transylvania, Stephen Báthory, was just as beholden to the sultan and did indeed present his candidacy for the vacant Polish throne. Another leading contender was Henry of Valois, the younger brother of Charles IX of France. The local estates enthusiastically welcomed the Valois prince's commitment to oppose Russian expansion into Poland.[73]

The prospect of a French ruler in Kraków may not have overly disturbed Maximilian, but the court in Madrid was worried. Granvella, quoting an Italian proverb, observed to Don Juan of Austria: "He who piles up a great deal is constrained by nothing."[74] Philip was as eager to have a Habsburg rule Poland as was his cousin. The Spanish monarch also had in mind the interests of his faith. He, the pope, and the Curia wished to curb the spread of evangelical factions in Poland, which, along with the royal government, opposed the tithe. Empress Maria, too, was fiercely engaged in the Habsburg quest for Poland, as both a Catholic and a mother. The cause of Christendom always quickened her deepest passions, and Philip and Maximilian had chosen her son Archduke Ernst as the family candidate. To win the votes of the Polish lower nobility, who thought that the Habsburg commitment to the elective principle was insincere, she began soliciting money for bribes from Rome. Habsburg chances did indeed brighten when news of the St. Bartholomew's Day Massacre weakened the appeal of the French royal line somewhat. In October 1572, two Bohemian magnates, Rožmberk and Pernstein, set off for the kingdom to their north, carrying a substantial sum to win support for the house of Austria in the upcoming election.[75]

All this largesse, however, was intended for the high lords of the kingdom, a signal to the lesser nobility, or *Szlachta,* that Maximilian had discounted their role in the process. The emperor would later much regret the oversight. In the meantime, rich or not, the great aristocrats took whatever was offered, then asked for more. Girding himself for a fight, Philip opened a separate credit line in Genoa for Maria to carry on her electoral activities.[76] Maximilian thought that the negotiations in Poland were going well, but what he meant by this is not clear. Maximilian liked copious reports, and the level of detail he was seeing pleased him very much.[77]

If he thought that the prospects for a favorable outcome were good, though, he was mistaken. The emperor's ambassadors could not have been more inept. They were never able to convince the Poles that the Habsburgs would respect their liberties. Maximilian's resident envoy, Johannes Cyrus, was actually imprisoned when he refused to leave the country after being ordered to do so. The emperor's personal spokesman, the normally skillful Wilhelm of Rožmberk, presented Archduke Ernst's qualifications with no great warmth. Maximilian's oversight of the candidacy from afar was just as haphazard. Instructions generated by the overburdened secretary Peter Obernburger were often vague and tardy.[78] Remarkably for him, Maximilian never used all of the large sums of money Philip had made available to advance Ernst's quest, in part because the emperor thought he would get nowhere.[79]

The Polish estates named Henry of Anjou their new king on 11 April 1573. The magnates supported Ernst, whereas the Szlachta opposed the archduke overwhelmingly. Maria blamed her husband and his lackadaisical conduct of the process. No one at the court, she observed, cared about much of anything other than personal convenience.[80] Maximilian himself had a familiar scapegoat for the botched Polish candidacy—Commendone. The emperor and his advisers in Vienna thought that Gregory XIII was backing Ernst; meanwhile, the papal nuncio, in addressing the Polish parliament during its deliberations, neglected to mention the archduke by name. In general the emperor did not seem upset by Henry's triumph, however, but pursued his relations with Poland as if nothing had ever happened. Confronted with such passivity, Philip began to think that his cousin's singular detachment had undermined the entire enterprise.[81]

The concern this turn of events provoked in Vienna and Madrid was shortlived. Henry reached Poland only in 1574, and within the year he was on the way back to Paris to replace his brother Charles IX, who had died.[82] The Habsburg candidacy was therefore still alive. Philip continued to support Archduke Ernst and leeched whatever money he could out of his dwindling treasury for the cause. His sister was equally committed.[83] Maximilian, however interested he was in the project, would be of little use, in their opinion. When Archduke Ferdinand in the Tyrol declared himself to be in the running, no one knew quite what to do. Even Monteagudo could not decide whom he favored.[84]

The emperor did indeed speak for his son, but the campaign, already faintly comic, became decidedly so. In December 1575, the majority in the Polish senate, the upper house in the parliament, once again selected a new ruler—Emperor Maximilian II himself. The lower house, where the more numerous lesser nobility sat, voted overwhelmingly for Báthory, who had pledged to marry the late Sigismund Augustus' fifty-year-old sister, Princess Anna. Maximilian was suddenly inspired to defend his improbable new title. Almost three months went by, as the emperor thrashed around for advice and money to support his role in a new kingdom. He was ready to accept the Polish senate's offer on 23 March 1576, and to commit himself to the *Pacta Conventa*, which set the conditions of monarchical rule in the kingdom. Báthory had already been crowned three weeks before, though, and was now in Kraków. The estates of Lower Austria turned down the emperor's request for aid to defend his claim in Poland, and Maximilian dropped the matter. What resources he had would best be spent against the Turks. He hoped all would work out for the best for Christendom; as far as Polish affairs went, he said a year later, he could make them neither better nor worse.[85] It was a comment that now applied to just about all his concerns.

fourteen

A Soul at Large

Maximilian had never been as sick as he was in the late fall of 1571, at least according to Monteagudo. The empress nursed her husband in her own chambers for more than two weeks, as he perspired and struggled to talk.[1] By the following year, it was said that the emperor never felt well. Cardiac seizures recurred, as did excessive sweating and difficulty speaking. Maximilian also had urinary stones and gravel, gout, which forced him to walk with a staff, and gastrointestinal upheavals.[2]

Though Maximilian's zest to accomplish great things was long gone, no one could predict when he would succumb to one of his ailments. The emperor could, according to Philip II's ambassador, look like a dead man one hour, but behave the next as if nothing had happened.[3] Ambassador Michele reported that Maximilian preserved to the very end the regal bearing and amiable public demeanor that so many of his contemporaries had admired. His beard was still chestnut and his color good, a sign of basic vitality. His memory was excellent; he seemed always busy. As late as 1573, his physicians declared that if he avoided excesses, Maximilian would have a long and happy life.[4] The emperor himself was less sure; indeed, he expected, and was ready for, the worst: "God Almighty, in whose hands all things rest, deals with me according to His Divine Will, wherefore I praise and thank Him for everything, since He knows best what [is] best or harmful to me. . . . I am forbearing, indeed, content with His Divine disposition, since it is unfortunately the way of the world that one has little pleasure and peace."[5] Such stoicism may have helped him find unlikely amusement during the little time he had left. Elector Augustus of Saxony showed up unannounced for a visit in the winter of 1573, reportedly to see for himself whether the emperor was alive or dead. Maximilian professed to have enjoyed his guest, despite the morbid question that had prompted the trip.[6]

His several physicians liked to think that they and higher powers were in league to restore the emperor's health. Good Friday of 1573 found them thanking the Almighty that their ministrations had rescued Maximilian from yet another seizure.[7] Some among them were men of learning and talent, especially Crato, whose treatise on palpitations certainly qualified him to treat his ailing prince.[8] He and his colleagues did all that contemporary protocols and their own experimental inclinations dictated. Plasters, salves, potions, and stimulants, along with more exotic remedies, were sought out to lighten the emperor's suffering. Some of these undoubtedly brought relief from the symptoms, others may have been no more than placebos, and some may even have aggravated Maximilian's suffering. There was, for example, "piedra bezar" (bezoar), used as antidote to poison. Found in the intestines of ruminant animals, it was a virtual cure-all, relieving everything from depression to carbuncles caused by the plague. Crato was not as enthusiastic about it as some physicians, but he did prescribe it on occasion. However sparingly used, it had a gravelly texture which could easily have worsened the emperor's urinary troubles.[9] Like many chronic patients, Maximilian became knowledgeable enough about drugs to guide his sister Anna on proper dosages of "saltza parrillia," or sarsaparilla, a root extract used for medical purposes. Probably the most helpful thing that the emperor did for himself was to take baths at Kaiserebersdorf, up to sixty hours' worth over the course of one visit.[10]

Throughout his life, Maximilian had been able to distract himself pleasurably from his ailments and responsibilities, and he continued to do so. His chief relief was traveling by coach to the orchard and garden of the Casa di Molino—the grounds surrounding what is today Schönbrunn palace.[11] As always, he enjoyed the company of his family, even Archduke Ferdinand, and genuinely regretted not seeing more of them,[12] with the exception of Archduchess Magdalena. Her costly piety—she was eventually said to have exhausted her entire income in religious and charitable causes—annoyed her eldest brother constantly. Their increasingly orthodox brother-in-law Albrecht V of Bavaria expressed the wish that he could have her around to chasten wayward monks—but then, he was not responsible for her debts.[13]

Maximilian enjoyed many other simple pleasures. Gifts arrived from far-away places to pique his abiding curiosity about matters beyond politics and sport. In 1572, the voivode of Transylvania sent elk and European bison (*Auerochsen*); the second animal was about to become extinct. Maximilian went to see the beasts when they first lumbered into the Vienna *Fleischmarkt*. From there, they went to the Hofburg, where the emperor and his family could continue to watch them from the ramparts.[14] He enjoyed giving as well. Carriage horses went to Albrecht in 1572 with Maximilian's reassurance that the animals were "spirited" but not "mean" (*boss*).[15] During the five or six years before his death, he was especially generous to members of his court and household and to visitors, both in Vienna and in his other capitals.[16] Social occasions provided frequent amusement. Sledding parties made up of members of the imperial family and the Viennese nobility offered happy moments. Foreign emissaries also dined frequently with him.[17] When a guest elsewhere, Maximilian did not sit quietly on the sidelines. In his visit to Dresden in 1575, he managed to dance with Electress Anna—going through Spanish and Italian steps, as well as German ones—even though he could barely walk.[18]

The Netherlands continued to weigh on the emperor's mind, but even that problem had its lighter moments. Maximilian laughed heartily over a hoax dreamed up by Don Francisco Mendoza, Monteagudo's son. Asked by his chaplain if anything newsworthy had recently come from the rebellious provinces, the young man had mischievously replied that William of Orange and Bergen oop Zoom had been captured. The story spread quickly around from the court to foreign ambassadors, who congregated daily at the Hofburg, and out into the city. Only after some skeptics queried postal officials, who had heard nothing from anyplace abroad, was the prank exposed.[19]

Maximilian's aesthetic interests never flagged. Even if political and administrative problems were unavoidable, he could face them in pleasant surroundings, such as the Vienna pheasant garden, where the emperor wrote letters in the spring.[20] He followed the construction of the Katterburg and the Neugebäude closely, though he would not have been happy about the fate of either project. The former, which was little more than a hunting-lodge and finished by 1570, went untended after his death. The uncompleted Neugebäude complex went to ruin in a relatively short time; as one writer has put it, it resembled some Arabian castle abandoned in the desert.[21] The recreational palace at Kaiserebersdorf met a truly unexpected fate: it became a modern prison. Only in Vienna did his architectural plans have a more lasting impact. He completed the Stallburg (now the winter stables of the Spanish Riding School) and began reconstruction of the Cillierhof, today's Amalienburg, as a residence for Archduke Ernst.[22]

When it came to sporting events, some of his activities caused him real physical harm. An avid hunter like his father, Maximilian chose to ignore the chills and soakings that hunting expeditions often entailed. Tournaments, another of his enthusiasms, could leave him with fingers or a hand "smashed" (*zerklopfte*), enough to keep him from writing for a time.[23] Even less strenuous pleasures, such as walking through the streets of Vienna, were fraught with dangers for a man in his delicate condition. Thoroughfares and public squares were centers of public infection, filled as they were with diseased and disorderly beggars.[24] His physicians also advised against such strolls in cold and snowy weather. The emperor did not hesitate to ignore them, at the expense of his gout.[25] Sometimes Maximilian forgot about doctors altogether, to his great regret. On a journey to Prague through deep snow during the winter of 1573, both he and Archduke Ernst developed colds. Having left their medical personnel behind and finding it impossible to turn up suitable substitutes locally, they had to summon both a doctor and a pharmacist from Vienna.[26]

But like his uncle Charles years before, the emperor overrode his physicians most routinely and recklessly in matters of diet and drink. Maximilian remained one of the most elegant and sociable diners of his age. He addressed his knights and courtiers by name. He began joking as soon as mealtime conversation turned away from affairs of state. Not only did he offer a wide array of foods and beverages at his court, but he ate in grand surroundings and was the object of exceptional courtesy from those who attended him. His table etiquette was not only "rare and remarkable in a German," according to Michele, but surpassed any the Venetian envoy had ever seen. The emperor served himself and rarely made use of a knife, apparently a token of good manners. He was no glutton, either.[27]

Nevertheless, almost anything he swallowed probably did something to aggravate one or another of his ailments. Figs, oranges, and raisins that he personally ordered from Italy probably did no great harm, being "completely fresh," as he delightedly reported.[28] Other items were more suspect. Gifts of aqua vitae, concocted according to a personal formula of Electress Anna of Saxony, were probably irresistible when they arrived from Dresden every New Year.[29] Sugar consumption at court was heavy.[30] Maximilian himself was probably not the chief culprit here—his wife Maria progressed from plumpness to corpulence in a remarkably short time—but it was easy for him to eat more than was good for him. Most unfortunate of all for a man with gout and urinary problems was his love of wine. The emperor assured Duke Christoph of Württemberg that vintages from the duke's domain were his sole *Mundgetränk,* but Maximilian's palate was far more cosmopolitan than this. He drank the products of many vineyards with gusto, but especially those from the South Tyrol.[31]

The emperor's brush with mortality in 1571 was a serious matter, but it would not have been fatal politically for his line of the house of Austria. He was well supplied with male heirs, however neglectful he had been of their future. What bothered Monteagudo most during Maximilian's seizure in 1571 was that the Habsburg ruler had not called for Catholic last rites. The Bohemian high chancellor, Vratislav of Pernstein, had spoken confidentially about the matter to the majordomo at the Vienna court, Hans Trautson, whose duty it was to inform his sovereign of the truth about his condition. All Monteagudo knew was that Maximilian may have been in touch with a Lutheran confessor earlier that Easter. The ambassador had no idea what the two men might have discussed.[32]

To the very end, relatives from Munich to Madrid were on the lookout for some clue to Maximilian's inner religious convictions. When searching for personal spiritual advisers, he usually did solicit recommendations from his family. During the years he was trying to replace Eisengrein, he asked for suggestions from his Bavarian brother-in-law. When Albrecht refused to give up his own pastor, Johann a Via, Maximilian declared himself willing to let Rome name someone for the office.[33] Nevertheless, his eventual appointee, Lambert Gruter, unsettled Protestants and Catholics alike, even though the devoutly Catholic Count Khevenhüller used him as a confessor and thought highly of him.[34]

No one took the emperor's uncertain religious commitment more to heart than did the empress. By 1574, she was said to have been almost single-handedly responsible for preserving what Catholic practice remained in her husband's lands, but, to her great distress, she had yet to accomplish her chief mission—the emperor's salvation.[35] She had long confided her worries to her brother in Spain. By 1570, she had already begun to think that her husband was a lost cause. He paid little attention at Mass and merely went through the motions of confession and Communion. He attributed his torpor to his political problems—his vassals had more control over him than he did over them. Maria remained disconsolate. Philip tried to intervene tactfully. He assured his cousin that he knew him to be a pure and Catholic spirit. But the rest of the world needed to see this as well. He accepted Maximilian's argument that the Reformation had been under way long before he became emperor; but this was no excuse for Maximilian to avoid public demonstrations of his faith and to let false teaching go unpunished. The emperor's very soul and reputation, said the king, were at stake.[36]

Maximilian, nevertheless, persisted on his own path. He continued to appear publicly at vespers, on feast days, and at other obligatory services in the Catholic religious calendar. At the same time, he ate meat freely. In the opinion of ambassador Michele, he knew his religious essentials and he knew God.[37] This was hardly enough for Maria, her brother, and his alter ego at Maximilian's court, Monteagudo. The count's instructions from Madrid were to further the interests of the Catholic Church wherever required. He was to consult with Maria on all important matters, a recommendation that was quite superfluous, given that he, too, knew little German and his Latin was insecure.[38] The ardor of his faith, however, more than offset his linguistic deficits. He had asked both Pius V and Spanish authorities for permission to read the Augsburg Confession and other Protestant texts so that he could negotiate effectively in his new position. He did not, he added emphatically, intend to use these materials for any other purpose.[39]

Philip's decision to replace Chantonnay in Vienna with Monteagudo had actually pleased the emperor; Maximilian's personal relations with the new envoy were remarkably cordial.[40] The count often dined privately with the imperial couple; at ceremonial appearances, for example, during a visit to Dresden in 1575, he would be the first notable on the emperor's right, standing ahead even of Elector August, the imperial marshal.[41] The Vienna posting was certainly no unbroken hardship for Monteagudo, either. He did not find Viennese Catholicism wholly offensive. Indeed, the ambassador considered that Holy Week in the Austrian Habsburg capital was observed in a far more serious fashion than in Spain. He also thought that Maximilian was still open to the traditional faith. At an early interview, the emperor commented angrily about the "accursed heretics" who had corrupted everything. Monteagudo was much encouraged. It was his relationship with Maria that sustained him, though, politically and religiously.[42]

The empress understood the difference between her faith and politics. In 1570, she regretted losing a discreet confessor who had performed his office "without involving himself in any other things."[43] Nonetheless, where her husband and children's place in eternity was at stake, the ardor of her belief knew few bounds. During Maximilian's illness in 1571, she was prominent among those who unsuccessfully begged him to prepare to die as a Catholic. A few months later, Philip weighed in, urging his cousin to give some outward sign of the pure Catholicism that the king was sure lay deep in Maximilian's heart. The emperor promised them nothing.[44]

Living with Maximilian was clearly a trial for a woman like Maria; during the winter of 1572, she admitted that she could never remember having been so tired. Her husband seemed indifferent not only to his own spiritual fate but to that of his younger sons as well. Maria had been after him for some time to allow Archdukes Matthias and Maximilian, to whom she was particularly close, to take their First Communion at Christmas in 1572. Maximilian had mischievously noted that she might ask if the two boys wished to commune in both kinds. The empress responded by advancing her deadline: perhaps the coming Easter would be a better date. By then, a Catholic tutor from Silesia would be on hand who could serve as confessor to the archdukes. Maria was not the only member of the imperial family who suffered in the confessional setting of the Vienna court. Before the Corpus Christi procession in June 1572, Archdukes Rudolph and Ernst had taken Communion at four in the morning in the chapel of the Hofburg before going to Mass. The procedure was unusual, they said, certainly unfamiliar in Spain. They thought it necessary, however, given the depraved atmosphere that now surrounded them.[45]

Christmas of 1573 came, and the issue of First Communion for Matthias and young Maximilian was still pending. Their father continued withholding his consent, even after long discussions with his wife. He wanted to instruct the boys thoroughly in the meaning of the sacraments, then leave it up to them whether they communed in one kind or both. The bull of Pius IV, which had given the emperor this dispensation, allowed him to extend the same privilege to his children, or at least he thought so.[46] Maria made known that if the two youths partook of the sacrament in both kinds, she would not speak to them; indeed, she declared she would rather see them dead. Hearing this from Monteagudo, the emperor yielded, "as he always has done," observed the ambassador.[47] Nevertheless, it was not until the summer of 1575 that the ceremony took place. By that time, or so speculation ran, Maximilian may have realized that his sons would have to remain orthodox Catholics to support themselves with church livings. The Austrian lands could not subsidize them, the Polish negotiations had ended in failure, and Philip now had male heirs of his own. Still, no one really knew for certain why he had relented.[48]

Maria also continued to work at winning her husband over to her faith. She pressed Adam von Dietrichstein into service; Philip was asked to pay for the ambassador's added duties. The strategy itself was sound. Dietrichstein both understood and respected the emperor's psychological makeup. He advised the king of Spain not to question his cousin's faith. Rather, he said, Maximilian should be treated as someone who could be trusted, even though he had done much to merit the suspicions that people had of him.[49]

However thoughtfully he approached his task, though, Dietrichstein got no further with Maximilian than had anyone else. According to Lambert Gruter, the emperor's spiritual performances had become, if anything, spottier. At one point in 1572, he heard no sermons for six months running, though his health had been stable enough for him to have done so.[50] His remarks about religion in family conversation could be shocking, especially to Catholics. During the spring of 1573, the subject of the Inquisition in Spain came up. The emperor pointed out approvingly that vernacular translations made biblical Scripture more accessible. This was particularly helpful to the Spanish, he said, among whom "ignorant people" (*idiotas*) abounded. The Law of God was for all, and all should be able to read it. Monteagudo, who was present, interjected that the Bible had no other exponent than the Holy Catholic Church. Maximilian allowed that Rome did indeed establish what was canonical, but the discussion became so heated that the ambassador worried lest he had overstepped the bounds. He need not have been concerned. Maximilian, at least in religious matters, continued to do as he wished, even as his health declined further. Despite the unwavering support of her brother, the empress grew even more despondent. Her husband now made light of the heresy all around him.[51]

Indeed, by 1574, Maximilian was laughing a great deal. He continued to avoid sermons, and if he attended Mass, his attention was elsewhere. He had drawn up neither a testament nor any instructions for his sons. To make matters worse for the empress, Philip and other Catholic sympathizers seemed to be gradually abandoning her husband as irredeemable. In spite of Maria's entreaties, Hans Trautson, the majordomo, refused to find a loyal Catholic confessor for the emperor. Such recommendations, he said, should come from the ecclesiastical authorities. Philip continued to applaud her efforts but at the same time advised her to back off.[52]

For all Maximilian's apparent nonchalance, he was clearly aware that he did not have long to live. In 1575 he sent a flurry of commendations of his court personnel, especially his musicians, to other establishments.[53] Presiding at the Bohemian diet in 1575, he could at first neither stand nor walk, though he later recovered a bit.[54] The luxuries of life still enchanted him. He was so taken by a "rare, foreign" fruit from Archduke Ferdinand in the summer of 1576 that he found time at the imperial diet in Regensburg to write to him to obtain its name. Others tried to alleviate his suffering, as well. His daughter Catherine sent him hunting dogs and a noble attendant in 1575. Her father, she thought, would enjoy hearing the young man blow his horn and cheer the animals on "in the French fashion."[55] Give up strenuous pursuits though he did, bodily misfortune continued to haunt him. During the winter of 1576, he organized a hunting party for the Polish ambassador on the outskirts of Vienna. Maximilian had to watch the sport from a carriage. One of the horses bolted, then the other, pulling the invalid and his chair down with them. The injured emperor could not get up, let alone walk.[56] Following Galen, conventional medical wisdom held that anyone who suffered from heart palpitations such as those Maximilian had experienced would never live to fifty. Age forty-nine, the product of the unlucky number seven multiplied by itself, was the "threshold year" (*Stufenjahr*), according to astrologers, and very dangerous. Those persons who passed it could breathe with some confidence awhile longer. In 1576, Adam von Dietrichstein congratulated the emperor on his birthday for having successfully crossed the treacherous divide. "For me, every year is a threshold year," was the weary, and wholly empirical, reply.[57]

But there were still responsibilities to meet at a diet to be held in Regensburg in 1576. The Turks were threatening once again. Shortly after Rudolph's election as German king in 1575, Maximilian had agreed to an eight-year truce with Constantinople. No one, however, was counting on the sultan to observe it.[58] Maximilian was increasingly disturbed by skirmishing along Archduke Charles's borders in the southwest. Such dangers made him more attentive to military details than he had been for some time, particularly when, to his annoyance, the Styrian estates decided to send a delegation to Regensburg to ask that the imperial diet earmark aid for their defense.[59] The diet was an important one, and Maximilian made sure that it took place in a proper environment. His orders—the most comprehensive of their kind to be issued in the sixteenth century—covered not only general police activities but provisioning, weights and measures in force during the session, fire prevention, prices, curfews for servants, gambling, conditions under which actors and soothsayers could ply their crafts, pub hours, garbage disposal, and much more.[60] Maximilian had announced that he would ask again for the Common Penny, a regular payment from the empire to maintain a more reliable army. The princes were predictably cool to the proposal; they wanted to discuss the contentious Ecclesiastical Reservation. Though Maximilian had said he would do so in return for Rudolph's election, he was no more eager to follow through on the matter than he had been in the past.[61]

Few princes of note were on hand when the emperor opened the proceedings on 25 June, but despite their absence, Maximilian gave a gripping account of the Turkish danger and the inability of his own lands to withstand it indefinitely. The imperial estates were prepared to plead poverty; they hoped for a settlement of the turbulence in the Netherlands so that commerce could resume again. They also insisted that whatever aid they granted was to be disbursed by a paymaster of their own choosing. They pointedly asked that, if members of Maximilian's war council supervised such a force, they should be people "with military experience."[62]

The religious issues that Maximilian wanted to downplay swiftly came to the fore at the gathering. Schwendi was there to advise on confessional matters; he urged the emperor to use the utmost leniency, given the threat of an attack from Constantinople. Presumably to dispel Protestant worries about the Habsburg's pro-Roman inclinations, the general himself assured the chancellor of Lutheran Braunschweig-Wolfenbüttel that Maximilian communed in both kinds privately once or twice a year. To no one's surprise, on the morning of 25 August Maximilian reconfirmed the Peace of Augsburg, saying that it was unthinkable to propose any serious changes in the imperial religious constitution when so few princes were in attendance. He let it be known informally that the Ecclesiastical Reservation was to stand as it was. The Protestants, who wanted the measure repealed, smelled Catholic advantage in this stratagem, and Maximilian moved to right the balance. Two days later he asked Germany's Catholic princes to avoid provoking the estates of neighboring territories. Oblique as the phrasing was, it was generally understood as a request that these rulers tolerate evangelicals in their territories—in other words, that they accept the spirit of the *Declaratio Ferdinandea*. The reaction of conservative Catholics was predictably negative. Throughout the diet they hoped to drive the emperor to more forceful moves against Protestants.[63]

Deliberations were still going on in early September. Maximilian's final word on religious policy to spokesmen from the Protestant estates was as

mild as it possibly could have been. He promised to do all he could to see
that religious peace endured and indicated that he was open to future discussions of evangelical grievances. Should these principalities continue to
resist larger contributions to the costs of the Turkish defense, however, he
would not go beyond the language he had already endorsed. In truth, he was
beginning to think that it was better to start negotiating with Constantinople
once again. To the Catholics, he made no reply at all.[64]

He issued these statements from the sickbed he had occupied for most of
the month. His signature had deteriorated badly in the short time between
the end of September and the beginning of October.[65] Five physicians had
been hovering over him, unable to agree on an appropriate treatment. Their
disputations had become so heated that Maximilian at one point ordered them
to reach some consensus. The emperor took his own pulse frequently, and
with the permission of one of his doctors, Julius Alexandrinus, he called in
a woman from Ulm, Magdalena Streicher, who was locally known as a
healer.[66] He sighed frequently, saying that no one could understand the pain
that he suffered, and begged the Almighty to release him from his agony.
Still, leave-taking—"the loss of beloved things," as he had long ago described
the process—was hard.[67] A few days before his death he took into his arms
the little daughter of a couple who worked for him and who was a great
favorite of both his and Maria's. "Cathy, we will never go to Katterberg
[Katterburg] again."[68] He became more melancholy by the day and had frequent heart palpitations, though these, unlike earlier episodes, left him free
of pain and breathlessness. Through all of this, he continued to receive delegations from the estates and drafts of the recess as they appeared.[69]

To the end the emperor's deepest beliefs remained hidden from his friends,
his relatives, and the common folk, whose curiosity his behavior had also
aroused. Protestants and Catholics told different stories of his passing on 12
October, the day of Maximilian the Martyr, at nine in the morning.[70] Only
by taking bits and pieces from several accounts can one form some approx-
imation of what happened. Despite the distraught entreaties of Maria, already
very upset by her husband's refusal to prepare a testament, Maximilian would
not take the last rites of the Roman Church. His sister Anna, brought in from
Bavaria for the purpose, could not prevail upon him, either. The relentless
pressure so irritated him that he refused for a time to see any members of
his family. Maria was at Mass, rather than at his bedside, when the emperor
actually died. Gruter, now bishop of Wiener Neustadt, had also been re-
buffed, though by this time he was suspect in all confessional quarters. At

the beginning of September, the emperor had received Communion, in both kinds. For many in the sixteenth century, this was sufficient preparation for death, and Maximilian may have been among them. When asked if he repented his sins and wished to die within the Church, he replied affirmatively. But just what church he meant, as Albrecht of Bavaria wrote in November to an inquiry from Elector August of Saxony, no one knew for sure.[71] An autopsy provided a meager explanation for the cause of death—it could not have been avoided.[72] Heart failure probably carried him off, but any one of several afflictions from which he had suffered could just as easily have been the culprit. Crato said simply that the power of nature had triumphed.[73]

The German princes, both Catholic and Protestant, sincerely mourned him. The Protestants were especially regretful; they feared that Rudolph, with his Spanish upbringing, would inaugurate a more sternly Catholic regime. Maximilian's eulogists did what they could to make him fit their confessional specifications. Gruter declared he had passed into "the total church of Christ" but made the deceased sound like a champion of Rome. In an unpublished essay, Crato tried to cull any hints of Protestantism he could from the emperor's utterances and policies.[74] Though he left no testament, Maximilian did give directions for his exequies in Vienna and Prague. They were modest by the standards of his house; an enormous *castrum doloris* in St. Stephen's Cathedral in Vienna was the sole exception to the general restraint of the occasion. The simplicity of the ceremony, however, hardly guaranteed a trouble-free burial. His body, which was to lie in state in Regensburg, was shunted from one location to another. Maximilian's officials told Rudolph that his late father had wished to be buried in Vienna; but it would be hard to raise the money to ship his remains down the Danube to Vienna in appropriate fashion. Perhaps thinking of it as his future residence, the new emperor chose to inter his father in Prague, where Ferdinand I and his consort, Anna, lay with earlier kings and queens of Bohemia in St. Vitus' Cathedral. It has been speculated that Rudolph made the choice to save money, but that is doubtful.[75] The platform supporting Ferdinand and Anna's sarcophagi was too small to hold a third. Their coffins had to be raised, and the entire structure, the work of the sculptor Alexander Colin, enlarged at considerable expense to make room for their eldest son. It was unusual, however, to deny a reigning emperor a burial monument of his own. Perhaps, as has also recently been suggested, the new emperor and king did not think his father was worthy of such recognition.[76]

Controversy, divisiveness, and even some minor violence marked Maximilian's transit to his resting place in the Bohemian capital. The funeral, in the church of St. James in Prague, took place on 22 March 1577. Most of his sons attended the burial rite, but none of his siblings. Archduke Charles was preoccupied with the estates in Graz. Illness kept Archduchess Anna away. Archduchess Magdalena was not well either, but above all, her cloistered state restricted her travels.[77] For some time before the funeral, quantities of Spanish arms had been arriving in the city, in all likelihood for ceremonial use by Rudolph's retinue. A rumor had begun to circulate among spectators that the new king, out of respect for his mother and on the urging of the Jesuits, was planning to attack the Utraquists. The scattering of coins began, as was customary at the burial of an emperor, and the crowd following the cortege turned rowdy. Soldiers moved to restrain them. Someone cried out that the duke of Alba's treatment of Antwerp was about to repeat itself, others that a second St. Barthomew's Day massacre was under way. A general melee ensued. Rudolph, standing beside his father's bier, drew his dagger, though someone grabbed the new emperor's hand before he hurt anyone. The uproar was finally quelled, but only with difficulty.[78]

Even in death, Maximilian continued to cause his family distress. Rudolph resented having to find livings for his unmarried brothers. None of the young men had any clerical education, even though Philip had urged Maximilian to provide such training for them.[79] Maria, now the dowager empress, had only the income from the interest on her dowry to support her. She was heavily in debt as well. This situation, along with her sons' reluctance to allow her to continue meddling in imperial politics, persuaded her to return to Spain in 1581. She and her brother, whom she had not seen for thirty years, had an emotional reunion. As their carriages drew close, they alighted, ran into one another's arms, and embraced at great length. Maria took up residence at the Carmelite cloister in Madrid, the burial place of her husband's grandmother, Joanna the Mad. The empress's interest in dynastic politics did not wane, even in the dark and otherworldly environment of her new retreat. When Archdukes Ernst and Maximilian resumed the Habsburg quest for the Polish crown in 1587, she waited impatiently for news of the outcome.[80] Her funeral in 1603 was designed for an empress. The royal chapel of the Carmelite cloister was hung in black and the imperial coats of arms were displayed for the occasion; an imperial crown was placed prominently on her tomb.[81]

Her husband's resting place at the front of St. Vitus' Cathedral is an altogether different affair. Of the three stone figures recumbent on the elevated surface over the vault, Maximilian's mother, on the far left, appears to be at perfect peace. Ferdinand I, in the center, lies in deep majesty, the imperial orb resting solidly above his left thigh. Maximilian, on his father's right, is very small—the space would not accommodate anything larger. Only the right hand, close to an imperial orb, seems to be expressing something. Is he trying to steady the globe with his fingers or to push it away? It is hard to say.

fifteen

Conclusion

Repeated failure's saddest end is loss of hope. As defeats accumulate, even the most resilient people give way to apathy and paralyzing skepticism. Issues that were once important lose their meaning, and ambition fades. Life's rituals are performed out of a sense of obligation rather than commitment.

Such feelings clearly haunted Maximilian in the last few years of his career. The confident enthusiasms of his youth had long been a thing of the past, and the tenacity and toughness with which he had once defended his religious views and his dynastic entitlements had weakened markedly. His stormy campaign for his thrones required both self-esteem and courage, as did his persistent religious unorthodoxy. But at the core, Maximilian may have been among those men whose reserves of psychic force are spent fairly early in their lives, never to be wholly renewed. The trait was apparently hereditary. His son Archduke Matthias poured a daunting amount of energy into wresting preeminence in his family from his elder brother Rudolph, only to turn into a remarkably passive emperor.[1]

Emotional weak spots, however, were not the chief cause of Maximilian's most crucial setbacks. Why would so intelligent and realistic a man foolishly stake his image as a leader on defeating so formidable a foe as the Turks? How could Maximilian have failed to see that the Protestants and Catholics were far more inclined to defend their respective confessional positions than to accommodate to the views of others? Did he not recognize that he could not reform his administration without a thoroughgoing commitment to substantial change; that his pan-European dynastic obligations could not be reconciled with the responsibilities of constitutional office; that his refusal to conform to any Christian orthodoxy would turn him into a kind of outcast within his family and in Germany as a whole? These questions raise problems of perception and judgment that can be answered only if one reflects on Maximilian's training, his worldview, and his offices, rather than on his inner demons. Such considerations are also the aspect of his career that makes him historically interesting.

Despite the grandiose manner in which Maximilian and his house could display their power, the Habsburgs operated under many constraints. Uncooperative estates and underfunding were only two of them. Just as restrictive were the subtler pressures of values and culture. Maximilian demanded a good deal from those who served him, but he was acutely sensitive to the expectations of others, too. To be sure, he was risking great disappointment against the Turks in Hungary in 1566, but he had many reasons to take them on. He belonged to a society that regarded leadership and feats of arms as virtually one and the same. Even the mock combat of the lists seemed indicative to audiences trying to evaluate princely prowess. Ferdinand I had always been in disrepute among the Turks because his armies were so ineffectual in the field. That he was a generally capable ruler was beside the point. Süleyman was a formidable adversary in 1566, but if Maximilian had not responded to him as vigorously as he did, Habsburg shame would have been still greater. Had the emperor won, of course (a reasonable expectation, given the size of the force at his command), he stood to gain great honor.

As archduke, king, and emperor, Maximilian enjoyed unique privileges and resources; but such status and its advantages did not encourage the habits of mind needed to realize serious administrative reform. For him and his Habsburg counterparts, government took place in a kind of timeless present. Having no reason to question a system that brought them the honor they enjoyed, they changed their way of ruling only when they believed they had to. When they did move, they did so on a case-by-case basis and not to alter the overall order that made them what they were, but to make that order work better for them. Like his great-grandfather and namesake, Maximilian could identify specific problems and construct imaginative remedies for them. The systematic and far-reaching innovation needed to carry out his vision was, however, beyond him. Nothing in his upbringing and career ever prepared him to rethink the values and institutional network that legitimated him. Maximilian recognized the administrative benefits of efficiency and general clerical orderliness; nevertheless, the cultural environment that would have validated such behavior was alien to the court and household that supported both his person and his offices.

How readily Maximilian would have delegated meaningful authority to subordinates in his extensive and politically complex holdings is also an open question. Personal rule was his style; indeed, he enjoyed the work that such a policy brought him. That outlook may also have warped his judgment in ways that left him open to disappointment. Even if he had been far richer than he was, Maximilian probably could not have found enough talented personnel to do all the assignments he had for them. His own father, as well as lesser German princes, suffered quite visibly from this lack of qualified assistants, and Maximilian should have factored this problem into his planning. Schooled as he was to command, he often seemed to think that giving orders was the equivalent of getting things done. This perception might have few negative consequences if one was ordering decorative shrubs from Italy, but not if one was staffing offices with intractable and self-interested human beings. In this respect, Maximilian anticipated the even more notorious failure of his eighteenth-century successor, Joseph II, who shared his ancestor's restless intellect, arrogance, and critical views of a successful parent.

Maximilian also badly overestimated the useful effect that the 1555 Augsburg settlement would have on his confessional policies. Once again, however, his alternatives were few, given his visceral dislike of religious conflict and its destabilizing effect on public life.[2] And he was not altogether wrong in his reading of the impact of the 1555 agreement. There were visible signs when he became emperor that the religious dualism had taken hold with both evangelicals and Catholics in the empire. Maximilian's endorsement of the peace clearly helped him win the confidence of both sides at his election in 1562. He therefore had reason to conclude that the imperial estates supported the arrangement as much as he did. His stubborn if ill-chosen commitment to confessional evenhandedness, therefore, flowed as much from a general atmosphere of political caution as it did from Maximilian's personality. Even as Calvinism became a serious problem in the late 1560s, the German electors, including Elector Palatine Frederick, respected the consensual process by which they arrived at decisions. They made it plain that they wanted religious peace and that it was the emperor's duty to uphold it. If the fractious Germans apparently thought this way, why could the Augsburg model not be exported to the Netherlands, where some thought it was applicable in any case, or even to France?

Indeed, if maintaining public tranquillity in Germany had been Maximilian's only charge, he might have realized his goal by means of the delicate balancing act he carried on between Lutherans and Catholics. By steadfastly refusing to identify himself with one side or the other in matters of religion, he probably kept Germany at peace internally and with its neighbors during his lifetime.[3] But the intractable political questions raised by first the conflict in the Netherlands and then the religious wars in France obscured that achievement. A vast inventory of scholarship, almost all of it from the second half of the twentieth century, now argues that the Holy Roman Empire, particularly on the regional and territorial level, ran a good deal better than some contemporaries believed.[4] However in need of correction our understanding of premodern German history may be, though, we should also recognize that imperial governance had seriously dysfunctional features, beginning with uncertainty over the locus and extent of the emperor's authority.[5]

Maximilian suffered from this confusion, particularly in his dealings with the Netherlands. Protecting each German principality's borders and maintaining general order in the empire were among his chief duties. Yet the imperial constitution gave no clear guidance to anyone trying to distinguish between Philip II's role as a German prince and his role as king of Spain. Philip himself exploited these ambiguities, to the discredit of his cousin and the office of emperor. Once again, though, if Maximilian had turned his back on these issues altogether, he would have been neglecting his chosen duty. Basic reform of the imperial office was the only productive course to take, but Maximilian had good political reasons not to attempt anything more radical in Germany than in his own lands and court. Charles V had given the princes a taste of authority in action in his treatment of Philip of Hesse and John Frederick of Saxony following the Schmalkaldic War, and he had lived to reap the consequences. His nephew was not about to repeat the performance. Maximilian pointed out several important areas for administrative reform in the empire, in particular as concerned military organization, yet he accomplished no more than had most of his predecessors.[6]

Maximilian's membership in the house of Austria also complicated his position in Germany. The imperial princes had long been uneasy with rulers whose dynastic loyalties ranged over much of Europe; the confessional split between Catholic and Protestant turned discomfort into mistrust. When Philip's problems in the Netherlands became Maximilian's as well, the emperor's dual heritage of house and office became as much a drawback as a benefit for him. The reverse was also true, however: the politics of the imperial office, over which Maximilian engaged in so many struggles, seriously upset his relationships with family members whose interests he never questioned and whose support was indispensable. Maximilian's religious policies, in both Germany and his Austrian lands, turned a sometimes difficult relationship with the king of Spain into one that was unremittingly so. Maximilian's enthusiasm for the Augsburg settlement, altogether necessary for his political survival in the empire, particularly displeased his house.[7] Yet he was also mindful, as were all sixteenth-century rulers, that land brought honor and prestige, and that all the territory he had he owed to the house of Habsburg. Maximilian's quarrels with Ferdinand I were never over the latter's paternal authority but rather over what the older man chose to do with it. If he was to keep his lands—or qualify for the Spanish inheritance, a thought that always lurked in his mind—Maximilian could never afford to alienate his relatives in Madrid.

Most of these difficulties will afflict anyone who, like Maximilian, takes central roles on every side of a many-sided conflict. Maximilian was pushed into that complex position by political necessity, responsibility, inheritance, and inclination, to name only the most important factors accounting for his career. There remains, however, the question of his personal religious views, for they do not neatly fit into a circumstantially conditioned assessment of his behavior. Unlike many in his era, Maximilian clearly did not think that confession defined the person—otherwise, how would he have been able to tolerate the Calvinist Crato at his court for his entire life, let alone remain on intimate terms with him and with scholars from both confessional camps? Institutionally and culturally, he was closer to the Catholicism in which he had been raised than to Protestantism, though his antipapalism set him apart sharply from his father. One can only agree with Maximilian's earlier biographer Viktor Bibl, who saw the emperor as a Christian without a real religion, in the sense of an elaborate confessional superstructure.[8]

However heterodox, Maximilian's religious views seem to have been the product of deeply independent thinking, of a kind that displayed itself only in flashes in other areas. For all the priority Maximilian assigned to dynastic matters throughout his career, he stood by his spiritual convictions for his entire life, in the face of his family's stony disapproval. Indeed, his confessional practice, not his politics, troubled them more than anything else.[9] Maximilian lived with Catholic ceremony on the one hand and evangelical inwardness on the other, regardless of what cousins, wife, and children thought.

Such behavior, however, was contrarian only among Habsburgs themselves. Maximilian was hardly atypical of his age. His personal juxtaposition of traditional and reformed belief had its counterpart in the humble parishes of his Austrian lands, where Catholics and evangelicals sometimes shared the same altar. Like many people of his time, he may never have stopped working through the doctrinal issues that the Reformation had raised. Like so many of his endeavors, this quest was one he probably did not complete. Indeed, in view of his political responsibilities, it is unlikely that he would have been altogether comfortable with the answers he found. He was not the only sixteenth-century ruler for whom a privately reconsidered faith became a public political problem. To have thought, however, that his family and his subjects would find some way to accommodate his positions, even to accept them, was one of his most serious miscalculations. Indeed, Maximilian's core mistakes all followed this pattern of misplaced expectations. The German princes were not disposed to rise above confessional partisanship, members of his dynasty were not ready to sacrifice their own agendas to advance his, and officials and court personnel throughout his life were as ill prepared as the emperor to exchange personal values for institutional ones in the name of administrative efficiency. Maximilian was indeed a very flawed ruler. His inadequacies, however, also made plain the limitations of the constitutional, societal, and cultural structures that gave him both his position and his problems.

Notes

INTRODUCTION

1. Thomas A. Brady, Jr., *The Politics of the Reformation in Germany: Jacob Sturm (1489–1553) of Strasbourg* (Atlantic Highlands, N.J.: Humanities Press, 1997), 3. On the issue of success and failure in Reformation history see Geoffrey Parker, "Success and Failure During the First Century of the Reformation," *Past and Present* 136 (1992), esp. 46–51.

2. Viktor Bibl, "Die Kulturblüte Wiens und seiner Umgebung unter Maximilian II.," *Monatsblatt des Vereins für Landeskunde von Niederösterreich* 17 (1918): 139.

3. R. J. W. Evans, *Rudolf II and His World: A Study in Intellectual History, 1576–1612* (Oxford: Oxford University Press, 1973), 52; R. J. W. Evans, "Culture and Anarchy in the Empire, 1540–1680," *Central European History* 18 (1985): 19.

4. See, e.g., Brady, *Politics,* passim; Jean-Louis Bourgeon, *Charles IX devant la Saint-Barthélemy* (Geneva: Droz, 1995), 12, 15; and Howard Louthan, *Johannis Crato and the Austrian Habsburgs: Reforming a Counter-Reform Court* (Princeton, N.J.: Princeton Theological Seminary, 1994), passim.

5. Viktor Bibl, "Zur Frage der religiösen Haltung Kaiser Maximilians II.," *AöG* 106 (1918): 291–328.

6. Bibl, "Frage," 322; Perez Zagorin, *Ways of Lying: Dissimulation, Persecution, and Conformity in Early Modern Europe* (Cambridge, Mass.: Harvard, 1990), 6–7, 11, 35.

7. Robert Holtzmann, *Kaiser Maximilian II. bis zu seiner Thronbesteigung, 1527–*

1564 (Berlin: Schwetschke, 1903), 10, 531; Andreas Edel, *Der Kaiser und Kurpfalz: Eine Studie zu den Grundelementen politischen Handelns bei Maximilian II.*, *1564–1576* (Göttingen: Vandenhoeck and Ruprecht, 1997), 159.

8. Bibl, "Frage," 385; Alois Brusatti, "Die Entwicklung der Reichskreise während der Regierungszeit Maximilians II." (dissertation, University of Vienna, 1950), 18; [?] Becker, "Die letzten Tage und der Tod Maximilians II.," *Blätter des Vereines für Landeskunde von Niederösterreich*, n.s. 11 (1877): 310, 312; Emanuel van Meteren, *Belgica: Historie der Neder-landen ende haerder Naburen Oorlogen ende Geschiedenissen . . .* , 2 vols. (The Hague: Jacobussz, 1614), 1: fo. 121, col. 2; Friedrich Schubert, *Die deutschen Reichstage in der Staatslehre der frühen Neuzeit*, Schriften des historischen Kommission der bayerischen Akademie der Wissenschaften, vol. 7 (1966): 325 and note 18.

9. See general comments of Evans, *Rudolf II*, 3–4, 92–93.

CHAPTER 1: A SON OF PROMISE

1. "Wellen wir so es ein Son ist das dan mit Shyessen unnd freudenfeuer auch ainen zimlichen pangket; wo es aber ein tochter ist, alain mit dem pangket fursehung bestech unnd freud gehaltn werde." Haus-, Hof- und Staatsarchiv, Vienna (hereafter HHStA), Familienarchiv (Family archive), Familienakten (Family documents), 2.1, Entbindungen und Taufen (Births and baptisms), box 18, fos. 8–9.

2. Ibid., fo. 5.

3. Paula Sutter Fichtner, *Ferdinand I of Austria* (Boulder, Colo.: East European Monographs, 1982), 38.

4. Hanns von Lamberg to Ferdinand, 8 Aug. 1527, HHStA, Familienarchiv, Familienakten, 2.1, Entbindungen und Taufen, box 18, fo. 10; Hanns von Lamberg to Ferdinand, 13 Aug. 1527, HHStA, Familienarchiv, Familienakten, 2.1, Entbindungen und Taufen, box 18, fo. 12; Lucian Groner of Carinthia to Hanns von Lamberg, n.d., HHStA, Familienarchiv, Familienakten, 2.1, Entbindungen und Taufen, box 18, fo. 19.

5. Fichtner, *Ferdinand I*, 103.

6. "Instruktion König Ferdinands I. für den Hofstaat der Erzherzöge Maximilian und Ferdinand," 13 Oct. 1538, HHStA, Hofarchiv (Household archive), Obersthofmeisteramt (Office of the grand master, hereafter OMeA), Sonderreihe (Special series), box 181/12, fos. 12–12a (draft).

7. "Mit ainem rütel . . . damit sie in der sorg und zuchtl gehalten werden." HHStA, Hofarchiv, OMeA, Sonderreihe, box 181/12, fos. 1, 3, 5–7, 10–11; and Veronika Pokorny, "Clementia Austriaca: Studien zur Bedeutung der Clementia Principis für die Habsburger im 16. und 17. Jahrhundert," *MIöG* 86 (1978): 349.

8. Instruktionen König Ferdinands . . . 1538, HHStA, Hofarchiv, OMeA, Sonderreihe, box 181/12, fo. 3; Instructions to the *Edelknaben* 1538, HHStA, Hofarchiv, OMeA, Sonderreihe, box 181/12, fo. 17; Joseph Hirn, *Erzherzog Ferdinand II. von Tirol*, 2 vols. (Innsbruck: Wagner, 1885–1888), 1: 5, 7.

9. Rosemarie Vocelka, "Die Begräbnisfeierlichkeiten für Kaiser Maximilian II., 1576–1577," *MIöG* 84 (1976): 135; Christine of Lorraine to Maximilian, 11 Jan. 1567, in *Die Korrespondenz des Kaisers Maximilian II.*, Viktor Bibl, ed., 2 parts in 2 vols., Veröffentlichungen der Kommission für neuere Geschichte Österreichs, vols. 14, 16 (Vienna: Holzhausen, 1916–1921), part 2: 92; Holtzmann, *Maximilian II.*, 22, note 3; Jaroslav Pánek, "Maximilian II. als König von Böhmen," in Friedrich Edelmayer and Alfred Kohler, eds., *Kaiser Maximilian II.: Kultur und Politik im 16. Jahrhundert*, Wiener Beiträge zur Geschichte der Neuzeit, vol. 19 (Vienna: Verlag für Geschichte und Politik, 1992), 37.

10. Viktor Bibl, *Maximilian II.: Der rätselhafte Kaiser* (Hellerau bei Dresden: Avalun, n.d.), 30; Fray Prudencio de Sandoval, *Historia de la vida y hechos del emperador Carlos V*, Biblioteca de autores españoles, vols. 80–82 (Madrid: Ediciones Atlas, 1955–1956), 82: 190; Joannis Crato a Kraftheim, *Epistola ad Joannem Sambucum de Morte Imperatoris Maximiliani Secundi* (Jena: Mauk, 1781), 14.

11. Fichtner, *Ferdinand I*, 110; Hirn, *Erzherzog Ferdinand*, 1: 7; Holtzmann, *Maximilian II.*, 18; Bibl, *Maximilian II.*, 30.

12. Holtzmann, *Maximilian II.*, 25–26.

13. "Ut paterno nomine infans in ipsius patris mores formandus decoraretur," Caspar Ursinus Velius, *De Bello Pannonico: Libri Decem*, Adam Francis Kollar, ed. (Vienna: Trattner, 1767), 100; Holtzmann, *Maximilian II.*, 17.

14. Giovanni Michele in Joseph Fiedler, ed., *Relationen venetianischer Botschafter über Deutschland und Österreich im sechzehnten Jahrhundert*, FRA, part 2, Diplomataria, vol. 30 (Vienna: Gerold, 1870), 286.

15. Fichtner, *Ferdinand I*, 102.

16. Gustav Turba, ed., *Venetianische Depeschen vom Kaiserhofe*, 4 vols. (Vienna: Tempsky, 1889), 2: 460–461. On primogeniture in Germany, see Paula Sutter Fichtner, *Protestantism and Primogeniture in Early Modern Germany* (New Haven, Conn.: Yale University Press, 1989), esp. chap. 1.

CHAPTER 2: AN ANGRY APPRENTICE

1. Holtzmann, *Maximilian II.*, 286–287.

2. Ibid., 38; Edel, *Kaiser*, 79.

3. Walter Pass, *Musik und Musiker am Hof Maximilians II.* (Tutzing: Schneider, 1980), 168.

4. Friedrich Edelmayer, "Die Beziehungen zwischen Maximilian II. und Philipp II." (philosophische Diplomarbeit, University of Vienna, 1982), 9; Holtzmann, *Maximilian II.*, 37, 42.

5. Bruno Thomas, "Die Harnischgarnitur Maximilians II. von Jörg Sensenhofer," *Belvedere* 13 (1938–1939): 77; Holtzmann, *Maximilian II.*, 46, 55.

6. Holtzmann, *Maximilian II.*, 46, 51; Fichtner, *Ferdinand I*, 244.

7. Alvise Mocenigo to the doge, 7 Feb. 1547, in Turba, *Depeschen*, 2: 169–17.

8. Winfried Eberhard, *Monarchie und Widerstand: Zur ständischen Oppositionsbildung im Herrschaftssystem Ferdinands I. in Böhmen*, Veröffentlichungen des Collegium Carolinum, vol. 54 (Munich: Oldenbourg, 1985), 429.

9. Holtzmann, *Maximilian II.*, 54–55; Grete Mecenseffy, "Maximilian II. in neuer Sicht," *Jahrbuch der Gesellschaft für die Geschichte des Protestantismus in Österreich* 92 (1976): 45; Matthias Koch, ed., *Quellen zur Geschichte des Kaisers Maximilian II.*, 2 vols. in 1 (Leipzig: Voigt and Günther, 1857–1861), 2: 119, note 1; Friedrich Edelmayer with the assistance of Arno Strohmeyer, ed., *Der Briefwechsel zwischen Ferdinand I., Maximilian II. und Adam von Dietrichstein, 1563–1565*, vol. 1 of *Die Korrespondenz der Kaiser mit ihren Gesandten in Spanien* (Vienna: Verlag für Geschichte und Politik, 1997), 73.

10. Fichtner, *Ferdinand I*, 244; Paula Sutter Fichtner, "Of Christian Virtue and a Practicing Prince: Emperor Ferdinand I and His Son Maximilian," *Catholic Historical Review* 61 (1975): 412–413.

11. Holtzmann, *Maximilian II.*, 60.

12. Edelmayer, "Beziehungen," 17.

13. Federico Chabod, "Milan o los Paises Bajos? Las discussiones en España sobre la 'alternativa' de 1544," in *Carlos V, 1500–1558: Homenaje de la Universidad de Granada* (Granada: La junta del centenario, 1958), 337; Holtzmann, *Maximilian II.*, 45.

14. Biblioteca nacional, Madrid (hereafter BN), Sección de manuscritos (Manuscript division), no. 6238, fos. 98–107. Dated 1613, this document appears to be a copy of one transmitted to Charles V. See also Alfred Kohler, "Vom habsburgischen Gesamtsystem Karls V. zu den Teilsystemen Philipps II. und Maximilians II.," in Edelmayer and Kohler, eds. *Maximilian II.*, 19.

15. Alvise Mocenigo to the doge, 18 June 1547, in Turba, *Depeschen*, 2: 286; Alvise Mocenigo to the doge, 16 July 1547, ibid., p. 311, note 1; Maximilian to Ernst of Krajk, 25 Jan. 1548, and Maximilian to Bohus Kostka of Postupic, 21 Jan. 1548, in Johann Loserth, ed., *Die Registratur Erzherzog Maximilians (Maximilians II.): 1547–1551 aus den Handschriften des Stifts Reun*, FRA, Diplomataria et Acta 48, part 2 (Vienna: Gerold, 1896): 402–404.

16. "Las rentas de las otras provincias," marriage capitulations of Maximilian and Maria, 24 April 1548, BN, Madrid, Sección de manuscritos, no. 6149,

fos. 166–167; Philip of Spain's confirmation of the marriage agreement, 2 May 1549, BN, Madrid, Sección de manuscritos, no. 1029, fos. 409–410.

17. Hans Habersack, *Die Krönungen Maximilians II. zum König von Böhmen, Römischen König und König von Ungarn (1562–1563) nach der Beschreibung des Hans Habersack*, Friedrich Edelmayer, Leopold Kammerhofer, Martin C. Mandlmayr, Walter Prenner, and Karl G. Vocelka, eds., FRA, part 1, Scriptores, 13, part 1 (Vienna: Österreichische Akademie der Wissenschaften, 1990), 24–25.

18. "Pro illustrando et ornando matrimonia," Philip of Spain's confirmation of the Bohemian marriage, 2 May 1549, BN, Madrid, Sección de manuscritos, no. 1029, fo. 409.

19. BN, Madrid, Sección de manuscritos, no. 7413, fos. 2–3, 39; Philip II to the head of the Council of Orders, 23 Mar. 1567, BN, Madrid, Sección de manuscritos, no. 781, fo. 114; Philip to the head of the Council of Orders, 10 May 1567, BN, Madrid, Sección de manuscritos, no. 781, fo. 120; Maria to the count of Benavente, 30 Nov. 1555, Archivo nacional, Madrid, Sección de Osuna (hereafter AN, Osuna), legajo 426(1), no. 4(2), no folio. See also AN, Osuna, legajo 2283(2), fo. 25.

20. Holtzmann, *Maximilian II.*, 73–74; "Matrimonialia Maximiliana . . . Maria," HHStA, Familienarchiv, Familienakten, 2.4, Vermählungen (marriages), box 20, fos. 43, 53; Alvise Mocenigo and Francesco Badoer to the doge, 19 Apr. 1548, in Turba, *Depeschen*, 2: 411.

21. "Dicitur erga pietatem et Germaniam non male affectus," Wolrad von Waldeck, *Tagebuch*, C. L. P. Tross, ed., Bibliothek des litterarischen Vereins in Stuttgart, vol. 59 (Stuttgart: Litterarischer Verein, 1861), 77, 157.

22. Holtzmann, *Maximilian II.*, 67; Loserth, *Registratur*, 422, note 2.

23. "Personas de calidad," Charles's Instructions of 8 June 1548, HHStA, Familienarchiv, Familienakten, 2.10, Reisen (Travel), box 86, fo. 2; Ferdinand Mencik, "Die Reise Kaiser Maximilians II. nach Spanien im Jahre 1548," *Archiv für österreichische Geschichte* (hereafter *AöG*) 86 (1899): 293–308.

24. Holtzmann, *Maximilian II.*, 82–84; Rafaela Rodríguez Raso, ed., *Maximiliano de Austria, gobernador de Carlos V en España: Cartas al emperador* (Madrid: Consejo superior de investigaciones cientificas, 1963), 17–18.

25. Giovanni Michele to [?] 1563[?], in Fiedler, *Relationen*, 30: 216; Maximilian to Albrecht V of Bavaria, 11 Oct. 1562, Hauptstaatsarchiv, Munich (hereafter HSA), Kurbayern (electoral Bavaria), Äußeres Archiv (Foreign affairs archive), no. 4461, fo. 127; Holtzmann, *Maximilian II.*, 85; Helga Widorn, "Die spanische Gemahlinnen der Kaiser Maximilian II., Ferdinand III. und Leopold I." (dissertation, University of Vienna, 1959), 5. For portraits of Maria in various stages of her life, see no. 2110 in the Prado Museum in

Madrid and depictions hung at the convent of the Carmelites, also in the Spanish capital.

26. Giovanni Michele to the senate[?], doge[?], 1563[?], in Fiedler, *Relationen*, 30: 216; Maximilian to Albrecht of Bavaria, St. Michael's Day 1563, HSA, Kurbayern, Äußeres Archiv, no. 4461, fo. 203; Widorn, "Gemahlinnen," 13–14.

27. Queen Maria to Maria of Hungary, 12 Nov. 1554, HHStA, Familienarchiv, Familienkorrespondenz (Family correspondence) A, box 31, bundle K. Maria Frau K. Max. II., fo. 7; Michele to [?] 1563 [?], in Fiedler, *Relationen*, 30: 216. Cf. Holtzmann, *Maximilian II.*, 85; and Edel, *Kaiser*, 157–158. Holtzmann's evaluation of Maria as reclusive and indifferent to politics may have been true of her first years in Vienna when her German was especially insecure. His study goes only to 1564, and therefore does not treat her later career, during which she was heavily involved in the political and religious scene at the court.

28. Rodríguez, *Maximiliano*, 19, note 36; Holtzmann, *Maximilian II.*, 8; Heinrich Noflatscher, "Erzherzog Maximilian Hoch- und Deutschmeister, 1585–90: Das Haus Habsburg, der deutsche Orden und das Reich im konfessionellen Zeitalter," 2 vols. (dissertation, University of Innsbruck, 1980), 1: 32; Peter Rassow, "Karls V. Tochter als Eventualerbin der spanischen Reiche," *Archiv für Reformationsgeschichte* 49 (1958): 164.

29. Report of Giovanni Michele, 1563, in Fiedler, *Relationen*, 30; 217; Maximilian to Queen Maria of Hungary, 2 May 1556, HHStA, Belgien (Belgium), Politisches Archiv (Political archive) 9, bundle 7, fo. 352,

30. Widorn, "Gemahlinnen," 30; Giovanni Michele to [?], 1571, in Fiedler, *Relationen*, 30: 282.

31. Matrimonialia Maximiliani . . . Maria, HHStA, Familienarchiv, Familienakten, 2.4, Vermählungen, box 20, fos. 83–86; Maximilian and Maria's marriage capitulations, 24 Apr. 1548, BN, Madrid, Sección de manuscritos, no. 6149, fo. 168; Rassow, "Tochter," 163; Maximilian and Maria to Charles, 6 July 1549, in Rodríguez, *Maximiliano*, 115–116; Edelmayer, "Beziehungen," 55.

32. Widorn, "Gemahlinnen," 1; Edelmayer, "Beziehungen," 48.

33. Holtzmann, *Maximilian II.*, 72; Rodríguez, *Maximiliano*, 4; Habersack, *Habersack*, 25, notes 18, 19. Cf. Henry Kamen, *Philip of Spain* (New Haven, Conn.: Yale University Press, 1997), 45.

34. "Dessen wir dann diser zeit am passten bedürftig," Maximilian to Duke William of Bavaria, 19 Sept. 1548, in Loserth, *Registratur*, 439. Cf. Maximilian to Mary of Hungary, 19 Sept. 1548, ibid., 437; and Maximilian to the elector of Mainz, 19 Sept. 1548, ibid., 346. See also Rodríguez, *Maximiliano*, 19.

35. "Welches uns dann nach gelegenhait und zeit unsers jetzigen newen standts,

in dem wir als ein junger und frommer angeender eeman getretten, zum höchsten beschwerlich sein will," Maximilian to Elector Palatine Frederick, 15 Nov. 1548, in Loserth, *Registratur*, 445; Rodríguez, *Maximiliano*, 19.

36. "Mit grossem schwangerm [?] leib beladen," Maximilian to Elector Palatine Frederick, 15 Nov. 1548, in Loserth, *Registratur*, 445.

37. Maximilian to Sigismund Lodron, 22 Dec. 1548, in Loserth, *Registratur*, 452; Maximilian to Maurice of Saxony, 2 Nov. 1549, ibid., 485; Holtzmann, *Maximilian II.*, 85.

38. Maximilian to Wenzel von Ludanitz, Hauptmann (captain) of Moravia, 9 Jan. 1550, in Loserth, *Registratur*, 497–498; Edelmayer, "Beziehungen," 132.

39. Rodríguez, *Maximiliano*, 25; Horst Rabe and Peter Marzahl, " 'Comme représentant nostre propre personne'—the Regency Ordinances of Charles V as a Historical Source," in E. I. Kouri and Tom Scott, eds., *Politics and Society in Reformation Europe* (London: Macmillan, 1987): 78–93.

40. See, e.g., Maximilian and Maria's bill of sale for the town of Villafranca, 7 Dec. 1549, AN, Osuna, legajo 2283(2), fos. 24–28.

41. Maximilian to Hanns Jergen Baumgartner, 8 June 1550, in Loserth, *Registratur*, 511; Maximilian to Albrecht of Bavaria, 31 May 1553, HSA, Kurbayern, Äußeres Archiv, no. 4460, no. 16. With few exceptions, materials in this fascicle are numbered by item rather than by folio. Those folio numbers which do exist are much older. I have used the item numbers.

42. Maximilian and Maria to Charles, 20 Apr. 1550, in Rodríguez, *Maximiliano*, 182–183; William S. Maltby, *Alba: A Biography of Fernando Alvarez de Toledo, Third Duke of Alba, 1507–1582* (Berkeley: University of California Press, 1983), 66–67. See also Rodríguez, *Maximiliano*, 29.

43. Maximilian to Hans Ungnad, 26 Apr. 1550, in Loserth, *Registratur*, 507–508; Maximilian and Maria to Charles, 9 Apr. 1550, in Rodríguez, *Maximiliano*, 175.

44. Maximilian and Maria to Charles, 10 Apr. 1549, Rodríguez, *Maximiliano*, 94; Maximilian and Maria to Charles, July 1550, ibid., 194, 200.

45. Maximilian to Wenzel Gämitzer [Jämnitzer], 18 Dec. 1548, in Loserth, *Registratur*, 450–451; Maximilian to Wolfgang Volandt, 18 Dec. 1548, ibid., 451–452.

46. Maximilian to Jacob Fugger, 28 June 1549, ibid., 466.

47. "Zu mererm gemainen nutz und aufnemen schifflich ze machen und zu gebrauchen sein möchte," Maximilian to Georg Broskofsky, 17 Aug. 1549, ibid., 476.

48. Maximilian to Georg Broskofsky, 17 Aug. 1549, ibid., 476–477; Ana Díaz Medina, "El gobierno en España de Maximiliano II (1548–1551)," in Edelmayer and Kohler, eds. *Maximilian II.*, 50. For a very suggestive analysis

of aquatic projects in European history, see Richard C. Hoffmann, "Economic Development and Aquatic Ecosystems in Medieval Europe," *American Historical Review* 101 (1996): 631–669.

49. "Auch wir hie ain gedechtnus hinder uns verlassen möchten," Maximilian to Jacob Fugger, 28 June 1549, in Loserth, *Registratur,* 467.

50. Maximilian to Matthess Frauenpreiss, 28 July 1549, ibid., 476.

51. Maximilian to Wolf der Ältere of Kreyg, 9 Jan. 1550, ibid., 496–497; Maximilian to Ferdinand, 18 June 1550, ibid., 508; Maximilian's Instructions for Christoph Wilhelm von Zelking et al. to Ferdinand, 17 Nov. 1549, ibid., 488–489.

52. "Und so wir also in unser vaterland komen in welches wir für all andere ding herzlich verlangen haben und das [es] der almechtige paldt schicken welle," Maximilian to Maurice of Saxony, 15 Jan. 1550, ibid., 494–495.

53. "Milt und lieblich," Maximilian to Christoph Haller zu Andorff, 31 Oct. 1549, ibid., 483; Holtzmann, *Maximilian II.,* 88.

54. Maximilian to the elector of Mainz et al., 21 July 1548, in Loserth, *Registratur,* 432–433; Maximilian to Vice-Chancellor Jonas, 16 Dec. 1548, ibid., 453; Maximilian to Hanns Jergen Baumgartner, 18 June 1550, ibid., 512.

55. Edelmayer, "Beziehungen," 24.

56. "Die loblich teutsch nation" and "unser geliebtes vatterlandt," Maximilian to the elector of Mainz, 19 Sept. 1548, in Loserth, *Registratur,* 436–437; Maximilian to Joachim of Brandenburg, 9 Jan. 1550, ibid., 492.

57. Fichtner, *Ferdinand I,* 172–174, 176.

58. Holtzmann, *Maximilian II.,* 91–92.

59. Ibid., 92–93, 146, 191; Maximilian to Joachim of Brandenburg, 9 Jan. 1550, in Loserth, *Registratur,* 492; Edelmayer in *Habersack,* 29.

60. Fichtner, *Ferdinand I,* 168.

61. Ibid., 169–170; Holtzmann, *Maximilian II.,* 110–114, 128.

62. Edelmayer in *Habersack,* 28–29, 31. Also Friedrich Edelmayer, "Kaisertum und Casa de Austria: Von Maximilian I. zu Maximilian II.," in *Hispania-Austria: Die katholischen Könige, Maximilian I. und die Anfänge der Casa de Austria in Spanien,* Friedrich Edelmayer and Alfred Kohler, eds. (Vienna: Verlag für Geschichte und Politik, 1993), 164; Holtzmann, *Maximilian II.,* 130–131.

63. Holtzmann, *Maximilian II.,* 128–129, 133–134, 145–146; Fichtner, *Ferdinand I,* 167; Geoffrey Parker, *Philip II* (London: Hutchison, 1979), 7, 21. Philip's tutor, Don Juan de Zuñiga, had indeed reported episodes of slovenliness, laziness, and laxity on the part of his charge in attending to religious obligations during 1548 and 1549; however, Maximilian himself had behaved much the same way at about the same time.

64. Holtzmann, *Maximilian II.,* 133–134.

65. Maximilian to Caspar Lindegg [secretary] 11 May 1551, in Loserth, *Registratur*, 561–562; Maximilian to Joseph von Lamberg and Wolfgang Volandt, 3 May 1551, ibid., 558–559.

66. Holtzmann, *Maximilian II.*, 142–144.

67. Maximilian to Ferdinand, 13 Nov. 1551, in Loserth, *Registratur*, 571; Maximilian to Ferdinand, 2 Dec. 1551, ibid., 573–574; Maximilian to Ferdinand, 19 Dec. 1551, ibid., 581; Maximilian's report to Ferdinand, 30 Dec. 1551, ibid., 587.

68. Holtzmann, *Maximilian II.*, 152–153, 155–156; Pánek, "Maximilian II," 58; Bibl, *Maximilian II.*, 59.

69. Widorn, "Gemahlinnen," 10–11.

70. Holtzmann, *Maximilian II.*, 155–156.

71. Maximilian to Maurice of Saxony, 17 Apr. 1551, in Loserth, *Registratur*, 551. The little Archduke Ferdinand died a little over a year later.

72. Maximilian to Philip of Hesse, 18 July 1547, ibid., 379; Maximilian to Philip of Hesse, 1 Aug. 1547, ibid., 384; Maximilian to Philip of Hesse, 5 Aug. 1547, ibid., 386; Maximilian to Count Palatine Ottheinrich, 12 June 1548, ibid., 423–424; Holtzmann, *Maximilian II.*, 63–65.

73. Fichtner, *Ferdinand I*, 189–190.

74. G. Heine, "Beiträge zur Geschichte im Zeitalter der Reformation aus spanischen und portugiesischen Archiven mitgetheilt," *Allgemeine Zeitschrift für Geschichte* 8 (1847): 8; Karlheinz Blaschke, *Moritz von Sachsen: Ein Reformationsfürst der zweiten Generation* (Göttingen: Muster-Schmidt, 1983), 27–28, 30, 46; Fichtner, *Ferdinand I*, 190–191; Bibl, *Maximilian*, 61.

75. Holtzmann, *Maximilian II.*, 168–170.

76. Ibid., 170–171.

77. Holtzmann, *Maximilian II.*, 133.

78. Maria to Queen Maria of Hungary, 12 Nov. 1554 (copy), HHStA, Familienarchiv, Familienkorrespondenz A, box 31, bundle K. Maria Frau K. Max. II, fo. 7; Ferdinand to Pedro Lasso, 24 June 1554, in *Briefe und Akten zur Geschichte des sechzehnten Jahrhunderts*, 5 vols. (Munich: Rieger: 1873–1896), 4: 492; Ferdinand to Alonso de Gamez, 10 Dec. 1552, ibid., 2: 830–831. Maria ordered that her letter to the queen of Hungary be destroyed, perhaps out of consideration for her husband's feelings.

79. Edelmayer, *Habersack*, 33.

80. Holtzmann, *Maximilian II.*, 212–213, 222; Edelmayer, "Beziehungen," 43, 46–47.

81. Maximilian to the count of Benavente, 2 August 1564, AN, Osuna, legajo 426/2, no. 12/2; Holtzmann, *Maximilian II.*, 247–248.

82. Holtzmann, *Maximilian II.*, 278–288.

83. Albrecht of Bavaria to Maximilian, 24 July 1558, HHStA, Staatenabteilungen

(Affairs of state), Bavarica (Bavaria), box 2, fo. 124; Holtzmann, *Maximilian II.*, 311.

84. Anton Gindely, ed., *Quellen ʒur Geschichte der böhmischen Brüder*, FRA, part 2, Diplomataria, vol. 19 (Vienna: Gerold, 1859), 136.

CHAPTER 3: A GERMAN PRINCE AND THE GERMAN RELIGION

1. Maximilian to Albrecht of Bavaria, 24 Mar. 1553 [?], HSA, Kurbayern, Äußeres Archiv, no. 4460, no. 49.

2. Pass, *Musik und Musiker*, 40–41; Maximilian to Albrecht of Bavaria, 12 Apr. 1564, HSA, Kurbayern, Äußeres Archiv, no. 4461, fo. 241.

3. Maximilian to Albrecht of Bavaria, 31 Mar. 1560, HSA, Kurbayern, Äußeres Archiv, no. 4461, fo. 5; Maximilian to Albrecht of Bavaria, 10 Apr. 1560, HSA, Kurbayern, Äußeres Archiv, no. 4461, fo. 9; Maximilian to Albrecht of Bavaria, 28 Apr. 1560, HSA, Kurbayern, Äußeres Archiv, no. 4461, fo. 14; Maximilian to Albrecht of Bavaria, 5 July 1560, HSA, Kurbayern, Äußeres Archiv, no. 4461, fo. 18; Maximilian to Albrecht of Bavaria, 14 Mar. 1564, HSA, Kurbayern, Äußeres Archiv, no. 4461, fo. 235; Maximilian to Albrecht of Bavaria, 26 June 1564, HSA, Kurbayern, Äußeres Archiv, no. 4461, fo. 257; Maximilian to Albrecht of Bavaria, 12 Aug. 1576, HSA, Kurbayern, Äußeres Archiv, no. 4462, fo. 164; Maximilian to Cardinal Caraffa, 2 Aug. 1557, HHStA, Familienarchiv, Familienakten, Sammelbände, box 1, vol. 1, fo. 20.

4. Maximilian to Albrecht of Bavaria, 26 Jan. 1561, HSA, Kurbayern, Äußeres Archiv, no. 4461, fo. 49; Maximilian to Albrecht of Bavaria, 19 Dec. 1564, HSA, Kurbayern, Äußeres Archiv, no. 4456, fos. 232–234; Maximilian to Albrecht of Bavaria, 20 Jan. 1569, HSA, Kurbayern, Äußeres Archiv, no. 4461, fo. 374; Maximilian to Albrecht of Bavaria, 11 Apr. 1570, HSA, Kurbayern, Äußeres Archiv, no. 4461, fo. 387.

5. See Albrecht of Bavaria to Maximilian, HHStA, Staatenabteilung, Bavarica, box 2, 22 May 1557, fo. 75; Albrecht of Bavaria to Maximilian, 6 July 1557, HHStA, Staatenabteilung, Bavarica, box 2, fo. 77; and Albrecht of Bavaria to Maximilian, 20 Sept. 1557, HHStA, Staatenabteilung, Bavarica, box 2, fo. 81.

6. Albrecht V of Bavaria to Maximilian, 11 Oct. 1557, HHStA, Staatenabteilung, Bavarica, box 2, fo. 86.

7. E.g., Maximilian to Philip II, n.d. July 1557, HHStA, Familienarchiv, Familienakten, Sammelbände, box 1, vol. 1, fos. 19, 86–87.

8. Gernot Heiß, "Die Jesuiten und die Anfänge der Katholisierung in den Ländern Ferdinands I.: Glaube, Mentalität, Politik," 2 vols. (Habilita-

tionsschrift, University of Vienna, 1986), 1: 106, 190–191; Volker Press, "The Habsburg Court as the Center of the Imperial Government," *Journal of Modern History* 58 (Supplement, 1986): S32; Bernd Zimmermann, "Hans Ungnads Beziehungen zu Reformatoren und Theologen," *Jahrbuch der Gesellschaft für die Geschichte des Protestantismus in Österreich* 103 (1987): 179–180, 187–188; Albrecht of Bavaria to Maximilian, 2 July 1561, HHStA, Staatenabteilung, Bavarica, box 2, fo. 182.

9. Holtzmann, *Maximilian II.,* 49–50, 79–80; Hans Ungnad to Maximilian, 1 Sept. 1561, HHStA, Familienarchiv, Familienkorrespondenz A, box 3, Konv. Kh.-W., fo. 536.

10. Mecenseffy, "Maximilian II.," 45; Holtzmann, *Maximilian II.,* 89; Friedrich Heer, *Die Dritte Kraft: Der europäische Humanismus zwischen den Fronten des konfessionellen Zeitalter* (Frankfurt a.M.: Fischer, 1959), 400.

11. Widorn, "Gemahlinnen," 5; Holtzmann, *Maximilian II.,* 89, 317; Rodríguez, *Maximiliano,* 84.

12. Maximilian to Charles, 7 Nov. 1549, in Rodríguez, *Maximiliano,* 149. Cf. Maximilian to Charles, 1 Dec. 1549, ibid., 152. See also Helmut Goetz, "Die Finalrelation des venezianischen Gesandter Michele Suriano, 1555," *Quellen und Forschungen aus italienischen Archiven und Bibliotheken* 41 (1961): 302–303.

13. Walter Goetz, "Der 'Kompromißkatholizismus' und Kaiser Maximilian II.," *Historische Zeitschrift* 77 (1896): 203; Alvise Mocenigo to the doge, 6 Sept. 1547, in Turba, *Depeschen,* 2: 336.

14. Holtzmann, *Maximilian II.,* 67–68, 146–147, 149.

15. Heine, "Beiträge," 16.

16. Maximilian to Albrecht of Bavaria V, 3 Aug. 1553, HSA, Kurbayern, Äußeres Archiv, no. 4460, fo. 22. Cf. Johann Joseph Ignaz Döllinger, *Beiträge zur politischen, kirchlichen und Cultur-geschichte der sechs letzten Jahrhunderte.* 3 vols. (Regensburg: Manz, 1862–1882), 1: no. 83.

17. Fichtner, *Ferdinand I,* 207–208; Holtzmann, *Maximilian II.,* 198.

18. "Dar bai ichs nun als der gehorsam son auch blaiwen haw lassen muessen," Maximilian to Albrecht of Bavaria, 1 Sept. 1553, HSA, Kurbayern, Äußeres Archiv, no. 4460, fo. 62.

19. Maximilian to Albrecht of Bavaria, 4 Sept. 1553, in *Briefe und Akten,* 4: 253–254; Holtzmann, *Maximilian II.,* 198; Maximilian to Albrecht of Bavaria, 18 Oct. 1553, HSA, Kurbayern, Äußeres Archiv, no. 4460, fo. 69.

20. Maximilian to Albrecht of Bavaria, 25 Feb. 1554, in *Briefe und Akten,* 4: 377, note 1. Also HSA, Kurbayern, Äußeres Archiv, no. 4460, fo. 43. Cf. Holtzmann, *Maximilian II.,* 216–217, for dating.

21. Maximilian to Christoph of Württemberg, 20 Dec. 1557, in Johann Friedrich

Le Bret, ed., *Maga*ʒ*in* ʒ*um Gebrauch der Staaten- und Kirchengeschichte* 9 (1785): 111; Maximilian to Christoph of Württemberg, 4 Sept. 1558, ibid., 139.

22. Wilhelm Maurenbrecher, "Beiträge zur Geschichte Maximilians II., 1548–1562," *Historische Zeitschrift* 32 (1874): 252–253; Bibl, *Maximilian II.*, 72–73; Goetz, " 'Kompromißkatholizismus,' " 202.

23. Pass, *Musik und Musiker*, 29–31; Mecenseffy, "Maximilian II.," 45; Holtzmann, *Maximilian II.*, 231–233.

24. Holtzmann, *Maximilian II.*, 234–235; Karl Brandi, *Deutsche Geschichte im Zeitalter der Reformation und Gegenreformation* (1927; reprint, Munich: Bruckmann, 1960), 340.

25. Fichtner, *Ferdinand I*, 248.

26. Fichtner, *Ferdinand I*, 249; Holtzmann, *Maximilian II.*, 235. An excellent discussion of the entire affair is in Heiß, "Jesuiten," 97–104.

27. Von Plienger, Iser, and Eisslinger to Duke Christoph of Württemberg, 20 June 1555, in Viktor Ernst, ed., *Briefwechsel des Her*ʒ*ogs Christoph von Wirtemberg*, 4 vols. (Stuttgart: Kohlhammer, 1899–1907), 3: 238; Goetz, "Kompromißkatholizismus," 201. Cf. Heinz Duchhardt, *Protestantisches Kaisertum und altes Reich: Die Diskussion über die Konfession des Kaisers in Politik, Publi*ʒ*istik und Staatsrecht*, Veröffentlichungen des Instituts für europäische Geschichte Mainz, Abteilung Universalgeschichte, vol. 87 (Wiesbaden: Steiner, 1977), 52.

28. Fichtner, "Christian Virtue," 411.

29. Holtzmann, *Maximilian II.*, 122–123.

30. Ibid., 238; Maximilian to Albrecht V of Bavaria, 30 May 1555, in *Briefe und Akten*, 4: 679.

31. Maximilian to Hans of Küstrin, 2 Feb. 1560, cited in Holtzmann, *Maximilian II.*, 351; Bibl, *Maximilian II.*, 257; Widorn, "Gemahlinnen," 21; Goetz, "Kompromißkatholizismus," 202.

32. Maximilian to Albrecht of Bavaria, 10 Dec. 1555, in *Briefe und Akten*, 4: 758; Koch, *Quellen*, 1: 6.

33. Holtzmann, *Maximilian II.*, 236–237, 267; Bibl, *Maximilian II.*, 267.

34. Mecenseffy, "Maximilian II.," 45.

35. "Anderen Theologen der wahren Religion Schriften übersenden," Maximilian to Christoph of Württemberg, 23 Feb. 1558, in Le Bret, *Maga*ʒ*in*, 9: 111–112. Cf. Christoph to Maximilian 16 Mar. 1558, ibid., 116–117; and Holtzmann, *Maximilian II.*, 324.

36. Maximilian to Hans Ungnad, 5 May 1561, in Otto Helmuth Hopfen, *Kaiser Maximilian II. und der Kompromißkatholi*ʒ*ismus* (Munich: Mühlthaler, 1895), 188–189; Maximilian to Christoph of Württemberg, 19 Feb. 1560, ibid., 172–174.

37. Christoph Haller von Hallerstein to Maximilian, 6 Jan. 1558, HHStA, Familienarchiv, Familienkorrespondenz A, box 3, bundle "Hallerstein," fo. 31; Christoph Haller von Hallerstein to Maximilian, 10 Mar. 1558, HHStA, Familienarchiv, Familienkorrespondenz A, box 3, bundle "Hallerstein," fo. 42.

38. Holtzmann, *Maximilian II.*, 205–206 and 206, note 1; Viktor Bibl, "Nidbruck und Tanner: Ein Beitrag zur Entstehungsgeschichte der Magdeburger Centurien und zur Charakteristik König Maximilians II.," *AöG* 85 (1898): 394–396, 401.

39. Holtzmann, *Maximilian II.*, 139; Heer, *Dritte Kraft*, 509–510.

40. "Oock seer familiaer metten keyser Maximiliaen," Simon Ruytinck, "Het Leven van Emanuel van Meteren," in van Meteren, *Belgica*, 2: n.p. See also Erich Hassinger, *Studien ʒu Jacobus Acontius*, Abhandlungen zur mittleren und neueren Geschichte, vol. 76 (Berlin: Verlag für Staatswissenschaften und Geschichte, 1934), 37.

41. Hassinger, *Acontius*, 44–46; Heer, *Dritte Kraft*, 511–512.

42. Acontius to Maximilian, 27 Nov. 1558 in *Acontiana: Abhandlungen und Briefe des Jacobus Acontius*, Walther Köhler and Erich Hassinger, eds., Abhandlungen der Heidelberger Akademie der Wissenschaften, philosophische-historische Klasse, no. 8 (Heidelberg: Carl Winter, 1932): 97; Brandi, *Reformation und Gegenreformation*, 66.

43. Acontius to Maximilian, 27 Nov. 1558, *Acontiana*, 97–98.

44. Hassinger, *Acontius*, 37–39, 43.

45. Holtzmann, *Maximilian II.*, 324; Pánek, "Maximilian II.," 59; Elector Ottheinrich to Maximilian, 4 Dec. 1557, HHStA, Staatenabteilung, Palatina (Palatine), 2, fo. 345; Maximilian to Duke Christoph of Württemberg, 9 Mar. 1559, in Le Bret, *Magaʒin*, 9: 156.

46. Edelmayer in *Habersack*, 35.

47. Ernst Trenkler, "War Kaiser Maximilian II. (1564–1576) tatsächlich Gründer der Hofbibliothek?" *Biblos* 19 (1970): 1–2. The collection would be the nucleus of the Bavarian State Library in Munich.

48. Fichtner, *Ferdinand I*, 227–228.

49. "Bestürmten den Sinn," Wilhelm Maurenbrecher, "Kaiser Maximilian II. und die deutsche Reformation," *Historische Zeitschrift* 7 (1862): 360.

50. Holtzmann, *Maximilian II.*, 332–333, 346–348, 358–359; Widorn, "Gemahlinnen," 21.

51. Edelmayer in *Habersack*, 36.

52. Maximilian to Cardinal Morone, 23 Jan. 1560, HHStA, Familienarchiv, Sammelbände, box 1, vol. 1, fo. 101.

53. Holtzmann, *Maximilian II.*, 342–346; Gindely, *Quellen*, 176; Maurenbrecher, "Beiträge," 264.

54. HHStA, Hofarchiv, OMeA, Sonderreihe, box 182, fo. 52; Bibl, *Maximilian II.*, 92.

55. Franz Bernhard von Bucholtz, *Geschichte der Regierung Ferdinands I*, 9 vols. (1831–1838; reprint, Graz: Akademische Druck- und Verlagsanstalt, 1971), 7: 502; Pass, *Musik und Musiker*, 33–34.

56. Holtzmann, *Maximilian II.*, 356–357, 367–370; Maurenbrecher, "Beiträge," 279; Bibl, *Maximilian II.*, 98.

57. Bibl, *Maximilian II.*, 90–91.

58. Bibl, "Frage," 313–315; Giacomo Soranzo to the doge, 19 Dec. 1559, in Turba, *Depeschen*, 3: 127.

59. Maurenbrecher, "Beiträge," 278–281; Bibl, *Maximilian II.*, 93–94.

60. Joseph Schlecht, "Das geheime Dispenzbreve Pius IV. für die römische Königskrönung Maximilians II.," *Historisches Jahrbuch* 14 (1893): 6–7, 13; Bibl, *Maximilian II.*, 95, 101; Fichtner, *Ferdinand I*, 252–253.

61. Viktor Bibl, "Die Organisation des evangelischen Kirchenwesens im Erzherzogtum Österreichs unter der Enns," *AöG* 87 (1899): 121–122; Eduard Reimann as cited in Maurenbrecher, "Beiträge," 222; Bibl, "Frage," 322.

62. Ferdinand to Pius IV, 4 Oct.[?] 1561, Schlecht, "Dispensbreve," 28–31.

63. Christoph Karlowitz to Maurice of Saxony, 11 Mar. 1551, in Loserth, *Registratur*, 550, note 1; Christoph of Württemberg to Maximilian, 24 May 1557, in Le Bret, *Magazin*, 9: 96; Maximilian to Virail, 11 June 1557, ibid., 103.

64. Holtzmann, *Maximilian II.*, 338.

65. Wilhelm Altmann, "Zur Geschichte der Wahl Maximilians II. zum römischen König," *MIöG* 13 (1892): 624; Philip de Croy to Margaret of Parma, 29 Nov. 1562, HHStA, Belgien, PA 62, bundle 3, fos. 234–235.

66. Margaret of Parma to Philipp II, 19 Dec. 1561, in *Correspondance de Marguerite d'Autriche, duchesse de Parme avec Philippe II*, L.-P. Gachard, ed., 3 vols. (Brussels: Muquardt, 1867–1881), 2: 39. Margaret was reporting here what she had heard from William of Orange.

67. Duchhardt, *Protestantisches Kaisertum*, 47, 67; Margaret of Parma to Philip II, 15 Feb. 1561, in Gachard, *Correspondance*, 2: 91–92; Maximilian to Christoph of Württemberg, 8 Mar. 1561, in Le Bret, *Magazin*, 9: 192–193; Report on Maximilian's election and coronation in Frankfurt 1560[*sic*], BN, Madrid, Sección de manuscritos, no. 7413, fo. 2.

68. Duchhardt, *Protestantisches Kaisertum*, 39; Altmann, "Geschichte," 619, note 1, and 623; Holtzmann, *Maximilian II.*, 401, 408.

69. Holtzmann, *Maximilian II.*, 76.

70. Duchhardt, *Protestantisches Kaisertum*, 48; Edel, *Kaiser*, 40–45.

71. Maximilian to Christoph of Württemberg, Jan. 1561, in Le Bret, *Magazin*, 9: 190–191; Holtzmann, *Maximilian II.*, 395; Maximilian to August of Saxony, 19 Aug. 1562; Hopfen, *Kompromißkatholizismus*, 195.

72. Maurenbrecher, "Kaiser Maximilian," 366; Maximilian to Christoph of Würt-

temberg, 22 June 1558, in Le Bret, *Magazin,* 9: 122; Maximilian to Christoph of Württemberg, 29 June 1558, ibid., 132.

73. Anonymous description in HSA, Kasten Schwarz (Black chest), fasc. 3727, fos. 2, 16; Manfred Rudersdorf, "Maximilian II., 1564–1576," in *Die Kaiser der Neuzeit, 1519–1918: Heiliges Römisches Reich, Österreich, Deutschland,* Anton Schindling and Walter Ziegler, eds. (Munich: Beck, 1990), 87; Edelmayer in *Habersack,* 129–178.

74. Holtzmann, *Maximilian II.,* 421–422; anonymous memorandum of 1562, HSA, Kasten Schwarz, fasc. 3727, fo. 17.

75. Heine, "Beiträge," 13; Maximilian to Albrecht of Bavaria, 28 Dec. 1561, HSA, Kurbayern, Äußeres Archiv, no. 4461, fo. 87; Fichtner, *Ferdinand I,* 255.

76. Maximilian to Philip, 27 June 1561, HHStA, Familienarchiv, Sammelbände, 1, vol. 1, fo. 148.

77. Fichtner, *Ferdinand I,* 255–256; Widorn, "Gemahlinnen," 26–27; Holtzmann, *Maximilian II.,* 451, 500–501.

78. Maximilian to Joachim of Ortenburg, 8 Nov. 1563, in *Briefe und Akten,* 6: 137, note 1.

79. Pass, *Musik und Musiker,* 6.

80. Maximilian to Albrecht of Bavaria, 25 May 1553, HSA, Kurbayern, Äußeres Archiv, no. 4460, no. 15; Holtzmann, *Maximilian II.,* 433–435, 457; Pánek, "Maximilian II.," in Edelmayer and Kohler, eds., *Maximilian II.,* 63; Edel, *Kaiser,* 177–178.

CHAPTER 4: FROM FATHER TO SON

1. Glenda Goss Thompson, "Mary of Hungary and Music Patronage," *Sixteenth Century Journal* 15 (1984): 407; Ferdinand to Maximilian, 12 Jan. 1557, HHStA, Familienarchiv, Familienkorrespondenz A, box 2, fo. 126.

2. Ferdinand to Maximilian, 6 June 1563, HHStA, Familienarchiv, Familienakten, Varia (Miscellaneous), box 108, fo. 8.

3. Ferdinand to Maximilian, 21 April 1555, HHStA, Familienarchiv, Familienkorrespondenz A, box 2, fo. 83; Ferdinand on Maximilian's household, 15 June 1555, HHStA, Familienarchiv, Familienakten, 1.7, Vermögensangelegenheiten (Financial affairs), box 15, fos. 20–22; Ferdinand to Maximilian, 15 June 1555 [?] 1559 [?], HHStA, Familienarchiv, Familienkorrespondenz A, box 2, fo. 169.

4. Count de Luna to Philip II, 28 Jan. 1561, *Colección de documentos inéditos para la historia de España* (hereafter CODOIN), 112 vols. (1842–1895; reprint, Vaduz: Kraus, 1966), 98: 130; Holtzmann, *Maximilian II.,* 389; cardinal of Lorraine to Ferdinand, 23 Apr. 1563, in Archivo general de Simancas, Estado, Alemania (State, Germany), legajo 652, fo. 15 (excerpts).

5. The Habsburg rulers, like the kings of medieval France, customarily ar-

ranged for their vital organs—heart, liver, intestines, and the like—to be distributed among their various provinces following their death. Baron von Presing to Ferdinand, 25 June 1556, HHStA, Familienarchiv, Familienakten, 2.6, Erziehung (Education), box 60, bundle 2, fo. 4; Ferdinand to baron von Presing, 28 June 1556, HHStA, Familienarchiv, Familienakten, 2.6, Erziehung, box 60, bundle 2, fo. 5. Presing was the governor (*Landeshauptmann*) in Austria above the Enns.

6. Baron von Presing to Ferdinand, 25 Aug. 1556, HHStA, Familienarchiv, Familienakten, 2.6, Erziehung, box 53, fo. 44; Ferdinand to Maximilian, 15 January 1557, HHStA, Familienarchiv, Familienakten, 2.6, Erziehung, box 53, fos. 26, 28, 46, 53.

7. Bibl, "Frage," 313–315.

8. Baron von Presing to Ferdinand, 1 July 1556, HHStA, Familienarchiv, Familienakten, 2.6, Erziehung, box 60, bundle 2, fo. 7.

9. Maximilian to Ferdinand, 2 Jan. 1564, HHStA, Familienarchiv, Familienakten, 2.10, Reisen, box 86, Reise der Erzherzöge Rudolf und Ernst, fo. 8.

10. "Sed non licet mihi condere leges," Maximilian to Albrecht of Bavaria, 19 Oct. 1562 (date in chancellory hand), HSA, Kurbayern, Äußeres Archiv, no. 4461, fo. 133. See also Maximilian to Albrecht of Bavaria, 21 Feb. 1554, HSA, Kurbayern, Äußeres Archiv, no. 4460, no. 8. With a few exceptions, the contents of this fascicle are recently numbered by item rather than by folio.

11. Holtzmann, *Maximilian II.*, 28–29; Ferdinand's Instructions to Chantonnay, 1548, HHStA, Familienarchiv, Familienakten, 2.4, Vermählungen, box 20, Matrimonialia Maximiliani, fo. 1.

12. Fichtner, *Ferdinand I*, 241–242.

13. Heine, "Beiträge," 2–3; Goetz, "Finalrelation," 297.

14. Maximilian to Albrecht of Bavaria, 28 Apr. 1554 [?], HSA, Kurbayern, Äußeres Archiv, no. 4460, no. 56; Maximilian to Albrecht of Bavaria, 26 Jan. 1556, HSA, Kurbayern, Äußeres Archiv, no. 4460, no. 76.

15. Heinrich Lutz, *Christianitas Afflicta: Europa, das Reich und die päpstliche Politik im Niedergang der Hegemonie Kaiser Karls V, 1552–1556* (Göttingen: Vandenhoeck and Ruprecht, 1964), 480, 499.

16. Goetz, "Finalrelation," 297, 304–307.

17. Zasius to Maximilian, 4 Nov. 1553, in *Briefe und Akten*, 4: 316–317; Maximilian to Albrecht of Bavaria, 15 Feb. 1554, ibid., 374.

18. Lutz, *Christianitas*, 480.

19. Holtzmann, *Maximilian II.*, 94, 113, 154, 186.

20. Maximilian to Albrecht of Bavaria, 13 May 1562, HSA, Kurbayern, Äußeres Archiv, no. 4461, fo. 99; Maximilian to Albrecht of Bavaria, 12 June 1563, in *Briefe und Akten*, 5: 263, note 2; Maximilian to Albrecht of Bavaria, 19 June 1563, HSA, Kurbayern, Äußeres Archiv, no. 4461, fo. 179.

21. Maximilian to Martin Guzman, 3 Oct. 1561, BN, Madrid, Sección de manuscritos, no. 3824, fo. 2.

22. Friedrich Firnhaber, "Zur Geschichte des österreichischen Militärwesens," *AöG* 30 (1864): 130, 97; Ferdinand to Maximilian, 12 Jan. 1557, HHStA, Familienarchiv, Familienkorrespondenz A, box 2, fo. 126.

23. Ferdinand to Maximilian, 20 Feb. 1558 [?], HHStA, Familienarchiv, Familienkorrespondenz A, box 2, fo. 142.

24. Maximilian to Albrecht of Bavaria, 16 Jan. 1564, HSA, Kurbayern, Äußeres Archiv, no. 4461, fo. 223.

25. Maximilian to Albrecht of Bavaria, 16 Dec. 1563, HSA, Kurbayern, Äußeres Archiv, no. 4461, fo. 217.

26. Maximilian to Christoph of Württemberg, 1 Oct. 1556, in Le Bret, *Magazin*, 9: 62; Maximilian to Albrecht of Bavaria, 18 Aug. 1559, HSA, Kurbayern, Äußeres Archiv, no. 4460, fo. 172; Maximilian to Albrecht of Bavaria, 23 July 1560, HSA, Kurbayern, Äußeres Archiv, no. 4461, fo. 24; Maximilian to Albrecht of Bavaria, 5 July 1560, HSA, Kurbayern, Äußeres Archiv, no. 4461, fo. 18; Maximilian to Albrecht of Bavaria, 23 Feb. 1562, HSA, Kurbayern, Äußeres Archiv, no. 4461, fo. 93.

27. Maximilian to Albrecht of Bavaria, 10 Sept. 1560, HSA, Kurbayern, Äußeres Archiv, no. 4461, fo. 36.

28. "Nolo me laudare," Maximilian to Albrecht of Bavaria, 28 Jan. 1564, HSA, Kurbayern, Äußeres Archiv, no. 4461, fo. 225.

29. Ferdinand to Maximilian, 2 Oct. 1555, HHStA, Familienarchiv, Familienkorrespondenz A, box 2, fo. 120.

30. Ferdinand to Maximilian, 2 Oct. 1555, HHStA, Familienarchiv, Familienkorrespondenz A, box 2, fo. 120; Ferdinand to Maximilian, 1 Feb. 1559 [?], HHStA, Familienarchiv, Familienkorrespondenz A, box 2, fo. 160.

31. Ferdinand to Maximilian, 29 Aug. 1559, HHStA, Familienarchiv, Familienkorrespondenz A, box 2, fo. 144.

32. Maximilian to Albrecht of Bavaria, 7 May 1563, HSA, Kurbayern, Äußeres Archiv, no. 4461, fo. 169; Maximilian to Albrecht of Bavaria, 15 June 1563, HSA, Kurbayern, Äußeres Archiv, no. 4461, fo. 177.

33. Margit Altfahrt, "Die politische Propaganda für Maximilian II.," part 1, *MIöG* 88 (1980): 308; Ferdinand to Charles, 9 Aug. 1548, HHStA, Handschriften (Manuscripts), Blau (Blue), 597/2, fos. 275–276; Edelmayer in *Habersack*, 37.

34. Holtzmann, *Maximilian II.*, 403.

35. Joachim of Neuhaus [Hradec] to Maximilian, 3 July 1562, HHStA, Familienarchiv, Familienakten, 1.3, Krönungen (Coronations), box 21, Berichte und Korrespondenzen betr. die Krönung Max. II. als König von Böhmen, no folio. Hradec was Bohemian chancellor. Jörg Neuhauser to Maximilian,

8 Aug. 1562, HHStA, Familienarchiv, Familienakten, 1.3, Krönungen, box 21, no folio; Fichtner, *Ferdinand I,* 256.

36. Altfahrt, "Propaganda," 303; Holtzmann, *Maximilian II.,* 413–414.

37. Holtzmann, *Maximilian II.,* 165; Gottfried of Scherffenberg to Maximilian, 16 July 1563, HHStA, Familienarchiv, Familienakten, 1.3, Krönungen, box 21, bundle Berichte u. Korrespondenzen betr. die Krönung Max. II. als König von Böhmen, no folio; Friedrich Firnhaber, "Die Krönung Kaiser Maximilians II. zum König von Ungarn," *AöG* 22 (1860): 313, 323, 326–327, 331.

38. "Ne timeatis, ego in praesentiarum neminem occidam," Firnhaber, "Krönung," 332–333; Holtzmann, *Maximilian II.,* 484–485.

39. Hofkammerarchiv (Court treasury archive), Vienna (hereafter HKA), Gedenkbücher (Memorandum books), 109 (1569–1570), fo. 93; Holtzmann, *Maximilian II.,* 404.

40. Holtzmann, *Maximilian II.,* 462, 489, 496; Maximilian to Albrecht of Bavaria, 10 Apr. 1563, HSA, Kurbayern, Äußeres Archiv, no. 4461, fo. 160. On Schwenkfeld, see George H. Williams, *The Radical Reformation* (London: Weidenfeld and Nicolson, 1962), 106–117.

41. Letter of Lower Austrian Estates of 31 Jan. 1552, HHStA, Familienarchiv, Familienakten, 2.6, Erziehung, box 60, bundle 1, fo. 3; Maximilian to Albrecht of Bavaria, 8 Oct. 4460, no. 124; Maximilian to Mary of Hungary, 15 Oct. 1555, HHStA, Familienarchiv, Familienkorrespondenz A, box 3, fo. 564; Maximilian to Albrecht of Bavaria, 23 Jan. 1559, in *Briefe und Akten,* 5: 144.

42. Maximilian to Albrecht of Bavaria, 5 July 1561, HSA, Kurbayern, Äußeres Archiv, no. 4461, fo. 63; Maximilian to Albrecht of Bavaria, 17 Aug. 1561, HSA, Kurbayern, Äußeres Archiv, no. 4461, fo. 67.

43. Maximilian to Albrecht of Bavaria, 4 Aug. 1563, HSA, Kurbayern, Äußeres Archiv, no. 4461, fo. 189; Maximilian to Albrecht of Bavaria, 20 Aug. 1563, HSA, Kurbayern, Äußeres Archiv, no. 4461, fo. 193.

44. "Ich khann E.L. nit alles schraiben was ier mat. in aner kurtzen zait herum fier seltzame gebart vnd sachen gethon hawen," Maximilian to Albrecht of Bavaria, 5 Sept. 1563, HSA, Kurbayern, Äußeres Archiv, no. 4461, fo. 197. Cf. *Briefe und Akten,* 5: 265, note 2; Rady, *Charles V,* 92.

45. Maximilian to Albrecht of Bavaria, 22 Oct. 1563, HSA, Kurbayern, Äußeres Archiv, no. 4461, fo. 207.

46. Maximilian to Albrecht of Bavaria, 12 Apr. 1564, HSA, Kurbayern, Äußeres Archiv, no. 4461, fo. 241; Holtzmann, *Maximilian II.,* 518.

47. Maximilian to Albrecht of Bavaria, 22 Apr. 1564, HSA, Kurbayern, Äußeres Archiv, no. 4461, fo. 243; Maximilian to Albrecht of Bavaria, 4 May 1564, HSA, Kurbayern, Äußeres Archiv, no. 4461, fo. 245; Fichtner, *Ferdinand I,* 257.

48. "Doch hawens ier Mt. noch nit in sin so bald endt zu machen," Maximilian

to Albrecht of Bavaria, 12 June 1564, HSA, Kurbayern, Äußeres Archiv, no. 4461, fo. 255.

49. Maximilian to Albrecht of Bavaria, 6 July 1564, HSA, Kurbayern, Äußeres Archiv, no. 4461, fo. 261.

50. HKA, Gedenkbücher, 124 (1569–1570), fo. 721.

51. Archduke Ferdinand to Maximilian, 21 Aug. 1564 and 28 Aug. 1564, Bibl, *Korrespondenz*, part 1: 8–9.

52. Maximilian to Archduke Ferdinand, 10 Oct. 1564, ibid., 37; Maximilian to William of Mantua, 21 Feb. 1565, ibid., 105.

53. Michele's Report of 1563, in Fiedler, *Relationen*, 30: 217, 241.

54. Friedrich Edelmayer, "Habsburgische Gesandte in Wien und Madrid in der Zeit Maximilians II.: Ein Vergleich der innerhabsburgischen Begegnung auf der Ebene der Diplomatie," in *Spanien und Österreich in der Renaissance*, Wolfram Krömer, ed., Innsbrucker Beiträge zur Kulturwissenschaft, special issue 66 (Innsbruck: Institut für Sprachwissenschaft, 1989), 60; Giovanni Michele's Reports of 1563 and 1564, in Fiedler, *Relationen*, 30: 216–217, 242.

55. Report of Giovanni Michele of 1563, in Fiedler, *Relationen*, 30: 217, 241–242.

56. Michele's report of 1564, ibid., 241; Gustave Constant, *Concession à l'Allemagne de la communion sous les deux espèces*, Bibliothèque des écoles françaises d'Athènes et Rom, vol. 128 (Paris: Bocard, 1923), 142–143; Count Hans Cobenzl to Archduke Ferdinand, 6 Oct. 1564, HHStA, Familienarchiv, Familienkorrespondenz A, box 38, Archduke Ferdinand, fo. 63.

57. Michele's Report of 1564, Fiedler, *Relationen*, 30: 242.

CHAPTER 5: A FLAWED INHERITANCE

1. Jürgen Bücking, *Frühabsolutismus und Kirchenreform in Tirol, 1566–1665: Ein Beitrag zum Ringen zwischen "Staat" und "Kirche" in der frühen Neuzeit*, Veröffentlichung des Instituts für europäische Geschichte, Mainz. Abhandlung für abendländische Religionsgeschichte, vol. 66 (Wiesbaden: Steiner, 1972), 240. On Ferdinand I's administrative model in Germany, see Eduard Rosenthal, *Die Behördeorganisation Kaiser Ferdinands I.: Das Vorbild der Verwaltungsorganisation in den deutschen Territorien*, AöG, vol. 69 (Vienna: Tempsky, 1887).

2. Friedrich Walter, *Österreichische Verfassungs- und Verwaltungsgeschichte von 1500–1955*, Adam Wandruszka, ed., Veröffentlichungen der Kommission für neuere Geschichte Österreichs, vol. 59 (Vienna: Böhlau, 1972), 36–39. See also Oskar Regele, "Der österreichische Hofkriegsrat, 1556–1848," MIöG, special issue 1, part 1 (1949): 17; Jean Bérenger, *Finances et absolutisme autrichien dans la seconde moitié du XVIIe siècle* (Paris: Imprimerie nationale,

1975), 186, 196, 248, 252; Kriegsarchiv, Vienna (hereafter KA), Alte Feldakten (Early campaign documents), 1570, 12–2, no folio; Ferdinand Mencik,
"Beiträge zur Geschichte der kaiserlichen Hofämter," *AöG* 87 (1899): 464;
and Hans Sturmberger, "Dualistischer Ständestaat und werdender Absolutismus: Die Entwicklung der Verfassung Österreichs," in Hans Sturmberger,
Land ob der Enns und Österreich: Aufsätze und Vorträge (Linz: Oberösterreichisches Landesarchiv, 1979), 256.

3. Emperor Maximilian II, Tagebuch (journal), HHStA, Familienakten 2.11,
   Aufzeichnungen (Notes), box 88, fos. 19, 60, 85; Heinrich Kretschmayr, "Das
   deutsche Reichsvicekanzleramt," *AöG* 84 (1898): 409, 411, 413–414, 416, 420,
   422; Maximilian to Archbishop Daniel of Mainz, 3 Jan. 1565, HHStA, Mainzer
   Erzkanzlerarchiv, Reichskanzlei und Taxamt (Imperial chancellory and tax
   office), fasc. 1, fo. 366; Helmut Neuhaus, *Reichsständische Repräsentationsformen im 16. Jahrhundert,* Schriften zur Verfassungsgeschichte, vol. 33 (Berlin: Duncker and Humblot, 1982), 284–298, 468. See also Edel, *Kaiser,* 153–
   156.

4. Maximilian to Archbishop Daniel of Mainz, 3 Jan. 1565 (copy), HHStA,
   Erzkanzlerarchiv, Reichskanzlei und Taxamt, fasc. 1, fo. 367; Maximilian to
   Albrecht of Bavaria, 8 Aug. 1565, HSA, Kurbayern, Äußeres Archiv, fasc.
   4465, fo. 235.

5. HHStA, Mainzer Erzkanzlerarchiv, Reichskanzlei und Taxamt, fasc. 1, fos.
   530–531; Ludwig Haberstock to Albrecht of Bavaria, HSA, Kasten Schwarz,
   no. 14893, 10 Oct. 1572, no folio; Ludwig Haberstock to Albrecht V of
   Bavaria, 14 Oct. 1572, HSA, Kasten Schwarz, no. 14893, no folio.

6. Albrecht V of Bavaria to Peter Obernburger, 4 Nov. 1573, Vienna, HHStA,
   Bavarica, 4, fo. 56; Ogier Busbecq to Maximilian, 9 Feb. 1575, in *Letters of
   Ogier Ghislain de Busbecq to the Holy Roman Emperor Maximilian II,* trans.
   from the Latin text of J. B. Howaert (Brussels 1632) by Robert C. Jones and
   Bernard C. Weber (New York: Bookman Associates, 1961), 77; Maximilian
   to Albrecht V of Bavaria, 17 May 1576, HSA, Äußeres Archiv, no. 4462, fo.
   242.

7. Delfino to Galli, 10 Oct. 1572, in *Nuntiaturberichte aus Deutschland,* part 3,
   vol. 6, Helmut Goetz, ed. (Tübingen: Niemeyer, 1982), 160; Delfino to Galli,
   17 Dec. 1572, ibid., 252. Citation in Peter Pierson, *Philip II of Spain* (London:
   Thames and Hudson, 1975), 92.

8. Kretschmayr, "Reichsvicekanzleramt," 413, 418; Günther Burkert, *Landesfürst und Stände: Karl V., Ferdinand I. und die österreichischen Erbländer im
   Ringen um Gesamtstaat und Landesinteressen,* Forschungen und Darstellungen
   zur Geschichte des steiermärkischen Landtages, vol. 1 (Graz: Historische
   Landeskommission für Steiermark, 1987), 147–148.

9. Kersten Krüger, "Public Finance and Modernisation: The Change from Do-

main State to Tax State in Hesse in the Sixteenth and Seventeenth Centuries—A Case Study," in *Wealth and Taxation in Central Europe: The History and Sociology of Public Finance,* Peter-Christian Witt, ed., German Historical Perspectives, vol. 2 (New York: St. Martin's, 1987), 52, table 3.1; Heide Wunder, "Finance in the 'Economy of Old Europe': The Example of Peasant Credit from the Late Middle Ages to the Thirty Years War," ibid., 27; Bérenger, *Finances et absolutisme,* 237.

10. Krüger, "Public Finance," 56, 60; Michael Mitterauer, "Die Wirtschaftspolitik der österreichischen Landesfürsten im Spätmittelalter und ihre Auswirkungen auf den Arbeitsmarkt," in *Wirtschaftspolitik und Arbeitsmarkt,* Hermann Kellenbenz, ed. (Vienna: Verlag für Geschichte und Politik, 1974), 19; Helmuth Feigl, *Die niederösterreichische Grundherrschaft vom ausgehenden Mittelalter bis zu den theresianisch-josephinischen Reformen,* Forschungen zur Landeskunde von Niederösterreich, vol. 16 (Vienna: Verein für Landeskunde von Niederösterreich und Wien, 1964), 46–47. On Hesse, see Ludwig Zimmermann, *Der ökonomische Staat Landgraf Wilhelms IV,* 2 vols., Veröffentlichungen der historischen Kommission für Hessen und Waldeck, vol. 17, parts 1 and 2 (Marburg: Elwert, 1933–1934).

11. Othmar Pickl, "Die Salzproduktion im Ostalpenraum am Beginn der Neuzeit," in Michael Mitterauer, ed. *Österreichisches Montanwesen, Produktion, Verteilung, Sozialformen* (Vienna: Verlag für Geschichte und Politik, 1974), 16–17, 19, 25–27.

12. Adam Swetkowycz to Maximilian, 7 Oct. 1563, HHStA, Familienarchiv, Familienakten 1.7, Vermögensangelegenheiten, box 15, "Berichte des Adam Swetkowycz an König Maximilian," no folio.

13. Fichtner, *Ferdinand I,* 238–239; HHStA, OMeA, Sonderreihe, box 181, Küniglicher Kinder Stat, fo. 1.

14. Hirn, *Ferdinand von Tirol,* 1: 4–5, note l.

15. Günther Burkert-Dottolo, "Die Landstände der österreichischen Erbländer auf dem Weg ins 'Reich': Die Entsendung ständischer Gesandtschaften zu Reichstagen," in Heinz Duchhardt and Matthias Schnettger, eds. *Reichsständische Libertät und habsburgisches Kaisertum* (Mainz: Philip von Zabern, 1999), 8, 24; Otto Stolz, *Geschichte des Landes Tirol,* vol. 1 (Innsbruck: Tyrolia, 1955), 533; Maximilian to Süleyman, 17 [?] 18 [?] Aug. 1564, in *Epistolae imperatorum et regum hungariae Ferdinandi I. et Maximiliani II. ad suos in porto ottomanica,* Jacob Ferdinand Miller, ed. (Pest, Hungary: Trattner, 1808), 178, 418–419. On German princes and partible inheritance, see Fichtner, *Protestantism,* esp. chap. 1.

16. Citation in Hirn, *Ferdinand von Tirol,* 2: 78; Maximilian to Charles, 28 Aug. 1566, ibid., 10. See also Hirn, *Ferdinand von Tirol,* 1: 34.

17. Bohemian treasury to Maximilian, 1564 [?], Státní ústřední archiv, Prague

(Central state archives, hereafter SÚA), Královská Registra (Royal register, hereafter Král. Reg.), 2c, vol. 75, Bericht an Hof (Court reports), fo. 235; Tagebuch, fos. 18, 21, 44, 48, 55.

18. Maximilian to Archduke Ferdinand, 11 Feb. 1569, Tiroler Landesarchiv, Innsbruck (hereafter TL), Geschäft von Hof (Business from court), 1569, fo. 59; Maximilian to Ferdinand, TL, Geschäft von Hof, 1569, fos. 95–96; Hans Khevenhüller, *Geheimes Tagebuch, 1548–1605,* Georg Khevenhüller-Metsch, ed., with the assistance of Günther Probszt-Obstorff (Graz: Akademische Druck- und Verlagsanstalt, 1971), 23; Hirn, *Ferdinand von Tirol,* 1: 44, 51.

19. Maximilian's accounting of Archduke Ferdinand's share, 28 June 1568, TL, Geschäft von Hof, 1568, fo. 289; Fichtner, *Ferdinand I,* 259.

20. See TL, Geschäft von Hof, 1565–1576, passim.

21. Archduke Ferdinand to Upper Austrian treasury, 1 Oct. 1573, TL, Geschäft von Hof, 1573, fo. 341; Maximilian's reply to Vanegas, 1567, CODOIN, 101: 333.

22. Hirn, *Ferdinand von Tirol,* 1: 421, 571.

23. Maximilian to Archduke Ferdinand, 31 Jan. 1568, TL, Geschäft von Hof, 1568, fo. 29; Archduke Ferdinand to [?], 20 Oct. 1568, TL, Geschäft von Hof, 1568, fo. 359; Archduke Ferdinand to his sisters, 11 Dec. 1568, TL, Geschäft von Hof, 1568, fo. 410; Maximilian to the Tyrolean treasury, 18 Jan. 1569, TL, Geschäft von Hof, 1569, fo. 31. See also TL, Geschäft von Hof, 1573, 163. The archival numeration in this series switches between folios and pages.

24. Maximilian to Ferdinand, 14 Nov. 1572, TL, Geschäft von Hof, 1572, fo. 383; Maximilian to the Tyrolean treasury, 26 Jan. 1573, TL, Geschäft von Hof, 1573, fos. 43–44.

25. Maximilian to Ferdinand, 16 July 1570, TL, Geschäft von Hof, 1570, fos. 129–130.

26. Maximilian to Ferdinand, 6 Mar. 1573, TL, Geschäft von Hof, 1573, fos. 60–61.

27. Khevenhüller, *Tagebuch,* 53; Hirn, *Ferdinand von Tirol,* 1: 428–429, 431, 557; Maximilian to Archduke Karl, 18 Mar. 1570, TL, Geschäft von Hof, 1570, fos. 41–43; Maximilian to Ferdinand, 8 Feb. 1571, TL, Geschäft von Hof, 1571, fo. 40; Maximilian to Archduke Ferdinand, 4 Oct. 1571, TL, Geschäft von Hof, 1571, fo. 240; Maximilian to Ferdinand, 11 Nov. 1571, fos. 256–257; Maximilian to Ferdinand, 22 Nov. 1571, TL, Geschäft von Hof, 1571, TL, Geschäft von Hof, 1571, fos. 288–289. An extensive correspondence on this issue is found in TL, Geschäft von Hof, vols. 1569–1572.

28. Hirn, *Ferdinand von Tirol,* 1: 44–45, 47.

29. See Johann Loserth, "Ständische Beziehungen zwischen Böhmen und Innerösterreich im Zeitalter Ferdinands I.," *Mitteilungen des Vereines für die Ge-*

schichte der Deutschen in Böhmen 50 (1911–1912): 1–41; and Johann Loserth and Franz von Mensi, "Die Prager Ländertagung von 1541–1542," *AöG* 103 (1913): 433–546.

30. Austrian officials to Maximilian, HHStA, Türkei (Turkey), 1, box 20, bundle 3, fos. 155–156; Jean Bérenger, *Histoire de l'empire des Habsbourg, 1273–1918* (Paris: Fayard, 1990), 191, 230.

31. Gerhard Kurzmann, *Kaiser Maximilian I. und das Kriegswesen der österreichischen Länder und des Reichs*, Militärgeschichtliche Dissertationen österreichischer Universitäten, vol. 5 (Vienna: Österreichischer Bundesverlag, 1985), 29–31, 40–41.

32. Wilhelm von Janko, *Lazarus Freiherr von Schwendi: Oberster Feldhauptmann und Rath Kaiser Maximilians II.* (Vienna: Braumüller, 1871), 43.

33. Maximilian to Archduke Ferdinand, 14 Aug. 1567, in Bibl, *Korrespondenz*, part 2: 216–217; Hirn, *Ferdinand von Tirol*, 2: 75, 92; Maximilian to Ferdinand, 31 Oct. 1574, TL, Geschäft von Hof, 1574, fo. 166; Helmuth Feigl, "Zur Rechtslage der unterbäuerlichen Schichten im 15., 16. und 17. Jahrhundert," *Wirtschafts- und sozialhistorische Beiträge: Festschrift für A. Hoffmann*, Herbert Knittler, ed. (Vienna: Oldenbourg, 1979), 256.

34. "In ander weeg mit obister Gelegenhaidt," HKA, Gedenkbücher, 109 (1569–1570), fo. 737; Karl Oberleitner, "Die Finanzlage Niederösterreichs im 16. Jahrhundert," *AöG* 30 (1864): 42; Bohemian treasury to Maximilian, 9 Aug. 1568, SÚA, Král. Reg. IIc, vol. 81, Bericht an Hof, fo. 344; Alfred Pribram, *Materialen zur Geschichte der Löhne und Preise in Österreich*, Veröffentlichungen des internationalen wissenschaftlichen Komitees für die Geschichte der Preise und Löhne, vol. 1 (Vienna: Karl Ueberreuter, 1938), 270, 322, 449–450, 488; Roman Sandgruber, "Die innerberger Eisenproduktion in der frühen Neuzeit," in Mitterauer, *Montanwesen*, 89. The Rhenish gulden, the Hungarian gold ducat, and the florin were very close in value to one another throughout the sixteenth century in the Habsburg lands. They were gradually replaced by the silver taler, minted since 1484 in the Tyrol, since 1524 in the other Austrian provinces, and since 1500 in Saxony, since 1518 in Bohemia. According to the imperial currency reform of 1510–1511, 1 gulden or florin = 60 Kreuzer = 240 Pfennige. See Pribram, *Materialen*, 3, note 4; 27.

35. Lazarus Schwendi to William of Orange, 27 Aug. 1564, Guillaume Groen van Prinsterer, *Archives ou correspondance inédite de la maison d'Orange-Nassau*, 27 vols. in 26 (Leide[n]: Luchtmans, 1835–1917), 1: 190. Cf. Schwendi to William of Orange, 16 Dec. 1564, ibid., 210.

36. "Dann soliches khumbt vnns zu grossem nachteill unnd spott," HHStA, Hofarchiv, OMeA, Sonderreihe, box 73, no. 3, fo. 85.

37. Maximilian's accounting of Archduke Ferdinand's share, 28 June 1568, TL, Geschäft von Hof, 1568, fo. 289.

38. HKA, Hofzahlamtsbücher (Court account books), 22 (1567), fos. 56, 167, 195, 557.

39. Mencik, "Hofämter," 483; Parker, *Philip II*, 123–124.

40. Maximilian to Albrecht of Bavaria, 1 July 1567, in Bibl, Korrespondenz, vol. 2, 199; Maximilian and Karl to Archduke Ferdinand, 23 May 1567, ibid., 183–184.

41. Tagebuch, fos. 44, 47–48.

42. Johann Newald, *Das österreichische Münzwesen unter den Kaisern Maximilian II., Rudolf II. und Matthias* (Vienna: K.u.k. Hof- und Staatsdruckerei, 1885), 49–51.

43. Maximilian's Instructions to the scrapmen (*Zuschrotter*), 6 Nov. 1553, HHStA, Hofarchiv, OMeA, Sonderreihe, box 74, Instruktionen, Varia (Miscellaneous instructions), no. 18, fos. 30–31; Maximilian's Kitchen Orders, 6 Oct. 1566, HHStA, Hofarchiv, OMeA, Sonderreihe, box 73, no. 3, fos. 84–87, 113.

44. Maximilian's "Liecht Cammer Ordnung," HHStA, Hofarchiv, OMeA, Sonderreihe, box 73, no. 3, fos. 108–110.

45. Mainzer Erzkanzlerarchiv, Reichskanzlei und Taxamt, fasc. 1, fo. 531.

46. Maximilian to the Tyrolean treasury, 20 Feb. 1569, TL, Geschäft von Hof, 1569, fo. 78; Maximilian to the Bohemian treasury, 25 May 1569, in Karl Köpl, ed., "Urkunden, Acten und Regesten aus dem Statthalterei-Archiv in Prag," *Jahrbücher der Kunstsammlungen des allerhöchsten Kaiserhauses* 12 (1891): 27. See also the account book for 1575–1576 of the court paymaster, David Hag, HHStA, Hofarchiv, OMeA, Sonderreihe, box 181, Handschrift (Manuscript) B520.

47. Austrian National Library (hereafter ÖNB), Handschriftensammlung (Manuscript collection), no. 9089, fos. 44, 52, 72, 92, 106–107.

48. Thomas Fellner and Heinrich Kretschmayr, *Die österreichische Zentralverwaltung*, 4 vols. (Vienna: Holzhausen, 1907–1925), 2: 330, note 1, 340–342, 353.

49. Maximilian's order for the regulation of tradespeople, 15 June 1572, HSA, Kurbayern, Äußeres Archiv, no. 4462, fos. 308–313, passim.

50. HHStA, Hofarchiv, OMeA, Sonderreihe, box 172, fos. 3–6.

51. HKA, Hofzahlamtsbücher, 20 (1565), fos. 71, 641; 21 (1566), fos. 40, 709; 22 (1567), fos. 56, 558; 23 (1568), fo. 82; 24 (1570), fos. 652, 883; 25 (1571), fos. 729, 785; 27 (1573), fo. 72; 28 (1574), fo. 84; 29 (1575), fo. 80; 30 (1576), fos. 88, 675. The volume for 1569 is missing; the one for 1572 covers only about half the year.

52. HHStA, Hofarchiv, OMeA, Sonderreihe, box 183, bundle 50, fos. 3–93; HKA, Hofzahlamtsbücher, 27 (1573), fo. 363; HKA, Hofzahlamtsbücher, 29 (1575), fos. 575, 685; HKA, Hofzahlamtsbücher, 30 (1576), fos. 450–451, 455.

53. HSA, Kurbayern, Äußeres Archiv, no. 4462, fos. 308–313, passim; HHStA, Hofarchiv, OMeA, Sonderreihe, box 183, no. 53, "Hofstaat König Rudolphs und des Erzherzogs Ernst," fo. 2; HHStA, Hofarchiv, OMeA, Sonderreihe, box 183, no. 50, Hofstaat Kaiser Maximilians, fos. 2–7, 40; HHStA, Hofarchiv, OMeA, Sonderreihe, box 183, no. 45, Hofstaat Kaiser Ferdinands, fos. 1–2, 15.

54. Winfried Schulze, *Landesdefension und Staatsbildung: Studien zum Kriegswesen des innerösterreichischen Territorialstaates, 1564–1619*, Veröffentlichungen der Kommission für neuere Geschichte Österreichs, vol. 60 (Vienna: Böhlau, 1973), 314–316.

55. Neuhaus, *Repräsentationsformen*, 382–383, 462; Tagebuch, fo. 48; Herbert Knittler, "Adelige Grundherrschaft im Übergang: Überlegungen zum Verhältnis von Adel und Wirtschaft in Niederösterreich um 1600," in Grete Klingenstein and Heinrich Lutz, eds., *Spezialforschung und "Gesamtgeschichte": Beispiele und Methodenfragen zur Geschichte der frühen Neuzeit*. Wiener Beiträge zur Geschichte der Neuzeit, vol. 8 (Vienna: Verlag für Geschichte und Politik, 1981), 97.

56. HKA, Hofzahlamtsbücher, 22 (1567), fos. 3–11; Bérenger, *Empire*, 233–234.

57. HKA, Hofzahlamtsbücher, 24, 1570.

58. HKA, Gedenkbücher, 109 (1569–1570), fo. 42.

59. Tagebuch, fo. 72.

60. Ibid., fo. 48.

61. Maximilian to the Moravian Estates, 30 Mar. 1565, SÚA, Morava (Moravia), no. 697, fo. 1; Maximilian to Archduke Ferdinand, 30 June 1565 (draft), SÚA, Morava, no. 697, fo. 7.

62. Jaroslav Pánek, "Das politische System des böhmischen Staates im ersten Jahrhundert der habsburgischen Herrschaft, 1526–1620," *MIöG* 97 (1989): 75; Valentin Urfus, "I moderni principi amministrativi in Boemia e l'assolutismo sovrano nei secoli XVI e XVII," *Annali della fondazione italiana per la storia amministrativa* (1965): 241–243; Jaroslav Pánek, *Stavovská opozice a její zápas s Habsburky 1547–1577* (Prague: Academia, 1982), 81.

63. Michael Mitterauer, "Produktionsweise, Siedlungsstruktur und Sozialformen im österreichischen Montanwesen des Mittelalters und der frühen Neuzeit," in Mitterauer, *Montanwesen*, 246, 250; Archduke Ferdinand to Maximilian, 22 Sept. 1565, SÚA, Král. Reg. IIc, vol. 79, Bericht an Hof, fo. 318.

64. Archduke Ferdinand to Maximilian, 19 Jan. 1566, SÚA, Král. Reg. IIc, vol. 37, Bericht an Hof, fos. 14–15; Newald, *Münzwesen*, 5–6, 9–10, 33, 38.

65. Accounting department of Maximilian's Bohemian treasury to [?], 1571, Köpl, "Statthalterei-Archiv," 12: 39–41, and report of 11 June 1571, ibid., 42.

66. Archduke Ferdinand to Maximilian, 9 Apr. 1565, SÚA, Král. Reg. IIc, vol. 79, Bericht an Hof, fos. 113–114.

67. Archduke Ferdinand to Maximilian, [?] Mar. 1565, SÚA, Král. Reg. IIc, vol. 79, Bericht an Hof, fos. 352–353; Ferdinand to Maximilian, 24 Oct. 1565, SÚA, Král. Reg. IIc, vol. 79, fo. 95; Ferdinand to Maximilian, 10 Nov. 1565, SÚA, Král. Reg. IIc, vol. 79, fo. 368; Archduke Ferdinand to Maximilian, 20 Apr. 1566, SÚA, Král. Reg. IIc, vol. 80, Bericht an Hof, fo. 104; Bohemian treasury to Maximilian, 24 Dec. 1566, SÚA, Král. Reg. IIc, vol. 80, Bericht an Hof, fo. 350. See also HKA, Gedenkbücher, 104 (1567–1568), fo. 41.

68. Bohemian treasury to Maximilian, 19 Sept. 1564, SÚA, Král. Reg., IIc, vol. 75, Bericht an Hof, fo. 278; Commission to Maximilian, 2 May 1566, SÚA, Král. Reg. IIc, vol. 80, Bericht an Hof, fos. 123–124.

69. E.g., HKA, Hofzahlamtsbücher, 22 (1567), fos. 6–11.

70. Ferdinand to Maximilian, 21 Feb. 1566, SÚA, Král. Reg. IIc, vol. 80, fo. 68; Ferdinand to Maximilian, 21 Mar. 1566, SÚA, Král. Reg. IIc, vol. 80, fo. 83; HKA, Hofzahlamtsbücher, 22 (1567), fos. 6–11.

71. Archduke Ferdinand to Maximilian, 21 Feb. 1566, SÚA, Král. Reg. IIc, vol. 80, Bericht an Hof, fos. 67–68; Archduke Ferdinand to Maximilian, 21 Mar. 1566, SÚA, Král. Reg. IIc, vol. 80, fos. 82–83; Archduke Ferdinand to Maximilian, 4 July 1566, SÚA, Král. Reg. IIc, vol. 80, fo. 178.

72. "Die prager sambt den andern schteten bitten umb erlassung des erblichen biers groschen—khan nitt sain," Tagebuch, fos. 85–86. See also ibid., fo. 42.

73. Tagebuch, fo. 26; Wolfgang Sittig, *Landstände und Fürstentum: Eine Krisenzeit als Anstoß für die Entwicklung der steierischen landständischen Verwaltung*, Veröffentlichungen des steiermärkischen Landesarchives, vol. 13 (Graz: Steiermärkisches Landesarchiv, 1982), 76, 86.

74. Archduke Ferdinand to Maximilian, 27 Feb. 1566, SÚA, Král. Reg. IIc, vol. 80, Bericht an Hof, fo. 76; Fellner, *Zentralverwaltung*, 2: 333.

75. Newald, *Münzwesen*, 10; Fellner, *Zentralverwaltung*, 2: 250, 337–338, 340–342; Adam von Dietrichstein to Maximilian, 30 June 1565, in Koch, *Quellen*, 1: 145–146.

76. Fellner, *Zentralverwaltung*, 2: 331; HHStA, Hofarchiv, OMeA, Sonderreihe, box 73, no. 3, fo. 113.

77. Fellner, *Zentralverwaltung*, 2: 342.

78. Ibid., 253, 259, 333–335, 338.

79. See HKA, Hofzahlamtsbücher, 24 (1570).

80. HKA, Hofzahlamtsbücher, 24 (1570), 352.

81. Mía Rodríguez-Salgado, *The Changing Face of Empire: Charles V, Philip II and Habsburg Authority, 1551–1559* (Cambridge: Cambridge University Press, 1988), 233–234.

82. Bohemian treasury to Maximilian, 25 June 1568, SÚA, Král. Reg. IIc, vol. 81, Bericht an Hof, fos. 278–279.
83. Bohemian treasury to Archduke Ferdinand, 7 Apr. 1566, SÚA, Král. Reg. IIc, vol. 80, Bericht an Hof, fo. 92.
84. Bohemian treasury to Maximilian, 30 Apr. 1568, SÚA, Král. Reg. IIc, vol. 81, Bericht an Hof, fos. 179–181; Bohemian treasury to Maximilian, 7 Aug. 1568, SÚA, Král. Reg. IIc, vol. 81, fo. 340; Pribram, *Materialen*, 312, 510; Newald, *Münzwesen*, 12.
85. Fellner, *Zentralverwaltung*, 1, part 2: 337.
86. "Diser ortten kheiner, sonst kheine haubtman vnd Ine, oder seinem [*sic*] gebiet nit hatt," Bohemian treasury to Maximilian, 30 Apr. 1568, SÚA, Král. Reg. IIc, vol. 81, Bericht an Hof, fo. 179.
87. "Tagebuch," fo. 55; Bohemian treasury to Maximilian, 2 June 1568, SÚA, Král. Reg. IIc, vol. 81, Bericht an Hof, fos. 232, 264; Bohemian treasury to Maximilian, 9 Aug. 1568, SÚA, Král. Reg. IIc, vol. 81, fos. 345–347.
88. Bohemian treasury to Maximilian, 2 June 1568, SÚA, Král. Reg. IIc, vol. 81, Bericht an Hof, fo. 244.
89. "Vnns darumben allerseits hin vnnd wider, wie wir khunnden vnnd mugen bewerben miessen," Maximilian to Wilhelm of Rožmberk [Rosenberg], 21 Mar. 1570, Třebon, Státní oblastní archiv (hereafter SOA, Třebon), Historica (History), no. 4766.
90. "Tagebuch," fos. 40, 44, 58, 63.
91. Karl Grossman, "Reichart Streun von Schwarzenau: Ein österreichischer Staatsmann und Gelehrter aus der Zeit der Renaissance, Reformation und Gegenreformation," *Jahrbuch für Landeskunde von Niederösterreich*, n.s. 20, part 2 (1927): 10.
92. Karl Helleiner, "Eine religionspolitische Denkschrift an Max. II. aus der Feder des Casp. Hirsch, 1574," *MIöG* 46 (1932): 203; Bohemian treasury [?] to Maximilian, 25 Mar. 1568, SÚA, Král. Reg. IIc, vol. 81, Bericht von Hof, fo. 110; Maximilian to Wilhelm of Rožmberk, 3 Oct. 1569, SOA, Třebon, *Historica*, no. 4758.6; Maximilian to Wilhelm of Rožmberk, 1570 [no further date], SOA, Třebon, Historica, no. 4778; Maximilian to Wilhelm of Rožmberk, 26 Mar. 1575, SOA, Třebon, Historica, no. 4902.
93. Maximilian to Wilhelm of Rožmberk, 21 Mar. 1570, SOA, Třebon, Historica, no. 4766; Maximilian to Wilhelm of Rožmberk, 26 Mar. 1575, SOA, Třebon, Historica, no. 4902.
94. Maximilian to Wilhelm of Rožmberk, 21 Mar. 1570, SOA, Třebon, Historica, no. 4766.
95. Maximilian to Johann von Lobkowitz, 1569 [no further date], Státní oblastní archiv, Litoměřice (hereafter SOA, Litoměřice), Lobkovic, B II, fo. 133.

96. Bohemian treasury to Maximilian, 19 Sept. 1564, SÚA, Král. Reg. IIc, Bericht an Hof, vol. 75, fo. 274.

97. Maximilian's order for the regulation of tradespeople, 15 June 1572, HSA, Kurbayern, Äußeres Archiv, no. 4462, fos. 308–313, passim.

98. For a stimulating discussion of this question, see Douglass C. North and Robert Paul Thomas, *The Rise of the Western World: A New Economic History* (Cambridge: Cambridge University Press, 1973), 132–145. See also Fellner, *Zentralverwaltung* 1: 253, 337–338.

99. Ernst Bruckmüller, *Sozialgeschichte Österreichs* (Vienna: Herold, 1985), 239.

100. Maximilian to Wilhelm of Rožmberk, 4 June [1567], SOA, Třebon, *Historica*, no. 4720.

101. HKA, Hofzahlamtsbücher, 27 (1573), fos. 472–571, and HKA, Hofzahlamtsbücher, 29 (1575), fos. 774–899.

102. Tagebuch, fo. 46.

CHAPTER 6: IMPERFECT MEN FOR AN IMPERFECT WORLD

1. Paula S. Fichtner, "To Rule Is Not to Govern: The Diary of Maximilian II," in *The Mirror of History: Essays in Honor of Fritz Fellner,* Solomon Wank, Heidrun Maschl, Brigitte Mazohl-Wallnig, and Reinhold Wagnleitner, eds. (Santa Barbara, Calif.: ABC-Clio, 1988), 258–259.

2. Archduke Ferdinand to Maximilian, 4 Feb. 1566, SÚA, Král. Reg. IIc., vol. 80, Bericht an Hof, fo. 39.

3. Bibl, *Maximilian II.,* 153.

4. Bérenger, *Empire,* 46; Karl Vocelka, *Die politische Propaganda Kaiser Rudolfs II., 1576–1612* (Vienna: Verlag der österreichischen Akademie der Wissenschaft, 1981), 98; Fellner, *Zentralverwaltung,* 1: 237; Firnhaber, "Militärwesens," 96–97. Cf. Helmut G. Koenigsberger, "Epilogue: Central and Western Europe," in R. J. W. Evans and T. V. Thomas, eds., *Crown, Church, and Estates: Central European Politics in the Sixteenth and Seventeenth Centuries* (New York: St. Martin's, 1991), 304.

5. "In diser geschwinden wildt," Archduke Ferdinand to Albrecht of Bavaria, Nov.[?] 1568, Geheimes Hausarchiv, Munich (hereafter GHA), Korrespondenz-Akten, no. 597/1, fo. 135; Albrecht of Bavaria to Archduke Charles, 25 Mar. 1573, GHA, Korrespondenz-Akten, no. 597/1, fo. 219; Albrecht of Bavaria to Archduke Charles, 25 Mar. 1573, GHA, Korrespondenz-Akten, no. 597/1, fo. 218.

6. David C. Goodman, *Power and Penury: Government, Technology, and Science in Philip II's Spain* (Cambridge: Cambridge University Press, 1988), 125–129.

7. E.g., Maximilian to Albrecht of Bavaria, 14 Nov. 1554 [?], HSA, Kurbayern, Äußeres Archiv, fasc. 4460, fo. 99; Maximilian to Philip, 24 Nov. 1568, HHStA, Familienarchiv, Sammelbände, box 1, vol. 2: fo. 141.

8. Albrecht to Archduke Charles, 25 Mar. 1573, GHA, Korrespondenz-Akten, no. 597/1, fo. 219.

9. Burkert, *Landesfürst und Stände*, 148; Pass, *Musik und Musiker*, passim.

10. ÖNB, Handschriftensammlung, fasc. 9089, fos. 60, 62, 65, 69, and passim. Dr. Robert Lindell kindly brought this material to my attention. Also Archduke Ferdinand to Maximilian, 23 Dec. 1560, HHStA, Familienarchiv, Familienakten 3.5, Jagdsachen (Hunt affairs), box 105, fo. 183.

11. HKA, Hofzahlamtsbücher, 20, 1565, fos. 116–121, 111–112.

12. Koch, *Quellen*, 2: 57–58.

13. Fellner, *Zentralverwaltung*, 2: 321.

14. Maximilian to Pius V, 19 June 1566, in Wilhelm Eberhard Schwarz, ed., *Briefe und Akten zur Geschichte Maximilians II.*, 2 vols. (Paderborn: Bonifacius-Druckerei, 1889, 1891), 1: 27.

15. E.g., the reports from France of Jerome de Cock, HHStA, Familienarchiv, Familienkorrespondenz A, box 2, bundle 3, fos. 436–438.

16. Alphons Lhotsky, *Festschrift des kunsthistorischen Museums zur Feier des fünfzigjährigen Bestandes*, 2 vols. in 3 (Vienna: Berger, 1941–1945), part 1, 160–162; Maximilian to Albrecht of Bavaria, 24 June 1566, HSA, Kurbayern, Äußeres Archiv, fasc. 4456, fo. 237; Maximilian to Christoph of Württemberg, 24 June 1566, in Le Bret, *Magazin*, 9: 250–251.

17. Josef Rübsam, "Nicholas Mameranus und sein Büchlein über den Reichstag zu Augsburg im Jahre 1566," *Historisches Jahrbuch* 10 (1889): 539 and note 1.

18. Fellner, *Zentralverwaltung*, 1: 77–79; Tagebuch, fo. 53.

19. Fellner, *Zentralverwaltung*, 2: 346, 348–349.

20. "Mit nichte," Tagebuch, fo. 58.

21. "Der camer presidentn ambt ist mit dem Bekhen nit gnuegsam versehen/ das camer wesen ist nie so hart geschteht [?] als jetzt vnd darf guetes rats vnd ainsehungs," Tagebuch, fo. 50. See also fo. 51. On Beck, see Bruno Schimetschek, *Der österreichische Beamte: Geschichte und Tradition* (Vienna: Verlag für Geschichte und Politik, 1984), 53; Gernot Heiß, "Bildungsverhalten des niederösterreichischen Adels im gesellschaftlichen Wandel: Zu Bildungsgang im 16. und 17. Jahrhundert," in Klingenstein and Lutz, eds., *Spezialforschung*, 149; and Karl Lind, "Die Chronik der Familie Beck von Leopoldsdorf," *Blätter des Vereines für Landeskunde von Niederösterreich* 11 (1877): 133–134.

22. "Weil der andern zwey unnd bey der Camer khiner verhanden ist," HHStA, Hofarchiv, OMeA, Sonderreihe, box 182, fo. 10.

23. Archduke Charles to Albrecht of Bavaria, 7 Apr. 1573, GHA, Korrespondenz-Akten, 597/1, fo. 223.

24. Hirn, *Ferdinand von Tirol*, *1: 553.*

25. This process has been very well studied in Austria above the Enns in Gerhard Putschögl, *Die landständische Behördeorganisation in Österreich ob der Enns vom Anfang des 16. bis zur Mitte des 18. Jahrhunderts: Ein Beitrag zur österreichischen Rechtsgeschichte*, Forschungen zur Geschichte Oberösterreichs, vol. 14 (Linz: Oberösterreiches Landesarchiv, 1978). See esp. 263, 287.

26. Hirn, *Ferdinand von Tirol*, 1: 461; Tagebuch, fo. 686.

27. Maximilian's Hofkammerdienerordnung (Court treasury order) of 1571, HHStA, Mainzer Erzkanzleramt, Reichskanzlei und Taxamt, fasc. 1, fo. 532.

28. "Nit an allen ortten sein kann," HKA, Gedenkbücher, 104 (1567–1568), fo. 3.

29. HHStA, Hofarchiv, OMeA, Sonderreihe, box 74, Instruktionen, Varia, no. 7, fos. 88–89, 92. Leonhard von Harrach served in this office until 1567, and then Hans Trautson served until the middle of 1575.

30. " 'Ich klage sehr dahin gebracht zu sein . . . dass ich weder an meine Gesundheit, noch an mein Leben irgend denken kann, . . . dass ich nicht weiss, ob es nicht besser wäre bald zu sterben und der menschlichen Dinge entledigt zu werden, als in diesem glänzenden Elend müde zu befinden,' " J. F. A. Gillet, *Crato von Krafftheim und seine Freunde: Ein Beitrag zur Kirchengeschichte*, 2 vols. (Frankfurt a.M: Brünner, 1860), 2: 6–8. Citation p. 10.

31. "Ich sey des Verzugs nit Vrsach," David Hag to Peter Workh [Vok] of Rožmberk [Rosenberg], 21 June 1567, Třebon, Historica, no. 4721.

32. Maximilian to [Hans] Rueber, 18 Nov. 1569 (copy), HHStA, Ungarn, fasc. 95, fo. 37.

33. Rübsam, "Mameranus," 538.

34. Ulrich de Vastalis to Maximilian, 28 Feb. 1567, Köpl, "Statthalterei-Archive," 12: XVII; Tagebuch, fos. 59, 65, 66.

35. Brady, *Reformation in Germany*, 18; Rolf Glawischnig, *Niederlande, Kalvinismus und Reichsgrafenstand, 1559–1584: Nassau-Dillenberg unter Graf Johann VI., 1559–1606*, Schriften des hessischen Landesamtes für geschichtliche Landeskunde, vol. 36 (Marburg: Elwert, 1973), 247; HKA, Hofzahlamtsbücher, 23 (1568), fos. 313–314; 24 (1570), fo. 241; 29 (1575), fos. 366–368; Ludwig Haberstock to William of Bavaria, 10 May 1573, HSA, Kasten Schwarz, no. 14893, no folio; Ludwig Haberstock to William of Bavaria, 9 Apr. 1574, HSA, Kasten Schwarz, no. 14893, no folio.

36. Robert Lindell, "Die Neubesetzung der Hofkapellmeisterstelle am Kaiserhof in den Jahren 1567–1568: Palestrina oder Monte?" *Studien zur Musikwissenschaft* 36 (1985): 36.

37. Archduke Ferdinand to Maximilian, 7 June 1566, Köpl, "Statthalterei-Archive," 12: VII.

38. Archduke Ferdinand to Maximilian, 27 Sept. 1565, SÚA, Král. Reg. IIc, vol. 79, Bericht an Hof, fos. 320–321.

39. Georg Eder to Albrecht V of Bavaria, 7 Sept. 1577, in Karl Schrauf, *Der Reichshofrath Dr. Georg Eder* (Vienna: Holzhausen, 1904), 111.

40. Rodríguez-Salgado, *Changing Face*, 53, 68–69.

41. Paula Sutter Fichtner, "Habsburg Household or Habsburg Government? A Sixteenth-Century Administrative Dilemma," *Austrian History Yearbook* 26 (1995): 45–60, passim.

42. E.g., the Bohemian treasury's commentary on the commission to reform the Jachýmov mines, 30 Apr. 1568, SÚA, Král. Reg. IIc, vol. 81, Bericht von Hof, fos. 182–183; Bohemian treasury to Maximilian, 6 May 1568, SÚA, Král. Reg. IIc, vol. 81, Bericht von Hof, fo. 193.

43. Albrecht of Bavaria to Maximilian, 14 Apr. 1562, HHStA, Staatenabteilung, Bavarica, 3, no folio; Albrecht of Bavaria to Maximilian, 24 May 1562, HHStA, Staatenabteilung, Bavarica, 3, no folio.

44. Press, "Habsburg Court," 533.

45. Maximilian to Archbishop Daniel of Mainz, 4 Apr. 1565, HHStA, Mainzer Erzkanzlerarchiv, Reichskanzlei und Taxamt, fasc. 1, fo. 490; Pierson, *Philip II*, 111; Winfried Schulze, *Reich und Türkengefahr im späten 16. Jahrhundert* (Munich: Beck, 1978), 317; Fellner, *Zentralverwaltung*, 1: 275–287, passim.

46. Volker Press, "The Imperial Court of the Habsburgs: From Maximilian I to Ferdinand III, 1493–1657," in *Princes, Patronage, and the Nobility: The Court at the Beginning of the Modern Age, c. 1450–1650*, Ronald G. Asch and Adolf M. Birke, eds. (London: Oxford University Press, 1991), 299.

47. Schrauf, *Eder*, xv–xvi.

48. SÚA, Patenty (Patents), box 3, patents of 24 Mar. 1569 and 26 January 1573; Chantonnay to Philip, 19 Nov. 1569, CODOIN, 103: 329.

49. Schrauf, *Eder*, xv–xvi.

50. Maximilian to Albrecht of Bavaria, 10 Mar. 1569, HSA, Kurbayern, Äußeres Archiv, no. 4462, fo. 69.

51. Zasius to Albrecht of Bavaria [?], July [?] 1576, HSA, Kurbayern, Äußeres Archiv, no. 4302. fo. 206. On the jurist's character and thought, see Walter Goetz, *Die bäyerische Politik im ersten Jahrzehnt der Regierung Herzog Albrechts von Bayern* (Munich: Rieger, 1896), 98, 100; and Hirn, *Ferdinand von Tirol*, 2: 94, note; and Viktor Bibl, "Die Erhebung Herzog Cosimos von Medici zum Grossherzog von Toskana und die kaiserliche Anerkennung, 1569–1576," *AöG* 103 (1913): 23.

52. Hirn, *Ferdinand von Tirol*, 2: 89–90; Khevenhüller, *Tagebuch*, 28–29.

53. Maximilian to Christoph of Württemberg, 4 Aug. 1552, Le Bret, *Magazin*, 9: 20; Tagebuch, fo. 86; Maximilian to Franz von Thurn, 30 Oct. 1567, HHStA, Familienarchiv, Sammelbände, box 1, vol. 2: fos. 96–97.

54. Fichtner, "Diary," 260; Hirn, *Ferdinand von Tirol*, 1: 462.

55. Ludwig Haberstock to Albrecht of Bavaria, 12 Aug. 1572, HSA, Kasten Schwarz, no. 14893, no folio; Ludwig Haberstock to Albrecht of Bavaria, 17 Aug. 1572, HSA, Kasten Schwarz, no. 14893, no folio; Ludwig Haberstock to Albrecht of Bavaria, 24 Aug. 1572, HSA, Kasten Schwarz, no. 14893, no folio; Johannes Kleinpaul, *Das Nachrichtenwesen der deutschen Fürsten im 16. und 17. Jahrhundert* (Leipzig: Klein, 1930), 126; Edel, *Kaiser*, 138–140.

56. Edelmayer, "Gesandte," 65–66; Bibl, "Organisation," 157. See also Friedrich Edelmayer, "Das Netzwerk Philipps II. von Spanien im Heiligen Römischen Reich," in Duchhardt and Schnettger, eds. *Reichsständische Libertät*, 57–80.

57. Widorn, "Gemahlinnen," 33. See also, Edelmayer, "Netzwerk," 63.

58. Bibl, "Erhebung," 82–83, 87, 93. On Weber, see Delfino to Galli, 27 Nov. 1572, *Nuntiaturberichte aus Deutschland*, part 3, vol. 6, 213.

59. Maximilian to Albrecht of Bavaria, 10 Mar. 1569, HSA, Kurbayern, Äußeres Archiv, no. 4462, fo. 69.

60. Maximilian to Albrecht of Bavaria, 6 Dec. 1566, HSA, Kurbayern, *Äußeres Archiv*, no. 4466, fo. 163.

61. Constant, *Concession*, 123; Kleinpaul, *Nachrichtenwesen*, 31–32.

62. Kleinpaul, *Nachrichtenwesen*, 13, 108, 120–121.

63. Constant, *Concession*, 113, note 1; Kleinpaul, *Nachrichtenwesen*, 106.

64. Fichtner, "Diary," 257; Tagebuch, 20.

65. E.g., Maximilian's nomination of Sigmund von Lodron to his council, 15 Jan. 1551, in Loserth, *Registratur*, 359; Maximilian's orders to his court comptroller, 1564–1579, HHStA, Hofarchiv, OMeA, Sonderreihe, Instruktionen, Varia, no. 7, fo. 91. For a stimulating discussion of this issue in modern times, but one that is relevant to the earlier period as well, see Leonore O'Boyle, "Some Recent Studies of Nineteenth-Century European Bureaucracy: Problems of Analysis," *Central European History* 19 (1986): 386–408.

66. "Mit Namen Monsr. de Grignac oder (wie Er auch sonst genent wirdet) de Gragnaque" (de Grignac or, as he is otherwise called, de Gragnaque), Maximilian to Albrecht of Bavaria, 24 Mar. 1568, HSA, Kurbayern, Äußeres Archiv, no. 4387, fo. 143. See also Edel, *Kaiser*, 151–159, for insightful commentary on Maximilian's style of government.

67. Lindell, "Neubesetzung," 39.

68. Maximilian's Quarantine Orders, 23 Aug. 1568, HSA, Kurbayern, Äußeres Archiv, no. 4459, fo. 284, and 1570 [?], fo. 290; Maximilian to Albrecht of Bavaria, 1 Apr. 1564, HSA, Kurbayern, Äußeres Archiv, no. 4461, fo. 229.

69. HHStA, Familienakten, Sammelbände, box 1, 2 vols.

70. Tagebuch, fos. 19, 66.

71. Tagebuch, fos. 70, 87; Ferdinand to Maximilian, 15 Apr. 1566, SÚA, Král. Reg. IIc, vol. 80, Bericht an Hof, fo. 103.

72. Tagebuch, fos. 22, 92–93.

73. Holtzmann, *Maximilian II.*, 526.

74. "Welche sich von Tag zu tag mehren, auch von Newem erwachsen," Maximilian to Albrecht of Bavaria, 9 Aug. 1567, Bibl, *Korrespondenz*, part 2: 215–216. See also Maximilian to the count of Benavente, 2 Aug. 1564, AN, Osuna, legajo 426/1, #12/2.

75. E.g., HSA, Kurbayern, Äußeres Archiv, no. 4462, fos. 102–110, 136–140; HHStA, Bavarica, 4, bundle 1573, fos. 1–141, and bundle 1574–1576, fos. 1–93.

76. Bohemian treasury to Maximilian, 3 Aug. 1568, SÚA, Král. Reg. IIc, Bericht an Hof, vol. 81, fos. 335–336; Bohemian treasury to Maximilian, 29 Dec. 1568, SÚA, Král. Reg. IIc, Bericht an Hof, vol. 81, fos. 491–492.

77. Zasius to Albrecht of Bavaria, 5 Dec. 1565, HSA, Kurbayern, Äußeres Archiv, no. 4300, fo. 207; Bohemian treasury to Maximilian, 25 July 1566, SÚA, Král. Reg. IIc, vol. 80, Bericht an Hof, fo. 197; Bohemian treasury to Maximilian, 30 Aug. 1566, SÚA, Král. Reg. IIc, vol. 80, Bericht an Hof, fos. 235–236; Tagebuch, fo. 28. Bohemian treasury to Maximilian, 6 Nov. 1566, SÚA, Král. Reg. IIc, vol. 80, Bericht an Hof, fos. 303–304.

78. SÚA, Patenty, box 3, patents of 8 July 1573 and 25 October 1574, November of 1575; Almut Bues, *Die habsburgische Kandidatur für den polnischen Thron während des ersten Interregnums in Polen, 1572–1573*, Dissertationen der Universität Wien, vol. 163 (Vienna: Verband der wissenschaftlichen Gesellschaften Österreichs, 1984), 112.

79. Maximilian to Wilhelm of Rožmberk, 4 June 1567, SOA, Třebon, Historica, no. 4720.

80. Zasius to Albrecht of Bavaria, 13 May 1568, *Briefe und Akten*, 5: 400; Parker, *Philip II*, 69–70.

81. E.g., Chantonnay to Philip, 6 Sept. 1567, CODOIN, 101: 269; Chantonnay to Philip, 20 Sept. 1567, ibid., 271; Vanegas to Philip, 11 Oct. 1568, ibid., 103: 3–4; Maximilian to Vratislav Pernstayn, 19 May 1568, SOA, Litoměřice, Lobkovic BII, fo. 96; Tagebuch, fo. 50.

82. Bohemian treasury [?] to Maximilian, 27 Apr. 1566, SÚA, Král. Reg. IIc, vol. 80, Bericht an Hof, fos. 123–126; commission on mining reform to Maximilian, 2 May 1566, SÚA, Král. Reg. IIc, vol. 80, Bericht an Hof, fos. 110–111. Cf. Bibl, "Haltung," 381.

83. Bibl, *Korrespondenz*, part 2: 254, note 2.

84. Monteagudo to Philip, 30 Nov. 1570, CODOIN, 110: 122.

85. Report of Michele, 1571, in Fiedler, *Relationen*, 30: 280.

86. E.g., William Beik, *Absolutism and Society in Seventeenth-Century France* (Cambridge: Cambridge University Press, 1985), chaps. 12–13 and passim; Thomas Robisheaux, *Rural Society and the Search for Order in Early Modern Germany* (Cambridge: Cambridge University Press, 1989), esp. chap. 9; Thomas Ertman, *Birth of the Leviathan* (Cambridge: Cambridge University Press, 1997), 107 and passim; John Lynch, *Spain Under the Habsburgs*, 2 vols. (Oxford: Blackwell, 1965–1969), 1: 184–186.

87. Beik, *Absolutism*, 303–307.

CHAPTER 7: THE PLEASURES AND IRONIES OF SPLENDOR

1. "Der Hof, der ist ein seltsames Spiel," "Das Hofleben," in Janko, *Schwendi*, 168.

2. Rodríguez-Salgado, *Changing Face*, 19–20; Leonhard von Harrach to Maximilian, 13 Apr. 1561, Vienna, HHStA, Familienarchiv, Familienkorrespondenz A, box 3, fos. 129–131.

3. Louthan, *Crato*, 32.

4. "Cum aliqua autoritate magna," Tagebuch, fo. 90.

5. Rübsam, "Mameranus," 540.

6. Chantonnay to Philip, 7 June 1567, CODOIN, 101: 230; Cf. Sophia Naguerin de Toledo to Maximilian, 24 July 1569, HHStA, Familienarchiv, Familienakten, 3, box 99, no folio.

7. Hanns Jäger-Sunstenau, "Über das Wiener Schützenfest, 1563," *Wiener Geschichtsblätter* 15 (1960): 142.

8. Description of 1560 festivities at court in GHA, Korrespondenz-Akten, no. 597/4, fo. 5.

9. Karl Vocelka, "Manier-Groteske-Fest-Triumph: Zur Geistesgeschichte der frühen Neuzeit," *Österreich in Geschichte und Literatur* 21 (1977): 142; Altfahrt, "Propaganda," part 1: 289–290; Thomas Da Costa Kaufmann, *Variations on the Imperial Theme: Studies in Ceremonial, Art, and Collecting in the Age of Maximilian II and Rudolph II* (New York: Garland, 1978), 81; Thomas Da Costa Kaufmann, *The Mastery of Nature* (Princeton, N.J.: Princeton University Press, 1993), 117–121.

10. Altfahrt, "Propaganda," part 1: 286–287.

11. Rainer A. Müller, *Der Fürstenhof in der frühen Neuzeit*, Enzyklopädie deutscher Geschichte, vol. 33 (Munich: Oldenbourg, 1995), 14–15; Maximilian's Kitchen Orders, 6 Oct. 1566, HHStA, Hofarchiv, OMeA, Sonderreihe, box 73, no. 3, fo. 85.

12. [Count] Hans Cobenzl to Archduke Ferdinand, 6 Oct. 1564, HHStA, Familienarchiv, Familienkorrespondenz A, box 38, "Erzherzog Ferdinand," fo.

61; anonymous report of 30 May 1568, HHStA, Familienarchiv, Familienakten, 8, Varia, box 108, fo. 76.

13. The chart is in HSA, Kurbayern, Äußeres Archiv, no. 4303, fos. 16–17. On
the reception of Sussex's embassy, see Johann Ulrich Zasius to Duke Albrecht
of Bavaria, 16 Aug. 1567, HSA, Kurbayern, Äußeres Archiv, no. 4302, fo.
216.

14. Rosemarie Aulinger, *Das Bild des Reichstages im 16. Jahrhundert: Beiträge zu
einer typologischen Analyse schriftlicher und bildlicher Quellen,* Schriftenreihe
des historischen Kommission bei der bayerischen Akademie der Wissenschaften, vol. 18 (Göttingen: Vandenhoeck und Ruprecht, 1980), 174; Alfred
Kohler, "Wohnen und Essen auf den Reichstagen des 16. Jahrhundert," in
*Alltag im 16. Jahrhundert: Studien zur Lebensformen in mitteleuropäischen Städ-
ten,* Alfred Kohler and Heinrich Lutz, eds., Wiener Beiträge zur Geschichte
der Neuzeit, vol. 14 (Vienna: Verlag für Geschichte und Politik, 1987), 225–
226.

15. Maximilian's orders to Ludwig Ungnad, 10 May 1564, HHStA, Hofarchiv,
Alte Akten des Hofmarschallamts (Early acts of the court marshal's office),
group 1, fasc. 1, bundle 1, 2.

16. A pregnant Tyrolean noblewoman of the time reported the following daily
intake. At three in the morning, an hour when digestion was thought to
function especially well, she drank a soup with three eggs and spices. At five
she had a kind of egg custard (*Eiermus*) and a chicken soup, the latter a
concession to the child she was bearing. Two more fresh eggs were downed
at seven and at nine a broth with egg yolks and spices along with several
biscuits (*Streiblen*) and a glass of wine—a Traminer. Three hours passed
until the noon meal where she ate from several kinds of fowl with bread,
wine, and sweets. At one there were cookies (*Brandkuchlein*) along with more
wine. Further substantial snacks came along at three and at five. Several
kinds of fish made up the evening meal around six. She ate again at seven
and nine, and awakening at midnight, put an end to this daunting intake
with more egg soup and spices. Hirn, *Ferdinand von Tirol,* 1: 486–488.

17. HHStA, Hofarchiv, OMeA, Sonderreihe, box 74, Instruktionen, Varia, no.
14, fo. 395.

18. Aulinger, *Reichstag,* 287, note 18.

19. Hilda Lietzmann, *Das Neugebäude in Wien: Sultan Süleymans Zelt—Kaiser
Maximilians Lustschloß. Ein Beitrag zur Kunst- und Kulturgeschichte der zweiten
Hälfte des sechzehnten Jahrhunderts* (Munich: Deutscher Kunstverlag, 1987),
48, note 30; Maximilian to Albrecht of Bavaria, 20 Oct. 1562, HSA, Kurbayern, Äußeres Archiv, no. 4461, fo. 135.

20. Tagebuch, fo. 28; Maximilian to Archduke Ferdinand, 5 Oct. 1570, TL,

Geschäft von Hof, 1570, fo. 214; Maximilian to the Tyrolean treasury, 1 and 15 Dec. 1570, TL, Geschäft von Hof, 1570, fo. 281. On Lower Austrian opposition to imported wines, see Hannelore Herold, "Die Hauptprobleme der Landtagshandlungen des Erzherzogthums unter der Enns zur Zeit der Regierung Kaiser Maximilians II., 1564–1576" (dissertation, University of Vienna, 1970), 209.

21. Peter Haller to Maximilian, 12 Oct. 1558, HHStA, Familienenarchiv, Familienakten, 1.7, Vermögensangelegenheiten, box 15, fos. 37–38; Adam Hoffman to Maximilian, 12 July 1563, HHStA, Familienarchiv, Familienakten, 8, Varia, box 108, fo. 37.

22. Archduke Ferdinand to Maximilian, 1 Mar. 1562, HHStA, Familienarchiv, Familienakten, 8, Varia, box 108, fo. 22.

23. Maximilian to Albrecht V of Bavaria, 27 Jan. 1563, HSA, Kurbayern, Äußeres Archiv, no. 4461, fo. 143; Aulinger, *Reichstag,* 27; Kaufman, *Imperial Theme,* 21.

24. Altfahrt, "Propaganda," 284, 296–297.

25. Franco Bonardo Perissone to Maximilian, 9 Oct. 1569, HHStA, Familienarchiv, Familienakten, 7, Bittschriften (Petitions), box 108, fos. 3–5.

26. Maximilian to Albrecht of Bavaria, 17 Sept. 1563, HSA, Kurbayern, Äußeres Archiv, no. 4461, fos. 201, 205.

27. Bibl, "Kulturblüte," 141–143; ÖNB, Handschriftensammlung, fo. 98; Albert Ilg, "Das Neugebäude bei Wien," *Jahrbuch der kunsthistorischen Sammlungen des allerhöchsten Kaiserhauses* 16 (1895): 91, 100.

28. Bibl, "Kulturblüte," 143.

29. "Ain wunderparlich, grausam, gros, scheisslich bestia, ist erst zwelf jar alt, wechst biz ins 30. jar, wurd noch gros als er ist," Bibl, "Kulturblüte," 142.

30. Lhotsky, *Festschrift,* 2, part 1: 170.

31. "Gar schen," Tagebuch, fo. 4.

32. William of Hesse to Maximilian, 22 June 1575, HHStA, Familienarchiv, Familienkorrespondenz A, box 2, fo. 346.

33. Lhotsky, *Festschrift,* 2, part 1: 172–173; ÖNB, Handschriftensammlung, no. 9089, fo. 106; Albrecht of Bavaria to Adam Dietrichstein, 4 Sept. 1566, HHStA, Staatenabteilung, Bavarica, 3, no folio.

34. Pass, *Musik und Musiker,* 215–216.

35. Maximilian to Stephen Rosetti[o], 18 Mar. 1575, HHStA, Familienarchiv, Sammelbände, box 1, vol. 2, fo. 317. Rosetti was the emperor's music librarian.

36. Thompson, "Mary of Hungary," 408; Lhotsky, *Festschrift* 2, part 1: 178; Maximilian to Stephano Rosetto, 20 Aug. 1574, HHStA, Familienarchiv, Sammelbände, box 1, vol. 2, fos. 302–303.

37. Maximilian to Don Diego Cordova, 16 Sept. 1574, HHStA, Familienarchiv, Sammelbände, box 1, vol. 2, fo. 314.

38. Report of Giovanni Michele, 1571, in Fiedler, *Relationen*, 30: 277.

39. For this issue generally, see Lietzmann, *Neugebäude*, passim.

40. Lhotsky, *Festschrift*, 2, part 1: 165–166; Howard Louthan, *The Quest for Compromise: Peacemakers in Counter-Reformation Vienna* (Cambridge: Cambridge University Press, 1997), 33–34. On Strada and Maximilian, see Dirk Jacob Jansen, "The Instruments of Patronage: Jacopo Strada at the Court of Maximilian II, A Case-Study," in Edelmayer and Kohler, eds., *Maximilian II*, 182–202.

41. Elisabeth Scheicher, *Die Kunst- und Wunderkammer der Habsburger* (Vienna: Molden, 1979), 137–140.

42. Rochus Kastner to Maximilian, 15 Aug. 1561, HHStA, Familienarchiv, Familienakten, 3.2, Kunstgegenstände (Art works and art holdings), box 103, fo. 207; Maximilian to Albrecht of Bavaria, 16 Oct. 1562, HHStA, Familienarchiv, Familienakten, Varia, box 108, fo. 131; Adam Swetkowycz to Maximilian, 30 Sept. 1563, HHStA, Familienarchiv, Familienakten, 1.7, Vermögensgegenstände, box 15, "Berichte des Adam Swetkowycz and König Maximilian," no folio; Christoph Friesinger to Maximilian, 8 Apr. 1564, HHStA, Familienarchiv, Familienkorrespondenz A, box 3, fos. 20–21.

43. Lhotsky, *Festschrift*, 2, part 1: 160, 165.

44. Lhotsky, ibid., 160, 165, 167; Bibl, "Kulturblüte," 146; Evans, *Rudolph II*, 166–167.

45. Archduke Ferdinand to Maximilian, 17 Jan. 1565, SÚA, Král. Reg. IIc, vol. 79, Bericht an Hof, fo. 11.

46. Lhotsky, *Festschrift*, 2, part 1: 5; Khevenhüller, *Tagebuch*, 30–32; Trenkler, "Hofbibliothek," 8, note 3.

47. Lhotsky, *Festschrift*, 2, part 1: 166; Archduke Ferdinand to Ferdinand, 4 May 1548, fos. 137–138; Archduke Ferdinand to King Ferdinand, 22 June 1548, SÚA, Král. Reg. IIc., vol. 37, Bericht an Hof, fo. 163; Archduke Ferdinand to King Ferdinand, 10 May 1550, SÚA, Král. Reg. IIc, vol. 45, Bericht an Hof, fo. 125; Archduke Ferdinand to Ferdinand I, 8 Nov. 1550, SÚA, Král. Reg. IIc, vol. 45, Bericht an Hof, fo. 231.

48. Archduke Ferdinand to Ferdinand, 10 May 1550, SÚA, Král. Reg. IIc, vol. 45, Bericht an Hof, fo. 125; Archduke Ferdinand to Maximilian, 6 Sept. 1565, SÚA, Král. Reg. IIc, vol. 79, Bericht an Hof, fo. 31, Archduke Ferdinand to Maximilian, 9 Oct. 1565, SÚA, Král. Reg. IIc, vol. 79, Bericht an Hof, fo. 343; Bohemian treasury to Maximilian, 29 Oct. 1566, SÚA, Král. Reg. IIc, vol. 80, Bericht an Hof, fos. 292–293; Lhotsky, *Festschrift* 2, part 1: 165–166; Scheicher, *Wunderkammer*, 137–138.

49. Bibl, "Kulturblüte," 145, 147.

50. "Porque ahoy es nra. voluntad," Maximilian to Pedro de Ansa, 17 Oct. 1572, HHStA, Familienarchiv, Sammelbände, box 1, vol. 2, fo. 262.

51. Lhotsky, *Festschrift* 2, part 1: 158–159; Ilg, "Neugebäude," 98.

52. E.g., Adam Swetkowycz to Maximilian, 26 Nov. 1563, HHStA, Familienarchiv, Familienakten 1.7, Vermögensangelegenheiten, box 15, "Berichte des Adam Swetkowycz," no folio.

53. Lietzmann, *Neugebäude*, 17–20; Bibl, "Kulturblüte," 140, 147–149; Becker, "Die letzten Tage," 321, note 3.

54. Tagebuch, fo. 67.

55. "Y son tantos los herrores que en ella se hallan por causa del auctor que no seria menos travajo enmendallos todos que hacer el libro de nuevo," Maximilian to Philip's ambassador in Venice, 18 Jan. 1566, HHStA, Familienarchiv, Sammelbände, box 1, vol. 2, fo. 18.

56. HHStA, Familienarchiv, Sammelbände, box 1, vol. 2, fo. 19.

57. Hermann Menhardt, *Das älteste Handschriftenverzeichnis der Wiener Hofbibliothek von Hugo Blotius, 1576*, Österreichische Akademie der Wissenschaften, philosophische-historische Klasse, Denkschriften, vol. 76 (Vienna: Rohrer, 1957), 3, 31; Johanna Ernuszt, "Die ungarische Beziehungen des Hugo Blotius," *Jahrbuch der Graf Klebelsberg Kun Instituts für ungarische Geschichtsforschung in Wien* 10 (1940): 14, 21; Busbecq to Maximilian, 9 Nov. 1574, *Letters*, 31–32.

58. Cited in Bibl, "Kulturblüte," 151.

59. Lietzmann, *Neugebäude*, 29, 73; Report of Giovanni Michele, 1571, in Fiedler, *Relationen*, 30: 280.

60. Maximilian to Albrecht of Bavaria, 20 Aug. 1563, HSA, Kurbayern, Äußeres Archiv, no. 4461, fo. 193.

61. "Los tempos frios y humedos a que esta tierra es la sujeta," Chantonnay to Philip, 22 Nov. 1568, CODOIN, 103: 32.

62. Louthan, *Quest*, 62, 92–93, 126; Charles L'Ecluse to Crato, 27 Apr. 1566, in *Caroli Clusii Atrebatis ad Thomam Redigerum et Joannem Cratonem epistolae*, F. X. de Ram, ed., Compte-Rendu des séances de la commission royale d'histoire vol. 12 (1847): 52.

63. On the contact between Johannes Crato, Maximilian's chief physician, and Innsbruck, see Crato, *Epistola*, 14; and the undated letter of the Siennese physician Petrus Andreas Matthiolis in L. Scholz, ed., *Johannis Cratonis a Kraftheim Consiliorum et Epistolarum* (Frankfurt: n.p., 1671), 118–159. See also Charles L'Ecluse, *Exoticorum Libri Decem: Quibus Animalium, Plantarum, Aromatum, aliorumque Peregrinorum Fructum Historiae Describuntur . . .* , ([Antwerp?]: Plantiniana Raphelengii, 1605), part 2: 289; and Andreae Camutius, *Medicinae svpraordinariam ac praecipvam . . . brevis excussio prae-*

cipui morbi, nempe cordis palpitationis Maximiliani secundi caesaris . . . (Florence: Marescori, 1580), 30. This letter is undated, but the context suggests that it was written sometime in 1576.

64. Leonhart Thurneisser zum Thurn, *Quinta essentia, das ist/Die hoechste subtilitet/krafft und wirckung/bey der fuertrefflichsten/vnd menschlichen geschlecht am nuetzlichsten kuensten/der Medecin vnd Alchemy/Auch wie nahe diese beyde mit sipschafft gefreund vnd versandt sind* (Leipzig: Steinman, 1574), book 1, chap. 3, 52–77; R. J. W. Evans, *The Making of the Habsburg Monarchy* (Oxford: Clarendon, 1979), 35 and note 81.

65. Louthan, *Quest,* 80.

66. Johannes Crato von Crafftheim, *Ordnung der Praeservation* (Nuremberg: Gerlach, 1585), part 2, unpaginated.

67. Bibl, "Kulturblüte, 143–144; Grete Mecenseffy, "Maximilian II" 51; Scheicher, *Wunderkammer,* 137; Lhotsky, *Festschrift* 2, part 1: 176.

68. L'Ecluse, *Exoticorum,* part 1: 1; part 2: 59, 80, 135; L'Ecluse to Crato, 10 April 1567, *Epistolae,* 55–56; L'Ecluse to Crato, 25 Nov. 1567, ibid., 59–60; L'Ecluse to Crato, 16 Aug. 1569, ibid., 61.

69. Ibid., 38, 41.

70. L'Ecluse, *Exoticorum,* part 1, 5, 14–16, 48, 51, 66, 70, 79.

71. Goodman, *Power and Penury,* 233–234.

72. Louthan, *Quest,* 89; Hubertus Languet to Count L. [Ludwig of Württemberg?] in *Decades tres epistolarum Huberti Langueti, Jo. Camerarii, Io. Cratonis et Casp. Peuceri* (Frankfurt: Johann Maximilian Sand, 1702), 10.

73. Crato, *Praeservation,* part 1, unpaginated.

74. Vivian Nutton, ed., *Medicine at the Courts of Europe, 1500–1837* (London: Routledge, 1990), 11; Hugh Trevor-Roper, "The Court Physician and Paracelsianism," ibid., 79; Bruce T. Moran, "Prince-Practitioning and the Direction of Medical Roles at the German Court: Maurice of Hesse-Kassel and His Physicians," ibid., 101–102.

75. Crato, *Praeservation,* parts 1 and 2 unpaginated.

76. E.g., Camutius, *Medicinae,* 25.

77. Crato, *Praeservation,* part 2 unpaginated. On the disputes surrounding astrology in the Renaissance, see Wayne Shumaker, *The Occult Sciences in the Renaissance* (Berkeley: University of California Press, 1972). See also Alan Chapman, "Astrological Medicine," in Charles Webster, ed., *Health, Medicine and Mortality in the Sixteenth Century* (Cambridge: Cambridge University Press, 1979), 275.

78. Trevor-Roper, "Court Physician," 79; Nutton, *Medicine,* 11.

79. Jo[hannis] Cratonis a Kraftheim, *III. Impp. Romanorum Medicii et Consiliarii Intimi, Consiliorum [et] Epistolarum Medicinalium . . . ,* 7 vols. (Frankfurt: Wechel, 1591–1611), 3: 14; Jo. Fermelii, *Ambiani, vniversa medicina,* 3rd ed.

(Frankfurt: Andreas Wechel, 1574), preface and introduction. Both are unpaginated. On Fernel, see James J. Bono, *The Word of God and the Languages of Man: Interpreting Nature in Early Modern Science and Medicine* (Madison: University of Wisconsin Press, 1995), 87, 89, 92–94, 98–99.

80. Tagebuch, fo. 35.

81. Evans, *Making*, 35; Heinrich von Rantzow, *Catalogus imperatorum, regum ac principium qui astrologicam artem amarunt, ornarunt et exercuerunt* (Antwerp: Plantin, 1580), 29. The title page of this volume in the Austrian National Library indicates that it was in the library of Archduke Ferdinand of the Tyrol. On Rantzow and Archduke Ferdinand, see Horst Fuhrmann, "Heinrich Rantzaus römische Korrespondenten," *Archiv für Kulturgeschichte* 41 (1959): 82, note 69.

82. Camutius, *Medicinae*, 10.

83. Crato, *Epistola*, 15.

84. Camutius, *Medicinae*, 13, 28–30.

85. Count Hans Cobenzl to Archduke Ferdinand, 10 Sept. 1564, HHStA, Familienarchiv, Familienkorrespondenz A, box 38, bundle Ferdinand Erzherzog von Tirol, fo. 54; Cobenzl to Archduke Ferdinand, 11 Mar. 1565, HHStA, Familienarchiv, Familienkorrespondenz A, box 38, bundle Ferdinand Erzherzog von Tirol, fo. 118; Johann Ulrich Zasius to Albrecht V, HSA, Kurbayern, Äußeres Archiv, no. 4303, fo. 14; Tagebuch, fos. 15, 47, 50.

86. Maximilian to Albrecht of Bavaria, 9 Oct. 1568, HSA, Kurbayern, Äußeres Archiv, no. 4462, fo. 41.

87. Maximilian to Albrecht of Bavaria, 19 Mar. 1562, HSA, Kurbayern, Äußeres Archiv, no. 4461, fo. 95; Maximilian to Albrecht of Bavaria, 5 May 1563, HSA, Kurbayern, Äußeres Archiv, no. 4461, fo. 166.

88. Maximilian to Albrecht of Bavaria, 4 July 1567, in Bibl, *Korrespondenz*, part 2, 201.

89. Maximilian to Albrecht of Bavaria, 5 Nov. 1567, GHA, Korrespondenz-Akten, 593/2, fo. 318.

90. L'Ecluse to Crato, 10 Apr. 1569, in *Epistolae*, 55–56; L'Ecluse to Crato, 25 Nov. 1567, ibid., 59–60; L'Ecluse to Crato, 16 Aug. 1569, ibid., 61.

CHAPTER 8: A SHAKY SOLIDARITY

1. "La calidad de sus padres," Maximilian to Adam von Dietrichstein, 17 Jan. 1569, HHStA, Familienarchiv, Sammelbände, box 1, vol. 2, fo. 149. See also Maximilian to Ferdinand, 3 Oct. 1565, SÚA, Stará manipulace (Old procedure), K1/#8, box 1051, fo. 70; maximilian to his officers and councillors in Prague, 2 Aug. 1567, SÚA, Stará manipulace, K1/#8, box 1051, fo. 72; and

Maximilian to his councillors in Bohemia, 8 Jan. 1574, SÚA, Stará manipulace, K1/#8, box 1051, fo. 74.

2. "Soro nullo modo potest remitti in polloniam nisi aliter tractetur quam hurusque," Tagebuch, fo. 89; Fichtner, *Ferdinand I,* 237. On the general details of Habsburg marriage politics in Poland during the reigns of Ferdinand I and Maximilian II, see Anna Sucheni-Grabowska, "Zu den Beziehungen zwischen den Jagiellonen und den Habsburgern: Katharina von Österreich, die dritte Gemahlin des Königs Sigismund August," *Historisches Jahrbuch der Stadt Linz* (1979): 59–100.

3. Maximilian to Albrecht of Bavaria, 13 May 1564, HSA, Kurbayern, Äußeres Archiv, no. 4461, fo. 247; Maximilian to Archduke Ferdinand, 28 Dec. 1566, in Bibl, *Korrespondenz,* part 2: 65–68.

4. Bibl, "Kulturblüte," 146.

5. "Haws auch billich und gern gethon, dan es mier ain fraid ist, wan ich E.L. was annemlichs verrichtn khan und nit alain in disem, sonder allen andern miglichen sachen," Maximilian to Albrecht of Bavaria, 4 June 1567, in Bibl, *Korrespondenz,* part 2: 191.

6. Vanegas to Philip, 3 Dec. 1567, CODOIN, 101: 323; Report of Giovanni Michele, 1574, in Fiedler, *Relationen,* 30: 365.

7. Tagebuch, fos. 73, 75–76; Archduke Ferdinand to Maximilian, 5 Sept. 1565, SÚA, Král. Reg. IIc, vol. 79, Bericht an Hof, fos. 313–314.

8. Ferdinand to Albrecht of Bavaria, Nov. 1568, GHA, Korrespondenz-Akten, 597/1, fo. 135; Count Cobenzl to Archduke Ferdinand, 30 Mar. 1565, HHSA, Familienarchiv, Familienkorrespondenz A, box 38, bundle Ferdinand, Erzherzog von Tirol, fo. 130; Count Cobenzl to Archduke Ferdinand, 27 Apr. 1565, HHSA, Familienarchiv, Familienkorrespondenz A, box 38, bundle Ferdinand, Erzherzog von Tirol, fo. 140; Count Cobenzl to Archduke Ferdinand, 9 May 1565, HHSA, Familienarchiv, Familienkorrespondenz A, box 38, bundle Ferdinand, Erzherzog von Tirol, fo. 144; Count Cobenzl to Archduke Ferdinand, 18 May 1565, HHSA, Familienarchiv, Familienkorrespondenz A, box 38, bundle Ferdinand, Erzherzog von Tirol, fo. 148; Count Cobenzl to Archduke Ferdinand, 2 May 1570, HHSA, Familienarchiv, Familienkorrespondenz A, box 38, bundle Ferdinand, Erzherzog von Tirol, fo. 233.

9. Maximilian to Ferdinand, 8 Dec. 1567, in Bibl, *Korrespondenz,* part 2: 275.

10. Archduke Ferdinand to Maximilian, 18 Jan. 1559, HHStA, Familienarchiv, Familienkorrespondenz A, box 2, bundle Ferdinand von Tirol an Maximilian, fo. 202; Archduke Ferdinand to Maximilian, 17 Sept. 1563, HHStA, Familienarchiv, Familienakten, 3.5, Jagdsachen, box 105, fo. 185; Archduke Ferdinand to Vratislav Pernsteyn, 28 Feb. 1566, SOA, Litoměřice, Lobkovic,

BII, fo. 204; Report of Giovanni Michele, 1574, in Fiedler, *Relationen*, 30: 365.

11. Maximilian Lanzinner, ed., *Deutsche Reichstagsakten: Reichsversammlungen, 1556–1662, Der Reichstag zu Speyer, 1570*, 2 vols. (Göttingen: Vandenhoeck and Ruprecht, 1988), 1: 130.

12. Maximilian to Albrecht of Bavaria, 27 Sept. 1568, HSA, Kurbayern, Äußeres Archiv, no. 4462, fo. 39; Chantonnay to Philip, 19 July 1567, CODOIN, 101: 253.

13. Heinz Noflatscher, "Deutschmeister und Regent der Vorlande Maximilian von Österreich, 1558–1618," in *Vorderösterreich in der frühen Neuzeit*, Hans Maier and Volker Press, eds. (Sigmaringen: Jan Thorbecke, 1989): 96–97; Polexna Lasso to Maximilian, 13 Jan. 1563, HHStA, Familienarchiv, Familienkorrespondenz A, box 3, bundle Kh.-W., fo. 303; Adam Swetkowycz to Maximilian, 6 Sept. 1563, HHStA, Familienarchiv, Familienkorrespondenz A, box 3, bundle Kh.-W., fo. 495; Vanegas to Philip, 3 Dec. 1567, CODOIN, 101: 323.

14. Adam von Dietrichstein to Maximilian, 26 Apr. 1567, in Koch, *Quellen*, 1: 186.

15. ÖNB, Handschriftensammlung, no. 9089, fo. 51.

16. "Quantum noceat discordia societati generis humani," Archduke Rudolph to Maximilian, 12 Sept. 1565, HHStA, Familienarchiv, Familienkorrespondenz A, box 2, bundle Erzherzog Rudolph, fo. 284.

17. Archduke Rudolph to Maximilian, 20 Nov. 1565, HHStA, Familienarchiv, Familienkorrespondenz A, box 2, bundle Erzherzog Rudolph, fo. 286, bundle 1, fos. 1–62, and bundle Erzherzog Rudolph (unnumbered), fos. 259–317, provide an illuminating picture of the educational program the two princes followed. See also ÖNB, Handschriftensammlung, Codex 8051, fos. 1–2, 8–9, 13–14, 31–32.

18. "Pueri bene nati," Rudolph to Maximilian, 3 Apr. 1568, ÖNB, Handschriftensammlung, Codex 8051, fos. 8, 40.

19. "Qui est valde amoenus locus," Rudolph to Matthias, Maximilian, Albert, and Wenzel, 19 May 1568, ÖNB, Handschriftensammlung, Codex 8051, fo. 14.

20. "Epistola Rudolphi ad amicum qui laudat Hispaliam civitatem magnam Hispaniae," 19 May 1570, ÖNB, Handschriftensammlung, Codex 8051, fos. 82–83; Kamen, *Philip*, 207.

21. Rudolph to [?], 15 June 1568, ÖNB, Handschriftensammlung, Codex 8051, fo. 15; Rudolph to Maximilian 2 Mar. 1570, ÖNB, Handschriftensammlung, Codex 8051, fos. 74–75, 79–81. On Philip and the Morisco uprising, see Kamen, *Philip*, 131.

22. Adam von Dietrichstein to Maximilian, 19 June 1564, in Edelmayer, *Brief-*

wechsel, 235; Archduke Rudolph to Maximilian, 26 June 1565, HHStA, Familienarchiv, Familienkorrespondenz A, box 2, bundle Erzherzog Rudolph, fo. 283.

23. Adam von Dietrichstein to Maximilian, 31 Mar. 1566, in Koch, *Quellen*, 1: 158–159; Bibl, "Frage," 384; Bibl, *Korrespondenz*, part 2: 254, note 2; Maximilian to Philip, 10 Nov. 1567, ibid., 254; Vanegas to Philip, 3 Dec. 1567, CODOIN, 101: 323.

24. Vanegas to Philip, 31 Jan. 1568, ibid., 360; Vanegas to Philip, 6 Mar. 1568, CODOIN, 101: p. 401.

25. Philip to Luis Vanegas, 28 Jan. 1568, ibid., 358; Chantonnay to Philip, 18 May 1568, ibid., 416; duke of Alba to Philip, 23 June 1568, ibid., 485. The excerpt of this letter in Alba's *Epistolario del III Duque de Alba Don Fernando Alvarez de Toledo*, duke of Berwick y de Alba, ed., 3 vols. (Madrid: n.p., 1952), 2: 68 does not contain this comment.

26. Kamen, *Philip*, 134, 206–207.

27. Report of Michele to the senate, 1564, in Fiedler, *Relationen*, 30: 261.

28. Maximilian and Maria to Charles, 21 Apr. 1550, in Rodríguez, *Maximiliano*, 185; Giovanni Michiel [Michele] to the doge, 28 June 1568, in Turba, *Depeschen*, 2: 441–442; L. J. Andrew Villalon, "Putting Don Carlos Together Again: Treatment of a Head Injury in Sixteenth-Century Spain," *Sixteenth Century Journal* 26 (1995): 347–365; Viktor Bibl, *Der Tod des Don Carlos* (Vienna: Braumüller, 1918), 318–319, 321; Kamen, *Philip*, 91–92; Edelmayer, *Briefwechsel*, 73.

29. "Die Informazion, so ich bisher hab, ist schlecht genueg," Adam von Dietrichstein to Maximilian, 22 Apr. 1564, Edelmayer, *Korrespondenz*, 1: 203. Cf. Adam von Dietrichstein to Maximilian, 29 June 1564, ibid., 230–231.

30. Adam von Dietrichstein to Maximilian, 5 June 1567, in Koch, *Quellen*, 1: 190.

31. "Don carlos nuevamente convertido de turco a n[uestr]a sancta fee catholica," Philip to the prior of Guadalupe, 26 Feb. 1564, BN, Madrid, Sección de manuscritos, no. 781, fo. 2.

32. "Segun su capacidad," BN, Madrid, Sección de manuscritos, no. 781, fo. 2.

33. Maximilian to Martin Guzmán, 24 Dec. 1561, HHStA, Familienarchiv, Sammelbände, box 1, vol. 1, fo. 170.

34. Dietrichstein to Maximilian, 2 and 8 Jan. 1567, in Koch, *Quellen*, 1: 178; Dietrichstein to Maximilian, 18 May 1567, ibid., 188.

35. E.g., Michele, Report of 1571, in Fiedler, *Relationen*, 30: 302.

36. Adam von Dietrichstein to Maximilian, 22 Apr. 1564, in Edelmayer, *Briefwechsel*, 1: 204.

37. Edelmayer, "Beziehungen," 121–122, 127–129; Marianne Strakosch, "Materialen zu einer Biographie Elisabeths von Österreich, Königin von Frank-

reich" (dissertation, University of Vienna, 1965), 23; Archduke Ferdinand to Maximilian, 19 Nov. 1567, in Bibl, *Korrespondenz*, part 2: 267; Maximilian's reply to Luis Vanegas, 20 July 1567, ibid., 212. Cf. CODOIN, 101: 331–332.

38. Edelmayer, "Beziehungen," 125, note 480, 130–131.

39. "In suma die Katz last des mausen nit," Maximilian to Albrecht of Bavaria, 16 Nov. 1567, in Bibl, *Korrespondenz* part 2: 258.

40. Ibid.

41. Adam von Dietrichstein to Maximilian, 2, 8 Jan. 1567, in Koch, *Quellen*, 1: 178; Adam von Dietrichstein to Maximilian, 18 May 1567, ibid., 188; Adam von Dietrichstein to Maximilian, 5 June 1567, ibid., 190 Maximilian's answer to Vanegas, 20 July 1567, in Bibl, *Korrespondenz* part 2: 212.

42. Philip to Luis Vanegas, 28 Jan. 1568, CODOIN, 101: 358.

43. Adam von Dietrichstein to Maximilian, 22 Jan. 1568, in Koch, *Quellen*, 1: 205.

44. Maximilian to Adam von Dietrichstein, 28 Feb. 1568, in Koch, *Quellen*, 2: 52.

45. Parker, *Philip II*, 91.

46. Vanegas to Philip II, 6 Mar. 1568, CODOIN, 101: 393–398, 401; Bibl, *Tod*, 306, 308–309, 316, 319, 322.

47. Adam von Dietrichstein to Maximilian, 5 June 1567, in Koch, *Quellen*, 1: 190; Bibl, *Tod*, 3; Maximilian to Adam von Dietrichstein, 5 Mar. 1568, in Koch, *Quellen*, 2: 52.

48. Vanegas to Philip, 31 Mar. 1568, CODOIN, 101: 405.

49. Adam von Dietrichstein to Maximilian, 13 Apr. 1568, in Koch, *Quellen*, 1: 210–211; duke of Alba to Philip, 23 June 1568, CODOIN, 101: 485.

50. Adam von Dietrichstein to Maximilian, 19 May 1568, in Koch, *Quellen*, 1: 216.

51. Bibl, *Tod*, 354–355; Maximilian to Adam von Dietrichstein, 27 July 1568, in Koch, *Quellen*, 2: 52–53; L. P. Gachard, *Don Carlos et Philippe II*, 2 vols. (Brussels: Emmanuel [?] Devroye, Imprimeur du Roi, 1863), 2: 572–574.

52. Maximilian to Albrecht of Bavaria, 1 Sept. 1568 [?], fo. 124. This document carries no date for the year. The contents clearly place it in 1568, but it has been numbered and stored among chronologically later materials on the microfiche.

53. Maximilian to Albrecht of Bavaria, 19 Sept. 1568, HSA, Kurbayern, Äußeres Archiv, no. 4462, fo. 37.

54. Robert Frettensattel, "Zu den Verhandlungen Maximilians II. mit Philipp II., 1568 und 1569," *MIöG* 24 (1903): 402; Bibl, "Frage," 384; Edelmayer, "Beziehungen," 144; Strakosch, "Materialen," 30–31.

55. Holtzmann, *Maximilian II.*, 115.

56. Philip to Maximilian, 6 Mar. 1567, in Bibl, *Korrespondenz*, part 2: 119; Max-

imilian to Albrecht of Bavaria, 16 Nov. 1567, ibid., 258; Memorandum [Dietrichstein?] to Philip, HHStA, Spanien, Varia (Spain, miscellaneous), 1527–1569, box 2, bundle 17, fo. 17; Chudoba, "Karl von Steiermark," 67.

57. Philip to Maximilian, 2 May 1563, BN, Madrid, Sección de manuscritos, no. 781, fos. 11–12. On Hungarian aid, see HHStA, Familienarchiv, Sammelbände, box 1, vol. 2, fos. 115–122. See also Viktor Bibl, "Die angebliche Textfälschung Kaiser Maximilians II. (Wortlaut einer Resolution König Philipps II. von Spanien)," *MIöG* 38 (1920): 438.

58. Report of Corraro, 1574, in Fiedler, *Relationen,* 30: 342; Bibl, "Textfälschung," 438.

59. Holtzmann, *Maximilian II.,* 191.

60. Philip to the head of the Council of Orders, 23 Mar. 1567, BN, Madrid, Sección de manuscritos, no. 781, fos. 114, 120; Maximilian to Albrecht of Bavaria, 6 Nov. 1568, HSA, Kurbayern, Äußeres Archiv, no. 4462, fo. 49; Edelmayer, "Gesandte," 63.

61. Constant, *Concession,* 103, 127; Adam von Dietrichstein to Maximilian, 6 June 1565, in Edelmayer, *Briefwechsel* 1: 393–394; Kamen, *Philip,* 232–233.

62. Granvella to Seld, 23 Jan. 1558, in *Briefe und Akten,* 5: 100–101.

63. Tagebuch, fo. 21.

64. Constant, *Concession,* 151, note 3.

65. Maximilian to the archbishop of Prague, 31 July 1564, SÚA, *Stará manipulace,* R109/1, part 1, box 1977, no folio; Count Hans Cobenzl to Archduke Ferdinand [?], 12 Oct. 1564, HHStA, Familienarchiv, Familienkorrespondenz A, box 38, fo. 67.

66. Susan Doran, "Religion and Politics at the Court of Elizabeth I: The Habsburg Marriage Negotiations of 1559–1567," *English Historical Review* 104 (1989): 915–916.

67. Maximilian to Ludwig Ungnad, 18 May 1564, HHStA, Hofarchiv, Alte Akten des Obersthofmarschallamtes, group 1, fasc. 1, bundle 1, fos. 8–9; Mandate of 1566 (copy) SOA, Třebon, Historica, no. 4621, no folio.

68. Maximilian to Pius V, 6 Oct. 1566, in Schwarz, *Briefe,* 2: 34–36; Maximilian to Pius V, 5 Dec. 1567, ibid., 77–78.

69. Robert Waissenberger, "Die hauptsächlichen Visitationen im Lande ob und unter der Enns sowie in Innerösterreich von 1528 bis 1580" (dissertation, University of Vienna, 1949), 5–6, 103–104.

70. Maximilian to Philip's ambassador in Rome, 17 Jan. 1567, HHStA, Familienarchiv, Sammelbände, box 1, vol. 2: fos. 61–65; Viktor Bibl, "Die Vorgeschichte der Religionskonzession Kaiser Maximilians II.," *Jahrbuch für Landeskunde von Niederösterreich,* n.s. 13–14 (1915): 403.

71. Constant, *Concession,* 676–679; Adam von Dietrichstein to Maximilian, 4–6 June 1565, in Edelmayer, *Briefwechsel,* 1: 393–394.

72. Edelmayer, "Beziehungen," 150; Maximilian to Archduchess Catherine, 1564 [?] 1565 [?] HHStA, Familienarchiv, Familienkorrespondenz A, box 3, fo. 552.

73. Maximilian and Archduke Charles to Archduke Ferdinand, 23 May 1567, in Bibl, *Korrespondenz*, part 2: 183.

74. For a detailed discussion, see Edelmayer, "Beziehungen," 146–156.

75. Constant, *Concession*, 119; Bibl, "Frage," 328–329; Edelmayer, "Beziehungen," 146 and note 562.

76. Zasius to Albrecht of Bavaria, [Jan. 1567?], in *Briefe und Akten*, 5: 378; Chantonnay to Philip, 25 Jan. 1567, CODOIN, 101: 154–155; Maria to Albrecht of Bavaria, 5 Nov. 1567, GHA, Korrespondenz-Akten, no. 593/2, fo. 321.

77. Vanegas to Philip, 6 Mar. 1568, CODOIN, 101: 397; Vanegas to Maximilian, 30 Sept. 1567, ibid., 290.

78. Chantonnay to Philip, 23 May 1567, CODOIN, 101: 218–219; Vanegas to Maximilian, 30 Sept. 1567, ibid., 290; Chantonnay to Philip, 28 Feb. 1568, ibid., 378; Chantonnay to Philip, 18 May 1568, ibid., 416, 418.

79. Ludwig Haberstock to Albrecht of Bavaria, 12 Oct. 1572, HSA, Kasten Schwarz, no. 14893, no folio. See also Haberstock to Albrecht of Bavaria, 10 Oct. 1572, HSA, Kasten Schwarz, no. 14893, no folio.

80. Chantonnay to Philip, 20 Sept. 1567, CODOIN, 101: 276.

81. Chantonnay to Philip, 12 Sept. 1569, CODOIN, 103: 283.

82. Heer, *Dritte Kraft*, 400; Philip to Vanegas, 23 May 1568, CODOIN, 101: 425; Philip to Chantonnay, 22 Oct. 1568, CODOIN, 103: 17–18.

83. Vanegas to Philip, 14 Oct. 1567, CODOIN, 101: 292; Philip to Vanegas, 28 Sept. 1568, ibid., 498; Vanegas to Philip, 23 Nov. 1568, CODOIN, 103: 54.

84. Holtzmann, *Maximilian II.*, 247; Widorn, "Gemahlinnen," 13–14; Noflatscher, "Erzherzog Maximilian," 1: 45.

85. Widorn, "Gemahlinnen," 14; Rodríguez-Salgado, *Changing Face*, 314; Maximilian to the count of Benavente, 10 Oct. 1564, AN, legajo 426/1, no. 12/3.

CHAPTER 9: DEFEATED AT ARMS, BROKEN IN SPIRIT

1. Maximilian to Philip, 7 Mar. 1567, in Bibl, *Korrespondenz*, part 2: 124; Gyula Káldy-Nagy, "The First Centuries of the Ottoman Military Organization," *Acta Orientalia Academiae Scientiarum Hungaricae* 31 (1977): 175.

2. Gernot Heiß, "Reformation und Gegenreformation, 1519–1618: Probleme und ihre Quellen," in *Die Quellen der Geschichte Österreichs*, Erich Zöllner, ed., Schriften des Instituts für Österreichkunde, vol. 40 (Vienna: Bundesverlag, 1982), 121; Karl Vocelka, "Die inneren Auswirkungen der Auseinandersetzungen Österreichs mit den Osmanen," *Südost-Forschungen* 36

(1977): 30; Rhoads Murphey, "Bigots or Informed Observers? A Periodization of Pre-Colonial English and European Writing on the Middle East," *Journal of the American Oriental Society* 110, no. 2 (1990): 301; C. Max Korpeter, "Habsburg and Ottoman in Hungary in the 16th and 17th Centuries," *Habsburgisch-osmanische Beziehungen*, Andreas Tietze, ed., Beihefte zur Wiener Zeitschrift für die Kunde des Morgenlandes, vol. 13 (Vienna: Verband der wissenschaftlichen Gesellschaften Österreichs, 1985), 55–56; Bérenger, *Empire*, 194.

3. Ferenc Szakály, "Der Wandel Ungarns in der Türkenzeit," in Tietze, *Habsburgisch-osmanische Beziehungen*, 36–38; Maximilian Grothaus, "Zum Türkenbild in der Kultur der Habsburgermonarchie zwischen dem 16. und 18. Jahrhundert," ibid., 71; and " 'Der Erbfeindt christlichen Namens': Studien zum Türken-Feindbild in der Kultur der habsburger Monarchie zwischen dem 16. und 18. Jahrhundert," 2 vols. (dissertation, University of Graz, 1986), 1: 37. See also, generally, Winfried Schulze, *Reich und Türkengefahr*.

4. Vernon J. Parry, "La manière de combattre," in *War, Technology and Society in the Middle East*, V. J. Parry and M. E. Yapp, eds. (London: Oxford University Press, 1975), 226; Halil Inalcik, "The Socio-Political Effects of the Diffusion of Fire-Arms in the Middle East," ibid., 198–199; Geoffrey Parker, *The Military Revolution: Military Innovation and the Rise of the West, 1500–1800* (Cambridge: Cambridge University Press, 1988), 126; and Káldy-Nagy, "Ottoman Military Organization," 169.

5. André Corvisier, *Armies and Societies in Europe, 1494–1789*, trans. Abigail T. Siddall (Bloomington: Indiana University Press, 1979), 47–48, 177. Similar systems existed in Poland and Hungary. See Parker, *Military Revolution*, 45–81.

6. Janko, *Schwendi*, 35–36; Regele, *Hofkriegsrat*, 17; Herold, "Hauptthemen," 184.

7. Regele, *Hofkriegsrat*, 16–17; Brusatti, "Reichskreise," 27, 70; Stephan Dworzak, "Georg Ilsung von Tratzberg" (dissertation, University of Vienna, 1954), 74–76.

8. "Unzucht, geschrey, schelten, Vexiren oder Leichtfertigkeit," Firnhaber, "Militärwesens," 140–141.

9. Ibid., 142–144; Fichtner, "Diary," 257; Tagebuch, fo. 66.

10. Maximilian Lanzinner, "Die Denkschrift des Lazarus von Schwendi zur Reichspolitik (1576)," *Zeitschrift für historische Forschung*, special series 3 (1987): 146; Eduard Heyck, "Briefe der Kaiser Maximilian II. und Rudolf II. an Lazarus Schwendi," *MIöG* 13 (1892): 164–165; Roman Schnur, "Lazarus von Schwendi, 1522–1583: Ein unerledigtes Thema der historischen Forschung," *Zeitschrift für historische Forschung* 14 (1987): 31, 38–40; Otto

Krabbe, *David Chyträus* (Rostock: Stiller, 1870), 219; Ernuszt, "Blotius," 12; Kleinpaul, *Nachrichtenwesen*, 12.

11. E.g., Lazarus Schwendi to Maximilian, 6 Oct. 1565, HHStA, Türkei (Turkey), 1, box 20, bundle 2, fo. 13; Janko, *Schwendi*, 54.

12. Janko, *Schwendi*, 36–42; Schwendi to Maximilian, 6 Oct. 1565, HHStA, Türkei, 1, box 20, bundle 2, fo. 13; Schwendi to Archduke Charles, 27 Jan. 1566 (copy), HHStA, Türkei, 1, box 21, bundle 1, fo. 69; Schulze, *Landesdefensionen*, 136, 143–144; Ertman, *Birth of the Leviathan*, 120.

13. Wolf Schreiber to Maximilian, 23 Apr. 1564, HHStA, Türkei, 1, box 18, bundle 2, fo. 199.

14. " 'Als wen sye der hagl hette an ire hals getroffen,' " Karl Vocelka, "Eine türkische Botschaft in Wien 1565," in *Beiträge zur neueren Geschichte Österreichs*, Heinrich Fichtenau and Erich Zöllner, eds. (Vienna: Böhlau, 1974), 103.

15. Eduard Wertheimer, "Zur Geschichte des Türkenkrieges Maximilians II., 1565 und 1566," *AöG* 53 (1875): 47; Kaufmann, *Imperial Theme*, 26–28.

16. Maximilian to the pasha of Buda, 26 June 1564, HHStA, Türkei, 1, box 18, bundle 3, fo. 21; Anton C. Schaendlinger and Claudia Römer, eds. *Die Schreiben Süleymans des Prächtigen an Karl V., Ferdinand I., und Maximilian II.*, Osmanisch-türkische Dokumente aus dem Haus-, Hof- und Staatsarchiv zu Wien, vol. 1 (Vienna: Österreichische Akademie der Wissenschaften, 1983), 91–93, 95–96.

17. Hungarian Council to Maximilian, 6 July 1564, HHStA, Türkei, 1, box 18, bundle 4, fo. 128; Süleyman to Maximilian, 21–30 July 1564, HHStA, Türkei, 1, box 18, bundle 4, fo. 141; Schaendlinger, *Schreiben*, 86.

18. Maximilian to Selim [?] pasha of Buda [?], 27 June 1564, HHStA, Türkei, 1, box 18, bundle 4, fo. 25; Maximilian to Süleyman, 17 [?]18 [?] August 1564, HHStA, Türkei, 1, box 18, bundle 4, fo. 178; Vocelka, "Botschaft," 104.

19. Herold, "Landtagshandlungen," 150; Hungarian councillors to Maximilian, 16 Aug. 1564, HHStA, Türkei, 1, box 18, bundle 4, fo. 168.

20. Wertheimer, "Türkenkrieg," 48–49; Count Hans Cobenzl to Archduke Ferdinand, 27 Sept. 1564, Vienna, HHStA, Familienarchiv, Familienkorrespondenz A, box 38, fo. 55; Archduke Ferdinand to Albrecht of Bavaria, 10 Nov. 1564, GHA, Korrespondenz-Akten, 597/1, fo. 51.

21. Janko, *Schwendi*, 46–50; Wertheimer, "Türkenkrieg," 48–49, 52, 55–56; Maximilian to Süleyman, 11 Oct. 1565, HHStA, Türkei, 1, box 20, bundle 2, fo. 52; Vocelka, "Botschaft," 109.

22. Lazarus von Schwendi to Maximilian, 15 Sept. 1565, HHStA, Türkei, 1, bundle 18, fos. 89–90; Lower Austrian Council to Maximilian, 4 Nov. 1565, HHStA, Türkei, 1, box 20, bundle 3, fos. 154–156; Parry, "Manière," 218–219, 223–224, 226–227.

23. "Muess man sich von des hohen fallens wegen, vor dem hohen steigen dest

mehr besorgen," Lazarus Schwendi to Maximilian, 15 Sept. 1565 [excerpt], HHStA, Türkei, 1, box 20, bundle 1, fo. 90; Lazarus Schwendi to Maximilian, 26 Sept. 1565, HHStA, Türkei, 1, box 20, bundle 1, fos. 81, 90–91; Archduke Ferdinand to Maximilian, 21 Feb. 1566, in Bibl, *Korrespondenz*, part 1: 417–418.

24. Zasius to Albrecht of Bavaria, 29 May 1565, HSA, Kurbayern, Äußeres Archiv, no. 4299, fo. 178.

25. Johann Petheu [Petho] to Maximilian, 30 Oct. 1565, HHStA, Türkei, 1, box 20, bundle 2, fo. 76; Maximilian to Johann Petheu, 3 Nov. 1565, HHStA, Türkei, 1, bundle 3, fo. 144; Johann Petheu to Maximilian, 13 Nov. 1565, HHStA, Türkei, 1, bundle 3, fo. 190; Alfred Sitte, "Tschausch Hedajets Aufenthalt in Wien, 1565," *Archiv für Kulturgeschichte* 6 (1908): 192–201; Wertheimer, "Türkenkrieg," 77. Petho (Petheu) was Maximilian's commandant in the fortress at Komorn.

26. Wertheimer, "Türkenkrieg," 69–70; Johannes Petheu [Petho] to Maximilian, 13 Nov. 1565, HHStA, Türkei, 1, box 20, bundle 3, fos. 190–191; Memorandum to Hosszútoti mission, Jan. 1566, HHStA, Türkei, 1, box 21, bundle 1, fo. 110; Vocelka, "Botschaft," 114.

27. Josef Zontar, "Michael Cernovic, Geheimagent Ferdinands I. und Maximilians II., und seine Berichterstattung," *Mitteilungen des österreichischen Staatsarchivs* 24 (1971): 216–217; Vocelka, "Botschaft," 112.

28. Archduke Ferdinand to Albrecht of Bavaria, 9 Mar. 1565, GHA, Korrespondenz-Akten, 597/1, fo. 59; Archduke Charles to Maximilian, 28 Nov. 1565, in Bibl, *Korrespondenz*, part 1: 323; Zontar, "Cernovic," 219.

29. HHStA, Türkei, 1, box 21, bundle 2, fo. 174.

30. Lower Austrian Estates to Archduke Charles, 24 Nov. 1565, HHStA, Türkei, 1, box 20, bundle 3, fos. 222, 227.

31. Lazarus Schwendi to Maximilian, 17 Nov. 1565, HHStA, Türkei, 1, box 20, bundle 3, fo. 206; Wertheimer, "Türkenkrieg," 52, 60.

32. Káldy-Nagy, "Ottoman Military Organization," 170, 178–181.

33. Rodríguez-Salgado, *Changing Face*, 29; Ernst Martin, "Lazarus von Schwendi und seine Schriften," *Zeitschrift für die Geschichte des Oberrheins*, n.s. 8 (1893): 399.

34. Endre Marosi, "Die ungarische Kampf gegen die Türken, 1352–1718: Ein historischer Überblick," *Die Türkenkriege in der historischen Forschung*, Zygmunt Abrahamowicz et al., eds. (Vienna: Deuticke, 1983), 130; Parker, *Military Revolution*, 8, 12, 130.

35. Walter Hollweg, *Der Augsburger Reichstag von 1566 und seine Bedeutung für die Entstehung der reformierten Kirche und ihres Bekenntnisses*, Beiträge zur Geschichte und Lehre der reformierten Kirchen, vol. 17 (1964), 301; Wertheimer, "Türkenkrieg," 64–67.

36. Schulze, *Reich und Türkengefahr*, 309.

37. Ibid., 63; Adam von Dietrichstein to Maximilian, 9 May 1566, in Koch, *Quellen*, 1: 164–165.

38. Adam von Dietrichstein to Maximilian, 16 Apr. 1565, in Koch, *Quellen*, 1: 138; Adam von Dietrichstein to Maximilian, [?] May 1565, ibid., 139; Adam von Dietrichstein to Maximilian, 30 June 1565, ibid., 145.

39. Bibl, "Erhebung," 12–13, 18–20; Koch, *Quellen*, 1: 108–109.

40. Maximilian to Albrecht of Bavaria, 13 Aug. 1565, *Freiherrn von Freybergs Sammlung historischer Schriften und Urkunden*, Wilhelm Freiherr von Freyberg, ed., 5 vols. (Stuttgart: Cotta, 1827–1836), 4: 144.

41. SÚA, Patenty, 1561–1566, box 2, patents of 15 Dec. 1564 and 14 Apr. 1565; Lazarus von Schwendi to Archduke Charles, 20 Mar. 1566, HHStA, Türkei, 1, box 21, bundle 2, fo. 224.

42. Maximilian's Instructions for Christoph Teufel, HKA, Gedenkbücher, 98 (1565), fos. 355–361.

43. Lazarus Schwendi to Maximilian, 14 Feb. 1566, HHStA, Türkei, 1, box 21, bundle 2, fo. 141; Lazarus Schwendi to Archduke Charles, 7 Apr. 1566, HHStA, Türkei, 1, box 21, bundle 3, fo. 21; Wertheimer, "Türkenkrieg," 81–82.

44. Franz von Thurn to Conrad zu Pappenheim, 14 Mar. 1566, HHStA, Türkei, 1, box 21, bundle 2, fo. 199; report of von Thurn's questioning, Mar. [?] Apr. [?] 1566, HHStA, Türkei, 1, box 21, bundle 3, fos. 41–43. See also report of Ogier de Busbecq, 29 May 1566, HHStA, Türkei, 1, box 21, bundle 3, fos. 67–69.

45. Hungarian councilors to Maximilian, 6 July 1564, HHStA, Türkei, 1, box 18, bundle 4, fos. 128–129; Michael Zarnoujgio [Cernovic] to Maximilian, 13 Aug. 1564, HHStA, Türkei, 1, box 18, bundle 4, fo. 155.

46. Johannes Petheu [Petho] to Maximilian, 8 May 1564, HHStA, Türkei, 1, box 18, bundle 2, fos. 213–214. This is undated. For evidence to support my dating, see Paulus de Palina to Maximilian, 8 May 1564, HHStA, Türkei, 1, box 18, bundle 2, fo. 215; and Johannes Petheu to Maximilian, 16 May 1564, HHStA, Türkei, 1, box 18, bundle 2, fo. 219. See also Johannes Petheu to Maximilian, 16 May 1564, HHStA, Türkei, 1, box 18, bundle 2, fo. 218; and Johann Petheu to Maximilian, 17 May 1564, HHStA, Türkei, 1, box 18, bundle 2, fo. 221.

47. Schulze, *Reich und Türkengefahr*, 23 and note 4, 29–30; Johannes Petheu to Maximilian, 22 Oct. 1565, HHStA, Türkei, 1, box 20, bundle 2, fo. 47. For evidence of the Turkish translators, see HHStA, Türkei, 1, box 18, bundle 4, fos. 141–142, 159.

48. Eck von Salm to Maximilian, 16 Dec. 1566, HHStA, Türkei, 1, box 21, bundle 5, fo. 74.

49. Zontar, "Cernovic," 212–213.

50. Albert de Wyss [?] to Maximilian, 31 Jan. 1566, HHStA, Türkei, 1, box 21, bundle 1, fo. 102; Káldy-Nagy, "Ottoman Military Organization," 182–183.

51. Count Hans Cobenzl to Archduke Ferdinand, 25 Oct. 1564, HHStA, Familienarchiv, Familienkorrespondenz A, box 38, "Erzherzog Ferdinand," fo. 68; Albert de Wyss [?] to Maximilian, 10 Feb. 1566 (copy), HHStA, Türkei 1, box 21, bundle 2, fo. 131; Albert de Wyss to Maximilian, 29 Apr. 1566 (copy), HHStA, Türkei, 1, box 21, bundle 3, fo. 48; Janko, *Schwendi,* 69.

52. Janko, *Schwendi,* 55, 64.

53. Maximilian to Wilhelm of Rožmberk, 25 July 1566, SOA, Třebon, Historica, no. 4658; Tagebuch, fo. 5; Hans Gerstinger, ed., *Aus dem Tagebuch des kaiserlichen Hofhistoriographen Johannes Sambucus, 1531–1584,* Österreichische Akademie der Wissenschaften, philosophische-historische Klasse, Sitzungsberichte 248, no. 2 (Graz: Böhlau, 1965), 16.

54. "Erliche lait," Maximilian to Albrecht of Bavaria, 9 Aug. 1566, GHA, Korrespondenz-Akten, 593/2, fo. 142.

55. "Und meniklich sehen sollen, das nix unterlassen sol werden, so an gefar und verletzung der reputation beschehen kan, wie man dan schan in der beratschlagung ist," Maximilian to Albrecht of Bavaria, 24 Aug. 1566, in Bibl, *Korrespondenz,* part 2: 7.

56. Maximilian to Count Frederick de Camerano, HHStA, Familienarchiv, Sammelbände, box 1, vol. 2, fos. 43–44; Maximilian to Wilhelm of Rožmberk, 6 Aug. 1566, SOA, Třebon, Historica, no. 4673; Tagebuch, fos. 3, 5.

57. "Mit hellen haufen in gottes namen," Khevenhüller, *Tagebuch,* 25; Report on troop movement in SOA, Třebon, Historica, no. 4677a; Tagebuch, fo. 5; Bibl, *Maximilian II.,* 145–146, 148.

58. Tagebuch, fo. 11; Bibl, *Maximilian II.,* 151–152; Wertheimer, "Türkenkrieg," 95–96. Cf. Georg Wagner, "Maximilian II., der Wiener Hof und die Belagerung von Sziget," in *Szigetvári Emlékönyv. Szigetvár 1566: Évi ostromának 400. Évfordulojára,* Lajos Rúzsás ed. (Budapest: Akadémiai Kiadó, 1966), 260, note 64. Wagner's comment (p. 245) that such behavior put Maximilian at considerable disadvantage militarily does not seem wholly justified. Some of the worst defeats Western armies suffered against the Turks were the result of reckless behavior. The battle of Mohács in 1526 was a conspicuous example. See Paula Sutter Fichtner, "An Absence Explained: Archduke Ferdinand of Austria and the Battle of Mohacs," *Austrian History Yearbook* 2 (1966): 11–17.

59. Wagner, "Sziget," 237, note 1, 249; Bibl, *Maximilian II.,* 145–146, 148; Wertheimer, "Türkenkrieg," 91; Khevenhüller, *Tagebuch,* 27.

60. Cf. Wagner, "Sziget," 242.

61. "Est homo periculosus et falsus," Tagebuch, fo. 11.

62. Kálman Benda, "Zrinyi Miklos, a szigetváry hős," in Rúzsás, *Szigetvári,* 46;

Wertheimer, "Türkenkrieg," 85–87; Bibl, *Maximilian II.*, 151–152; Wagner, "Sziget," 257; Koch, *Quellen*, 1: 100; Tagebuch, fo. 12.

63. Koch, *Quellen*, 1: 100; Káldy-Nagy, "Ottoman Military Organization," 171.

64. "Ich wolt, das die prekin in einen sackh schtekt und was nit wo ware," Maximilian to Albrecht of Bavaria, 18 Oct. 1566, in Bibl, *Korrespondenz*, part 2: 36. See also ibid., 38, note 3; Tagebuch, fo. 15; and H. C. Erik Midelfort, *Mad Princes of Renaissance Germany* (Charlottesville: University of Virginia Press, 1994), 128–129.

65. Maximilian to Albrecht of Bavaria, 29 Sept. 1568, in Bibl, *Korrespondenz*, part 2: 28–30; Maximilian to Albrecht of Bavaria, 18 Oct. 1566, ibid., 35; Hirn, *Ferdinand von Tirol*, 2: 293–295; Wertheimer, "Türkenkrieg," 92.

66. Wagner, "Sziget," 257, 261; Koch, *Quellen*, 1: 100; Tagebuch, fos. 15–16.

67. "Ist alles betrug," Tagebuch, fo. 69.

68. Ibid., fos. 16, 18, 26.

69. Zasius to Albrecht of Bavaria, 18 Oct. 1566, HSA, Kurbayern, Äußeres Archiv, no. 4301, fo. 257; Tagebuch, fo. 31.

70. In 1604, Karl von Liechtenstein, briefly the *Obersthofmeister* for Rudolph II, was still asking for a civilian war commissioner to oversee musters, loans, and payments, as well as to facilitate communications between the war council and the treasury. Fellner, *Zentralverwaltung*, 1: 243.

71. Maximilian to Albrecht of Bavaria, 15 Feb. 1568, HSA, Kurbayern, Äußeres Archiv, no. 4462, fo. 21; Herold, "Hauptthemen," 136–137.

72. Archduke Ferdinand to Maximilian, 23 Apr. 1567, in Bibl, *Korrespondenz*, part 2: 158, 160.

73. Maximilian's Instructions to Verantius, Wyss, and Teuffenbach, 25 June 1567, Miller, *Epistolae*, 213; Tagebuch, fos. 51, 56; Zontar, "Cernovic," 213–214.

74. Tagebuch, fos. 34–35.

75. Wertheimer, "Türkenkrieg," 92–93; Rodríguez-Salgado, *Changing Face*, 74–75; Report of Giovanni Michele, 1571, in Fiedler, *Relationen*, 30: 282.

76. Maximilian to Ferdinand and Charles, 23 Oct. 1566, in Bibl, *Korrespondenz*, part 2: 38–42; Biglia to Alessandrino, 28 Nov. 1566, in *Nuntiaturberichte aus Deutschland*, Ignaz Philip Dengel, ed., part 2, vol. 6 (Vienna: Holzhausen, 1939): 27–28.

77. "Tol und unsinnig," Maximilian to Albrecht of Bavaria, 29 Sept. 1566, in Bibl, *Korrespondenz*, part 2: 28–30.

78. Hungarian councillors to Maximilian, Nov.–Dec. 1566, HHStA, Türkei, 1, box 21, bundle 5, fo. 138; Austrian memorandum, 28 Dec. 1566, HHStA, Türkei, 1, box 21, bundle 5, fos. 100–105; Bohemian council of princes [*sic*], councillors, officers of the kingdom to Maximilian, 29 Dec. 1566, HHStA, Türkei, 1, box 21, bundle 5, fos. 115–118; Albrecht of Bavaria to Maximilian, 8 Jan. 1567, in Bibl, *Korrespondenz*, part 2: 88–90; Charles to Maximilian, 19

Nov. 1567, HHStA, Türkei, 1, box 21, bundle 5, 260; Ferdinand to Maximilian, 19 Nov. 1567, HHStA, Türkei, 1, box 21, bundle 5, 266–267; Ferdinand to Maximilian, 24 Nov. 1567, HHStA, Türkei, 1, box 21, bundle 5, 271. See also Tagebuch, fo. 72.

79. Tagebuch, fo. 61; Bibl, "Erhebung," 21, 23–24; Schwarz, *Briefe*, 1: 105, 107; Maximilian to Pius V, 3 Feb. 1570, ibid., 153–154; Opinion of Cardinal Delfino, 15 Dec. 1566, HHStA, Türkei 1, box 21, bundle 5, fo. 68.

80. Chantonnay to Philip, 30 Aug. 1567, CODOIN, 101, 265; Lazarus Schwendi to Archduke Charles, 4 Mar. 1566, HHStA, Türkei, 1, box 21, bundle 2, fo. 176; Lazarus Schwendi to Maximilian, 10 Mar. 1568 (excerpt), HHStA, Ungarn, fasc. 95, fo. 48.

81. Karl Teply, "Das österreichische Türkenkriegszeitalter," in Abrahamowicz, *Türkenkriege*, 31; Herold "Hauptthemen," 172, 182.

82. Maximilian to Albrecht of Bavaria, 29 Sept. 1566, in Bibl, *Korrespondenz*, part 2: 28–30; Report of Hungarian campaign to leaders of the imperial German circles in Erfurt, 1567, in Koch, *Quellen*, 1: 99.

83. Janko, *Schwendi*, frontispiece.

CHAPTER 10: CHRISTIANS DIVIDED

1. "Sekty, Bludy, Ruznice a Nejednoty," Patent of 21 May 1567, SÚA, Patenty, 1567–1579, box 3, no folio. This particular order carries Maximilian's personal signature.

2. Mandate against Jews trading in the mining cities of Bohemia, 6 Aug. 1568 (copy), SÚA, Patenty, 1567–1579, box 3, no folio.

3. Theodor Wiedemann, *Geschichte der Reformation und Gegenreformation im Lande unter der Enns*, 5 vols. (Prague: Tempsky, 1879–1886), 1: 351.

4. Winfried Schulze, "Concordia, Discordia, Tolerantia: Deutsche Politik im konfessionellen Zeitalter," *Zeitschrift für historische Forschung* special issue 3 (Berlin: Duncker and Humblot, 1987): 51; Maximilian to Archbishop Johann Jakob of Salzburg, 4 Nov. 1564, in Hopfen, *Kompromißkatholizismus*, 215–217.

5. Ulrich Eisenhardt, as cited in Hartmut Lehmann, *Das Zeitalter des Absolutismus: Gottesgnadentum und Kriegsnot* (Stuttgart: Kohlhammer, 1980), 53.

6. Ibid., 52.

7. Bibl, "Frage," 365–366; Volker Press, "Wilhelm von Oranien, die deutschen Reichsstände und der niederländische Aufstand," *Bijdragen en Mededelingen betreffende de Geschiedenis der Nederlanden* 99 (1984): 679; Fritz Dickmann, "Das Problem der Gleichberechtigung der Konfessionen im Reich im 16. und 17. Jahrhundert," *Historische Zeitschrift* 201 (1965): 276, 278; Maximilian to Prosper d'Arco, 30 Aug. 1565, in Hopfen, *Kompromißkatholizismus*, 227.

8. Gustav Reingrabner, "Zur Geschichte der flacianische Bewegung im Lande unter der Enns," *Jahrbuch für Landeskunde von Niederösterreich,* n.s. 54–55 (1988–1989): 268; Oliver K. Olson, "Matthias Flacius Illyricus, 1520–1575," *Shapers of Religious Traditions in Germany, Switzerland, and Poland, 1560–1600,* Jill Raitt, ed. (New Haven, Conn.: Yale University Press, 1981): 13; Hollweg, *Reichstag,* 107.

9. "Wie dan in ainer klainen zeit draierla vnterschidliche confessiones saind aufgericht worden," Tagebuch, fo. 1. See also fo. 53.

10. John Hesselink, "The Dramatic Story of the Heidelberg Catechism," in *Later Calvinism: International Perspectives,* W. Fred Graham, ed., Sixteenth Century Essays and Studies, vol. 22 (Kirksville, Mo.: Sixteenth Century Journal, 1994): 285; Fred H. Klooster, "Calvin's Attitude to the Heidelberg Catechism," in Graham, ibid., 312–313; Lazarus Schwendi to Maximilian, 4 May 1560, HHStA, Familienarchiv, Familienkorrespondenz A, box 3, bundle Kh.-W., fo. 397; Lazarus von Schwendi to Maximilian, 22 June 1560, HHStA, Familienarchiv, Familienkorrespondenz A, box 3, bundle Kh.-W., fo. 401.

11. Jerome de Cock to Maximilian, 26 June 1562, HHStA, Familienarchiv, Familienkorrespondenz A, box 2, bundle 3, fo. 453; Silliers to Maximilian (excerpt), Mar. 1563, HHStA, Familienarchiv, Familienkorrespondenz A, box 3, bundle Kh.-W, fo. 443.

12. Holtzmann, *Maximilian II.,* 426, 439.

13. "Die verdamliche vnd aus dem gemainen Reichs Religion vnd prophan friden außgeschaidner vnd excludierte bose Sect Suinglianismj vnd Calvinismj viler stenden vnd deren zugethanen Christen Menschn Conscientz unnd gewüssen zum hogstn zuwid [?], und mitt gantz beschwärlicher unzimblicher betrangnuss derselben Irer gewüssen einzufüren und mitt zwang und gewaldt ansurichten [?] . . . velliches alles zum maisten thaill dem claaren Innhalt und Puechstab nitt allain unsers und des Hailln. Reiches Religie [?] und prophanfridens sonder auch der augspurgischen Confession selbst gestrackhs entgegen und zuwider," Maximilian's Instructions for Timotheus Jung, 1565 (copy), HSA, Kurbayern, Äußeres Archiv, no. 4289, fo. 322.

14. Hollweg, *Reichstag,* 107–108; Hesselink, "Story," 277–278; Henry J. Cohn, "The Territorial Princes in Germany's 'Second Reformation,'" in Menna Prestwich, ed., *International Calvinism, 1541–1715* (Oxford: Clarendon Press, 1985), 148. On the development of Maximilian's positions with the elector palatine and the attitude of German princes toward the spread of Calvinism, see Edel, *Kaiser,* 191–203.

15. Maximilian to Archbishop Daniel of Mainz, 4 Apr. 1565, HHStA, Mainzer Erzkanzlerarchiv, Reichskanzlei und Taxamt, fasc. 1, fo. 490; Maximilian to Peter of Rožmberk, 22 Nov. 1565, SOA, Třebon, Historica, no. 4564.

16. For a detailed analysis of the recreational and social aspects of diets, see

Aulinger, *Reichstag,* esp. parts 3 and 5; and Kohler, "Wohnen und Essen," passim.

17. Hollweg, *Reichstag,* 246; Aulinger, *Reichstag,* 197, note 18; 206–207, 303, 353.

18. Rübsam, "Mameranus," 540–541; Nikolaus Didier, *Nikolaus Mameranus: Ein luxemburger Humanist des XVI. Jahrhunderts am Hofe der Habsburger, sein Leben und seine Werke* (Freiburg: Herder, 1915), 177–178.

19. Rudersdorf, "Maximilian II.," 89–90; Press, "Wilhelm von Oranien," 679; Edel, *Kaiser,* 208.

20. " 'Zu richtigen verstand zu bringen,' " Bibl, *Maximilian II.,* 132.

21. Cited in Hollweg, *Reichstag,* 343.

22. Ibid., 284; SOA, Třebon, Historica, no. 4569; Edel, *Kaiser,* 209, 220.

23. Neuhaus, *Representationsformen,* 26–27.

24. Hollweg, *Reichstag,* 246–247, 269, 280, 292.

25. Ibid., 266, 298.

26. Pius to Maximilian, 25 Jan. 1566, in Schwarz, *Briefe,* 1: 6; Maximilian to Pius, 27 Mar. 1566, ibid., 17.

27. The details of these discussions are found in Hollweg, *Reichstag,* 331–386. See also Edel, *Kaiser,* 210–234.

28. Maximilian to Pius, 1 July 1566 (summary), in Schwarz, *Briefe,* 1: 30; Pius to Maximilian, 12 July 1566 (summary), ibid., 33.

29. *Nuntiaturberichte aus Deutschland,* Ignaz Philip Dengel, ed., part 2, vol. 5 (Vienna: Hölder/Pichler/Tempsky, 1926): 232, note 2; Tagebuch, fo. 57. Cf. Tagebuch fo. 78.

30. Maximilian to Albrecht of Bavaria, 19 Jan. 1567, in Bibl, *Korrespondenz,* part 2: 97.

31. Albrecht of Bavaria to Maximilian, 27 Apr. 1564, HHStA, Staatenabteilung, Bavarica, fasc. 3, no folio; Rudersdorf, "Maximilian II.," 90, 94; Volker Press, "Wilhelm von Grumbach und die deutsche Adelskrise der 1560en Jahre," *Blätter für deutsche Landesgeschichte* 113 (1977): 399, 401, 408–416, 429. For a detailed account of the conspiracy, see Friedrich Ortloff, *Geschichte der grumbachischen Handel,* 4 vols. (Jena: Fromann, 1868–1870). Koch, *Quellen,* 1: 42–53, has a useful summary.

32. Tagebuch, fo. 25; Press, "Grumbach," 416; Brusatti, "Reichskreise," 22.

33. Maximilian to Margaret of Parma, 9 Mar. 1567, in Bibl, *Korrespondenz,* part 2: 134, 135, note 3; Ortloff, *Handel,* 4: 247; Tagebuch, fo. 74; Press, "Grumbach," 417.

34. Citation of Maximilian to Margaret of Parma, 9 Mar. 1567, in Bibl, *Korrespondenz,* part 2: 134. See also Bibl, "Frage," 368; and Maximilian to Christoph of Württemberg, 13 Mar. 1567, in Koch, *Quellen,* 1: 53.

35. Tagebuch, fo. 86.

36. Press, "Grumbach," 430; Chantonnay to Philip II, 24 May 1567, in Koch, *Quellen*, 2: 39–40. See also Biglia to Alessandrino, 27 June 1567, in *Nuntiaturberichte*, part 2, vol. 6: 79; and Bibl, *Maximilian II.*, 123.

37. Fichtner, *Protestantism*, 19; Tagebuch, fo. 41; HKA, Gedenkbücher, 109 (1569–1570), passim.

38. Maximilian to Albrecht of Bavaria, 17 Apr. 1567, in Bibl, *Korrespondenz*, part 2: 151.

39. Archduke Ferdinand to Maximilian, 23 Apr. 1567, ibid., 159.

40. Da du empfingest die gülden kron,
    Has du das Evangelion zugesagt.
    Denk, ob es denn auch Gott so behagt
    Wenn izt die Hur von Babylon
    Gefördert wird durch deine Kron.
    Der Höchste sitzt in seinem Thron,
    Und hat für lengst gezelet schon
    Die Tag und Stund des Szepters Dein.
    Die Zeit, di ist hie kurz und klein.

    Bibl, *Maximilian II.*, 165. A copy of the pamphlet is in HHStA, Staatenabteilung, Saxonica, 5, fos. 10–21.

41. Sigmund Melanthon to Elector Frederick, n.d. 1567 [?], HSA, Kurbayern, Äußeres Archiv, no. 4302, fo. 290; Johann Ulrich Zasius to Albrecht of Bavaria, 15 Nov. 1567, HSA, Kurbayern, Äußeres Archiv, no. 4302, fos. 342–344; Edel, *Kaiser*, 263–266.

42. Maximilian to Christoph of Württemberg, 12 Apr. 1567, in Le Bret, *Magazin*, 9: 257–258; Josef Benzing, *Die Buchdrucker des 16. und 17. Jahrhunderts im deutschen Sprachgebiet* (Wiesbaden: Harrassowitz, 1963), 183.

43. Maximilian to the Frankfurt city council, 10 Apr. 1567, in Koch, *Quellen*, 1: 7–9, 20, 24; Robert M. Kingdon, *Myths About the St. Bartholomew's Day Massacre, 1572–1576* (Cambridge, Mass.: Harvard University Press, 1988), 15.

44. Koch, *Quellen*, 2: 25.

45. Wolfgang Brückner, "Die Gegenreformation im politischen Kampf um die Frankfurter Buchmessen: Die kaiserliche Zensur zwischen 1567 und 1619," *Archiv für Frankfurts Geschichte und Kunst* 48 (1960): 68; Edel, *Kaiser*, 267–270.

46. Chantonnay to Philip, 20 Sept. 1567, in Koch, *Quellen*, 2: 46–47.

47. Maximilian to Pius V, 10 Aug. 1567, in Schwarz, *Briefe*, 1: 65; Maximilian to Pius V, 3 Sept. 1567, ibid., 68–70; Walter Platzhoff, "Vom Interregnum bis zur französischen Revolution, 1250–1789," in Hermann Aubin, Theodor Fimas, and Josef Müller, *Geschichte des Rheinlandes von der ältesten Zeit bis zur Gegenwart*, 2 vols. (Essen: Baedeker, 1922), 1: 212.

48. Maximilian to Archduke Ferdinand, 31 Aug. 1567, in Bibl, *Korrespondenz*, part 2: 220; Maximilian to Archduke Ferdinand, 9 Nov. 1567, ibid., 275; Vanegas to Philip, 31 Mar. 1568, CODOIN, 101: 409.

49. "Wenn die predig auss wär, solt niemand, Er auch selbs, nit wissen was er predigt hett," HHStA, Familienarchiv, Familienkorrespondenz A, box 3, bundle Kh.-W., fo. 285. See also Tagebuch, fo. 1.

50. Theodor von Sickel, "Das Reformationslibell des Kaisers Ferdinand I. vom Jahre 1562 bis zur Absendung nach Trient," *AöG* 45 (1871): 6–7; Grete Mecenseffy, *Geschichte des Protestantismus in Österreich* (Graz: Böhlau, 1956), 44–49.

51. Bibl, *Maximilian II.*, 127, 198.

52. "Bese lait," Tagebuch, fo. 39.

53. KA, Alte Feldakten, 1566–1569, VII-1; Joseph F. Patrouch, "The Investiture Controversy Revisited: Religious Reform, Emperor Maximilian II, and the Klosterrat," *Austrian History Yearbook* 25 (1994): 59–68. Cf. Hopfen, *Kompromißkatholizismus*, 385, 402–406. See also Theodor Brückler, "Zum Problem der katholischen Reform in Niederösterreich in der zweiten Hälfte des 16. Jahrhunderts," *Österreich in Geschichte und Literatur* 21 (1977): 153.

54. "Est talis qualis," Tagebuch, fo. 47.

55. Tagebuch, fos. 1, 43, 45, 76. Cf. Eisengrein to Albrecht of Bavaria, 6 Feb. 1569, in Hopfen, *Kompromißkatholizismus*, 316–317.

56. Maximilian to Prosper d'Arco, 2 Feb. 1565, in Hopfen, *Kompromißkatholizismus*, 223. See also Maximilian to Prosper d'Arco, 13 Mar. 1565, ibid., 224–225; Maximilian to Prosper d'Arco, 4 Dec. 1565, ibid., 231–232; Tagebuch, fo. 29; and Waissenberger, "Visitationen," 104.

57. Tagebuch, fo. 37. Anna is not specifically mentioned in the entry, but she was the only one of Maximilian's sisters to have a son by that name.

58. Maximilian to Pius V, 4 Mar. 1567, in Schwarz, *Briefe*, 1: 553; Constant, *Concession*, 680, 682–683.

59. Waissenberger, "Visitationen," 104–113; Maximilian to Pius V, 3 Mar. 1568, in Schwarz, *Briefe*, 1, 96–97, 99; Patrouch, "Klosterrat," 68–71.

60. Oswald von Gschliesser, *Der Reichshofrat: Bedeutung und Verfassung, Schicksal und Besetzung einer obersten Reichsbehörde von 1559–1806*, Veröffentlichungen der Kommission für neuere Geschichte Österreichs, vol. 33 (Vienna: Holzhausen, 1942): 112–113, 135.

61. Mecenseffy, "Maximilian II," 48; Bibl, "Organisation," 177.

62. Tagebuch, fo. 43.

63. Herbert Krimm, "Die Agende der niederösterreichischen Stände im Jahre 1571," *Jahrbuch für die Geschichte des Protestantismus in Österreich* 55 (1934): 5; Bibl, "Organisation," 135–136; Reingrabner, "Flacianische Bewegung,"

269–270. Cf. Georg Loesche, *Geschichte des Protestantismus in Österreich* (Vienna: Manz, 1921), 25–26.

64. Schwendi to William of Orange, 9 Nov. 1565, van Prinsterer, *Archives* 1: 288; Evans, *Making*, 13.

65. Mecenseffy, *Protestantismus*, 50–51; Karl Gutkas, *Geschichte des Landes Niederösterreich*, 3 vols. (St. Pölten, Austria: Kulturreferat der niederösterreichischen Landesregierung, 1957–1959), 2: 207; Bibl, "Organisation," 119–121; Karin J. MacHardy, "Social Mobility and Noble Rebellion in Early Modern Habsburg Austria," in *Nobilities in Central and Eastern Europe: Kinship, Property and Privilege*, János M. Bak, ed., History and Society in Central Europe 2/ vol. 29 (Budapest: Hajnal Society, 1994), 103.

66. " 'Sonst nicht die suppen vermöchten, wann es on der k. Mt. dienst wäre,' " cited in Helleiner, "Denkschrift," 201. For the financial position of the nobility, ibid., 201–202.

67. "Ow ichs auch ex plena potestate den schtenden mög auflegen oder ow es mit den lantlaitn zu beratschlagen sai ow auch auf kunftigen lantag ich solliches welle an die schtend langen lassen ante in vel post dietam," Tagebuch, fo. 1.

68. Herold, "Hauptprobleme," 111, 113–115, 133. Ferdinand I's permission for this had extended only to the diocese of Vienna.

69. Herold, "Hauptprobleme," 140; Otto Krabbe, *David Chyträus* (Rostock: Stiller, 1870), 195, 204–205; Hans Sturmberger, *Adam Graf Herberstorff: Herrschaft und Freiheit im konfessionellen Zeitalter* (Vienna: Verlag für Geschichte und Politik, 1976), 73.

70. Tagebuch, fos. 68–69; Maximilian to Albrecht of Bavaria, 5 Aug. 1564, HSA, Kurbayern, Äußeres Archiv, no. 4231, fo. 230.

71. Karl Gutkas, "Landesfürst, Landtag und Städte Niederösterreichs im 16. Jahrhundert," *Jahrbuch für Landeskunde von Niederösterreich*, n.s. 36 (1964): 311, 313–315, 319; Viktor Bibl, "Maximilians II Erklärung vom 18. Aug. 1568 über die Ertheilung des Religions-Concession," *MIöG* 20 (1899): 637–638; Tagebuch, fo. 29.

72. "Vor allen dingen die er gottes befurdern sünd schand vnd laster awschtellen vnd sich mit gott verainigen vnd versienen sine qua re factum est nihil," Tagebuch, fo. 27.

73. Krabbe, *Chyträus*, 195, 198, 204–205; Bibl, "Organisation," 133–134; Krimm, "Agende," part 1, 8; Mecenseffy, *Protestantismus*, 52.

74. "Piscis putrescit in capite," in Hopfen, *Kompromißkatholizismus*, 273; Tagebuch, fos. 50, 56; Philip Soergel, *Wondrous in His Saints: Counter-Reformation Propaganda in Bavaria* (Berkeley: University of California Press, 1993), 105–107, 109–110.

75. Martin Eisengrein to Albrecht of Bavaria, 17 Sept. 1568, in Hopfen, *Kompromißkatholizismus*, 279–282.

76. Martin Eisengrein to Albrecht of Bavaria, 23 Oct. 1568, HSA, Kurbayern, Äußeres Archiv, no. 4233, fo. 335, postscript.

77. Martin Eisengrein to Albrecht of Bavaria, 25 Sept. 1568, in Hopfen, *Kompromißkatholizismus*, 286–287; Martin Eisengrein to Albrecht of Bavaria, 26 Nov. 1568, ibid., 303–304.

78. Chantonnay to Philip II, 22 Nov. 1568, CODOIN, 103: 34; Constant, *Concession*, 684 and note 3.

79. "Ich red zu schwäbisch," Martin Eisengrein to Albrecht of Bavaria, 6 Feb. 1569, in Hopfen, *Kompromißkatholizismus*, 316–317.

80. "Vnd die leut nit also ga[r] an Kopf schlagen," Martin Eisengrein to Albrecht of Bavaria, 6 Mar. 1569, HSA, Kurbayern, Äußeres Archiv, no. 4423, fo. 383.

81. "Martin Eisengrein," *Allgemeine Deutsche Biographie*, vol. 5.

82. Philip to Alba, 17 Oct. 1568, CODOIN, 103: 15–16; Philip to Chantonnay, 22 Oct. 1568, ibid., 17.

83. Maximilian to Archduke Ferdinand, 6 Sept. 1568, HSA, Äußeres Archiv, no. 4233, fos. 180–187 (copy); Bibl, "Organisation," 13; Constant, *Concession*, 684 and note 3; Philip to Maximilian, 22 Nov. 1568, CODOIN, 103: 30; Chantonnay to Philip, 22 Nov. 1568, CODOIN, 103: 32–34.

84. Schwarz, *Briefe*, 1: ix–x.

85. " 'Der Papst wäre gut zum Inquisitor und' um ein Kloster zu regieren, aber die Welt regieren ist ein anderes Metier,' " cited in Schwarz, *Briefe*, 1: xi; Eisengrein to Albrecht of Bavaria, 15 Oct. 1568, HSA, Kurbayern, Äußeres Archiv, no. 4233, fo. 33.

86. Gillet, *Crato*, 2: 33; Bibl, "Organisation," 141; Wiedemann, *Reformation und Gegenreformation*, 1: 359–360.

87. Maximilian to Pius V, 4 Mar. 1567, in Schwarz, *Briefe*, 1: 53–54; Edelmayer, "Beziehungen," 148.

88. Krimm, "Agende," part 1: 11; Maximilian to Albrecht of Bavaria, 3 Dec. 1568, HSA, Kurbayern, Äußeres Archiv, no. 4233, fo. 275.

89. Chantonnay to Philip, 18 Dec. 1568, CODOIN, 103: 63.

90. Eisengrein to Albrecht V, 30 Oct. 1568, HSA, Kurbayern, Äußeres Archiv, no. 4233, fo. 336.

91. Wiedemann, *Reformation und Gegenreformation*, 1: 359–360; Bibl, "Organisation," 141, note 1.

92. Gillet, *Crato*, 2: 34–35; Krabbe, *Chyträus*, 207; Großman, "Streuen von Schwarzenau," 12–14; Krimm, "Agende," part 1: 15.

93. Krimm, "Agende," part 1: 16–18, 26 and part 2: 68. Cf. Wiedemann, *Reformation und Gegenreformation*, 1: 361–362. See also Bibl, "Organisation," 147; Gillet, *Crato*, 2: 34–35; and Mecenseffy, *Protestantismus*, 52.

94. Eisengrein to Albrecht of Bavaria, 15 Jan. 1569, HSA, Äußeres Archiv, no.

4233, fo. 369; Krabbe, *Chyträus*, 214; Krimm, "Agende," part 1: 16–19. On the character of Weber, see Helmut Goetz, "Die geheimen Ratgeber Ferdinands I.," *Quellen und Forschungen in italienischen Archiven und Bibliotheken* 42–43 (1964): 487–488.

95. Krabbe, *Chyträus*, 211–213.

96. Ibid., 214; Reingrabner, "Flacianische Bewegung," 273.

97. Chantonnay to Philip, 29 May 1569, CODOIN, 103: 215; Chantonnay to Philip 8 June 1569, ibid., 224; Eisengrein to Albrecht of Bavaria, 18 June 1569, HSA, Kurbayern, Äußeres Archiv, no. 4233, fo. 396.

98. "Como los de Austria pretendian instituir su religion," Philip [?] to Chantonnay, 12 Sept. 1569, CODOIN, 103: 283.

99. Philip to Maximilian, 26 Oct. 1569, CODOIN, 103: 302–303. On the confessional makeup of the *Reichshofrat*, see Gschliesser, *Reichshofrat*, 112–113, 135.

100. Helleiner, "Denkschrift," 197; Maximilian to Archduke Charles, 30 Oct. 1569, HSA, Kurbayern, Äußeres Archiv, no. 4233, fos. 403–405; Maximilian to Archduke Charles, 5 Nov. 1569, HSA, Kurbayern, Äußeres Archiv, no. 4233, fos. 414–415. Cf. Johann Loserth, *Die Reformation und Gegenreformation in den innerösterreichischen Ländern im 16. Jahrhundert* (Stuttgart: Cotta, 1898), 147.

101. Heiß, "Anfänge," 301–305, 314–315.

102. Bibl, "Organisation," 148–149.

103. Loesche, *Protestantismus in Österreich*, 26; Reingrabner, "Flacianische Bewegung," 279 Krimm, "Agende," part 1: 21, and part 2: 70–84.

104. Bibl, "Organisation," 183–185; Krimm, "Agende," part 3: 51–59; Reingrabner, "Flacianische Bewegung," 290–291.

105. *Ausbund aller Frosche so wider die Oesterreichische Agende*, Wiedemann, *Reformation und Gegenreformation*, 1: 377.

106. Bibl, "Organisation," 163–164; Walter, *Verfassungsgeschichte*, 59; Krabbe, *Chyträus*, 215–216; Gustav Reingrabner, *Adel und Reformation: Beiträge zur Geschichte des protestantischen Adels im Lande unter der Enns während des 16. und 17. Jahrhunderts*, Forschungen zur Landeskunde von Niederösterreich, vol. 21 (St. Pölten, Austria: Verein für Landeskunde von Niederösterreich und Wien, 1976), 60.

107. Heiß, "Konfession," 44.

CHAPTER 11: TWO HABSBURGS AND THE NETHERLANDS

1. "Das sich die sachen in niderlandt der religion halwer nuer besern," *Tagebuch*, fo. 6.

2. Geoffrey Parker, *The Dutch Revolt* (London: Penguin Books, 1985), 27–29; Felix Rachfall, *Wilhelm von Oranien und der niederländische Aufstand*, 3 vols. (Halle: Niemeyer, 1906–1908, and The Hague: Martinus Nijhoff, 1924), 1: 509. For general background on government in the Netherlands, see Rachfall, 1: 494–576; Martin Van Gelderen, *The Political Thought of the Dutch Revolt, 1555–1590* (Cambridge: Cambridge University Press, 1992), chap. 1; and Henri Pirenne, *Histoire de Belgique*, 5 vols. (reprint, n.p.: La Renaissance du Livre, 1972–1975), 2: 27–47.

3. Pieter Geyl, *The Revolt of the Netherlands* (1932; reprint, London: Ernest Benn, 1958), 75–76; Brusatti, "Reichskreise," 42; Press, "Wilhelm von Oranien," 682.

4. Edelmayer, "Beziehungen," 89–90; Brusatti, "Reichskreise," 29–35; Nicolette Mout, "Die Niederlande und das Reich im 16. Jahrhundert," *Alternativen zur Reichsverfassung in der frühen Neuzeit?* Volker Press, ed., Schriften des historischen Kollegs, vol. 23 (Munich: Oldenbourg, 1995): 146–147, 154, 156–157.

5. Rodríguez-Salgado, *Changing Face*, 54–60; Parker, *Revolt*, 38–40, 61; James D. Tracy, *Holland Under Habsburg Rule, 1506–1566* (Berkeley: University of California Press, 1990), 44–52, 115–117.

6. Khevenhüller, Tagebuch, 28; van Meteren, *Belgica*, 1: fo. 47r., col. 1.

7. Pierson, *Philip II*, 164; Parker, *Revolt*, 44, 61.

8. Parker, *Revolt*, 53–86; Pierson, *Philip II*, 83, 167; Edelmayer, "Beziehungen," 94; Van Gelderen, *Political Thought*, 34–36; Lynch, *Spain*, 1: 190–192; Kamen, *Philip*, 93–94.

9. Rodríguez-Salgado, *Changing Face*, 330.

10. Pierson, *Philip II*, 167–168, 224; Parker, *Revolt*, 58; Herbert H. Rowen, "The Dutch Revolt: What Kind of Revolution?" *Renaissance Quarterly* 43 (1990): 573–574; Kamen, *Philip*, 114–115.

11. Philip to Maximilian, 13 Aug. 1566, in Bibl, *Korrespondenz*, part 2: 2–6; Maximilian Lanzinner, *Friedenssicherung und politische Einheit des Reiches unter Kaiser Maximilian II., 1564–1576* (Göttingen: Vandenhoeck and Ruprecht, 1993), 79–80; Kamen, *Philip*, 101.

12. Maximilian's Instructions to Chantonnay for Philip, 31 Aug. 1566, in Bibl, *Korrespondenz*, part 2: 13–14; Chantonnay to Philip, 2 July 1567, in Koch, *Quellen*, 2: 42; Chantonnay to Philip, 20 Sept. 1567, ibid., 47. Cf. CODOIN, 101: 272–273. On Habsburg inclinations toward personal government, see remarks on Charles the Bold of Burgundy in Bernd Rill, *Friedrich III.: Habsburgs europäischer Durchbruch* (Graz: Styria Verlag, 1987), 220.

13. Tagebuch, fo. 35.

14. Maximilian to Philip, 7 Mar. 1567, in Bibl, *Korrespondenz*, part 2: 121.

15. Tagebuch, fo. 8. Cf. Lanzinner, *Friedenssicherung*, 80.

16. Margaret of Parma to Maximilian, 22 Mar. 1567, in Bibl, *Korrespondenz*, part 2: 140.

17. Brusatti, "Reichskreise," 37–38; Parker, *Revolt*, 90–91.

18. Alba to Figueroa, 10 May 1555, *Epistolario*, 1: 95; Alba to Figueroa, 14 June 1555, ibid., 174–175; Maximilian's Answer to Chantonnay for Philip, 31 Aug. 1566, in Bibl, *Korrespondenz*, part 2: 13–14; Edelmayer, "Beziehungen," 66; Lanzinner, *Friedenssicherung*, 79, 82–83; Ertman, *Leviathan*, 95.

19. Lazarus Schwendi to William of Orange, 9 Nov. 1565; Van Prinsteren, *Archives*, 1: 288; Kohler, "Gesamtsystem," 33; Maximilian's Instructions to Chantonnay for Philip, 31 Aug. 1566, in Bibl, *Korrespondenz*, part 2: 12–18, 246, note; Bibl, "Textfälschung," 427.

20. Maximilian to Margaret of Parma, 21 Sept. 1566, in Bibl, *Korrespondenz*, part 2: 26. See also ibid., 96, note 2; Philip II to Chantonnay, 3 Jan. 1567, CODOIN, 101: 141–142.

21. Adam von Dietrichstein to Maximilian, 16 Dec. 1566, in Koch, *Quellen*, 1: 176; Adam von Dietrichstein to Maximilian, 2 Jan. 1567, and 8 Jan. 1567, ibid., 177; Charles L'Ecluse to Crato, 10 Apr. 1567, in *Epistolae*, 55.

22. Bohdan Chudoba, "Karl von Steiermark und der Spanische Hof," in *Innerösterreich, 1564–1619*, Joannea III (Graz: Universitätsdruckerei Styria, 1967), 67; Mout, "Niederlande," 159.

23. Pierson, *Philip II*, 225–226; Parker, *Revolt*, 78.

24. Tagebuch, fos. 12, 21, 50; Adam von Dietrichstein to Maximilian, 10 Aug. 1567 in Koch, *Quellen*, 1: 192; Kamen, *Philip*, 111.

25. Adam von Dietrichstein to Maximilian, 4 Nov. 1566, in Koch, *Quellen*, 1: 170–171.

26. Philip to Maximilian, 7 Jan. 1567, in Bibl, *Korrespondenz*, part 2: 81–87.

27. " 'Perversita e la licenza,' " in Paolo Prodi, *Il sovrano pontifice—un corpo e due anime: La monarchia papale nella prima età moderna* (Bologna: Il Mulino, 1982), 319, note 54; Adam von Dietrichstein to Maximilian, 4 Nov. 1566, in Koch, *Quellen*, 1: 172.

28. "Est zelosissimus," Adam von Dietrichstein to Maximilian, 14 Dec. 1567, in Koch, *Quellen*, 1: 200.

29. Maximilian to Philip, 7 Mar. 1567, in Bibl, *Korrespondenz*, part 2: 124; Tagebuch, fo. 53.

30. Maximilian to Philip II, 7 Mar. 1567, in Bibl, *Korrespondenz*, part 2: 128–129.

31. Archduke Charles's Reply to Philip, 22 Jan. 1569, CODOIN, 103: 111. See also Margaret to Maximilian, 27 Oct. 1566, in Bibl, *Korrespondenz*, part 2: 43, 44 and note 2; Margaret of Parma to Maximilian, 17 Dec. 1566, ibid.: 60–61; Maximilian's Answer to Chantonnay for Margaret of Parma, 31 Dec.

1566, ibid.: 71–72; and Lanzinner, *Friedenssicherung*, 81–82; Brusatti, "Reichskreise," 39.

32. Koch, *Quellen*, 1: 54–55, 82; Chantonnay to Philip, 8 May 1567, CODOIN, 101: 164–165; Maximilian to Philip, 9 July 1567, in Bibl, *Korrespondenz*, part 2: 204–205.

33. R. Po-Chi Hsia, *Social Discipline in the Reformation: Central Europe, 1550–1750* (London: Routledge, 1989), 174–175; Robert Bireley, *Maximilian von Bayern, Adam Contzen S.J. und die Gegenreformation in Deutschland, 1624–1635*, Schriftenreihe der historischen Kommission bei der bayerischen Akademie der Wissenschaften, vol. 13 (Göttingen: Vandenhoeck and Ruprecht, 1975), 20.

34. "Oltros algunos Principados," Archduke Charles's Reply to Philip, 22 Jan. 1569, CODOIN, 103: 111. Frisia, Guelders, and Zutphen, along with Utrecht, Groningen, and Drente had been conquered and incorporated into the Netherlands between 1524 and 1543 by Charles V. They were part of the imperial Westphalian Circle until 1548. I am grateful to Professor Paul Rosenfeld for clarifying these details for me.

35. Chantonnay to Philip, 20 Mar. 1567, CODOIN, 101: 181.

36. Philip to Maximilian, 25 Apr. 1567, ibid., 163–169; Mout, "Niederlande," 156.

37. Chantonnay to Philip, 31 Mar. 1567, CODOIN, 101: 190–191.

38. Albrecht P. Luttenberger, *Kurfürsten, Kaiser und Reich: Politische Führung und Friedenssicherung unter Ferdinand I. und Maximilian II.*, Veröffentlichungen des Instituts für Europäische Geschichte Mainz, Abteilung Universalgeschichte, vol. 149 (Mainz: Philipp von Zabern, 1994), 203.

39. Christoph of Württemberg to Maximilian, 29 Apr. 1567, in Koch, *Quellen*, 1: 286–287.

40. Adam von Dietrichstein to Maximilian, 10 Mar. 1567, in Koch, *Quellen*, 1: 180–181. On the Erfurt *Kreistag* of 1567, see Luttenberger, *Kurfürsten*, 365–384.

41. Chantonnay to Philip, 8 May 1567, CODOIN, 101: 164–165.

42. Maximilian to Philip, 7 Mar. 1567, in Bibl, *Korrespondenz*, part 2: 121, 123–125; Philip to Maximilian 25 Apr. 1567, ibid., 165; Chantonnay's Report of conversation with Maximilian, 2 July 1567, in Koch, *Quellen*, 2: 41–42; Maximilian to Philip, 9 July 1567, in Bibl, *Korrespondenz*, part 2: 202–203. See also Pokorny, "Clementia Austriaca," 348.

43. Margaret of Parma to Maximilian, 23 Feb. 1567, in Bibl, *Korrespondenz*, part 2: 112; Chantonnay to Philip, 2 July 1567, in Koch, *Quellen*, 2: 42; Chantonnay to Philip, 20 Sept. 1567, ibid., 47; Philip to Maximilian, 12 Dec. 1567, in Bibl, *Korrespondenz*, part 2: 278–279.

44. Koch, *Quellen*, 1: 271.

45. Maltby, *Alba*, 156. Cf. Geyl, *Revolt*, 102–104; Van Gelderen, *Political Thought*, 40; and Kamen, *Philip*, 145.

46. Chantonnay to Philip, 28 Sept. 1567, CODOIN, 101: 282.

47. Koch, *Quellen*, 1: 262; Maximilian to Philip, 30 Sept. 1567, in Bibl, *Korrespondenz*, part 2: 230, 232, note 2.

48. Maximilian to Philip, 30 Sept. 1567, in Bibl, *Korrespondenz*, part 2: 228, 230.

49. Chantonnay to Philip, 16 Oct. 1567, CODOIN, 101: 302; Maximilian to Philip, 20 Oct. 1567, in Bibl, *Korrespondenz*, part 2: 243–244; Zasius to Albrecht of Bavaria, 21 Oct. 1567, HSA, Kurbayern, Äußeres Archiv, no. 4302, fo. 292.

50. Maximilian to Albrecht of Bavaria, 14 Oct. 1567, in Bibl, *Korrespondenz*, part 2: 242.

51. Tagebuch, fo. 57.

52. Brusatti, "Reichskreise," 43–44.

53. Lanzinner, *Friedenssicherung*, 86; Maximilian to Margaret of Parma, 23 Oct. 1567, in Bibl, *Korrespondenz*, part 2: 246; Maximilian to Albrecht of Bavaria, 23 Oct. 1567, ibid., 247.

54. Maximilian to the king of France, 30 Jan. 1568 (copy), HSA, Kurbayern, Äußeres Archiv, no. 4387, fos. 150–151; Tagebuch, fo. 56; SOA, Třebon, Historica, no. 4730, fos. 44–47.

55. Lanzinner, *Friedenssicherung*, 88–89.

56. Maximilian Lanzinner, "Friedenssicherung und Zentralisierung der Reichsgewalt: Ein Reformsuch auf dem Reichstag zu Speyer, 1570," *Zeitschrift für historische Forschung* 12 (1985): 289; Helmut Neuhaus, "Zwänge und Entwicklungsmöglichkeiten reichsständischer Beratungsformen in der zweiten Hälfte des 16. Jahrhunderts," *Zeitschrift für historische Forschung* 10 (1983): 287.

57. Neuhaus, "Zwänge," 291.

58. Schulze, "Concordia," 59–69; Luttenberger, *Kurfürsten*, 234–235.

59. Tagebuch, fo. 57.

60. Chantonnay to Philip, 20 Mar. 1567, CODOIN, 101: 179; Maximilian's Instructions to Johann Achilles Ilsung for Elector Palatine Frederick, 20 Nov. 1567, HSA, Äußeres Archiv, no. 4456, fos. 289–293; Maximilian to William of Jülich, 21 Nov. 1567, in Bibl, *Korrespondenz*, part 2: 270; Lanzinner, *Friedenssicherung*, 94, note 1. A thorough discussion of imperial politics and the issue of aiding Calvinists in France and the Netherlands is found in Edel, *Kaiser*, 292–307.

61. Luttenberger, *Kurfürsten*, 215; Lanzinner, *Friedenssicherung*, 94, note 60, 97.

62. Brusatti, "Reichskreise," 41–42; Nicola Sutherland, *The Huguenot Struggle for Recognition* (New Haven, Conn.: Yale University Press, 1988), 156; Brandi, *Reformation und Gegenreformation*, 366–367.

63. "Ex istis moribus gallicis" Maximilian's Reply to a French ambassador, 16 Oct. 1568 (copy), GHA, Korrespondenz-Akten, 597/1, fo. 129. See also Maximilian to Albrecht of Bavaria, 24 Mar. 1568, HSA, Kurbayern, Äußeres Archiv, no. 4387, fos. 143, 145.

64. Van Gelderen, *Political Thought*, 39; Philip to Maximilian, 12 Dec. 1567, in Bibl, *Korrespondenz*, part 2: 278–283; Philip to Luis Vanegas, 28 Jan. 1568, CODOIN, 101: 358; Report of letter of Maximilian to Philip, 2 Mar. 1568, ibid., 387; Vanegas to Philip, 6 Mar. 1568, ibid., 399.

65. Brusatti, "Reichskreise," 51–52, 55; Alba to Philip, 5 Nov. 1573, in *Epistolario*, 3: 552; Pierson, *Philip II*, 168. On the behavior of Spanish troops in the Low Countries, see "Cabos succintos que se tocan de las causas y origen de los males succedidos desde el 1568 por todo el 1573 en los Payses baxos," BN, Madrid, Sección de manuscritos, no. 1009, fo. 112.

66. Brusatti, "Reichskreise," 55; Perrenot [Chantonnay] to Philip II, 11 Aug. 1568, CODOIN, 101: 470, 472; Maximilian to Albrecht of Bavaria, 12 Aug. 1568, in *Briefe und Akten*, 5: 408; Maximilian to Albrecht of Bavaria, 14 Sept. 1568[?], HSA, Kurbayern, Äußeres Archiv, no. 4462, fo. 128; Maximilian to Adam von Dietrichstein, 1568 (no further date), in Koch, *Quellen*, 2:53.

67. Maximilian to Archduke Ferdinand, 25 July 1568, in Hirn, *Ferdinand von Tirol*, 2: 232, note 5, 233; Lanzinner, *Friedenssicherung*, 88–89. On the constitutional thinking of the princes generally, see Luttenberger, *Kurfürsten*.

68. Koch, *Quellen*, 1: 258–260; Adam von Dietrichstein to Maximilian, 22 Jan. 1568, ibid., 206–207; Report of a letter written by Maximilian [Vanegas? Chantonnay?] to Philip, 2 Mar. 1568, CODOIN, 101: 383.

69. Maximilian to Alba, n.d. May 1568, HHStA, Familienarchiv, Belgische Korrespondenz (Belgian correspondence), box 3, fo. 13; Alba to Maximilian, 5 June 1568, HHStA, Familienarchiv, Belgische Korrespondenz, box 3, fos. 24–25; Maximilian's Mandate to the imperial commissioners in Trier, HHStA, Familienarchiv, Belgische Korrespondenz, box 3, fo. 2.

70. "Aus . . . der nahennden Plutssipschafft," Maximilian to Alba, 4 Sept. 1568, HHStA, Familienarchiv, Belgische Korrespondenz, box 3, fo. 52. See also Maximilian to Alba, 7 Aug. 1568, HHStA, Familienarchiv, Belgische Korrespondenz, box 3, fo. 44.

71. Maximilian to Alba, 16 May 1568, HHStA, Familienarchiv, Belgische Korrespondenz, box 3, fo. 5; Maximilian to Alba, 4 Sept. 1568, HHStA, Familienarchiv, Belgische Korrespondenz, box 3, fo. 53; Alba to Maximilian, 23 Sept. 1568 (draft), HHStA, Familienarchiv, Belgische Korrespondenz, box 3, fo. 99.

72. Maximilian to Don Fadrique de Toledo [Alba], 30 Sept. 1569, HHStA, Fa-

milienarchiv, Sammelbände, box 1, vol. 2, fo. 172; Maximilian to Alba, 23 Feb. 1572, HHStA, Familienarchiv, Belgische Korrespondenz, box 4, bundle 1571–1573, fo. 46.

73. Vanegas to Philip, 11 Oct. 1568, CODOIN, 103: 9–10.

74. Alba to Maximilian, 24 July 1568, HHStA, Familienarchiv, Belgische Korrespondenz, box 3, fo. 38; Maximilian to Alba, 7 Aug. 1568, HHStA, Familienarchiv, Belgische Korrespondenz, box 3, fo. 44; Maximilian to Alba, 4 Sept. 1568, HHStA, Familienarchiv, Belgische Korrespondenz, box 3, fo. 54.

75. Maximilian to Alba, 6 Oct. 1568, HHStA, Familienarchiv, Belgische Korrespondenz, box 3, fos. 67–68.

76. Maximilian to Alba, 9 Dec. 1568, HHStA, Familienarchiv, Belgische Korrespondenz, box 3, fos. 107–110; Maximilian Lanzinner, "Der Aufstand der Niederlande und der Reichstag zu Speyer, 1570," in *Fortschritte in der Geschichtswissenschaft durch Reichstagsaktenforschung,* Heinz Angermeier and Erich Meuthen, eds., Schriftenreihe der bayerischen Akademie der Wissenschaften, vol. 35 (Göttingen: Vandenhoeck and Ruprecht, 1988), 106–107, 116.

77. Memorandum to the prince of Orange, 24 Sept. 1568, HSA, Kurbayern, Äußeres Archiv, no. 4837, fos. 164–165.

78. "Bej disen trübseligen und sorgsamen mißlichen zeitten," Maximilian to Elector Palatine Frederick, 29 June 1568, HHStA, Staatenabteilung, Palatina, 3, no folio.

CHAPTER 12: CONFRONTING INADEQUACY

1. Cf. Lanzinner, *Friedenssicherung,* 92, 520.

2. Friedrich Edelmayer, *Maximilian II., Philipp II. und Reichsitalien: Die Auseinandersetzungen um das Reichslehen Finale in Ligurien* (Stuttgart: Franz Steiner, 1988), 4; Karl Othmar von Aretin, *Das Reich: Friedensgarantie und europäische Gleichgewicht, 1648–1806* (Stuttgart: Klett-Cotta, 1986), 76–91.

3. In general, Gerhard Rill, "Reichsvikar und Kommisar: Zur Geschichte der Verwaltung Reichsitaliens im Spätmittelalter und in der frühen Neuzeit," *Annali della Fondazione italiana per la storia amministrativa* 2 (1965): 173–198.

4. Giorgio Spini, "The Medici Principality and the States of Europe in the Sixteenth Century," *Journal of Italian History* 2 (1979): 430, 432, 434–435; Bibl, "Erhebung," 56; BN, Madrid, Sección de manuscritos, no. 813, esp. fos. 201–202.

5. Chantonnay to Philip, 25 Mar. 1570, CODOIN, 103: 468, 472; Gerhard Rill, *Geschichte der Grafen von Arco, 1487–1614: Reichsvasallen und Landsassen* (Horn, Austria: Ferdinand Berger, 1975), 120.

6. Luttenberger, *Kurfürsten,* 183, note 375; Schwarz, *Briefe,* part 1: xi; Montea-

gudo to Philip, 27 May 1574, CODOIN, 111: 415; Spini, "Medici Principality," 438–439.

7. Edelmayer, *Finale,* 13–20, 39–40, 96, note 199.

8. Ibid., 29–30, 45–47, 53, 56, 69–70.

9. Ibid., 44–45; Maximilian to Archduke Ferdinand, 5 July 1573, TL, Geschäft von Hof, 1573, fo. 161.

10. Edelmayer, *Finale,* 105, note 11, 118.

11. Ibid., 104.

12. Ibid., 122, 127, 129, 135, 153, 164–165, 167, 174, 192–194, 201, 203, 205, 217.

13. Koch, *Quellen,* 1: 258–260; Lanzinner, *Friedenssicherung,* 145–147; Vanegas to Philip, 11 Oct. 1568, CODOIN, 103: 7.

14. Philip to Maximilian, 26 Oct. 1568, in Koch, *Quellen,* 2: 93–95; Philip to Maximilian, 22 Nov. 1568, CODOIN, 103: 29.

15. Philip to the duke of Feria, 17 Nov. 1568, CODOIN, 103: 86.

16. Philip to Maximilian, 22 Nov. 1568, CODOIN, 103: 28; Edelmayer, "Beziehungen," 107.

17. Philip's Reply to Archduke Charles, n.d. Jan. 1569, CODOIN, 103: 129; Maximilian to Philip, 16 Jan. 1569, ibid., 74–75; Archduke Charles's Reply to Philip, 22 Jan. 1569, ibid., 108–119; Memorandum of Archduke Charles to Philip, 25 Feb. 1569, ibid., 150; Oratio Rudolphi ad Regem Hispaniarum . . . , ÖNB, Handschriftensammlung, 8051, fo. 37; Mout, "Niederlande," 159; Kamen, *Philip,* 125–126.

18. Chantonnay and Vanegas to Philip, 12 Sept. 1569, CODOIN, 103: 274–275; van Meteren, *Oorloge,* 1: fo. 64r, col. 2; Frettensattel, "Verhandlungen," 392–393, 395–396. Cf. Kohler, "Gesamtsystem," in *Maximilian II,* 36. See also Chudoba, "Karl von Steiermark," 70; Bibl, "Frage," 330–331.

19. Koch, *Quellen,* 1: 257; Brusatti, "Reichskreise," 48–49; Philip to Chantonnay, 16 Aug. 1569, CODOIN, 103: 266–267; Philip to Maximilian, 26 Oct. 1569, in Koch, *Quellen,* 2: 95.

20. Geoffrey Parker, *The Army of Flanders and the Spanish Road, 1567–1659* (Cambridge: Cambridge University Press, 1972), 53; Archduke Ferdinand to Maximilian, 5 Feb. 1569, HSA, Kurbayern, Äußeres Archiv, no. 4837, fos. 166–167; Lanzinner, *Friedenssicherung,* 519, and *Reichstagsakten,* 1: 114–115.

21. Maximilian to Archduke Ferdinand, 11 Feb. 1569 (copy), HSA, Kurbayern, Äußeres Archiv, no. 4387, fos. 172–175; Mandate of 17 Mar., HSA, Kurbayern, Äußeres Archiv, no. 4387, fo. 254; Vanegas to Philip, 19 Mar. 1569, CODOIN, 103: 174–175. Cf. Chantonnay to Philip, 2 Apr. 1569, ibid., 182.

22. Luttenberger, *Kurfürsten,* 406, note 99; Lanzinner, *Friedenssicherung,* 186–187, 518–519; Maximilian to Schwendi, 6 Apr. 1570 [?], in Heyck, "Briefe," 165–166.

23. Lanzinner, *Reichstag* 1: 117, 123–127; 2: 921.

24. Maximilian Lanzinner, "Friedenssicherung," 293–295, 521–522; Maximilian Lanzinner, "Die Denkschrift des Lazarus von Schwendi (1570)," in *Zeitschrift für Historische Forschung*, special supplement 3 (1984), 144–145, 148–150; Bibl, "Erhebung," 80–81; Brusatti, "Reichskreise," 66–67; Lanzinner, *Reichstag*, 1: 118, 162.

25. Brusatti, "Reichskreise," 70, 72, 74, 83, 87; Maximilian to Archduke Charles, 7 Mar. 1570, HHStA, Familienakten, Familienkorrespondenz A, box 39, bundle "Karl von Steiermark," no folio; Lanzinner, *Reichstag*, 1: 117, 123–127; 2: 921.

26. On German opinion concerning Maximilian, see Lazarus Schwendi's "Discourse," of 1574 in Schwendi, "Denkschrift," 13. See also Luttenberger, *Kurfürsten*, 246.

27. E.g., Mandate of 24 Oct. 1572 (copy), HSA, Kasten Schwarz, no. 14893.

28. William of Orange to Maximilian, 27 Aug. 1572, (copy), HHStA, Familienarchiv, Familienakten, Belgische Korrespondenz, box 4, bundle 1571–1573, fo. 89.

29. "Passionierte hitzige affectionen," Maximilian to Albrecht of Bavaria, 6 Feb. 1569, HSA, Kurbayern, Äußeres Archiv, no. 4461, fos. 338–340. Citation fo. 340. Also, *Briefe und Akten*, 5: 432–436, has an excerpt of this letter.

30. Maximilian to Biglia, 12 Oct. 1570, in Schwarz, *Briefe*, 1, 167; "Isenberg, Salentin von," *Allgemeine Deutsche Biographie*, vol. 30.

31. "Dem Reich Christj," Maximilian to Julius of Braunschweig, 17 July 1571 (draft), HHStA, Familienarchiv, Familienkorrespondenz A, box 3, fo. 562; Maximilian to Julius of Braunschweig-Wolfenbüttel, 18 July 1571, HHStA, Familienarchiv, Familienkorrespondenz A, box 3, fo. 577.

32. Alba to Maximilian, 15 Mar. 1571 (unsigned draft), HHStA, Familienarchiv, Belgische Korrespondenz, box 3, fo. 215; Maximilian to Alba, 11 Apr. 1571, HHStA, Familienarchiv, Belgische Korrespondenz, box 3, fo. 329; Maximilian to Alba, 4 June 1572, HHStA, Familienarchiv, Belgische Korrespondenz, box 4, bundle 1571–1573, fo. 59; Maximilian to Alba, 6 June 1572, HHStA, Familienarchiv, Belgische Korrespondenz, box 4, fo. 65.

33. Maximilian to Alba, 27 June 1571, HHStA, Familienarchiv, Belgische Korrespondenz, box 3, fo. 367; Maximilian to Alba, 26 Feb. 1572, HHStA, Familienarchiv, Belgische Korrespondenz, box 4, bundle 1571–1573, fo. 48; Maximilian to Requesens, 12 Apr. 1574, Familienarchiv, Belgische Korrespondenz, box 4, bundle 1574–1576, fo. 33.

34. Monteagudo to Philip, 22 July 1570, CODOIN, 110: 37; Monteagudo to Philip, 31 Dec. 1570, ibid., 137.

35. Monteagudo to Philip, 9 Feb. 1572, ibid., 376; Alba to Philip, 29 July 1573, in *Epistolario*, 3: 475; Bibl, "Frage," 368; Press, "Wilhelm von Oranien," 693–694.

36. Maximilian to Albrecht of Bavaria, 11 May 1571, HSA, Kurbayern, Äußeres Archiv, no. 4462, fo. 132.

37. Max Spindler, ed., *Handbuch der bayerischen Geschichte*, 2d ed., 4 vols. (Munich: Beck, 1977–1981), 2: 339. See also Günther von Lojewski, *Bayerns Weg nach Köln: Geschichte der bayerischen Bistumspolitik in der 2. Hälfte des 16. Jahrhunderts*, Bonner historische Forschungen, vol. 21 (Bonn: Röhrscheid, 1962), 47 ff.; and Platzhoff, "Interregnum," 210.

38. Monteagudo to Alba, 27 May 1571, in *Briefe und Akten*, 5: 778–779; Platzhoff, "Interregnum," 210.

39. Monteagudo to Philip, 14 Dec. 1570, CODOIN, 110: 134–135; Monteagudo to Philip, 14 Apr. 1571, ibid., 196–197; Brusatti, "Reichskreise," 96. See also Maximilian to Alba, 12 Feb. 1572, HHStA, Familienarchiv, Belgische Korrespondenz, box 4, bundle 1571–1573, fo. 42.

40. Maximilian's circular to the German princes, HHStA, Familienarchiv, Belgische Korrespondenz, box 4, bundle 1571–1573, fo. 79; Maximilian's Orders for the empire, 1 June 1572, Kurbayern, HSA, Äußeres Archiv, no. 4459, fo. 306; Maximilian's declaration of 15 July 1572, CODOIN, 110: 482–483.

41. Maximilian's Instructions to his ambassadors, Mar. 1569, HSA, Kasten Schwarz, no. 6440, no folio; Sutherland, *Struggle*, 174–177; Maximilian's Instructions to Friedrich Truchsess, 14 Mar. 1570, HHStA, Staatenabteilung, Frankreich, Varia (France, miscellaneous), box 4, fos. 2–3; Bourgeon, *Charles IX*, 12, 15.

42. Maximilian to Albrecht of Bavaria, 24 Mar. 1568, HSA, Kurbayern, Äußeres Archiv, no. 4387, fos. 143, 145; Sutherland, 122–123; Barbara Diefendorf, *Beneath the Cross: Catholics and Huguenots in Sixteenth-Century Paris* (New York: Oxford University Press, 1991), 62–63, 179.

43. Barbara Diefendorf, "Prologue to a Massacre: Popular Unrest in Paris, 1557–1572," *American Historical Review* 90 (1985): 1083–1085; Sutherland, *Struggle*, 206.

44. Vanegas to Philip, 23 Apr. 1569, CODOIN, 103: 198; Philip to Chantonnay, [?] May 1569, ibid., 223.

45. Description of de la Rivière, 1 Aug. 1572, HHStA, Staatenabteilung, Frankreich, Varia, box 4, fo. 27; Sutherland, *Struggle*, 207–210; Monteagudo to Philip, 8 Oct. 1572, CODOIN, 111: 15.

46. J. Dostál, "Ohlas Bartholomějské noci na dvoře Maximiliána II.," *Český časopis historický* 37 (1931): 337–339, 343–344.

47. Charles Petrie, *Philipp II. von Spanien*, trans. Ursula Gmelin (Stuttgart: Kohlhammer, 1965), 211–212.

48. Monteagudo to Philip, 12 Oct. 1572, CODOIN, 111: 38, 40–41.

49. Dostál, "Ohlas," 340; Ludwig Haberstock to Albrecht of Bavaria, 8 Nov. 1572, HSA, Kasten Schwarz, no. 14893, no folio.

50. Martin, "Schwendi," 400.

51. Maximilian to Alba, 5 Apr. 1573, HHStA, Familienarchiv, Belgische Korrespondenz, box 4, bundle 1571–1573, fo. 115; Maximilian to Alba, 18 Apr. 1573, HHStA, Familienarchiv, Belgische Korrespondenz, box 4, bundle 1571–1573, fo. 119.

52. Maximilian to Wolfgang Rumplio [Rumpler], 13 Sept. 1574, HHStA, Familienarchiv, Sammelbände, box 1, vol. 2, fo. 312.

53. Dostál, "Ohlas," 341, 344–346; Sutherland, *Struggle*, 210.

54. Monteagudo to Philip, 12 Oct. 1572, CODOIN, 111: 32. On Maximilian's supplying Philip, see document dated 18 Aug. 1573 in HHStA, Familienarchiv, Belgische Korrespondenz, box 4, bundle 1574–1576, fo. 5. This folder actually contains materials running from 1573 to 1576. For Maximilian and Archduke Ferdinand, see Maximilian to Ferdinand, 18 Oct. 1572, TL, Geschäft von Hof, 1572, fo. 282; Maximilian to Alba, 15 Nov. 1572, HHStA, Familienarchiv, Sammelbände, box 1, vol. 2, fo. 266. Maximilian to Archduke Ferdinand, 15 July 1573, TL, Geschäft von Hof, 1573, fos. 147–148; Maximilian to Archduke Ferdinand, 31 Aug. 1573, TL, Geschäft von Hof, 1573, fo. 220.

55. Pierson, *Philip II*, 170; Maximilian to the marquis of Requesens, 14 Jan. 1574, HHStA, Familienarchiv, Belgische Korrespondenz, box 4, bundle 1574–1576, fos. 18–19.

56. Monteagudo to Philip, 18 Apr. 1573, CODOIN, 111: 187–194.

57. Report of Giovanni Corraro, 1574, in Fiedler, *Relationen*, 30: 331.

58. Brandi, *Reformation und Gegenreformation*, 371.

59. "El remedio que parece seria conveniente para las cosas de Flandes: El año 1573," BN, Madrid, Sección de manuscritos, no. 1009, fo. 116.

60. "Und ist in der Wahrheit nicht anders, als wie ich ihr vernünftiglich schreibet, dass Religions-Sachen nicht mit dem Schwerdt wollen gerichtet und gehandelt werden. . . . Zu dem so hat Christus und seine Apostel viel ein anders gelehret. Denn ihr Schwerd ist die Zung, Lehre Gottes Wort und christlicher Wandel gesesst: Auch ihr Leben unsdahin reizen solle, wie sie und so weit sie Christo nachgefolgt, ihnen nachzufolgen. . . . In Summa, Spanien und Frankreich machen es, wie sie wollen, so werden sies [*sic*] gegen gott, dem gerechten Richter müssen verantworten. Ich will, so Gott will, für meine Person erbar, christlich, treulich, und auf richtig handeln. Hoff gänzlich, Gott werde mir seinen Seegen darzu verleichen, damit ich mein thung[?] und Willen geegen Gott und der Welt könne verantworten. Und wenn ich das thue, so bekümmere ich mich um diese böse und heillose Welt gar nichts," Martin, "Schreiben," 454–457. Cf. Maximilian to Schwendi, 22 Feb. 1574 [?], SOA, Třebon, Historica, no. 4845.

61. E.g., Bibl, "Frage," 389, and Howard Louthan, "A *via media* in Central

Europe: Irenicism in Habsburg Vienna" (dissertation, Princeton University, 1994), 73–74, 74, note 9.

62. Lanzinner, "Denkschrift," 5–34, passim. See also Rudolf Krone, *Laʒarus von Schwendi, 1522–1584, kais. General und geheimer Rat, seine kirchenpolitische Tätigkeit und seine Stellung ʒur Reformation*, Schriften des Vereins für Reformationsgeschichte, vol. 29, no. 107 (1912): 141–143.

63. Heyck, "Briefe," 166.

64. Monteagudo to Philip, 20 Mar. 1574, CODOIN, 111: 382, 386–387.

65. Monteagudo to Philip, 27 May 1574, ibid., 414; Kamen, *Philip*, 155–156.

CHAPTER 13: STAYING AFLOAT

1. Delfino to Galli, 16 Sept. 1572, in *Nuntiaturberichte*, part 3, vol. 6: 132; Report of Corraro, 1574, in Fiedler, *Relationen*, 30: 350.

2. Johann Rueber to Caspar Bebes, 1 Nov. 1569, HHStA, Ungarn, Allgemeine Akten (General documents), fasc. 95, fos. 24, 28.

3. Brusatti, "Reichskreise," 86, note 8.

4. Archduke Charles to Maximilian, 30 June 1570, HHStA, Ungarn, Allgemeine Akten, fasc. 96, bundle Jan.–June 1570, fos. 73–74; Salentin to Maximilian, 23 Apr. 1571, HHStA, Ungarn, Allgemeine Akten, fasc. 97, fo. 75; Philip Freiherr of Winnenberg and Beilstein to Maximilian, 26 Apr. 1571, HHStA, Ungarn, Allgemeine Akten, fasc. 97, fo. 80. Winnenberg was the president of Maximilian's court council.

5. Monteagudo to Philip, 28 Apr. 1571, CODOIN, 110: 218–219.

6. Hans Rueber to Maximilian, 13 May 1571, HHStA, Ungarn, Allgemeine Akten, fasc. 97, bundle Jan.–June, fos. 94, 6–97; Relation of Dimitri Zemeri, 4 June 1571, HHStA, Ungarn, Allgemeine Akten, fasc. 97, bundle Jan.–June, fo. 109; Christoph Teuffenbach to Maximilian, 7 Nov. 1571, HHStA, Ungarn, Allgemeine Akten, fasc. 97, bundle July–Dec., fo. 111; Herold, "Hauptthemen," 183; Ernuszt, "Blotius," 36.

7. Schwarz, *Briefe*, 1: 115; Schulze, *Landesdefension*, 53–54.

8. Khevenhüller, *Tagebuch*, 63; Kamen, *Philip*, 138–139; Sanseverino, "Letteria," 1570, BN, Madrid, Sección de manuscritos, no. 783, fo. 48.

9. Pius V to Maximilian, 31 May 1571, and Delfino's description of Maximilian's reaction, in Schwarz, *Briefe*, 1: 179–180.

10. Monteagudo to Philip, 27 Nov. 1571, CODOIN, 10: 321; Leonhardt von Harrach to Maximilian, 13 Feb. 1572, HHStA, Ungarn, Allgemeine Akten, fasc. 98, bundle Jan.–Feb., fo. 62.

11. Maximilian to Pius V, 26 Oct. 1571, in Schwarz, *Briefe*, 1: 188–189; Maximilian to Don Juan of Austria, 21 Dec. 1571, HHStA, Familienarchiv, Sammelbände, box 1, vol. 2, fo. 225.

12. Maximilian to Prospero Colonna, 21 Dec. 1571, HHStA, Familienarchiv, Sammelbände, box 1, vol. 2, fo. 226; Maximilian to Pius V, 15 Jan. 1572, in Schwarz, *Briefe*, 1: 197; and Delfino to Galli, 7 Oct. 1572, in *Nuntiaturberichte*, part 3, vol. 6: 158.

13. Maximilian to Albrecht of Bavaria, 8 Feb. 1572, HSA, Kurbayern, Äußeres Archiv, no. 4466, fos. 289–290. Cf. Monteagudo to Philip, 13 Feb. 1572, CODOIN, 110: 38. See also Maximilian to Albrecht of Bavaria, 13 Nov. 1571, HSA, Kurbayern, Äußeres Archiv, no. 4462, fo. 142[?] (last digit indistinct); Delfino to Galli, 10 Oct. 1572, in *Nuntiaturberichte*, part 3, vol. 6: 161; and Bibl, "Erhebung," 124–125.

14. Delfino to Rusticucci, 21 Nov. 1571, in *Nuntiaturberichte aus Deutschland*, part 2, vol. 8, Johann Rainer, ed. (Graz: Böhlau, 1967): 173–174; Maximilian to Albrecht of Bavaria, 1 Oct. 1572, HSA, Kurbayern, Äußeres Archiv, no. 4462, fo. 150; and Khevenhüller, *Tagebuch*, 77.

15. Monteagudo to Philip, 10 Jan. 1573, CODOIN, 111: 108–109; Monteagudo to Philip, 25 Jan. 1573, ibid., 128; Maximilian to Albrecht of Bavaria, 24 Feb. 1573, HSA, Kurbayern, Äußeres Archiv, no. 4462, fo. 158; Monteagudo to Philip, 18 Apr. 1573, CODOIN, 111: 198; Maximilian to Albrecht of Bavaria, 23 Nov. 1573, HSA, Kurbayern, Äußeres Archiv, no. 4462, fo. 152[?], 153[?] (last digits in each set of numbers indistinct).

16. Maximilian to Albrecht of Bavaria, 18 May 1574, HSA, Kurbayern, Äußeres Archiv, no. 4462, fo. 160.

17. Pius to Maximilian, 15 Sept. 1568, in Schwarz, *Briefe*, 1: 119; Pius to Maximilian, 1 Dec. 1568, ibid., 127–128; Maximilian to Pius, 20 Jan. 1569, ibid., 130; Hirn, *Ferdinand von Tirol*, 2: 93 and note 2, 94 and note 3; Koch, *Quellen*, 2: 119.

18. Maximilian to Philip, 20 Nov. 1569, in Koch, *Quellen*, 2: 97–99.

19. Philip to Chantonnay for Monteagudo, 24 June 1570, CODOIN, 110: 23; Monteagudo to Philip, 15 Aug. 1570, ibid., 49–50.

20. Maximilian's Visitation Order 1574, HSA, Kurbayern, Äußeres Archiv, no. 4459, fos. 323–325.

21. HKA, Gedenkbücher, 109 (1569–1570), fo. 36; Maximilian to Archduke Charles, 30 Aug. 1570, HKA, Gedenkbücher, 109 (1569–1570), fo. 674.

22. Orders to the Landeshauptmann of Upper Austria, 28 Dec. 1573, Kurbayern, Äußeres Archiv, no. 4459, fos. 327–328.

23. Mecenseffy, "Maximilian II.," 50; Monteagudo to Philip, 18 Oct. 1573, CODOIN, 111: 332–335; Maximilian's University Decree of 3 Dec. 1573, HSA, Kurbayern, Äußeres Archiv, no. 4459, fo. 334; Maximilian to Georg Gienger "the Old," 7 Dec. 1573, HSA, Kurbayern, Äußeres Archiv, no. 4459, fo. 339; Maximilian to the provincial or vicar of the Friars Minor, HSA, Kurbayern, Äußeres Archiv, no. 4459, fo. 318.

24. Tagebuch, fo. 86; Eberhard, *Monarchie und Widerstand*, 202–264, 374–398;

Pánek, "Maximilian II.," 62–64; Pánek, *Opozice*, 91; Joachim Bahlcke, *Regionalismus und Staatsintegration im Widerstreit: Die Länder der böhmischen Krone im ersten Jahrhundert der habsburger Herrschaft, 1526–1619*, Schriften des Bundesinstituts für ostdeutsche Kultur und Geschichte, vol. 3 (Munich: Oldenbourg, 1994), 170, 178, 188.

25. Maximilian's Bohemian treasury to Maximilian, 25 May 1568, SÚA, Král. Reg. IIc, vol. 81, Bericht an Hof, fos. 220–221.

26. Gillet, *Crato*, 2: 15–17.

27. Josef Kollman, "Berní registřiky a berně roku 1567," *Sborník archivních prací* 13/I (1963): 170, 176, 188–189, 190–191.

28. Heiß, "Anfänge," 129; Pánek, "Maximilian II.," 64–65; Monteagudo to Philip, 22 May 1571, CODOIN, 110: 226–227.

29. Monteagudo to Philip, 26 June 1571, CODOIN, 110: 262; Philip to Monteagudo, 7 Sept. 1571, ibid., 298; Gillet, *Crato*, 2: 17.

30. Bibl, "Frage," 366.

31. Monteagudo to Philip, 23 Sept. 1571, CODOIN, 110: 305.

32. Theodor Brückler, "Zum Problem der katholischen Reform in Niederösterreich in der zweiten Hälfte des 16. Jahrhunderts," *Österreich in Geschichte und Literatur* 16 (1977): 151–163.

33. Monteagudo to Philip, 27 Nov. 1571, CODOIN, 110: 323; Maximilian to Fabian von Schenaich [?] 13 Aug. 1572, SÚA, Stará manipulace, K1/#12, box 1052, fo. 170; Maximilian to the Estates of Silesia and the Lusatias, 1 June 1572, SÚA, Stará manipulace, K1/#12, box 1052, fo. 110; Monteagudo to Philip, 12 Oct. 1572, CODOIN, 111: 37–38.

34. Monteagudo to Philip, 10 Jan. 1573, CODOIN, 111: 103–104; Monteagudo to Philip, 14 May 1573, ibid., 230.

35. "Die fest lant althergebrachtes löbliches christliches guetes brauchs," Khevenhüller, *Tagebuch*, 74.

36. Schrauf, *Eder*, 22. The full title was Evangelische/INQUISITION/Wahrer und falscher Religion/Wider/Das gemain vnchristliche Clagge/schray, Dass schier niemands mehr wissen/künde, wie oder was er glauben solle:/ In Form aines/Christlichen Rathschlags/Wie ein jeder Christen Mensch seines Glaubens halben gäntzlich vergewisst vnd gesichert/sein möge: Dermassen, dass er leichtlich nit künde/betrogen noch verführt werden./

37. Schrauf, *Eder*, xv–xvi; Bibl, "Frage," 345–346; Louthan, *Quest*, 127–128.

38. Schrauf, *Eder*, xxxiii; Hegenmüller to Albrecht of Bavaria, 7 Nov. 1573, ibid., 40, 42.

39. Ibid., x–xi, note 2, and xxi–xxiii.

40. Ibid., xiv; Monteagudo to Philip, 25 Dec. 1573, CODOIN, 111: 346–347.

41. Schrauf, *Eder*, xii–xiii. The text of the mandate is on pp. 1–3. See also Maximilian to Johann Egulf, bishop of Augsburg, 3 Oct. 1573, ibid., 4.

42. Ibid., xiv.

43. Ibid., xxviii.
44. Monteagudo to Philip, 18 Apr. 1573, CODOIN, 111: 201.
45. Schrauf, *Eder*, xxix, xxxi; Monteagudo to Philip, 18 Oct. 1573, CODOIN, 111: 337–338.
46. Monteagudo to Philip, 18 Oct. 1573, CODOIN, 111: 332–335.
47. Herold, "Hauptprobleme," 148; Bibl, "Organisation," 170–172, 214–215, 217–221.
48. Maximilian to the Utraquist administrator and consistory, 6 May 1572 (draft), SÚA, Stará manipulace, R 109/13–14, vol. 1, box 1988, fo. 218.
49. Pánek, *Opozice*, 50, 97, 871–872; Bahlcke, *Regionalismus*, 71–85, 152, 170; Maximilian to the archbishop of Prague, 15 May 1573, draft, SÚA, Stará manipulace, R 109/1, vol. 2, box 1977, no folio.
50. Pánek, *Opozice*, 874–875; Pánek, "Maximilian II.," 65–67; Maximilian to Wilhelm of Rožmberk, 28 Dec. 1573, SOA, Třebon, Historica, no. 4868; Maximilian to Wilhelm of Rožmberk, 14 November 1574, SOA, Třebon, Historica, no. 4895.
51. Pánek, *Opozice*, 102; Hugo Moritz, *Die Wahl Rudolfs II.: Der Reichstag zu Regensburg (1576) und die Freistellungsbewegung* (Marburg: Elwert, 1895), 117.
52. Alois Míka, *Stoletý zápas o charakter českého státu, 1526–1627* (Prague: Státní pedagogické nakladatelství, 1974), 113–114, 116; Pánek, *Opozice*, 101.
53. Bahlcke, *Regionalismus*, 182; Louthan, *Crato*, 21–23.
54. Bahlcke, *Regionalismus*, 182; Pánek, *Opozice*, 881–882; Pánek, "Maximilian II.," 66–67; Gillet, *Crato*, 2:27.
55. Pánek, *Opozice*, 877; Pánek, "Maximilian II.," 66–67.
56. Pánek, "Maximilian II.," 67; Míka, *Stoletý zápas*, 117; Gillet, *Crato*, 2: 27.
57. Pánek, "Maximilian II.," 64; Guzmán de Silva to Don Juan of Austria, 22 Oct. 1575, BN, Madrid, Sección de manuscritos, no. 783, fo. 610.
58. Ceremonial order for Rudolf's coronation in Bohemia, 1575, SOA, Třebon, Historica, no. 4899.
59. Moritz, *Wahl*, 50–51.
60. Moritz, *Wahl*, 50–51; Vocelka, *Propaganda*, 121; Philip to Maximilian, 10 Mar. 1569, CODOIN, 103: 159; Chantonnay and Vanegas to Philip, 29 May 1569, ibid., 219; Monteagudo to Philip, 30 Nov. 1570, CODOIN, 110: 123; Maria to Philip, 10 July 1574, CODOIN, 111: 437.
61. Monteagudo to Philip, 6 Apr. 1572, CODOIN, 110: 431.
62. Vocelka, *Propaganda*, 123; Moritz, *Wahl*, 52–54.
63. Monteagudo to Philip, 25 Feb. 1573, CODOIN, 111: 161–162; Monteagudo to Philip, 14 May 1573, ibid., 227; Moritz, *Wahl*, 52–55.
64. Vocelka, *Propaganda*, 122; Moritz, *Wahl*, 68, 72, 75.
65. Moritz, *Wahl*, 52, 141, 162; Edel, *Kaiser*, 367–370.

66. Report of October 1575, BN, Madrid, Sección de manuscritos, no. 7413, fos. 53, 56–57; citation, fo. 56. See also fos. 27–28.

67. *Porträtgalerie zur Geschichte Österreichs von 1400 bis 1800* (Vienna: Kunsthistorisches Museum, 1982), Rudolph II (no. 130); Ernst (no. 131); Matthias (nos. 134, 136, and 137); Albrecht (no. 128); Maximilian (no. 129).

68. Philip to Maximilian, 10 Mar. 1569, CODOIN, 103: 159–160. To Rudolf's annoyance, Isabel would eventually marry Maximilian's youngest son, Archduke Albrecht. Midelfort, *Mad Princes*, 129. See also Monteagudo to Philip, 30 Nov. 1570, CODOIN, 110: 123; Maria to Philip, s.d., 1573, CODOIN, 111: 357; and Report of Hieronymus Soranzo, 1614, in Fiedler, *Relationen*, 26: 2.

69. Moritz, *Wahl*, 95.

70. Pass, *Musik und Musiker*, 80–81; Rudolph's Instructions for Johann Hegenmüller to the archbishop of Mainz, 6 Aug. 1577, HHStA, Familienarchiv, Familienakten, Varia, box 108, fo. 12.

71. Bahlcke, *Regionalismus*, 195; Bues, *Kandidatur*, 5–9; Bibl, *Maximilian II.*, 350; Sucheni-Grabowska, "Beziehungen," 63, 66, 68.

72. *Tagebuch*, fo. 25.

73. Eduard Winter, "Die polnische Königswahlen 1575 und 1587 in der Sicht der Habsburger," *Innsbrucker Historische Studien* 1 (1978): 63.

74. "Y dize le vulgaramente en Italia che chi molto abarca nulla stringe," Granvella to Don Juan of Austria, 28 Aug. 1573, BN, Madrid, Sección de manuscritos, no. 783, fo. 469.

75. Winter, "Polnische Königswahlen," 61–63; Bues, *Kandidatur*, 124; Bibl, *Maximilian II.*, 360–361; Dostál, "Ohlas," 336; Maria to Pius V, 29 Apr. 1572 (draft), HHStA, Ungarn, Allgemeine Akten, fasc. 98, bundle April, fo. 78; Monteagudo to Philip, 8 Oct. 1572, CODOIN, 111: 16.

76. Bues, *Kandidatur*, 55–62; Maria to Philip, 12 Feb. 1573, CODOIN, 111: 141–142; Monteagudo to Philip, 14 Feb. 1573, ibid., 145; Monteagudo to Philip, 12 May 1573, ibid., 216–217.

77. Bues, *Kandidatur*, 84–85, 127, 130, 142–144, 147, 158, 171; Philip to Monteagudo, 6 July 1573, CODOIN, 111: 278–279; Maximilian to Philip, 12 Feb. 1573, CODOIN, 111: 139.

78. Bues, *Kandidatur*, 65–66, 73, 77–80, 90–92, 94–95, 101–114.

79. Monteagudo to Philip, 31 July 1573, CODOIN, 111: 286.

80. Maria to Philip, 4 June 1573, CODOIN, 111: 248–249; Monteagudo to Philip, 31 July 1573, ibid., 286.

81. Bues, *Kandidatur*, 158, 171; Philip to Monteagudo, 6 July 1573, CODOIN, 111, 278–279.

82. Monteagudo to Philip, 18 Oct. 1573, CODOIN, 111: 327.

83. Philip to Monteagudo, 15 Oct. 1574, CODOIN, 479; Philip to Monteagudo,

27 Aug., ibid., 455; Monteagudo to Philip, 13 Oct. 1574, ibid., 472; Monteagudo to Philip, 26 June 1574, ibid., 434.

84. Monteagudo to Philip, 20 June 1574, ibid., 422–423; Monteagudo to Philip, 16 or 26 Nov. 1574, ibid., 487.

85. Moritz, *Wahl*, 230–231; Herold, "Hauptprobleme," 15–16; Khevenhüller, *Tagebuch*, 89; Maximilian to Albrecht of Bavaria, 29 May 1575 [?], HSA, Kurbayern, Äußeres Archiv, no. 4462, fo. 178; Maximilian to Albrecht of Bavaria, 18 July 1576, HSA, Kurbayern, Äußeres Archiv, no. 4462, fo. 162.

CHAPTER 14: A SOUL AT LARGE

1. Monteagudo to Philip, 5 Dec. 1571, CODOIN, 110: 325–326.

2. Maximilian to Archduke Charles, 21 May 1570, HHStA, Familienarchiv, Familienkorrespondenz A, box 39, bundle Karl von Steiermark, no folio; Maximilian to Archduke Charles, 20 June 1570, HHStA, Familienarchiv, Familienkorrespondenz A, box 39, bundle Karl von Steiermark, no folio; Monteagudo to Philip, 5 Dec. 1571, CODOIN, 110: 325; Monteagudo to Philip, 23 Aug. 1572, ibid., 497; Monteagudo to Philip, 17 Nov. 1572, CODOIN, 111: 55; Leopold Senfelder, "Kaiser Maximilian's II. letzte Lebensjahr und Tod," *Blätter für Landeskunde von Niederösterreich*, n.s. 32 (1898): 49, 54–63.

3. Monteagudo to Philip, 5 Dec. 1571, CODOIN, 110: 325–326.

4. Report of Giovanni Michele, 1571, in Fiedler, *Relationen*, 30: 277; Monteagudo to Philip, 18 Oct. 1573, CODOIN, 111: 326.

5. "Der Allmechtige Gott zu dessen hennden alle ding stehen, der machts mit mir nach seinem Gottlichem Willen, dann Ich Ihme umb alles lob unnd danck sage, dann er am besten weiss was mir nutzlich oder schätlich, unnd Ich mitt sein Gottlichen willen geduldig, unnd nur gar wohlzufriedenn bin, den es leider auff dieser welt dermassenzugehet, dass einer darbei wenig lust unnd rue hatt," Maximilian to Lazarus Schwendi, 22 Feb. 1573 (copy), SOA, Třebon, Historica, no. 4845.

6. Ludwig Haberstock to William of Bavaria, 23 Feb. 1573, HSA, Kasten Schwarz, no. 4893, no folio; Maximilian to Albrecht of Bavaria, 24 Feb. 1573, HSA, Äußeres Archiv, no. 4462, fo. 158.

7. Ludwig Haberstock to William of Bavaria, 30 Mar. 1573, HSA, Kasten Schwarz, no. 14893, no folio.

8. Becker, "Letzte Tagen," 318–320; Menhardt, *Handschriftenverzeichnis*, 47.

9. Monteagudo to Philip, 5 Dec. 1571, CODOIN, 110: 327; Crato, *Consiliorum*, 2: 92; L'Ecluse, *Exoticorum*, 216.

10. Maximilian to Albrecht of Bavaria, 3 Feb. 1569, HSA, Äußeres Archiv, no. 4462, fo. 65; Monteagudo to Philip, 12 May 1572, CODOIN, 110: 434.

11. Monteagudo to Philip, 23 Aug. 1572, CODOIN, 110: 497.

12. Maximilian to Albrecht of Bavaria, 31 Aug. 1573, GHA, Korrespondenz-Akten, no. 597/1, fo. 239; Maximilian to Archduke Ferdinand, 4 Nov. 1573, TL, Geschäft von Hof, 1573, fo. 277.

13. Albrecht of Bavaria to Archduke Ferdinand, 23 June 1568, GHA, Korrespondenz-Akten, 597/I, fo. 122; Maximilian to Archduke Ferdinand, 7 June 1571, TL, Geschäft von Hof, 1571, fos. 158–159; Maximilian to Archduke Ferdinand, 20 Sept. 1574, TL, Geschäft von Hof, 1574, fo. 170; and Hirn, *Ferdinand von Tirol*, 2: 465–466.

14. Ludwig Haberstock to Albrecht of Bavaria, 5 Nov. 1572, HSA, Kasten Schwarz, no. 14893, no folio.

15. Maximilian to Albrecht of Bavaria, 1 Oct. 1572, HSA, Kurbayern, Äußeres Archiv, no. 4462, fo. 150.

16. Lhotsky, *Festschrift*, 2, part 1: 169; Vanegas to Philip, 26 Feb. 1570, CODOIN, 103: 460.

17. Ludwig Haberstock to Albrecht of Bavaria, 29 Nov. 1572, HSA, Kasten Schwarz, no. 14893, no folio (document heavily damaged). Cf. Ludwig Haberstock to William of Bavaria, 29 Nov. 1572, HSA, Kasten Schwarz, no. 14893, no folio. See also Monteagudo's report to Philip [?], 16 June 1573, CODOIN, 111: 255.

18. Moritz, *Wahl*, 50 and 51, note 1; SOA, Třebon, Historica, no. 4906.

19. Kaufmann, *Imperial Theme*, 36; Ludwig Haberstock to Albrecht of Bavaria, 10 Oct. 1572, HSA, Kasten Schwarz, no. 14893, no folio.

20. Maximilian to Albrecht of Bavaria, 18 May 1574, HSA, Äußeres Archiv, no. 4462, fo. 160.

21. Herbert Knöbl, *Das Neugebäude und sein baulicher Zusammenhang mit Schloß Schönbrunn* (Vienna: Böhlau, c. 1988), 9.

22. Hans Tietze, *Wien, Kultur, Kunst, Geschichte* (Vienna: Epstein, 1931), 193–194.

23. Maximilian to Albrecht, Nov.[?] Dec.[?] 1569, HSA, Äußeres Archiv, no. 4462, fo. 90; Maximilian to Archduke Charles, 22 Jan. 1570 [?], HHStA, Familienarchiv, Familienkorrespondenz A, box 39, bundle Karl von Steiermark, no folio; Maximilian to Archduke Charles, 7 Mar. 1570, HHStA, Familienarchiv, Familienkorrespondenz A, box 39, bundle Karl von Steiermark, no folio.

24. Sanitary Order of the Lower Austrian chamber, 28 July 1571, HSA, Äußeres Archiv, no. 4459, fo. 206.

25. Ludwig Haberstock to William of Bavaria, 29 Nov. 1572, HSA, Kasten Schwarz, no. 14893, no folio.

26. Ludwig Haberstock to William of Bavaria, 30 Jan. 1573, HSA, Kasten Schwarz, no. 14893, no folio.

27. Report of Giovanni Michele, 1571, in Fiedler, *Relationen*, 30: 277.

28. "Gannz frisch," Maximilian to the Tyrolean treasury, 3 Nov. 1570, TL, Geschäft von Hof, 1570, fo. 244; Maximilian to the Tyrolean treasury, 15 Dec. 1570, TL, Geschäft von Hof, 1570, fo. 281.

29. Electress Anna to Empress Maria, 3 Jan. 1576, HHStA, Familienarchiv, Familienkorrespondenz A, box, 31 bundle "K. Maria Frau/K. Max. II.," fo. 25.

30. In 1576 he ordered 4,598 pounds of the sweetener, and use never fell below 2,558 pounds. Rudolph II used far less—2,738 pounds was the biggest order in 1578. HHStA, OMeA, Sonderrreihe, box 172, Hofrechnungen (Court accounts), 1531–1780, fos. 271–275.

31. Maximilian to Christoph of Württemberg, 16 Feb. 1568, in Le Bret, *Magazin*, 9: 260–261; Maximilian to Archduke Ferdinand, 5 Oct. 1570, TL, Geschäft von Hof, 1570, fo. 214.

32. Monteagudo to Philip, 9 Dec. 1571, CODOIN, 110: 328–329.

33. Maximilian to Albrecht V of Bavaria, 17 Dec. 1569, HSA, Kurbayern, Äußeres Archiv, no. 4462, fo. 92.

34. Khevenhüller, *Tagebuch*, 62; Vocelka, "Begräbnisfeierlichkeiten," 132–133.

35. Report of Giovanni Corraro, 1574, in Fiedler, *Relationen*, 30: 336.

36. Philip II's Memorandum to Adam von Dietrichstein, 6 Apr. 1573, in Bibl, "Frage," 403; Memorandum of Philipp, 4 Jan. 1570, CODOIN, 103: 411; Philip to Maximilian, 5 Feb. 1570, ibid., 428–429.

37. Report of Giovanni Michele, 1571, in Fiedler, *Relationen*, 30: 281.

38. Bibl, "Frage," 335; Monteagudo to Philip, 25 Feb. 1573, CODOIN, 111: 159; Edelmayer, "Gesandte," 61.

39. Monteagudo to Philip, 30 Aug. 1570, CODOIN, 110: 59.

40. Chantonnay to Philip, 28 June 1570, CODOIN, 103: 523.

41. Description of the journey, SOA, Třebon, Historica, no. 4906.

42. Monteagudo to Philip, 23 Apr. 1570, CODOIN, 110: 18–19; Monteagudo to Philip, 26 May 1574, CODOIN, 111: 410.

43. "Sin meterse en ninguna otra cose," Maria to Philip, 2 Mar. 1570, CODOIN, 103: 463–464.

44. Monteagudo to Philip, 19 Jan. 1572, CODOIN, 110: 342; Philip to Maximilian, 4 Mar. 1572, ibid., 396–397.

45. Monteagudo to Philip, 19 Jan. 1572, ibid., 345; Maria to Philip, 8 Feb. 1572, ibid., 369; Monteagudo to Philip, 5 June 1572, ibid., 447–448; Noflatscher, "Erzherzog Maximilian," 1: 33.

46. Noflatscher, "Erzherzog Maximilian," 1: 47–48.

47. "Como siempre lo ha hecho," Monteagudo to Philip, 25 Dec. 1573, CODOIN, 111: 348–349.

48. Noflatscher, "Erzherzog Maximilian," 1: 48; Report of Giovanni Corraro, 1574, in Fiedler, *Relationen*, 30: 319.

49. Bibl, "Frage," 338, 341–342.

50. Monteagudo to Philip, 10 Jan. 1573, CODOIN, 111: 100, 102.

51. Monteagudo to Philip, 14 May 1573, ibid., 231–232, 234–237; Philip to Monteagudo, 24 June 1573, ibid., 277–278.

52. Maria to Philip, 10 July 1574, ibid., 440; Monteagudo to Maximilian, 16 Nov. 1574, ibid., 490; Philip to Monteagudo, 27 Dec. 1574, ibid., 502–503.

53. E.g., Maximilian to the governor of Milan, 5 July 1575, HHStA, Familienarchiv, Sammelbände, box 1, vol. 2, fos. 324–326.

54. Maximilian to Lazarus Schwendi, 22 Feb. 1574, "Eigenhändiges Schreiben Kaiser Maximilians II. an seinen General und Freund Lazarus von Schwendi, die Religionsverfolgungen in Frankreich, den Niederlanden und Böhmen betreffend, dd. Wien den 12. Febr. 1574," Friedrich C. Moser, ed., *Patriotisches Archiv für Deutschland* 6 (1787): 457; Maximilian to Albrecht of Bavaria, 4 Feb. 1575, HSA, Kurbayern, Äußeres Archiv, no. 4462, fo. 172.

55. Maximilian to Archduke Ferdinand, 12 June 1576, TL, Geschäft von Hof, 1576, fo. 367; Maximilian to the Tyrolean treasury, 6 Aug. 1576, TL, Geschäft von Hof, 1576, fo. 581. Citation in Busbecq, *Letters*, 155.

56. William of Bavaria to Albrecht of Bavaria, 16 Feb. 1576, HSA, Äußeres Archiv, no. 4457, fo. 150.

57. Senfelder, "Tod," 56 and note 2. For a contemporary commentary on the climacteric year, see Rantzow, *Catalogus*, 57, 60–64.

58. Moritz, *Wahl*, 229–230; Biglia to Alessandrino, 5 June 1568, *Nuntiaturberichte*, part 2, vol. 5: 148–149. For a detailed discussion of the diet in 1576, see Edel, *Kaiser*, 371–444.

59. Maximilian to Wilhelm of Rožmberk, 13 May 1573 [?], SOA, Třebon, Historica, no. 4851; Maximilian to Albrecht of Bavaria, 9 Oct. 1575, HSA, Kurbayern, Äußeres Archiv, no. 4462, fo. 186; Maximilian to Archduke Charles, 24 July 1576, KA, AFA, 7–1 (1576), no folio; Maximilian to Archduke Charles, 8 Aug. 1576, HKA, AFA, 8–1 (1576), no folio; Maximilian to the land marshal of Lower Austria, 8 Aug. 1576, HKA, AFA, 8–1 (1576), no folio; Maximilian to Archduke Charles, 25 Sept. 1576, KA, AFA, 9–1 (1576), no folio; *Graz als Residenz: Innerösterreich, 1564–1619*, exhibition catalogue (Graz: Universitäts-Buchdruckerei, 1964), 293.

60. Aulinger, *Reichstag*, 175–180.

61. Moritz, *Wahl*, 232.

62. "Etlich Kriegsverfarne Personnen," Reply of the German estates to Maximilian, 1576, KA, AFA, 7–3 (1576), fos. 10, 13, 22. Citation fo. 13.

63. Moritz, *Wahl*, 279–281, 291, 361–362, 366–367, 383–385, 401; Edel, *Kaiser*, 439; Maximilian to Albrecht of Bavaria, 18 July 1576, HSA, Kurbayern, Äußeres Archiv, no. 4462, fo. 162.

64. Moritz, *Wahl*, 401–403; Maximilian to Archduke Charles, 25 Sept. 1576, KA, AFA, 9–1 (1576), no folio.

65. Cf. Maximilian to Archduke Charles, 25 Sept. 1576, KA, AFA, 9–1 (1576), no folio; and Maximilian to Archduke Ernst, 3 Oct. 1576, KA, AFA, 10–2 (1576), no folio.

66. Senfelder, "Tod," 51, 62, note 2; Becker, "Letzte Tagen," 321, note 4, 322.

67. Maximilian to Duchess Jacobea of Bavaria, 18 June 1550, in Loserth, *Registratur,* 509.

68. Cited in Bibl, "Kulturblüte," 152. See also Becker, "Letzte Tagen," 313; and Vocelka, "Begräbnisfeierlichkeiten," 110.

69. Report of the Marquis d'Almazon to Philip on Maximilian's death, in Koch, *Quellen,* 2: 101; Aulinger, *Reichstag,* 318–319.

70. Vocelka, "Begräbnisfeierlichkeiten," 108–109; Aulinger, *Reichstag,* 317.

71. Widorn, "Gemahlinnen," 37–38; Almazon's Report, in Koch, *Quellen,* 2: 103–107; Vocelka, "Begräbnisfeierlichkeiten," 108; Becker, "Letzte Tagen," 324–327, note 10; Edel, *Kaiser,* 13; Aulinger, *Reichstag,* 319–320.

72. Excerpts from the Protocols of Maximilian's privy council, n.d., HHStA, Familienarchiv, Familienakten 2.7, Todesfälle (Deaths), 60, bundle 7, fo. 8.

73. Crato, *Sambucum,* 20.

74. Louthan, *Crato,* 29–36. Cf. Vocelka, "Begräbnisfeierlichkeiten," 130–133. See also Aulinger, *Reichstag,* 322.

75. Excerpts from the Protocols of Maximilian's privy council, n.d., HHStA, Familienarchiv, Familienakten, 2.7, Todesfälle, 60 bundle 7, fo. 9; Prague, SÚA, Stará manipulace, K1/#15, box 1052, no folio; Anonymous Report of Maximilian's funeral 1576, HSA, Kasten Schwarz, no. 4048, no folio; Ludwig Haberstock to Albrecht of Bavaria, 30 Oct. 1576, HSA, Kasten Schwarz, no. 4048, no folio; Memorandum to Emperor Rudolph, 30 Oct. 1576, HSA, Kasten Schwarz, no. 4048, no folio.

76. Lietzmann, *Neugebäude,* 200 and note 205.

77. Becker, "Letzte Tagen," 333, 335.

78. Vocelka, *Propaganda,* 41; Becker, "Letzte Tagen," 336–338; [?] Zimmerman, "Leichenbegräbniss weiland Kaiser Maximilians II. gehalten zu Prag am 22. März 1577," *Archiv für Geschichte, Statistik, Literatur und Kunst* 14 (1823): 469–470.

79. Max Lossen, *Der Kölnische Krieg* (Gotha: Perthes, 1882); Munich: Franz, 1897), 1: 474–483; Noflatscher, "Erzherzog Maximilian," 1: 52–53.

80. Widorn, "Gemahlinnen," 41–42, 47; Report of Michele et al., 1581, in Fiedler, *Relationen,* 30: 394; Parker, *Philip II,* 79. On Maria's political activities in Spain, see Magdalena S. Sánchez, *The Empress, the Queen, and the Nun: Women and Power at the Court of Philip III of Spain* (Baltimore, Md.: Johns Hopkins University Press, 1998), passim.

81. BN, Madrid, Sección de manuscritos, no. 11773, fos. 573 (a), 575. This manuscript is misfoliated. There are 2 folios numbered 573.

CHAPTER 15: CONCLUSION

1. Alfred Kohler, "Kontinuität oder Diskontinuität im frühneuzeitlichen Kaisertum: Ferdinand II.," in Duchhardt and Schnettger, *Reichständische Libertät*, 110.
2. Cf. Edel, *Kaiser*, 57–63.
3. Lanzinner, *Friedenssicherung*, 513, 518.
4. Paula Sutter Fichtner, "The Holy Roman Empire: Did It Really Hold Together?" paper delivered to the Columbia University Seminar on the History of Political and Legal Thought and Institutions, 23 April 1998. For an excellent historiographical introduction to these issues, see Helmut Neuhaus, *Das Reich in der frühen Neuzeit* (Munich: Oldenbourg, 1997), 57–101.
5. For a useful discussion of this enduring problem, see Rudolf Hoke, "Prokaiserliche und antikaiserliche Reichspublizistik," in Duchhardt and Schnettger, *Reichsständische Libertät*, 119–132. Neuhaus, *Reich*, 86, has observed that recent scholarship has paid far less attention to the office of emperor than the role of the estates.
6. Lanzinner, *Friedenssicherung*, 515.
7. Cf. ibid., 520.
8. Duchhardt, *Protestantisches Kaisertum*, 53. Cf. Edel, *Kaiser*, 86–87.
9. Edel, *Kaiser*, 17–18.

References

ARCHIVAL AND LIBRARY COLLECTIONS

Innsbruck
  Tiroler Landesarchiv
    Geschäft von Hof
Litoměřice
  Státní oblastní archiv: pobočka Žitenice
    Lobkovicové roudnictí rodinný archiv
Madrid
  Archivo Historico Nacional
    Sección de Osuna
  Biblioteca nacional
    Sección de Manuscritos
Munich
  Bayerisches Hauptstaatsarchiv
    Kasten Schwarz
    Kurbayern, Äußeres Archiv
  Geheimes Hausarchiv
    Korrespondenzakten und Urkunden
    Österreichische Sachen
New York
  Pierpont Morgan Library
    Rulers of Holy Roman Empire

Prague
    Státní ústřední archiv
        Královicá registra
        Patenty
        Morava
        Stará manipulace
Simancas
    Archivo Nacional
        Estado
            Alemania
Třebon
    Státní oblastní archiv
        Historica
Vienna
    Haus-, Hof- und Staatsarchiv
        Belgien, Politisches Archiv
        Familienarchiv
            Belgien: Belgische Korrespondenz
            Familienakten
                Entbindungen und Taufen
                Familienkorrespondenz A
                Grabstätten und Leichenübertragungen
                Hofstaatssachen, Supplicationen
                Jagdsachen
                Kunstgegenstände
                Privilegien, Krönungen
                Ritterorden
                Varia
                Vermählungen
                Vermögensangelegenheiten
            Sammelbände
        Hofarchiv
            Alte Akten des Oberstmarschallamtes: group 1
            Ältere Zeremonialakten
            Obersthofmeisteramt, Sonderreihe
        Mainzer Erzkanzleramt
            Reichshofrathsacten
            Reichskanzlei und Taxamt
        Staatenabteilung
            Bavarica
            Frankreich
            Palatina

Saxonica
Spanien
Türkei
Ungarn
  Allgemeine Akten
Hofkammerarchiv
  Gedenkbücher
  Hofzahlamtsbücher
  Reichsakten
Kriegsarchiv
  Alte Feldakten
Österreichische Nationalbibliothek
  Handschriftensammlung

PUBLISHED SOURCES

Acontiana: Abhandlungen und Briefe des Jacobus Acontius. Ed. Walther Köhler and
  Erich Hassinger. Abhandlungen der Heidelberger Akademie der Wissen-
  schaften, philosophische-historische Klasse 8. Heidelberg: Carl Winter, 1932.
Briefe und Akten zur Geschichte des sechzehnten Jahrhunderts. 5 vols. Munich: Rie-
  ger, 1873–1896.
Busbecq, Ogier Ghislain de. *Letters of Ogier Ghislain de Busbecq to the Holy Roman
  Emperor Maximilian II.* Trans. Robert C. Jones and Bernard C. Weber. New
  York: Bookman Associates, 1961.
Camutius, Andreae. *Medicinae supraordinariam ac Praecipvam . . . brevis excussio
  praecipui morbi, nempe cordis palpitationis Maximiliani secundi caesaris . . . .*
  Florence: Marescori, 1580.
Colección de documentos inéditos para la historia de España. 112 vols. 1842–1895.
  Reprint, Vaduz: Kraus, 1966.
Crato von Crafftheim, Johannes. *Ordnung der Praeservation: Wie man sich zur zeit
  der Infeccion verwahren/Auch bericht/wie die rechte Pestilentia erkandt und curirt
  werden sol: Mit einer lehre/von dem vorsorg der Geschwieren.* Nuremberg: Ger-
  lach, 1585.
Crato a Kraftheim, Jo[hannis]. *Epistola ad Joanneum Sambucum de Morte Impe-
  ratoris Maximiliani Secundi.* Jena: Mauk, 1781.
———. *III. Impp. Romanorum Medicii et Consiliarii Intimi, Consiliorum [et]
  Epistolarum Medecinialium . . . .* 7 vols. Frankfurt: Andreas Wechel, 1591–
  1611.
*Decades tres epistolarum Huberti Langueti, Jo. Camerarii, Io. Cratonis et Casp.
  Peuceri.* Frankfurt: Johann Maximilian Sand, 1702.
Deutsche Reichstagsakten: Reichsversammlungen, 1556–1662, Der Reichstag zu

Speyer, 1570. 2 vols. Ed. Maximilian Lanzinner. Göttingen: Vandenhoeck and Ruprecht, 1988.

Döllinger, Johann Joseph Ignaz, ed. *Beiträge zur politischen, kirchlichen und Culturgeschichte der sechs letzten Jahrhunderte.* 3 vols. Regensburg: Manz, 1862–1882.

Edelmayer, Friedrich, ed., with the assistance of Arno Strohmayer. *Die Korrespondenz der Kaiser mit ihren Gesandten in Spanien.* Vol. 1: *Der Briefwechsel zwischen Ferdinand I., Maximilian II. und Adam von Dietrichstein, 1563–1565.* Vienna: Verlag für Geschichte und Politik, 1997.

"Eigenhändiges Schreiben Kaiser Maximilians II. an seinen General und Freund Lazarus von Schwendi, die Religionsverfolgungen in Frankreich, den Niederlanden und Böhmen betreffend, dd. Wien den 12. Febr. 1574." In Friedrich C. Moser, ed. *Patriotisches Archiv für Deutschland,* vol. 6. (1787): 453–457.

Epistolae imperatorum et regum hungariae Ferdinandi I. et Maximiliani II. ad suos in porto ottomanica. Ed. Jacob Ferdinand Miller. Pest: Trattner, 1808.

Epistolario del III Duque de Alba Don Fernando Alvarez de Toledo. Ed. duke of Berwick y de Alba. 3 vols. Madrid: n.p., 1952.

Ernst, Viktor, ed. *Briefwechsel des Herzogs Christoph von Wirtemberg [sic].* 4 vols. Stuttgart: Kohlhammer, 1899–1907.

Fernelii, Io. *Ambiani, vniversa medicina.* 3d ed. Frankfurt: Andreas Wechel, 1574.

Fiedler, Joseph, ed. *Relationen venetianischer Botschafter über Deutschland und Österreich im sechzehnten Jahrhundert.* Fontes Rerum Austriacarum, part 2, Diplomataria, vol. 26. Vienna: Gerold, 1866. Fontes Rerum Austriacarum, part 2, Diplomataria, vol. 30. Vienna: Gerold, 1870.

Freiherrn von Freybergs Sammlung historischer Schriften und Urkunden. Ed. Wilhelm Freiherr von Freyberg. 5 vols. Stuttgart: Cotta, 1827–1836.

Gachard, L. P., ed. *Correspondance de Marguerite d'Autriche, duchesse de Parme, avec Philippe II.* 3 vols. Brussels: Muquardt, 1867–1881.

Gerstinger, Hans, ed. *Aus dem Tagebuch des kaiserlichen Hofhistoriographen Johannes Sambucus, 1531–1584.* Österreichische Akademie der Wissenschaften, philosophische-historische Klasse, Sitzungsberichte 248, no. 2. Graz: Böhlau, 1965.

Gindely, Anton, ed. *Quellen zur Geschichte der böhmischen Brüder.* Fontes Rerum Austriacarum, part 2, Diplomataria, vol. 19. Vienna: Gerold, 1859.

Groen van Prinsterer, Guillaume, ed. *Archives ou correspondance inédite de la maison d'Orange-Nassau.* 27 vols. in 26. Leide[n]: Luchtmans, 1835–1917.

Habersack, Hans. *Die Krönungen Maximilians II zum König von Böhmen, Römischen König und König von Ungarn (1562–1563) nach der Beschreibung des Hans Habersack.* Ed. Friedrich Edelmayer, Leopold Kammerhofer, Martin C. Mandlmayr, Walter Prenner, and Karl G. Vocelka. Fontes Rerum Austriacarum, part 1, Scriptores, vol. 13. Vienna: Österreichische Akademie der Wissenschaften, 1990.

Helleiner, Karl. "Eine religionspolitische Denkschrift an Maximilian II. aus der Feder des Casp. Hirsch, 1574." *Mitteilungen des Instituts für österreichische Geschichtsforschung* 46 (1932): 196–215.

Heyck, Eduard, ed. "Briefe der Kaiser Maximilian II. und Rudolf II. an Lazarus Schwendi." *Mitteilungen des Instituts für österreichische Geschichtsforschung* 13 (1892): 164–168.

Khevenhüller, Hans. *Geheimes Tagebuch, 1548–1605.* Ed. Georg Khevenhüller-Metsch and prepared for publication by Günther Probszt-Obstorff. Graz: Akademische Druck- und Verlagsanstalt, 1971.

Koch, Matthias, ed. *Quellen zur Geschichte des Kaisers Maximilian II.* 2 vols. in 1. Leipzig: Voigt and Günther, 1857–1861.

Köpl, Karl, ed. "Urkunden, Acten und Regesten aus dem Statthalterei-Archive in Prag." *Jahrbücher der Kunstsammlungen des allerhöchsten Kaiserhauses* 10 (1889), entries 5925–6230; 12 (1891), entries 7939–7977.

Die Korrespondenz des Kaisers Maximilian II. Ed. Viktor Bibl. 2 parts in 2 vols. Veröffentlichungen der Kommission für neuere Geschichte Österreichs 14, 16. Vienna: Holzhausen, 1916–1921.

Le Bret, Johann Friedrich, ed. *Magazin zum Gebrauch der Staaten- und Kirchengeschichte* 9 (1785): 1–262.

L'Ecluse, Charles. *Caroli Clusii Atrebatis ad Thomam Redigerum et Joannem Cratonem epistolae.* Ed. F. X. de Ram. Compte-Rendu des Séances de la Commission Royale d'Histoire 12 (1847): 1–104.

———. *Exoticorum Libri Decem: Quibus Animalium, Plantarum, Aromatum, aliorumque Peregrinorum Fructuum Historiae Describuntur . . . .* N.p.: Plantiniana Raphelengii, 1605. 2 parts.

Loserth, Johann, ed. *Die Registratur Erzherzog Maximilians (Maximilians II) 1547–1551 aus den Handschriften des Stifts Reun.* Fontes Rerum Austriacarum, Diplomataria et Acta, vol. 48, part 2 (1896): 361–600.

Nuntiaturberichte aus Deutschland. Part 2, 5, 1560–1572. Ed. Ignaz Philip Dengel. Vienna: Hölder/Pichler/Tempsky, 1926.

Part 2, 6, 1560–1572. Ed. Ignaz Philip Dengel. Vienna: Holzhausen, 1939.

Part 2, 8, 1560–1572. Ed. Johann Rainer. Graz: Böhlaus, 1967.

Part 3, 6, 1572–1585. Ed. Helmut Goetz. Tübingen: Niemeyer, 1982.

Rantzow, Heinrich von. *Catalogus imperatorum, regum ac principium qui astrologicam artem amarunt, ornarunt & exercuerunt.* Antwerp: Plantin, 1580.

Rodríguez, Rafaela Raso, ed. *Maximiliano de Austria, gobernador de Carlos V en España: Cartas al emperador.* Madrid: Consejo superior de investigaciones cientificas, 1963.

Sandoval, Fray Prudencio de. *Historia de la vida y hechos del emperador Carlos V.* Biblioteca de autores españoles, vols. 80–82. Madrid: Ediciones Atlas, 1955–1956.

Schaendlinger, Anton C., and Claudia Römer, eds. *Die Schreiben Süleymans des Prächtigen an Karl V., Ferdinand I., und Maximilian II.* Osmanisch-türkische Dokumente aus dem Haus-, Hof- und Staatsarchiv zu Wien, vol. 1. Vienna: Österreichische Akademie der Wissenschaften, 1983.

Scholz, L., ed. *Johannis Cratonis à Krafteim Consiliorum et Epistolarum.* Frankfurt: n.p., 1671.

Schwarz, Wilhelm Eberhard, ed. *Briefe und Akten zur Geschichte Maximilians II.* 2 vols. Paderborn: Bonifacius-Druckerei, 1889–1891.

Thurneisser zum Thurn, Leonhart. *Quinta Essentia, Das ist/Die hoechste subtilitet/krafft und wirckung/bey der fuertrefflichsten /vnd menschlichen geschlecht am nuetzlichsten kuensten/der Medecin vnd Alchemy/Auch wie nahe diese beyde mit sippschafft gefreund vnd verwandt sind.* Leipzig: Steinman, 1574.

Turba, Gustav, ed. *Venetianische Depeschen vom Kaiserhofe.* 4 vols. Vienna: Tempsky, 1889.

Van Meteren, Emanuel. *Belgica: Historie der Neder-landen ende haerder Na-buren Oorlogen ende Geschiedenissen* . . . . 2 vols. The Hague: Jacobussz, 1614.

Velius, Caspar Ursinus. *De Bello Pannonico: Libri Decem.* Ed. Adam Francis Kollar. Vienna: Trattner, 1767.

Waldeck, Wolrad von. *Tagebuch.* Ed. C. L. P. Tross. Bibliothek des litterarischen Vereins in Stuttgart 59. Stuttgart: Litterarischer Verein, 1861.

Zimmermann, [?]. "Leichenbegräbniss weiland Kaiser Maximilians II. gehalten zu Prag am 22. März 1577." *Archiv für Geschichte, Statistik, Literatur und Kunst* 14 (1823): 469–470.

SECONDARY LITERATURE

Abrahamowicz, Zygmunt, Vojtech Kopčan, Metin Kunt, Endre Marosi, Nenad Moačanin, Constantin Serban, and Karl Teply. *Die Türkenkriege in der historischen Forschung.* Forschungen und Beiträge zur Wiener Stadtgeschichte 13. Vienna: Deuticke, 1983.

Altfahrt, Margit. "Die politische Propaganda für Maximilian II." 2 parts. *Mitteilungen des Instituts für österreichische Geschichtsforschung* 88 (1980): 283–312, and 89 (1981): 53–92.

Altmann, Wilhelm. "Zur Geschichte der Wahl Maximilians II. zum römischen König." *Mitteilungen des Instituts für österreichische Geschichtsforschung* 13 (1892): 619–625.

Aretin, Karl Othmar von. *Das Reich: Friedensgarantie und europäische Gleichgewicht, 1648–1806.* Stuttgart: Klett-Cotta, 1986.

Asch, Ronald G., and Adolf M. Birke. *Princes, Patronage and the Nobility: The Court at the Beginning of the Modern Age, c. 1450–1650.* London: Oxford, 1991.

Aulinger, Rosemarie. *Das Bild des Reichstages im 16. Jahrhundert: Beiträge zu einer typologischen Analyse schriftlicher und bildlicher Quellen.* Schriftenreihe des historischen Kommission bei der bayerischen Akademie der Wissenschaften 18. Göttingen: Vandenhoeck und Ruprecht, 1980.

Bahlcke, Joachim. *Regionalismus und Staatsintegration im Widerstreit: Die Länder der böhmischen Krone im ersten Jahrhundert der habsburger Herrschaft, 1526–1619.* Schriften des Bundesinstituts für ostdeutsche Kultur und Geschichte 3. Munich: Oldenbourg, 1994.

Bak, János, ed. *Nobilities in Central and Eastern Europe: Kinship, Property and Privilege.* History and Society in Central Europe no. 2 (1994).

Becker, [?]. "Die letzten Tage und der Tod Maximilians II." *Blätter des Vereines für Landeskunde von Niederösterreich,* n.s. 11 (1877): 308–343.

Beik, William. *Absolutism and Society in Seventeenth-Century France.* Cambridge: Cambridge University Press, 1985.

Benda, Kálmán. "Zrinyi Miklos, a szigetváry hős." In Lajos Rúzsás, ed., *Szigetvári Emlékönyv. Szigetvár, 1566: Évi ostromának 400. Évfordulojára.* Budapest: Akadémiai Kiadó, 1966.

Benzing, Josef. *Die Buchdrucker des 16. und 17. Jahrhunderts im deutschen Sprachgebiet.* Wiesbaden: Harrassowitz, 1963.

Bérenger, Jean. *Finances et absolutisme autrichien dans la seconde moitié du XVIIe siècle.* Paris: Imprimerie nationale, 1975.

————. *Histoire des l'empire des Habsbourg, 1273–1918.* Paris: Fayard, 1990.

Bibl, Viktor. "Die angebliche Textfälschung Kaiser Maximilians II. (Wortlaut einer Resolution König Philipps II. von Spanien)." *Mitteilungen des Instituts für österreichische Geschichtsforschung* 38 (1920): 423–449.

————. "Die Erhebung Herzog Cosimos von Medici zum Großherzog von Toskana und die kaiserliche Anerkennung, 1569–1576." *Archiv für österreichische Geschichte* 103 (1913): 1–162.

————. "Die Kulturblüte Wiens und seiner Umgebung unter Maximilian II." *Monatsblatt des Vereins für Landeskunde von Niederösterreich* 17 (1918): 139–153.

————. *Maximilian II.: Der rätselhafte Kaiser.* Hellerau bei Dresden: Avalun, n.d.

————. "Maximilian's II. Erklärung vom 18. Aug. 1568 über die Ertheilung der Religions-Concession." *Mitteilungen des Instituts für österreichische Geschichtsforschung* 20 (1899): 635–640.

————. "Nidbruck und Tanner: Ein Beitrag zur Entstehungsgeschichte der Magdeburger Centurien und zur Charakteristik König Maximilians II." *Archiv für österreichische Geschichte* 85 (1898): 379–430.

————. "Die Organisation des evangelischen Kirchenwesens im Erzherzogtum Österreich unter der Enns." *Archiv für österreichische Geschichte* 87 (1899): 115–228.

————. *Der Tod des Don Carlos.* Vienna: Braumüller, 1918.

————. "Die Vorgeschichte der Religionskonzession Kaiser Maximilians II."
Jahrbuch für Landeskunde von Niederösterreich, n.s. 13–14 (1915): 400–431.

————. "Zur Frage der religiösen Haltung Kaiser Maximilians II." *Archiv für
österreichische Geschichte* 106 (1918): 289–425.

Bireley, Robert. *Maximilian von Bayern, Adam Contzen, S.J., und die Gegenreformation in Deutschland, 1624–1635.* Schriftenreihe der historischen Kommission
bei der bayerischen Akademie der Wissenschaften, 13. Göttingen: Vandenhoeck and Ruprecht, 1975.

Blaschke, Karlheinz. *Moritz von Sachsen: Ein Reformationsfürst der zweiten Generation.* Göttingen: Muster-Schmidt, 1983.

Bono, James J. *The Word of God and the Languages of Man: Interpreting Nature
in Early Modern Science and Medicine.* Madison: University of Wisconsin Press,
1995.

Bourgeon, Jean-Louis. *Charles IX devant la Saint-Barthélemy.* Geneva: Droz,
1995.

Brady, Thomas A., Jr. *The Politics of the Reformation in Germany: Jacob Sturm
(1489–1553) of Strasbourg.* Atlantic Highlands, N.J.: Humanities Press, 1997.

Brandi, Karl. *Deutsche Geschichte im Zeitalter der Reformation und Gegenreformation.* 1927. Reprint, Munich: Bruckmann, 1960.

Brückler, Theodor. "Zum Problem der katholischen Reform in Niederösterreich
in der zweiten Hälfte des 16. Jahrhunderts." *Österreich in Geschichte und Literatur* 21 (1977): 151–163.

Bruckmüller, Ernst. *Sozialgeschichte Österreichs.* Vienna: Herold, 1985.

Brückner, Wolfgang. "Die Gegenreformation im politischen Kampf um die
Frankfurter Buchmessen: Die kaiserliche Zensur zwischen 1567 und 1619."
Archiv für Frankfurts Geschichte und Kunst 48 (1968): 67–86.

Brusatti, Alois. "Die Entwicklung der Reichskreise während der Regierungszeit
Maximilians II." Dissertation, University of Vienna, 1950.

Buchholtz, Franz Bernhard von. *Geschichte der Regierung Ferdinands I.* 9 vols.
1831–1838. Reprint, Graz: Akademische Druck- und Verlagsanstalt, 1971.

Bücking, Jürgen. *Frühabsolutismus und Kirchenreform in Tirol, 1566–1665: Ein
Beitrag zum Ringen zwischen "Staat" und "Kirche" in der frühen Neuzeit.* Veröffentlichung des Instituts für abendländische Religionsgeschichte, Abhandlung für abendländische Religionsgeschichte, 66. Wiesbaden: Steiner, 1972.

Bues, Almut. *Die habsburgische Kandidatur für den polnischen Thron während des
ersten Interregnums in Polen, 1572–1573.* Dissertationen der Universität Wien,
vol. 163. Vienna: Verband der wissenschaftlichen Gesellschaften Österreichs,
1984.

Burkert, Günther. *Landesfürst und Stände: Karl V., Ferdinand I. und die österreichischen Erbländer im Ringen um Gesamtstaat und Landesinteressen.* Forschungen

und Darstellungen zur Geschichte des steiermärkischen Landtages, 1. Graz: Historische Landeskommission für Steiermark, 1987.

Burkert-Dottolo, Günther. "Die Landstände der österreichischen Erbländer auf dem Weg ins "Reich": Die Entsendung ständischer Gesandtschaften zu Reichstagen." In Heinz Duchhardt and Matthias Schnettger, eds., *Reichsständische Libertät und habsburgisches Kaisertum*. Mainz: Philipp von Zabern, 1999, 3–24.

Chabod, Federico. "Milan o los Paises Bajos? Las discussiones en España sobre la 'alternativa' de 1544." In *Carlos V, 1500–1558: Homenaje de la Universidad de Granada*. Granada: La Junta del centenario, 1958.

Chapman, Allan. "Astrological Medicine." In Charles Webster, ed., *Health, Medicine and Mortality in the Sixteenth Century*. Cambridge: Cambridge University Press, 1979, 275–300.

Chudoba, Bohdan. "Karl von Steiermark und der spanische Hof." In *Innerösterreich, 1564–1619*. Joannea 3. Graz: Universitätsdruckerei Styria, 1967, 63–72.

Cohn, Henry J. "The Territorial Princes in Germany's 'Second Reformation.'" In Menna Prestwich, ed., *International Calvinism, 1541–1715*. Oxford: Clarendon Press, 1985, 135–165.

Constant, Gustave. *Concession à l'Allemagne de la communion sous les deux espèces*. Bibliothèque des écoles françaises d'Athènes et Rom, 128. Paris: Bocard, 1923.

Corvisier, André. *Armies and Societies in Europe, 1494–1789*. Trans. Abigail T. Siddall. Bloomington: Indiana University Press, 1979.

Díaz Medina, Ana. "El Gobierno en España de Maximiliano II, 1548–1551." In Friedrich Edelmayer and Alfred Kohler, eds., *Kaiser Maximilian II.: Kultur und Politik im 16. Jahrhundert*. Wiener Beiträge zur Geschichte der Neuzeit, 19. Vienna: Verlag für Geschichte und Politik, 1992, 38–54.

Dickmann, Fritz. "Das Problem der Gleichberechtigung der Konfessionen im Reich im 16. und 17. Jahrhundert." *Historische Zeitschrift* 201 (1965): 265–305.

Didier, Nikolaus. *Nikolaus Mameranus, Ein luxemburger Humanist des XVI. Jahrhunderts am Hofe der Habsburger: Sein Leben und seine Werke*. Freiburg: Herder, 1915.

Diefendorf, Barbara. *Beneath the Cross: Catholics and Huguenots in Sixteenth-Century Paris*. New York: Oxford University Press, 1991.

———. "Prologue to a Massacre: Popular Unrest in Paris, 1557–1572." *American Historical Review* 90 (1985): 1067–1091.

Doran, Susan. "Religion and Politics at the Court of Elizabeth I: The Habsburg Marriage Negotiations of 1559–1567." *English Historical Review* 104 (1989): 908–926.

Dostál, J. "Ohlas Bartholomějské noci na dvoře Maximiliána II." *Český časopis historický* 37 (1931): 335–349.

Duchhardt, Heinz. *Protestantisches Kaisertum und altes Reich: Die Diskussion über*

die Konfession des Kaisers in Politik, Publizistik und Staatsrecht. Veröffentlichungen des Instituts für europäische Geschichte Mainz, Abteilung Universalgeschichte, 87. Wiesbaden: Steiner, 1977.

————, and Matthias Schnettger, eds. *Reichständische Libertät und habsburgisches
Kaisertum.* Mainz: Philipp von Zabern, 1999.

Dworzak, Stephan. "Georg Ilsung von Tratzberg." Dissertation, University of
Vienna, 1954.

Eberhard, Winfried. *Monarchie und Widerstand: Zur ständischen Oppositionsbildung
im Herrschaftssystem Ferdinands I. in Böhmen.* Veröffentlichungen des Collegium Carolinum, 54. Munich: Oldenbourg, 1985.

Edel, Andreas. *Der Kaiser und Kurpfalz: Eine Studie zu den Grundelementen politischen Handelns bei Maximilian II., 1564–1576.* Göttingen: Vandenhoeck and
Ruprecht, 1997.

Edelmayer, Friedrich. "Die Beziehungen zwischen Maximilian II. und Philipp
II." Thesis, University of Vienna, 1982.

————. "Habsburgische Gesandte in Wien und Madrid in der Zeit Maximilians
II.: Ein Vergleich der innerhabsburgischen Begegnung auf der Ebene der Diplomatie." In Wolfram Krömer, ed., *Spanien und Österreich in der Renaissance.*
Innsbrucker Beiträge zur Kulturwissenschaft, special issue 66. Innsbruck: Institut für Sprachwissenschaft, 1989, 57–70.

————. "Kaisertum und Casa de Austria: Von Maximilian I. zu Maximilian II."
In Friedrich Edelmayer and Alfred Kohler, eds., *Hispania-Austria: Die katho-
lischen Könige, Maximilian I. und die Anfänge der Casa de Austria in Spanien.*
Vienna: Verlag für Geschichte und Politik, 1993, 157–171.

————. *Maximilian II., Philipp II. und Reichsitalien: Die Auseinandersetzungen
um das Reichslehen Finale in Ligurien.* Stuttgart: Franz Steiner, 1988.

————. "Das Netzwerk Philipps II. von Spanien im Heiligen Römischen
Reich." In Heinz Duchhardt and Matthias Schnettger, eds., *Reichständische
Libertät und habsburgisches Kaisertum.* Mainz: Philipp von Zabern, 1999, 57–
80.

————, and Alfred Kohler, eds. *Hispania-Austria: Die katholischen Könige, Maximilian I. und die Anfänge der Casa de Austria in Spanien.* Vienna: Verlag für
Geschichte und Politik, 1993, 157–171.

————. *Kaiser Maximilian II.: Kultur und Politik im 16. Jahrhundert.* Wiener
Beiträge zur Geschichte der Neuzeit, 19. Vienna: Verlag für Geschichte und
Politik, 1992.

Ernuszt, Johanna. "Die ungarische Beziehungen des Hugo Blotius." *Jahrbuch der
Graf Klebelsberg Kun Instituts für ungarische Geschichtsforschung in Wien* 10
(1940): 7–53.

Ertman, Thomas. *Birth of the Leviathan.* Cambridge: Cambridge University
Press, 1997.

Evans, R. J. W. "Culture and Anarchy in the Empire, 1540–1680," *Central European History* 18 (1985): 14–30.

———. *The Making of the Habsburg Monarchy 1550–1700.* Oxford: Clarendon, 1979.

———. *Rudolf II and His World: A Study in Intellectual History.* Oxford: Oxford University Press, 1973.

———, and T. V. Thomas, eds. *Crown, Church and Estates: Central European Politics in the Sixteenth and Seventeenth Centuries.* New York: St. Martin's, 1991.

Feigl, Helmuth. *Die niederösterreichische Grundherrschaft vom ausgehenden Mittelalter bis zu den theresianisch-josephinischen Reformen.* Forschungen zur Landeskunde von Niederösterreich, 16. Vienna: Verein für Landeskunde von Niederösterreich und Wien, 1964.

———. "Zur Rechtslage der unterbäuerlichen Schichten im 15., 16. und 17 Jahrhundert." In Herbert Knittler, ed., *Wirtschafts- und sozialhistorische Beiträge: Festschrift für A. Hoffmann.* Vienna: Oldenbourg, 1979, 247–271.

Fellner, Thomas, and Heinrich Kretschmayr. *Die österreichische Zentralverwaltung.* 4 vols. Vienna: Holzhausen, 1907–1925.

Fichtner, Paula Sutter. "An Absence Explained: Archduke Ferdinand of Austria and the Battle of Mohacs." *Austrian History Yearbook* 2 (1966): 11–17.

———. "Of Christian Virtue and a Practicing Prince: Emperor Ferdinand I and His Son Maximilian." *Catholic Historical Review* 61 (1975): 409–416.

———. *Ferdinand I of Austria.* Boulder, Colo.: East European Monographs, 1982.

———. "Habsburg Household or Habsburg Government? A Sixteenth-Century Administrative Dilemma." *Austrian History Yearbook* 26 (1995): 45–60.

———. *Primogeniture and Protestantism in Early Modern Germany.* New Haven, Conn.: Yale University Press, 1989.

———. "To Rule Is Not to Govern: The Diary of Maximilian II." In Solomon Wank, Heidrun Maschl, Brigitte Mazohl-Wallnig, and Reinhold Wagnleitner, eds., *The Mirror of History: Essays in Honor of Fritz Fellner.* Santa Barbara, Calif.: ABC-Clio, 1988, 255–264.

Firnhaber, Friedrich. "Die Krönung Kaiser Maximilians II. zum König von Ungarn." *Archiv für österreichische Geschichte* 22 (1860): 305–338.

———. "Zur Geschichte des österreichischen Militärwesens." *Archiv für österreichische Geschichte* 30 (1864): 91–1778.

Frettensattel, Robert. "Zu den Verhandlungen Maximilians II. mit Philipp II., 1568 und 1569." *Mitteilungen des Instituts für österreichische Geschichtsforschung* 24 (1903): 389–411.

Fuhrmann, Horst. "Heinrich Rantzaus römische Korrespondenten." *Archiv für Kulturgeschichte* 41 (1959): 63–89.

Gachard, L. P. *Don Carlos et Philippe II.* 2 vols. Brussels: Emmanuel [?] Devroye, Imprimeur du Roi, 1863.

Geyl, Pieter. *The Revolt of the Netherlands.* 1932. Reprint, London: Ernest Benn, 1958.

Gillet, J. F. A. *Crato von Krafftheim und seine Freunde: Ein Beitrag zur Kirchengeschichte.* 2 vols. Frankfurt: Brünner, 1860.

Ginhart, Karl. *Wiener Kunstgeschichte.* Vienna: Paul Neff, 1948.

Glawischnig, Rolf. *Niederlande, Kalvinismus und Reichsgrafenstand 1559–1584: Nassau-Dillenberg unter Graf Johann VI., 1559–1606.* Schriften des hessischen Landesamtes für geschichtliche Landeskunde, 36. Marburg: Elwert, 1973.

Goetz, Helmut. "Die Finalrelation des venezianischen Gesandter Michele Suriano, 1555." *Quellen und Forschungen aus italienische Archiven und Bibliotheken* 41 (1961): 235–322.

——. "Die geheimen Ratgeber Ferdinands I." *Quellen und Forschungen in italienischen Archiven und Bibliotheken* 42–43 (1964): 453–494.

Goetz, Walter. *Die bayerische Politik im ersten Jahrzehnt der Regierung Herzog Albrechts von Bayern.* Munich: Rieger, 1896.

——. "Der 'Kompromisskatholizismus' und Kaiser Maximilian II." *Historische Zeitschrift* 77 (1896): 193–206.

Goodman, David C. *Power and Penury: Government, Technology and Science in Philip II's Spain.* Cambridge: Cambridge University Press, 1988.

Graham, W. Fred, ed. *Later Calvinism: International Perspectives.* Sixteenth Century Essays and Studies, no. 22. Kirksville, Mo.: Sixteenth Century Journal, 1994.

Graz als Residenz: Innerösterreich, 1564–1619. Exhibition Catalogue. Graz: Universitäts-Buchdruckerei Styria, 1964.

Grossman, Karl. "Reichart Streun von Schwarzenau: Ein österreichischer Staatsmann und Gelehrter aus der Zeit der Renaissance, Reformation und Gegenreformation." *Jahrbuch für Landeskunde von Niederösterreich,* n.s. 20 (1927, part 2): 1–37.

Grothaus, Maximilian. "'Der Erbfeindt christlichen Namens': Zum Türken-Feindbild in der Kultur der habsburger Monarchie zwischen dem 16. und 18. Jahrhundert." 2 vols. Dissertation, University of Graz, 1986.

——. "Zum Türkenbild in der Kultur der Habsburgermonarchie zwischen dem 16. und 18. Jahrhundert." In Andreas Tietze, ed., *Habsburgisch-osmanische Beziehungen.* Beihefte zur Wiener Zeitschrift für die Kunde des Morgenlandes, 13. Vienna: Verband der wissenschaftlichen Gesellschaften Österreichs, 1985, 67–89.

Gschliesser, Oswald von. *Der Reichshofrat: Bedeutung und Verfassung, Schicksal und Besetzung einer obersten Reichsbehörde von 1559–1806.* Veröffentlichungen der Kommission für neuere Geschichte Österreichs, 33. Vienna: Holzhausen, 1942.

Gutkas, Karl. *Geschichte des Landes Niederösterreich.* 3 vols. St. Pölten, Austria: Kulturreferat der niederösterreichischen Landesregierung, 1957–1959.

———. "Landesfürst, Landtag und Städte Niederösterreichs im 16. Jahrhundert." *Jahrbuch für Landeskunde von Niederösterreich,* n.s. 36. (1964): 311–319.

Hassinger, Erich. *Studien zu Jacobus Acontius.* Abhandlungen zur mittleren und neueren Geschichte, no. 76. Berlin: Verlag für Staatswissenschaften und Geschichte, 1934.

Heer, Friedrich. *Die Dritte Kraft: Der Europäische Humanismus zwischen den Fronten des konfessionellen Zeitalters.* Frankfurt: Fischer, 1959.

Heine, G. "Beiträge zur Geschichte im Zeitalter der Reformation aus spanischen und portugiesischen Archiven mitgetheilt." *Allgemeine Zeitschrift für Geschichte* 8 (1847): 1–38; 9 (1848): 139–180.

Heiß, Gernot. "Bildungsverhalten des niederösterreichischen Adels im gesellschaftlichen Wandel: Zum Bildungsgang im 16. und 17. Jahrhundert." In Grete Klingenstein and Heinrich Lutz, eds., *Spezialforschung und "Gesamtgeschichte": Beispiele und Methodenfragen zur Geschichte der Neuzeit.* Wiener Beiträge zur Geschichte der Neuzeit, no. 8. Vienna: Verlag für Geschichte und Politik, 1981, 139–157.

———. "Die Jesuiten und die Anfänge der Katholisierung in den Ländern Ferdinands I.: Glaube, Mentalität, Politik." 2 vols. Habilitationsschrift, University of Vienna, 1986.

———. "Reformation und Gegenreformation, 1519–1618: Probleme und ihre Quellen" In Erich Zöllner, ed., *Die Quellen der Geschichte Österreichs.* Schriften des Instituts für Österreichkunde, 40. Vienna: Bundesverlag, 1982.

Herold, Hannelore. "Die Hauptprobleme der Landtagshandlungen des Erzherzogthums unter der Enns zur Zeit der Regierung Kaiser Maximilians II., 1564–1576." Dissertation, University of Vienna, 1970.

Hesselink, John. "The Dramatic Story of the Heidelberg Catechism." In W. Fred Graham, ed., *Later Calvinism International Perspectives.* Sixteenth Century Essays and Studies, 22. Kirksville, Mo.: Sixteenth Century Journal, 1994, 273–288.

Hirn, Joseph. *Erzherzog Ferdinand II. von Tirol.* 2 vols. Innsbruck: Wagner, 1885–1888.

Hoffmann, Richard C. "Economic Development and Aquatic Ecosystems in Medieval Europe." *American Historical Review* 101 (1996): 631–669.

Hoke, Rudolph. "Prokaiserliche und antikaiserliche Reichspublizistik." In Heinz Duchhardt and Matthias Schnettger, eds., *Reichsständische Libertät und habsburgisches Kaisertum.* Mainz: Philipp von Zabern, 1999, 119–132.

Hollweg, Walter. *Der Augsburger Reichstag von 1566 und seine Bedeutung für die Entstehung der reformierten Kirche und ihres Bekenntnisses.* Beiträge zur Geschichte und Lehre der reformierten Kirche 17 (1964).

Holtzmann, Robert. *Kaiser Maximilian II. bis zu seiner Thronbesteigung, 1527–1564.* Berlin: Schwetschke, 1903.

Hopfen, Otto Helmuth. *Kaiser Maximilian II. und der Kompromißkatholizismus.* Munich: Mühlthaler, 1895.

Hsia, R. Po-Chi. *Social Discipline in the Reformation: Central Europe, 1550–1570.* London: Routledge, 1989.

Ilg, Albert. "Das Neugebäude bei Wien." *Jahrbuch der kunsthistorischen Sammlungen des allerhöchsten Kaiserhauses* 16 (1895): 81–121.

Inalcik, Halil. "The Socio-Political Effects of the Diffusion of Fire-Arms in the Middle East." In Vernon J. Parry and M. E. Yapp, eds., *War, Technology and Society in the Middle East.* London: Oxford University Press, 1975, 195–217.

"Isenberg, Salentin von." *Allgemeine Deutsche Biographie,* vol. 30.

Jäger-Sunstenau, Hanns. "Über das Wiener Schützenfest, 1563." *Wiener Geschichtsblätter* 15 (1960): 138–143.

Janko, Wilhelm von. *Lazarus Freiherr v. Schwendi: Oberster Feldhauptmann und Rath Kaiser Maximilians II.* Vienna: Braumüller, 1871.

Jansen, Dirk Jacob. "The Instruments of Patronage: Jacopo Strada at the Court of Maximilian II, a Case Study." In Friedrich Edelmayer and Alfred Kohler, eds., *Kaiser Maximilian II.: Kultur und Politik im 16. Jahrhundert.* Wiener Beiträge zur Geschichte der Neuzeit 19 (1992): 182–202.

Káldy-Nagy, Gyula. "The First Centuries of the Ottoman Military Organization." *Acta Orientalia Academiae Scientiarum Hungaricae* 31 (1977): 147–183.

Kamen, Henry. *Philip of Spain.* New Haven, Conn.: Yale University Press, 1997.

Kaufmann, Thomas da Costa. *The Mastery of Nature.* Princeton, N.J.: Princeton University Press, 1993.

———. *Variations on the Imperial Theme: Studies in Ceremonial, Art and Collecting in the Age of Maximilian II and Rudolph II.* New York: Garland, 1978.

Kellenbenz, Hermann, ed. *Wirtschaftspolitik und Arbeitsmarkt.* Vienna: Verlag für Geschichte und Politik, 1974.

Kingdon, Robert. *Myths About the St. Bartholomew's Day Massacre, 1572–1576.* Cambridge, Mass.: Harvard University Press, 1988.

Kleinpaul, Johannes. *Das Nachrichtenwesen der deutschen Fürsten im 16. und 17. Jahrhundert.* Leipzig: Klein, 1930.

Klingenstein, Grete, and Heinrich Lutz, eds. *Spezialforschung und "Gesamtgeschichte": Beispiele und Methodenfragen zur Geschichte der frühen Neuzeit.* Wiener Beiträge zur Geschichte der Neuzeit, 8. Vienna: Verlag für Geschichte und Politik, 1981.

Klooster, Fred H. "Calvin's Attitude to the Heidelberg Catechism." In W. Fred

Graham, ed., *Later Calvinism: International Perspectives*. Sixteenth Century Essays and Studies, 22. Kirksville, Mo.: Sixteenth Century Journal, 1994, 311–33.

Knittler, Herbert. "Adelige Grundherrschaft im Übergang: Überlegungen zum Verhältnis von Adel und Wirtschaft in Niederösterreich um 1600." In Grete Klingenstein and Heinrich Lutz, eds., *Spezialforschung und "Gesamtgeschichte."* Wiener Beiträge zur Geschichte der Neuzeit, no. 8. Vienna: Verlag für Geschichte und Politik, 1981, 84–111.

Knöbl, Herbert. *Das Neugebäude und sein baulicher Zusammenhang mit Schloß Schönbrunn*. Vienna: Böhlau, c. 1988.

Koenigsberger, Helmut G. "Epilogue: Central and Western Europe." In R. J. W. Evans and T. V. Thomas, eds., *Crown, Church and Estates: Central European Politics in the Sixteenth and Seventeenth Centuries*. New York: St. Martin's, 1991, 300–310.

Kohler, Alfred, and Heinrich Lutz, eds. *Alltag im 16. Jahrhundert: Studien zur Lebensformen in mitteleuropäischen Städten*. Wiener Beiträge zur Geschichte der Neuzeit, 14. Vienna: Verlag für Geschichte und Politik, 1987.

———. "Kontinuität oder Diskontinuität im frühneuzeitlichen Kaisertum: Ferdinand II." In Heinz Duchhardt and Matthias Schnettger, eds., *Reichständische Libertät und habsburgisches Kaisertum*. Mainz: Philipp von Zabern, 1999, 107–118.

———. "Vom habsburgischen Gesamtsystem Karls V. zu den Teilsystemen Philipps II. und Maximilians II." In Friedrich Edelmayer and Alfred Kohler, eds., *Kaiser Maximilian II.: Kultur und Politik im 16. Jahrhundert*. Wiener Beiträge zur Geschichte der Neuzeit, 19. Vienna: Verlag für Geschichte und Politik, 1992, 13–24.

———. "Wohnen und Essen auf den Reichstagen des 16. Jahrhundert." In Alfred Kohler and Heinrich Lutz, eds., *Alltag im 16. Jahrhundert: Studien zur Lebensformen in mitteleuropäischen Städten*. Wiener Beiträge zur Geschichte der Neuzeit, 14. Vienna: Verlag für Geschichte und Politik, 1987, 222–257.

Kollman, Josef. "Berní registříky a berně roku 1567." *Sborník archivních prací* 13, no. 1 (1963): 169–246.

Korpeter, C. Max. "Habsburg and Ottoman in Hungary in the 16th and 17th Centuries." In Andreas Tietze, ed., *Habsburgisch-osmanische Beziehungen*. Vienna: Verband der wissenschaftlichen Gesellschaften Österreichs, 1985, 55–67.

Kouri, E. I., and Tom Scott, eds. *Politics and Society in Reformation Europe*. London: Macmillan, 1987.

Krabbe, Otto. *David Chyträus*. Rostock: Stiller, 1870.

Kretschmayr, Heinrich. "Das deutsche Reichsvicekanzleramt." *Archiv für österreichische Geschichte* 84 (1898): 381–502.

Krimm, Herbert. "Die Agende der niederösterreichischen Stände im Jahre 1571."

Jahrbuch für die Geschichte des Protestantismus in Österreich 55 (1934): 3–64; 56 (1935): 52–87; 57 (1936): 51–70.

Krömer, Wolfram, ed. *Spanien und Österreich in der Renaissance*. Innsbrucker Beiträge zur Kulturwissenschaft, special issue 66 (Innsbruck, Austria: Institut für Sprachwissenschaft, 1989).

Krone, Rudolf. *Lazarus von Schwendi, 1522–1584, kais. General und geheimer Rat, seine kirchenpolitische Tätigkeit und seine Stellung zur Reformation*. Schriften des Vereins für Reformationsgeschichte, 29, no. 107 (1912): 129–166.

Krüger, Kersten. "Public Finance and Modernisation: The Change from Domain State to Tax State in Hesse in the Sixteenth and Seventeenth Centuries—A Case Study." In Peter-Christian Witt, ed., *Wealth and Taxation in Central Europe: the History and Sociology of Public Finance*. German Historical Perspectives, 2. Leamington Spa: Berg and St. Martin's, 1987, 49–62.

Kurzmann, Gerhard. *Kaiser Maximilian I. und das Kriegswesen der österreichischen Länder und des Reichs*. Militärgeschichtliche Dissertationen österreichischer Universitäten, vol. 5. Vienna: Österreichischer Bundesverlag, 1985.

Lanzinner, Maximilian. "Der Aufstand der Niederlande und der Reichstag zu Speyer, 1570. In *Fortschritte in der Geschichtwissenschaft durch Reichstagsaktenforschung*. Schriftenreihe der historischen Kommission bei der bayerischen Akademie der Wissenschaften, 35. Göttingen: Vandenhoeck and Ruprecht, 1988, 102–117.

———. "Die Denkschrift des Lazarus von Schwendi zur Reichspolitik (1576)." *Zeitschrift für historische Forschung*, special supplement 3 (1987): 141–185.

———. *Friedenssicherung und politische Einheit des Reiches unter Kaiser Maximilian II., 1564–1576*. Göttingen: Vandenhoeck und Ruprecht, 1993.

———. "Friedenssicherung und Zentralisierung der Reichsgewalt: Ein Reformsuch auf dem Reichstag zu Speyer, 1570." *Zeitschrift für historische Forschung*, 12 (1985): 287–310.

Lehmann, Hartmut. *Das Zeitalter des Absolutismus: Gottesgnadentum und Kriegsnot*. Stuttgart: Kohlhammer, 1980.

Lhotsky, Alphons. *Festschrift des kunsthistorischen Museums zur Feier des fünfzigjährigen Bestandes*. 2 vols. in 3. Vienna: Berger, 1941–1945.

Lietzmann, Hilda. *Das Neugebäude in Wien: Sultan Süleymans Zelt—Kaiser Maximilians Lustschloß. Ein Beitrag zur Kunst- und Kulturgeschichte der zweiten Hälfte des sechzehnten Jahrhunderts*. Munich: Deutscher Kunstverlag, 1987.

Lind, Karl. "Die Chronik der Familie Beck von Leopoldsdorf." *Blätter des Vereines für Landeskunde von Niederösterreich* 9 (1875): 129–134, 221–224, 329–339; 10 (1876): 96–101, 210–218; 11 (1877): 131–142.

Lindell, Robert. "Die Neubesetzung der Hofkapellmeisterstelle am Kaiserhof in den Jahren 1567–1568: Palestrina oder Monte?" *Studien zur Musikwissenschaft* 36 (1985): 35–52.

Loesche, Georg. *Geschichte des Protestantismus in Österreich*. Vienna: Manz, 1921.

Lojewski, Günther von. *Bayerns Weg nach Köln: Geschichte der bayerischen Bistumspolitik in der 2. Hälfte des 16. Jahrhunderts*. Bonner historische Forschungen, 21. Bonn: Röhrscheid, 1962.

Loserth, Johann. *Die Reformation und Gegenreformation in den innerösterreichischen Ländern im 16. Jahrhundert*. Stuttgart: Cotta, 1898.

―――. "Ständische Beziehungen zwischen Böhmen und Innerösterreich im Zeitalter Ferdinands I." *Mitteilungen des Vereines für die Geschichte der Deutschen in Böhmen*, 50 (1911–1912): 1–141.

―――, and Franz von Mensi. "Die Prager Ländertagung von 1541–42." *Archiv für österreichische Geschichte*, 103 (1913): 433–546.

Lossen, Max. *Der Kölnische Krieg*. Vol. 1. Gotha: Perthes, 1882. Vol. 2, Munich: Franz, 1897.

Louthan, Howard. *Johannis Crato and the Austrian Habsburgs: Reforming a Counter-Reform Court*. Princeton, N.J.: Princeton Theological Seminary, 1994.

―――. *The Quest for Compromise: Peacemakers in Counter-Reformation Vienna*. Cambridge: Cambridge University Press, 1997.

―――. "A *via media* in Central Europe: Irenicism in Habsburg Vienna." Dissertation, Princeton University, 1994.

Luttenberger, Albrecht P. *Kurfürsten, Kaiser und Reich: Politische Führung und Friedenssicherung unter Ferdinand I. und Maximilian II*. Veröffentlichungen des Instituts für Europäische Geschichte Mainz, Abteilung Universalgeschichte, 149. Mainz: Philipp von Zabern, 1994.

Lutz, Heinrich. *Christianitas Afflicta: Europa, das Reich und die päpstliche Politik im Niedergang der Hegemonie Kaiser Karls V, 1552–1556*. Göttingen: Vandenhoeck und Ruprecht, 1964.

Lynch, John. *Spain Under the Habsburgs*. 2 vols. Oxford: Blackwell, 1965–1969.

Machardy, Karin J. "Social Mobility and Noble Rebellion in Early Modern Habsburg Austria." In János M. Bak, ed., *Nobilities in Central and Eastern Europe: Kinship, Property and Privilege*. History and Society in Central Europe, 2. Budapest: Hajnal Society, 1994, 97–139.

Maier, Hans, and Volker Press, eds. *Vorderösterreich in der frühen Neuzeit*. Sigmaringen: Thorbecke, 1989.

Maltby, William S. *Alba: A Biography of Fernando Alvarez de Toledo, Third Duke of Alba, 1507–1582*. Berkeley: University of California Press, 1983.

Marosi, Endre. "Die ungarische Kampf gegen die Türken, 1352–1718: Ein historischer Überblick." In Zygmunt Abrahamowicz, et al., eds., *Die Türkenkriege in der historischen Forschung*. Forschungen und Beiträge zur Wiener Stadtgeschichte, 13. Vienna: Deuticke, 1983, 119–142.

"Martin Eisengrein." *Allgemeine Deutsche Biographie*, vol. 5.

Martin, Ernst. "Lazarus von Schwendi und seine Schriften." *Zeitschrift für die Geschichte des Oberrheins*, n.s. 8 (1893): 389–418.

Maurenbrecher, Wilhelm. "Beiträge zur Geschichte Maximilians II., 1548–1562." *Historische Zeitschrift* 32 (1874): 221–297.

———. "Kaiser Maximilian II. und die deutsche Reformation." *Historische Zeitschrift* 7 (1862): 351–380.

Mecenseffy, Grete. *Geschichte des Protestantismus in Österreich*. Graz: Böhlau, 1956.

———. "Maximilian II. in neuer Sicht." *Jahrbuch der Gesellschaft für die Geschichte des Protestantismus in Österreich* 92 (1976): 42–54.

Mencik, Ferdinand. "Beiträge zur Geschichte der kaiserlichen Hofämter." *Archiv für österreichische Geschichte* 87 (1899): 447–564.

———. "Die Reise Kaiser Maximilians II. nach Spanien im Jahre 1548." *Archiv für österreichische Geschichte* 86 (1899): 293–308.

Menhardt, Hermann. *Das älteste Handschriftenverzeichnis der Wiener Hofbibliothek von Hugo Blotius 1576*. Österreichische Akademie der Wissenschaften, philosophische-historische Klasse, Denkschriften, 76. Vienna: Rohrer, 1957.

Midelfort, H. C. Erik. *Mad Princes of Renaissance Germany*. Charlottesville: University of Virginia Press, 1994.

Míka, Alois. *Stoletý zápas o charakter českého státu, 1526–1527*. Prague: Státní pedagogické nakladatelství, 1974.

Mitterauer, Michael. "Produktionsweise, Siedlungsstruktur und Sozialformen im österreichischen Montanwesen des Mittelalters und der frühen Neuzeit." In Michael Mitterauer, ed., *Österreichisches Montanwesen: Produktion, Verteilung, Sozialformen*. Vienna: Verlag für Geschichte und Politik, 1974, 234–315.

Mitterauer, Michael, ed. *Österreichisches Montanwesen: Produktion, Verteilung, Sozialformen*. Vienna: Verlag für Geschichte und Politik, 1974.

———. "Die Wirtschaftspolitik der österreichischen Landesfürsten im Spätmittelalter und ihre Auswirkungen auf den Arbeitsmarkt." In Hermann Kellenbenz, ed., *Wirtschaftspolitik und Arbeitsmarkt*. Vienna: Verlag für Geschichte und Politik, 1974, 15–46.

Moran, Bruce T. "Prince-Practitioning and the Direction of Medical Roles at the German Court: Maurice of Hesse-Kassel and His Physicians." In Vivian Nutton, ed., *Medicine at the Courts of Europe, 1500–1837*. London: Routledge, 1990, 95–116.

Moritz, Hugo. *Die Wahl Rudolfs II.: Der Reichstag zu Regensburg (1576) und die Freistellungsbewegung*. Marburg: Elwert, 1895.

Mout, Nicolette. "Die Niederlande und das Reich im 16. Jahrhundert." In Volker Press, ed., *Alternativen zur Reichsverfassung in der frühen Neuzeit?* Schriften des historischen Kollegs, 23. Munich: Oldenbourg, 1995, 143–168.

Müller, Rainer A. *Der Fürstenhof in der frühen Neuzeit*. Enzyklopädie deutscher Geschichte, vol. 33. Munich: Oldenbourg, 1995.

Murphey, Rhoads. "Bigots or Informed Observers? A Periodization of Pre-Colonial English and European Writing on the Middle East." *Journal of the American Oriental Society* 110, no. 2 (1990): 291–303.

Neuhaus, Helmut. *Das Reich in der frühen Neuzeit.* Munich: Oldenbourg, 1997.

———. *Reichsständische Repräsentationsformen im 16. Jahrhundert.* Schriften zur Verfassungsgeschichte, 33. Berlin: Duncker und Humblot, 1982.

———. "Vom Reichstag(en) zu Reichtstag: Reichsständische Beratungsformen von der Mitte des 16. bis zur Mitte des 17. Jahrhunderts." In Heinz Duchhardt and Matthias Schnettger, eds., *Reichsständische Libertät und habsburgisches Kaisertum.* Mainz: Philipp von Zabern, 1999, 135–150.

———. "Zwänge und Entwicklungsmöglichkeiten reichsständischer Beratungsformen in der zweiten Hälfte des 16. Jahrhunderts." *Zeitschrift für historische Forschung* 10 (1983): 279–298.

Newald, Johann. *Das österreichische Münzwesen unter den Kaisern Maximilian II. Rudolf II. und Matthias.* Vienna: K.u.k. Hof- und Staatsdruckerei, 1885.

Noflatscher, Heinz. "Deutschmeister und Regent der Vorlande: Maximilian von Österreich, 1558–1618." In Hans Maier and Volker Press, eds., *Vorderösterreich in der frühen Neuzeit.* Sigmaringen: Thorbecke, 1989, 93–130.

———. "Erzherzog Maximilian Hoch- und Deutschmeister, 1585–90: Das Haus Habsburg, der deutsche Orden und das Reich im konfessionellen Zeitalter." 2 vols. Dissertation, University of Innsbruck, 1980.

North, Douglass C., and Robert Paul Thomas. *The Rise of the Western World: A New Economic History.* Cambridge: Cambridge University Press, 1973.

Nutton, Vivian, ed. *Medicine at the Courts of Europe, 1500–1837.* London: Routledge, 1990.

Oberleitner, Karl. "Die Finanzlage Niederösterreichs im 16. Jahrhundert." *Archiv für österreichische Geschichte* 30 (1864): 3–90.

O'Boyle, Leonore. "Some Recent Studies of Nineteenth-Century European Bureaucracy: Problems of Analysis." *Central European History* 19 (1986): 386–408.

Olson, Oliver K. "Matthias Flacius Illyricus, 1520–1575." In Jill Raitt, ed., *Shapers of Religious Traditions in Germany, Switzerland, and Poland, 1560–1600.* New Haven, Conn.: Yale University Press, 1981.

Ortloff, Friedrich. *Geschichte der grumbachischen Handel.* 4 vols. Jena: Fromann, 1868–1870.

Pánek, Jaroslav. "Maximilian II. als König von Böhmen." In Edelmayer and Kohler, eds., *Kaiser Maximilian II.: Kultur und Politik im 16. Jahrhundert.* Wiener Beiträge zur Geschichte der Neuzeit, 19. Vienna: Verlag für Geschichte und Politik, 1992: 55–69.

———. "Das politische System des böhmischen Staates im ersten Jahrhundert der habsburgischen Herrschaft, 1526–1620." *Mitteilungen des Instituts für österreichische Geschichtsforschung* 97 (1989): 53–82.

————. *Stavovská opozice a její zápas s Habsburky, 1547–1577.* Prague: Academia, 1982.

Parker, Geoffrey. *The Army of Flanders and the Spanish Road, 1567–1659.* Cambridge: Cambridge University Press, 1972.

————. *The Dutch Revolt.* London: Penguin Books, 1985.

————. *The Military Revolution: Military Innovation and the Rise of the West, 1500–1800.* Cambridge: Cambridge University Press, 1988.

————. *Philip II.* London: Hutchison, 1979.

————. "Success and Failure During the First Century of the Reformation." *Past and Present* 136 (1992): 43–82.

Parry, Vernon J. "La manière de combattre." In Vernon J. Parry and M. E. Yapp, eds., *War, Technology and Society in the Middle East.* London: Oxford University Press, 1975, 218–256.

Pass, Walter. *Musik und Musiker am Hof Maximilians II.* Wiener Veröffentlichungen zur Musikwissenschaft, 20. Tutzing: Schneider, 1980.

Patrouch, Joseph F. "The Investiture Controversy Revisited: Religious Reform, Emperor Maximilian II and the Klosterrat." *Austrian History Yearbook* 25 (1994): 59–78.

Petrie, Charles. *Philipp II. von Spanien.* Trans. Ursula Gmelin. Stuttgart: Kohlhammer, 1965.

Pickl, Othmar. "Die Salzproduktion im Ostalpenraum am Beginn der Neuzeit." In Michael Mitterauer, ed., *Österreichisches Montanwesen: Produktion, Verteilung, Sozialformen.* Vienna: Verlag für Geschichte und Politik, 1974, 11–28.

Pierson, Peter. *Philip II of Spain.* London: Thames and Hudson, 1975.

Pirenne, Henri. *Histoire de Belgique.* 5 vols. Reprint: n.p., La Renaissance du Livre, 1972–1975.

Platzhoff, Walter. "Vom Interregnum bis zur französischen Revolution, 1250–1789." In Hermann Aubin, Theodor Fings, and Josef Müller, eds., *Geschichte des Rheinlandes von der ältesten Zeit bis zur Gegenwart.* 2 vols. Essen: Baedeker, 1922, 1: 169–238.

Pokorny, Veronika. "Clementia Austriaca: Studien zur Bedeutung der Clementia Principis für die Habsburger im 16. und 17. Jahrhundert." *Mitteilungen des Instituts für österreichische Geschichtsforschung* 86 (1978): 310–364.

Porträtgalerie zur Geschichte Österreichs von 1400 bis 1800. Vienna: Kunsthistorisches Museum, 1982.

Press, Volker. "The Habsburg Court as the Center of the Imperial Government." *Journal of Modern History* 58 (supplement, 1986): S23–45.

————. "The Imperial Court of the Habsburgs: From Maximilian I to Ferdinand III, 1493–1657." In Ronald G. Asch and Adolf M. Birke, *Princes, Patronage and the Nobility. The Court at the Beginning of the Modern Age, c. 1450–1650.* London: Oxford University Press, 1991, 289–314.

―――. "Wilhelm von Grumbach und die deutsche Adelskrise der 1560en Jahre." *Blätter für deutsche Landesgeschichte* 113 (1977): 396–431.

―――. "Wilhelm von Oranien, die deutschen Reichsstände und der niederländische Aufstand." *Bijdragen en Mededelingen betreffende de Geschiedenis der Nederlanden* 99 (1984): 677–707.

Prestwich, Minna, ed. *International Calvinism, 1541–1715*. Oxford: Clarendon, 1979.

Pribram, Alfred. *Materialen zur Geschichte der Löhne und Preise in Österreich*. Veröffentlichungen des internationalen wissenschaftlichen Komitees für die Geschichte der Preise und Löhne, 1. Vienna: Carl Ueberreuter, 1938.

Prodi, Paolo. *Il sovrano pontifice, un corpo e due anime: La monarchia papale nella prima età moderna*. Bologna: Il Mulino, 1982.

Putschögl, Gerhard. *Die landständische Behördeorganisation in Österreich ob der Enns vom Anfang des 16. bis zur Mitte des 18. Jahrhunderts: Ein Beitrag zur österreichischen Rechtsgeschichte*. Forschungen zur Geschichte Oberösterreichs, 14. Linz: Oberösterreichisches Landesarchiv, 1978.

Rabe, Horst, and Peter Marzahl, " 'Comme représentant nostre propre personne'—the Regency Ordinances of Charles V as a Historical Source." In E. I. Kouri and Tom Scott, eds., *Politics and Society in Reformation Europe*. London: Macmillan, 1987: 78–93.

Rachfall, Felix. *Wilhelm von Oranien und der niederländische Aufstand*. 3 vols. Halle: Niemeyer, 1906–1908; and The Hague: Martinus Nijhoff, 1924.

Raitt, Jill, ed. *Shapers of Religious Traditions in Germany, Switzerland, and Poland, 1560–1600*. New Haven, Conn.: Yale University Press, 1981.

Rassow, Peter. "Karls V. Tochter als Eventualerbin der spanischen Reiche." *Archiv für Reformationsgeschichte* 49 (1958): 161–168.

Regele, Oskar. "Der österreichische Hofkriegsrat, 1556–1848." *Mitteilungen des Instituts für österreichische Geschichtsforschung*, special issue 1, part 1 (1949): 1–91.

Reingrabner, Gustav. *Adel und Reformation: Beiträge zur Geschichte des protestantischen Adels im Lande unter der Enns während des 16. und 17. Jahrhunderts*. Vienna: Verein für Landeskunde von Niederösterreich und Wien, 1976.

―――. "Zur Geschichte der flacianische Bewegung im Lande unter der Enns." *Jahrbuch für Landeskunde von Niederösterreich*, n.s. 54–55 (1988–1989): 265–301.

Rill, Bernd. *Friedrich III. Habsburgs europäischer Durchbruch*. Graz: Styria, 1987.

Rill, Gerhard. *Geschichte der Grafen von Arco, 1487–1614: Reichsvasallen und Landsassen*. Horn, Austria: Berger, 1975.

―――. "Reichsvikar und Kommisar: Zur Geschichte der Verwaltung Reichsitaliens im Spätmittelalter und in der frühen Neuzeit." *Annali della Fondazione italiana per la storia amministrativa* 2 (1965): 173–198.

Robisheaux, Thomas. *Rural Society and the Search for Order in Early Modern Germany.* Cambridge: Cambridge University Press, 1989.

Rodríguez-Salgado, Mía. *The Changing Face of Empire: Charles V, Philip II and Habsburg Authority, 1551–1559.* Cambridge: Cambridge University Press, 1988.

Rosenthal, Eduard. *Die Behördeorganisation Kaiser Ferdinands I.: Das Vorbild der Verwaltungsorganisation in den deutschen Territorien. Archiv für österreichische Geschichte,* vol. 69. Vienna: Tempsky, 1887.

Rowen, Herbert H. "The Dutch Revolt: What Kind of Revolution?" *Renaissance Quarterly* 43 (1990): 570–590.

Rudersdorf, Manfred. "Maximilian II., 1564–1576." In Anton Schindling and Walter Ziegler, eds., *Die Kaiser der Neuzeit, 1519–1918: Heiliges Römisches Reich, Österreich, Deutschland.* Munich: Beck, 1990.

Rübsam, Josef. "Nicholas Mameranus und sein Büchlein über den Reichstag zu Augsburg im Jahre 1566." *Historisches Jahrbuch* 10 (1889): 525–554.

Rúzsás, Lajos, ed. *Szigetvári Emlékönyv. Szigetvár, 1566: Évi ostromának 400. Évfordulojára.* Budapest: Akadémiai Kiadó, 1966.

Sánchez, Magdalena. *The Empress, the Queen, and the Nun: Women and Power at the Court of Philip III of Spain.* Baltimore, Md.: Johns Hopkins University Press, 1998.

Sandgruber, Roman. "Die innerberger Eisenproduktion in der frühen Neuzeit." In Michael Mitterauer, ed., *Österreichisches Montanwesen: Produktion, Verteilung, Sozialformen.* Vienna: Verlag für Geschichte und Politik, 1974, 72–105.

Scheicher, Elisabeth. *Die Kunst- und Wunderkammer der Habsburger.* Vienna: Molden, 1979.

Schimetschek, Bruno. *Der österreichische Beamte: Geschichte und Tradition.* Vienna: Verlag für Geschichte und Politik, 1984.

Schlecht, Joseph. "Das geheime Dispenzbreve Pius IV für die römische Königskrönung Maximilians II." *Historisches Jahrbuch* 14 (1893): 1–38.

Schnur, Roman. "Lazarus von Schwendi, 1522–1583: Ein unerledigtes Thema der historischen Forschung." *Zeitschrift für historische Forschung* 14 (1987): 27–46.

Schrauf, Karl. *Der Reichshofrath Dr. Georg Eder.* Vienna: Holzhausen, 1904.

Schubert, Friedrich. *Die deutschen Reichstage in der Staatslehre der frühen Neuzeit.* Schriften der historischen Kommission der bayerischen Akademie der Wissenschaften, 7. Göttingen: Vandenhoeck and Ruprecht, 1966.

Schulze, Winfried. "Concordia, Discordia, Tolerantia: Deutsche Politik im konfessionellen Zeitalter." *Zeitschrift für historische Forschung,* special issue 3 (1987): 43–80.

———. *Landesdefension und Staatsbildung: Studien zum Kriegswesen des innerösterreichischen Territorialstaates, 1564–1619.* Veröffentlichungen der Kommission für neuere Geschichte Österreichs, 60. Vienna; Böhlau, 1973.

———. *Reich und Türkengefahr im späten 16. Jahrhundert.* Munich: Beck, 1978.

Senfelder, Leopold. "Kaiser Maximilians letzte Lebensjahr und Tod." *Blätter für Landeskunde von Niederösterreich,* n.s. 32 (1898): 47–75.

Shumaker, Wayne. *The Occult Sciences in the Renaissance.* Berkeley: University of California Press, 1972.

Sickel, Theodor von. "Das Reformationslibell des Kaisers Ferdinand I. vom Jahre 1562 bis zur Absendung nach Trient." *Archiv für österreichische Geschichte* 45 (1871): 1–96.

Sitte, Alfred. "Tsausch Hedajets Aufenthalt in Wien, 1565." *Archiv für Kulturgeschichte* 6 (1908): 192–201.

Sittig, Wolfgang. *Landstände und Fürstentum: Eine Krisenzeit als Anstoß für die Entwicklung der steierischen landständischen Verwaltung.* Veröffentlichungen des steiermärkischen Landesarchives, 13. Graz: Steiermärkisches Landesarchiv, 1982.

Soergel, Philip. *Wondrous in His Saints: Counter-Reformation Propaganda in Bavaria.* Berkeley: University of California Press, 1993.

Spindler, Max. *Handbuch zur bayerischen Geschichte,* 2d ed. 4 vols. Munich: Beck, 1977–1981.

Spini, Giorgio. "The Medici Principality and the States of Europe in the Sixteenth Century." *Journal of Italian History* 2 (1979): 420–447.

Stolz, Otto. *Geschichte des Landes Tirol,* vol. 1 (no further vols. published). Innsbruck: Tyrolia, 1955.

Strakosch, Marianne. "Materialen zu einer Biographie Elisabeths von Österreich, Königin von Frankreich." Dissertation, University of Vienna, 1965.

Sturmberger, Hans. *Adam Graf Herberstorff: Herrschaft und Freiheit im konfessionellen Zeitalter.* Vienna: Verlag für Geschichte und Politik, 1976.

———. "Dualistischer Ständestaat und werdender Absolutismus: Die Entwicklung der Verfassung Österreichs." In Hans Sturmberger, ed., *Land ob der Enns und Österreich: Aufsätze und Vorträge.* Linz: Oberösterreichisches Landesarchiv, 1979, 246–272.

Sucheni-Grabowska, Anna. "Zu den Beziehungen zwischen den Jagiellonen und den Habsburgern: Katharina von Österreich, die dritte Gemahlin des Königs Sigismund August," *Historisches Jahrbuch der Stadt Linz* (1979): 59–100.

Sutherland, Nicola. *The Huguenot Struggle for Recognition.* New Haven, Conn: Yale University Press, 1988.

Szakály, Ferenc. "Der Wandel Ungarns in der Türkenzeit." In Andreas Tietze, ed., *Habsburgisch-osmanische Beziehungen.* Vienna: Verband der wissenschaftlichen Gesellschaften Österreichs, 1985, 35–55.

Teply, Karl. "Das österreichische Türkenzeitalter." In Zygmunt Abrahamowicz, et al., eds., *Die Türkenkriege in der historischen Forschung.* Forschungen und Beiträge zur Wiener Stadtgeschichte, no. 13. Vienna: Deuticke, 1983: 5–52.

Thomas, Bruno. "Die Harnischgarnitur Maximilians II. von Jörg Sensenhofer." *Belvedere* 13 (1938–1939): 73–82.

Thompson, Glenda Goss. "Mary of Hungary and Music Patronage." *Sixteenth Century Journal* 15 (1984): 401–418.

Tietze, Andreas, ed. *Habsburgisch-osmanische Beziehungen.* Beihefte zur Wiener Zeitschrift für die Kunde des Morgenlandes, no. 13. Vienna: Verband der wissenschaftlichen Gesellschaften Österreichs, 1985.

Tietze, Hans. *Wien, Kultur, Kunst, Geschichte.* Vienna: Epstein, 1931.

Tracy, James D. *Holland Under Habsburg Rule, 1506–1566.* Berkeley: University of California Press, 1990.

Trenkler, Ernst. "War Kaiser Maximilian II. (1564–1576) tatsächlich Gründer der Hofbibliothek?" *Biblos* 19 (1970): 1–11.

Trevor-Roper, Hugh. "The Court Physician and Paracelsianism." In Vivian Nutton, ed., *Medicine at the Courts of Europe, 1500–1837.* London: Routledge, 1990, 79–95.

Urfus, Valentin. "I moderni principi amministrativi in Boemia e l'assolutismo sovrano nei secoli XVI e XVII." *Annali della fondazione italiana per la storia amministrativa* (1965): 237–247.

Van Gelderen, Martin. *The Political Thought of the Dutch Revolt, 1555–1590.* Cambridge: Cambridge University Press, 1992.

Vaughn, Richard. *Valois Burgundy.* London: Allen Lane, 1975.

Villalon, L. J. Andrew. "Putting Don Carlos Together Again: Treatment of a Head Injury in Sixteenth-Century Spain." *Sixteenth Century Journal* 26 (1995): 347–365.

Vocelka, Karl. "Die inneren Auswirkungen der Auseinandersetzungen Österreichs mit den Osmanen." *Südost-Forschungen* 36 (1977): 13–34.

———. "Manier-Groteske-Fest-Triumph: Zur Geistesgeschichte der frühen Neuzeit." *Österreich in Geschichte und Literatur* 21 (1977): 137–150.

———. *Die politische Propaganda Kaiser Rudolfs II., 1576–1612.* Vienna: Verlag der österreichischen Akademie der Wissenschaft, 1981.

———. "Eine türkische Botschaft in Wien, 1565." In Heinrich Fichtenau and Erich Zöllner, eds., *Beiträge zur neueren Geschichte Österreichs.* Vienna: Böhlau, 1974, 102–114.

Vocelka, Rosemarie. "Die Begräbnisfeierlichkeiten für Kaiser Maximilian II., 1576–1577." *Mitteilungen des Instituts für österreichische Geschichtsforschung* 84 (1976): 105–136.

Wagner, Georg. "Maximilian II., der Wiener Hof und die Belagerung von Sziget." In Lajos Rúzsás, ed., *Szigetvári Emlékönyv. Szigetvár, 1566: Évi ostromának 400. Évfordulojára.* Budapest: Akadémiai Kiadó, 1966, 237–268.

Waissenberger, Robert. "Die hauptsächlichen Visitationen im Lande ob und unter der Enns sowie in Innerösterreich von 1528 bis 1580." Dissertation, University of Vienna, 1949.

Walter, Friedrich. *Österreichische Verfassungs- und Verwaltungsgeschichte von 1500–1955.* Ed. Adam Wandruszka. Veröffentlichungen der Kommission für neuere Geschichte Österreichs, 59. Vienna: Böhlau, 1972.

Wank, Solomon, Heidrun Maschl, Brigitte Mazohl-Wallnig, and Reinhold Wagnleitner, eds. *The Mirror of History: Essays in Honor of Fritz Fellner.* Santa Barbara, Calif.: ABC-Clio, 1988.

Webster, Charles, ed. *Health, Medicine and Mortality in the Sixteenth Century.* Cambridge: Cambridge University Press, 1979.

Wertheimer, Eduard. "Zur Geschichte des Türkenkrieges Maximilians II., 1565 und 1566." *Archiv für österreichische Geschichte* 53 (1875): 43–101.

Widorn, Helga. "Die spanischen Gemahlinnen der Kaiser Maximilian II., Ferdinand III. und Leopold I." Dissertation, University of Vienna, 1959.

Wiedemann, Theodor. *Geschichte der Reformation und Gegenreformation im Lande unter der Enns.* 5 vols. Prague: Tempsky, 1879–1886.

Williams, George H. *The Radical Reformation.* London: Weidenfeld and Nicolson, 1962.

Winter, Eduard. "Die polnische Königswahlen 1575 und 1587 in der Sicht der Habsburger." *Innsbrucker Historische Studien* 1 (1978): 61–76.

Witt, Peter-Christian, ed. *Wealth and Taxation in Central Europe: The History and Sociology of Public Finance.* German Historical Perspectives, 2. New York: St. Martin's Press, 1987.

Wunder, Heide. "Finance in the 'Economy of Old Europe': The Example of Peasant Credit from the Late Middle Ages to the Thirty Years War." In Peter-Christian Witt, ed., *Wealth and Taxation in Central Europe: The History and Sociology of Public Finance.* German Historical Perspectives, 2. New York: St. Martin's Press, 1987, 19–48.

Zagorin, Perez. *Ways of Lying: Dissimulation, Persecution and Conformity in Early Modern Europe.* Cambridge, Mass.: Harvard, 1990.

Zimmermann, Bernd. "Hans Ungnads Beziehungen zu Reformatoren und Theologen." *Jahrbuch der Gesellschaft für die Geschichte des Protestantismus in Österreich* 103 (1987): 179–191.

Zimmermann, Ludwig. "Moderne Staatsbildung in Deutschland." *Herrschaft und Staat im Mittelalter.* Wege der Forschung, 2. Darmstadt: Genther, 1956, 365–409.

———. *Der ökonomische Staat Landgraf Wilhelms IV.* 2 vols. Veröffentlichungen der historischen Kommission für Hessen und Waldeck, 17, parts 1 and 2. Marburg: Elwert, 1933–1934.

Zontar, Josef. "Michael Cernovic, Geheimagent Ferdinands I. und Maximilians II., und seine Berichterstattung." *Mitteilungen des österreichischen Staatsarchivs* 24 (1971): 169–222.

Index

tion history, and his era of war, religious division, political conflict, and administrative stress.

PAULA SUTTER FICHTNER is professor of history emerita from Brooklyn College and the Graduate Center, City University of New York. She is the author of *Protestantism and Primogeniture in Early Modern Germany*, published by Yale University Press.